Kubernetes Cookl

Second Edition

Practical solutions to container orchestration

Hideto Saito
Hui-Chuan Chloe Lee
Ke-Jou Carol Hsu

BIRMINGHAM - MUMBAI

Kubernetes Cookbook
Second Edition

Commissioning Editor: Gebin George
Acquisition Editor: Divya Poojari
Content Development Editor: Dattatraya More
Technical Editor: Sayali Thanekar
Copy Editor: Safis Editing
Project Coordinator: Shweta H Birwatkar
Proofreader: Safis Editing
Indexer: Priyanka Dhadke
Graphics: Jisha Chirayil
Production Coordinator: Deepika Naik

First published: June 2016
Second edition: May 2018

Production reference: 1290518

Published by Packt Publishing Ltd.
Livery Place
35 Livery Street
Birmingham
B3 2PB, UK.

ISBN 978-1-78883-760-6

www.packtpub.com

`mapt.io`

Mapt is an online digital library that gives you full access to over 5,000 books and videos, as well as industry leading tools to help you plan your personal development and advance your career. For more information, please visit our website.

Why subscribe?

- Spend less time learning and more time coding with practical eBooks and Videos from over 4,000 industry professionals

- Improve your learning with Skill Plans built especially for you

- Get a free eBook or video every month

- Mapt is fully searchable

- Copy and paste, print, and bookmark content

PacktPub.com

Did you know that Packt offers eBook versions of every book published, with PDF and ePub files available? You can upgrade to the eBook version at `www.PacktPub.com` and as a print book customer, you are entitled to a discount on the eBook copy. Get in touch with us at `service@packtpub.com` for more details.

At `www.PacktPub.com`, you can also read a collection of free technical articles, sign up for a range of free newsletters, and receive exclusive discounts and offers on Packt books and eBooks.

Contributors

About the authors

Hideto Saito has around 20 years of experience in the computer industry. In 1998, while working for Sun Microsystems Japan, he was impressed by Solaris OS, OPENSTEP, and Sun Ultra Enterprise 10000 (also known as StarFire). He then decided to pursue UNIX and macOS operating systems. In 2006, he relocated to southern California as a software engineer to develop products and services running on Linux and macOS X. He was especially renowned for his quick Objective-C code when he was drunk. He is also an enthusiast of Japanese anime, drama, and motorsports, and he loves Japanese Otaku culture.

Hui-Chuan Chloe Lee is a DevOps and software developer. She has worked in the software industry on a wide range of projects for over five years. As a technology enthusiast, she loves trying and learning about new technologies, which makes her life happier and more fulfilling. In her free time, she enjoys reading, traveling, and spending time with the people she loves.

Ke-Jou Carol Hsu has three years of experience working as a software engineer and is currently a PhD student in the area of computer systems. Not only involved programming, she also enjoys getting multiple applications and machines perfectly working together to solve big problems. In her free time, she loves movies, music, cooking, and working out.

About the reviewer

Stefan Lapers started his career almost 20 years ago as a support engineer and quickly grew into Linux/Unix system engineering, security, and network positions. Over the years, he accumulated experience in developing, deploying, and maintaining hosted applications while working for great customers, such as MTV and TMF. In his spare time, he enjoys spending time with his family, tinkering with electronics, and flying model helicopters.

Packt is searching for authors like you

If you're interested in becoming an author for Packt, please visit authors.packtpub.com and apply today. We have worked with thousands of developers and tech professionals, just like you, to help them share their insight with the global tech community. You can make a general application, apply for a specific hot topic that we are recruiting an author for, or submit your own idea.

Table of Contents

Preface

With the trend of microservices architecture in the recent years, a monolithic application is refactored into multiple microservices. Container simplifies the deployment of the application build from microservices. Container management, automation, and orchestration have become crucial problems. Kubernetes is here to solve these.

This book is a practical guide that provides step-by-step tips and examples to help you build and run your own Kubernetes cluster in both private and public clouds. Following along with the book will lead you to understanding how to deploy and manage your application and services in Kubernetes. You will also gain a deep understanding of how to scale and update live containers, and how to do port forwarding and network routing in Kubernetes. You will learn how to build a robust high-availability cluster with the book's hands-on examples. Finally, you will build a Continuous Delivery pipeline by integrating Jenkins, Docker registry, and Kubernetes.

Who this book is for

If you've been playing with Docker containers for a while and want to orchestrate your containers in a modern way, this book is the right choice for you. This book is for those who already understand Docker and container technology, and want to explore further to find better ways to orchestrate, manage, and deploy containers. This book is perfect for going beyond a single container and working with container clusters, learning how to build your own Kubernetes, and making it work seamlessly with your Continuous Delivery pipeline.

What this book covers

Chapter 1, *Building Your Own Kubernetes Cluster*, explains how to build your own Kubernetes cluster with various deployment tools and run your first container on it.

Chapter 2, *Walking through Kubernetes Concepts*, covers both basic and advanced concepts we need to know about Kubernetes. Then, you will learn how to combine them to create Kubernetes objects by writing and applying configuration files.

Chapter 3, *Playing with Containers*, explains how to scale your containers up and down and perform rolling updates without affecting application availability. Furthermore, you will learn how deploy containers for dealing with different application workloads. It will also walk you through best practices of configuration files.

Chapter 4, *Building High-Availability Clusters*, provides information on how to build High Availability Kubernetes master and etcd. This will prevent Kubernetes components from being the single point of failure.

Chapter 5, *Building Continuous Delivery Pipelines*, talks about how to integrate Kubernetes into an existing Continuous Delivery pipeline with Jenkins and private Docker registry.

Chapter 6, *Building Kubernetes on AWS*, walks you through AWS fundamentals. You will learn how to build a Kuberentes cluster on AWS in few minutes.

Chapter 7, *Building Kubernetes on GCP*, leads you to the Google Cloud Platform world. You will learn the GCP essentials and how to launch a managed, production-ready Kubernetes cluster with just a few clicks.

Chapter 8, *Advanced Cluster Administration*, talks about important resource management in Kubernetes. This chapter also goes through other important cluster administration, such as Kubernetes dashboard, authentication, and authorization.

Chapter 9, *Logging and Monitoring*, explains how to collect both system and application logs in Kubernetes by using Elasticsearch, Logstash, and Kibana (ELK). You will also learn how to leverage Heapster, InfluxDB, and Grafana to monitor your Kubernetes cluster.

To get the most out of this book

Throughout the book, we use at least three servers with a Linux-based OS to build all of the components in Kubernetes. At the beginning of the book, you could use one machine, whether it is Linux or Windows, to learn about the concepts and basic deployment. From a scalability point of view, we recommend you start with three servers in order to scale out the components independently and push your cluster to the production level.

Download the example code files

You can download the example code files for this book from your account at `www.packtpub.com`. If you purchased this book elsewhere, you can visit `www.packtpub.com/support` and register to have the files emailed directly to you.

You can download the code files by following these steps:

1. Log in or register at `www.packtpub.com`.
2. Select the **SUPPORT** tab.
3. Click on **Code Downloads & Errata**.
4. Enter the name of the book in the **Search** box and follow the onscreen instructions.

Once the file is downloaded, please make sure that you unzip or extract the folder using the latest version of:

- WinRAR/7-Zip for Windows
- Zipeg/iZip/UnRarX for Mac
- 7-Zip/PeaZip for Linux

The code bundle for the book is also hosted on GitHub at `https://github.com/PacktPublishing/Kubernetes-Cookbook-Second-Edition`. In case there's an update to the code, it will be updated on the existing GitHub repository.

We also have other code bundles from our rich catalog of books and videos available at `https://github.com/PacktPublishing/`. Check them out!

Download the color images

We also provide a PDF file that has color images of the screenshots/diagrams used in this book. You can download it here: `https://www.packtpub.com/sites/default/files/downloads/KubernetesCookbookSecondEdition_ColorImages.pdf`.

Conventions used

There are a number of text conventions used throughout this book.

`CodeInText`: Indicates code words in text, database table names, folder names, filenames, file extensions, pathnames, dummy URLs, user input, and Twitter handles. Here is an example: "Prepare the following YAML file, which is a simple Deployment that launches two `nginx` containers."

A block of code is set as follows:

```
# cat 3-1-1_deployment.yaml
apiVersion: apps/v1
kind: Deployment
metadata:
  name: my-nginx
```

When we wish to draw your attention to a particular part of a code block, the relevant lines or items are set in bold:

```
Annotations:          deployment.kubernetes.io/revision=1
Selector:             env=test,project=My-Happy-Web,role=frontend
Replicas:             5 desired | 5 updated | 5 total | 5 available | 0
unavailable
StrategyType:         RollingUpdate
```

Any command-line input or output is written as follows:

```
//install kubectl command by "kubernetes-cli" package
$ brew install kubernetes-cli
```

Bold: Indicates a new term, an important word, or words that you see onscreen. For example, words in menus or dialog boxes appear in the text like this. Here is an example: "Installation is straightforward, so we can just choose the default options and click **Next**."

Warnings or important notes appear like this.

Tips and tricks appear like this.

Sections

In this book, you will find several headings that appear frequently (*Getting ready*, *How to do it...*, *How it works...*, *There's more...*, and *See also*).

To give clear instructions on how to complete a recipe, use these sections as follows:

Getting ready

This section tells you what to expect in the recipe and describes how to set up any software or any preliminary settings required for the recipe.

How to do it...

This section contains the steps required to follow the recipe.

How it works...

This section usually consists of a detailed explanation of what happened in the previous section.

There's more...

This section consists of additional information about the recipe in order to make you more knowledgeable about the recipe.

See also

This section provides helpful links to other useful information for the recipe.

Get in touch

Feedback from our readers is always welcome.

General feedback: Email `feedback@packtpub.com` and mention the book title in the subject of your message. If you have questions about any aspect of this book, please email us at `questions@packtpub.com`.

Errata: Although we have taken every care to ensure the accuracy of our content, mistakes do happen. If you have found a mistake in this book, we would be grateful if you would report this to us. Please visit www.packtpub.com/submit-errata, selecting your book, clicking on the Errata Submission Form link, and entering the details.

Piracy: If you come across any illegal copies of our works in any form on the internet, we would be grateful if you would provide us with the location address or website name. Please contact us at copyright@packtpub.com with a link to the material.

If you are interested in becoming an author: If there is a topic that you have expertise in and you are interested in either writing or contributing to a book, please visit authors.packtpub.com.

Reviews

Please leave a review. Once you have read and used this book, why not leave a review on the site that you purchased it from? Potential readers can then see and use your unbiased opinion to make purchase decisions, we at Packt can understand what you think about our products, and our authors can see your feedback on their book. Thank you!

For more information about Packt, please visit packtpub.com.

Building Your Own Kubernetes Cluster

1

In this chapter, we will cover the following recipes:

- Exploring the Kubernetes architecture
- Setting up a Kubernetes cluster on macOS by minikube
- Setting up a Kubernetes cluster on Windows by minikube
- Setting up a Kubernetes cluster on Linux by kubeadm
- Setting up a Kubernetes cluster on Linux by Ansible (kubespray)
- Running your first container in Kubernetes

Introduction

Welcome to your journey into Kubernetes! In this very first section, you will learn how to build your own Kubernetes cluster. Along with understanding each component and connecting them together, you will learn how to run your first container on Kubernetes. Having a Kubernetes cluster will help you continue your studies in the chapters ahead.

Exploring the Kubernetes architecture

Kubernetes is an open source container management tool. It is a Go language-based (`https://golang.org`), lightweight and portable application. You can set up a Kubernetes cluster on a Linux-based OS to deploy, manage, and scale Docker container applications on multiple hosts.

Getting ready

Kubernetes is made up of the following components:

- Kubernetes master
- Kubernetes nodes
- etcd
- Kubernetes network

These components are connected via a network, as shown in the following diagram:

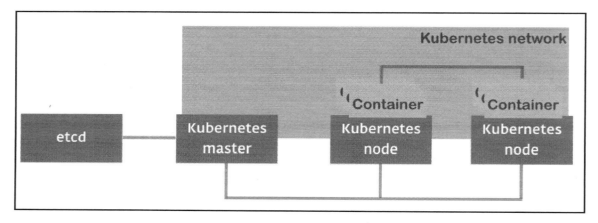

The preceding diagram can be summarized as follows:

- **Kubernetes master**: It connects to etcd via HTTP or HTTPS to store the data
- **Kubernetes nodes**: It connect to the Kubernetes master via HTTP or HTTPS to get a command and report the status
- **Kubernetes network**: It L2, L3 or overlay make a connection of their container applications

How to do it...

In this section, we are going to explain how to use the Kubernetes master and nodes to realize the main functions of the Kubernetes system.

Kubernetes master

The Kubernetes master is the main component of the Kubernetes cluster. It serves several functionalities, such as the following:

- Authorization and authentication
- RESTful API entry point
- Container deployment scheduler to Kubernetes nodes
- Scaling and replicating controllers
- Reading the configuration to set up a cluster

The following diagram shows how master daemons work together to fulfill the aforementioned functionalities:

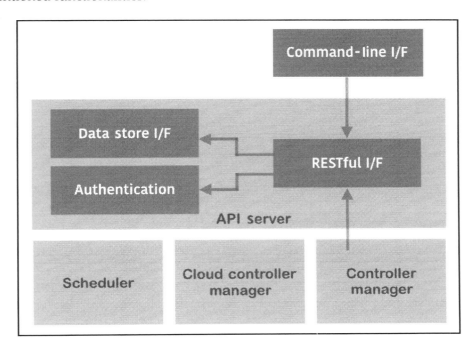

There are several daemon processes that form the Kubernetes master's functionality, such as `kube-apiserver`, `kube-scheduler` and `kube-controller-manager`. Hypercube, the wrapper binary, can launch all these daemons.

In addition, the Kubernetes command-line interface, kubect can control the Kubernetes master functionality.

API server (kube-apiserver)

The API server provides an HTTP- or HTTPS-based RESTful API, which is the hub between Kubernetes components, such as kubectl, the scheduler, the replication controller, the etcd data store, the kubelet and kube-proxy, which runs on Kubernetes nodes, and so on.

Scheduler (kube-scheduler)

The scheduler helps to choose which container runs on which nodes. It is a simple algorithm that defines the priority for dispatching and binding containers to nodes. For example:

- CPU
- Memory
- How many containers are running?

Controller manager (kube-controller-manager)

The controller manager performs cluster operations. For example:

- Manages Kubernetes nodes
- Creates and updates the Kubernetes internal information
- Attempts to change the current status to the desired status

Command-line interface (kubectl)

After you install the Kubernetes master, you can use the Kubernetes command-line interface, kubectl, to control the Kubernetes cluster. For example, kubectl get cs returns the status of each component. Also, kubectl get nodes returns a list of Kubernetes nodes:

```
//see the Component Statuses
# kubectl get cs
NAME                    STATUS     MESSAGE              ERROR
controller-manager      Healthy    ok                   nil
scheduler               Healthy    ok                   nil
etcd-0                  Healthy    {"health": "true"}   nil


//see the nodes
# kubectl get nodes
```

NAME	LABELS	STATUS	AGE
kub-node1	kubernetes.io/hostname=kub-node1	Ready	26d
kub-node2	kubernetes.io/hostname=kub-node2	Ready	26d

Kubernetes node

The Kubernetes node is a slave node in the Kubernetes cluster. It is controlled by the Kubernetes master to run container applications using Docker (http://docker.com) or rkt (http://coreos.com/rkt/docs/latest/). In this book, we will use the Docker container runtime as the default engine.

Node or slave?

The term slave is used in the computer industry to represent the cluster worker node; however, it is also associated with discrimination. The Kubernetes project uses minion in the early version and node in the current version.

The following diagram displays the role and tasks of daemon processes in the node:

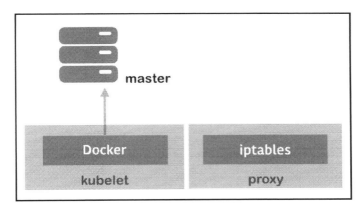

The node also has two daemon processes, named kubelet and kube-proxy, to support its functionalities.

kubelet

kubelet is the main process on the Kubernetes node that communicates with the Kubernetes master to handle the following operations:

- Periodically accesses the API controller to check and report
- Performs container operations
- Runs the HTTP server to provide simple APIs

Proxy (kube-proxy)

The proxy handles the network proxy and load balancer for each container. It changes Linux iptables rules (nat table) to control TCP and UDP packets across the containers.

After starting the kube-proxy daemon, it configures iptables rules; you can use `iptables -t nat -L` or `iptables -t nat -S` to check the nat table rules, as follows:

```
//the result will be vary and dynamically changed by kube-proxy
# sudo iptables -t nat -S
-P PREROUTING ACCEPT
-P INPUT ACCEPT
-P OUTPUT ACCEPT
-P POSTROUTING ACCEPT
-N DOCKER
-N FLANNEL
-N KUBE-NODEPORT-CONTAINER
-N KUBE-NODEPORT-HOST
-N KUBE-PORTALS-CONTAINER
-N KUBE-PORTALS-HOST
-A PREROUTING -m comment --comment "handle ClusterIPs; NOTE: this must be
before the NodePort rules" -j KUBE-PORTALS-CONTAINER
-A PREROUTING -m addrtype --dst-type LOCAL -m comment --comment "handle
service NodePorts; NOTE: this must be the last rule in the chain" -j KUBE-
NODEPORT-CONTAINER
-A PREROUTING -m addrtype --dst-type LOCAL -j DOCKER
-A OUTPUT -m comment --comment "handle ClusterIPs; NOTE: this must be
before the NodePort rules" -j KUBE-PORTALS-HOST
-A OUTPUT -m addrtype --dst-type LOCAL -m comment --comment "handle service
NodePorts; NOTE: this must be the last rule in the chain" -j KUBE-NODEPORT-
HOST
-A OUTPUT ! -d 127.0.0.0/8 -m addrtype --dst-type LOCAL -j DOCKER
-A POSTROUTING -s 192.168.90.0/24 ! -o docker0 -j MASQUERADE
-A POSTROUTING -s 192.168.0.0/16 -j FLANNEL
-A FLANNEL -d 192.168.0.0/16 -j ACCEPT
```

```
-A FLANNEL ! -d 224.0.0.0/4 -j MASQUERADE
```

How it works...

There are two more components to complement Kubernetes node functionalities, the data store etcd and the inter-container network. You can learn how they support the Kubernetes system in the following subsections.

etcd

etcd (https://coreos.com/etcd/) is the distributed key-value data store. It can be accessed via the RESTful API to perform CRUD operations over the network. Kubernetes uses etcd as the main data store.

You can explore the Kubernetes configuration and status in etcd (/registry) using the curl command, as follows:

```
//example: etcd server is localhost and default port is 4001
# curl -L http://127.0.0.1:4001/v2/keys/registry
{"action":"get","node":{"key":"/registry","dir":true,"nodes":[{"key":"/regi
stry/namespaces","dir":true,"modifiedIndex":6,"createdIndex":6},{"key":"/re
gistry/pods","dir":true,"modifiedIndex":187,"createdIndex":187},{"key":"/re
gistry/clusterroles","dir":true,"modifiedIndex":196,"createdIndex":196},{"k
ey":"/registry/replicasets","dir":true,"modifiedIndex":178,"createdIndex":1
78},{"key":"/registry/limitranges","dir":true,"modifiedIndex":202,"createdI
ndex":202},{"key":"/registry/storageclasses","dir":true,"modifiedIndex":215
,"createdIndex":215},{"key":"/registry/apiregistration.k8s.io","dir":true,"
modifiedIndex":7,"createdIndex":7},{"key":"/registry/serviceaccounts","dir"
:true,"modifiedIndex":70,"createdIndex":70},{"key":"/registry/secrets","dir
":true,"modifiedIndex":71,"createdIndex":71},{"key":"/registry/deployments"
,"dir":true,"modifiedIndex":177,"createdIndex":177},{"key":"/registry/servi
ces","dir":true,"modifiedIndex":13,"createdIndex":13},{"key":"/registry/con
figmaps","dir":true,"modifiedIndex":52,"createdIndex":52},{"key":"/registry
/ranges","dir":true,"modifiedIndex":4,"createdIndex":4},{"key":"/registry/m
inions","dir":true,"modifiedIndex":58,"createdIndex":58},{"key":"/registry/
clusterrolebindings","dir":true,"modifiedIndex":171,"createdIndex":171}],"m
odifiedIndex":4,"createdIndex":4}}
```

Kubernetes network

Network communication between containers is the most difficult part. Because Kubernetes manages multiple nodes (hosts) running several containers, those containers on different nodes may need to communicate with each other.

If the container's network communication is only within a single node, you can use Docker network or Docker compose to discover the peer. However, along with multiple nodes, Kubernetes uses an overlay network or **container network interface (CNI)** to achieve multiple container communication.

See also

This recipe describes the basic architecture and methodology of Kubernetes and the related components. Understanding Kubernetes is not easy, but a step-by-step learning process on how to set up, configure, and manage Kubernetes is really fun.

Setting up the Kubernetes cluster on macOS by minikube

Kubernetes consists of combination of multiple open source components. These are developed by different parties, making it difficult to find and download all the related packages and install, configure, and make them work from scratch.

Fortunately, there are some different solutions and tools that have been developed to set up Kubernetes clusters effortlessly. Therefore, it is highly recommended you use such a tool to set up Kubernetes on your environment.

The following tools are categorized by different types of solution to build your own Kubernetes:

- Self-managed solutions that include:
  - minikube
  - kubeadm
  - kubespray
  - kops

- Enterprise solutions that include:
  - OpenShift (`https://www.openshift.com`)
  - Tectonic (`https://coreos.com/tectonic/`)
- Cloud-hosted solutions that include:
  - Google Kubernetes engine (`https://cloud.google.com/kubernetes-engine/`)
  - Amazon elastic container service for Kubernetes (Amazon EKS, `https://aws.amazon.com/eks/`)
  - Azure Container Service (AKS, `https://azure.microsoft.com/en-us/services/container-service/`)

A self-managed solution is suitable if we just want to build a development environment or do a proof of concept quickly.

By using minikube (`https://github.com/kubernetes/minikube`) and kubeadm (`https://kubernetes.io/docs/admin/kubeadm/`), we can easily build the desired environment on our machine locally; however, it is not practical if we want to build a production environment.

By using kubespray (`https://github.com/kubernetes-incubator/kubespray`) and kops (`https://github.com/kubernetes/kops`), we can also build a production-grade environment quickly from scratch.

An enterprise solution or cloud-hosted solution is the easiest starting point if we want to create a production environment. In particular, the **Google Kubernetes Engine (GKE)**, which has been used by Google for many years, comes with comprehensive management, meaning that users don't need to care much about the installation and settings. Also, Amazon EKS is a new service that was introduced at AWS re: Invent 2017, which is managed by the Kubernetes service on AWS.

Kubernetes can also run on different clouds and on-premise VMs by custom solutions. To get started, we will build Kubernetes using minikube on macOS desktop machines in this chapter.

Getting ready

minikube runs Kubernetes on the Linux VM on macOS. It relies on a hypervisor (virtualization technology), such as VirtualBox (`https://www.virtualbox.org`), VMWare fusion (`https://www.vmware.com/products/fusion.html`), or hyperkit (`https://github.com/moby/hyperkit`) In addition, we will need to have the Kubernetes **command-line interface (CLI)** `kubectl`, which is used to connect through the hypervisor, to control Kubernetes.

With minikube, you can run the entire suite of the Kubernetes stack on your macOS, including the Kubernetes master, node, and CLI. It is recommended that macOS has enough memory to run Kubernetes. By default, minikube uses VirtualBox as the hypervisor.

In this chapter, however, we will demonstrate how to use hyperkit, which is the most lightweight solution. As Linux VM consumes 2 GB of memory, at least 4 GB of memory is recommended. Note that hyperkit is built on the top of the hypervisor framework (`https://developer.apple.com/documentation/hypervisor`) on macOS; therefore, macOS 10.10 Yosemite or later is required.

The following diagram shows the relationship between kubectl, the hypervisor, minikube, and macOS:

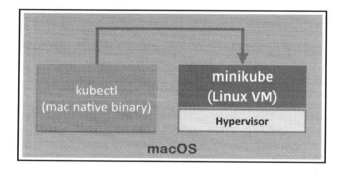

How to do it...

macOS doesn't have an official package management tool, such as yum and apt-get on Linux. But there are some useful tools available for macOS. Homebrew (`https://brew.sh`) is the most popular package management tool and manages many open source tools, including minikube.

In order to install `Homebrew` on macOS, perform the following steps:

1. Open the Terminal and then type the following command:

```
$ /usr/bin/ruby -e "$(curl -fsSL
https://raw.githubusercontent.com/Homebrew/install/master/insta
ll)"
```

2. Once installation is completed, you can type `/usr/local/bin/brew help` to
   see the available command options.

> If you just install or upgrade Xcode on your macOS, the `Homebrew`
> installation may stop. In that case, open Xcode to accept the license
> agreement or type `sudo xcodebuild -license` beforehand.

3. Next, install the `hyperkit driver` for minikube. At the time of writing
   (February 2018), HomeBrew does not support hyperkit; therefore type the
   following command to install it:

```
$ curl -LO
https://storage.googleapis.com/minikube/releases/latest/docker-
machine-driver-hyperkit \
&& chmod +x docker-machine-driver-hyperkit \
&& sudo mv docker-machine-driver-hyperkit /usr/local/bin/ \
&& sudo chown root:wheel /usr/local/bin/docker-machine-driver-
hyperkit \
&& sudo chmod u+s /usr/local/bin/docker-machine-driver-hyperkit
```

4. Next, let's install the Kubernetes CLI. Use Homebrew with the following
   comment to install the `kubectl` command on your macOS:

```
//install kubectl command by "kubernetes-cli" package
$ brew install kubernetes-cli
```

Finally, you can install minikube. It is not managed by Homebrew; however,
Homebrew has an extension called `homebrew-cask` (https://github.com/
caskroom/homebrew-cask) that supports minikube.

5. In order to install minikube by `homebrew-cask`, just simply type the following
   command:

```
//add "cask" option
$ brew cask install minikube
```

6. If you have never installed **Docker for Mac** on your machine, you need to install it via `homebrew-cask` as well

```
//only if you don't have a Docker for Mac
$ brew cask install docker

//start Docker
$ open -a Docker.app
```

7. Now you are all set! The following command shows whether the required packages have been installed on your macOS or not:

```
//check installed package by homebrew
$ brew list
kubernetes-cli


//check installed package by homebrew-cask
$ brew cask list
minikube
```

How it works...

minikube is suitable for setting up Kubernetes on your macOS with the following command, which downloads and starts a Kubernetes VM stet, and then configures the kubectl configuration (`~/.kube/config`):

```
//use --vm-driver=hyperkit to specify to use hyperkit
$ /usr/local/bin/minikube start --vm-driver=hyperkit
Starting local Kubernetes v1.10.0 cluster...
Starting VM...
Downloading Minikube ISO
 150.53 MB / 150.53 MB [=========================================]
100.00% 0s
Getting VM IP address...
Moving files into cluster...
Downloading kubeadm v1.10.0
Downloading kubelet v1.10.0
Finished Downloading kubelet v1.10.0
Finished Downloading kubeadm v1.10.0
Setting up certs...
Connecting to cluster...
Setting up kubeconfig...
Starting cluster components...
Kubectl is now configured to use the cluster.
```

```
Loading cached images from config file.


//check whether .kube/config is configured or not
$ cat ~/.kube/config
apiVersion: v1
clusters:
- cluster:
    certificate-authority: /Users/saito/.minikube/ca.crt
    server: https://192.168.64.26:8443
  name: minikube
contexts:
- context:
    cluster: minikube
    user: minikube
  name: minikube
current-context: minikube
kind: Config
preferences: {}
users:
- name: minikube
  user:
    as-user-extra: {}
    client-certificate: /Users/saito/.minikube/client.crt
    client-key: /Users/saito/.minikube/client.key
```

After getting all the necessary packages, perform the following steps:

1. Wait for a few minutes for the Kubernetes cluster setup to complete.
2. Use `kubectl version` to check the Kubernetes master version and `kubectl get cs` to see the component status.
3. Also, use the `kubectl get nodes` command to check whether the Kubernetes node is ready or not:

```
//it shows kubectl (Client) is 1.10.1, and Kubernetes master
(Server) is 1.10.0
$ /usr/local/bin/kubectl version --short
Client Version: v1.10.1
Server Version: v1.10.0


//get cs will shows Component Status
$ kubectl get cs
NAME                 STATUS    MESSAGE              ERROR
controller-manager   Healthy   ok
scheduler            Healthy   ok
```

```
etcd-0                          Healthy   {"health": "true"}


//Kubernetes node (minikube) is ready
$ /usr/local/bin/kubectl get nodes
NAME        STATUS    ROLES     AGE      VERSION
minikube    Ready     master    2m       v1.10.0
```

4. Now you can start to use Kubernetes on your machine. The following sections describe how to use the `kubectl` command to manipulate Docker containers.

5. Note that, in some cases, you may need to maintain the Kubernetes cluster, such as starting/stopping the VM or completely deleting it. The following commands maintain the minikube environment:

Command	Purpose
`minikube start --vm-driver=hyperkit`	Starts the Kubernetes VM using the hyperkit driver
`minikube stop`	Stops the Kubernetes VM
`minikube delete`	Deletes a Kubernetes VM image
`minikube ssh`	ssh to the Kubernetes VM guest
`minikube ip`	Shows the Kubernetes VM (node) IP address
`minikube update-context`	Checks and updates `~/.kube/config` if the VM IP address is changed
`minikube dashboard`	Opens the web browser to connect the Kubernetes UI

For example, minikube starts a dashboard (the Kubernetes UI) by the default. If you want to access the dashboard, type `minikube dashboard`; it then opens your default browser and connects the Kubernetes UI, as illustrated in the following screenshot:

See also

This recipe describes how to set up a Kubernetes cluster on your macOS using minikube. It is the easiest way to start using Kubernetes. We also learned how to use kubectl, the Kubernetes command-line interface tool, which is the entry point to control our Kubernetes cluster!

Setting up the Kubernetes cluster on Windows by minikube

By nature, Docker and Kubernetes are based on a Linux-based OS. Although it is not ideal to use the Windows OS to explore Kubernetes, many people are using the Windows OS as their desktop or laptop machine. Luckily, there are a lot of ways to run the Linux OS on Windows using virtualization technologies, which makes running a Kubernetes cluster on Windows machines possible. Then, we can build a development environment or do a proof of concept on our local Windows machine.

You can run the Linux VM by using any hypervisor on Windows to set up Kubernetes from scratch, but using minikube (https://github.com/kubernetes/minikube) is the fastest way to build a Kubernetes cluster on Windows. Note that this recipe is not ideal for a production environment because it will set up a Kubernetes on Linux VM on Windows.

Getting ready

To set up minikube on Windows requires a hypervisor, either VirtualBox (https://www.virtualbox.org) or Hyper-V, because, again, minikube uses the Linux VM on Windows. This means that you cannot use the Windows virtual machine (for example, running the Windows VM on macOS by parallels).

However, kubectl, the Kubernetes CLI, supports a Windows native binary that can connect to Kubernetes over a network. So, you can set up a portable suite of Kubernetes stacks on your Windows machine.

The following diagram shows the relationship between kubectl, Hypervisor, minikube, and Windows:

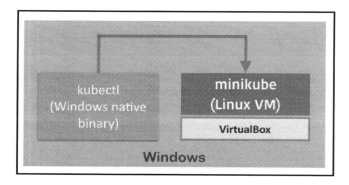

Hyper-V is required for Windows 8 Pro or later. While many users still use Windows 7, we will use VirtualBox as the minikube hypervisor in this recipe.

How to do it...

First of all, VirtualBox for Windows is required:

1. Go to the VirtualBox website (`https://www.virtualbox.org/wiki/Downloads`) to download the Windows installer.
2. Installation is straightforward, so we can just choose the default options and click **Next**:

3. Next, create the `Kubernetes` folder, which is used to store the minikube and kubectl binaries. Let's create the `k8s` folder on top of the `C:` drive, as shown in the following screenshot:

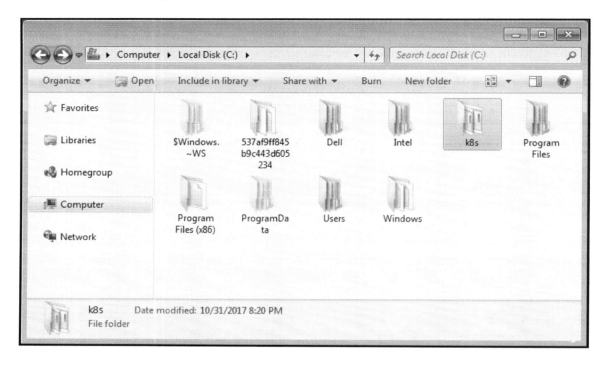

4. This folder must be in the command search path, so open **System Properties**, then move to the **Advanced** tab.

5. Click the **Environment Variables...** button, then choose **Path** , and then click the **Edit...** button, as shown in the following screenshot:

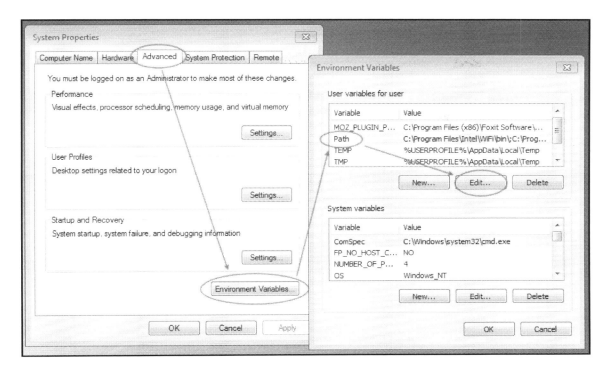

6. Then, append `c:\k8s` , as follows:

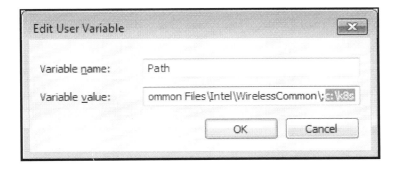

7. After clicking the **OK** button, log off and logo on to Windows again (or reboot) to apply this change.

8. Next, download minikube for Windows. It is a single binary, so use any web browser to download `https://github.com/kubernetes/minikube/releases/download/v0.26.1/minikube-windows-amd64` and then copy it to the `c:\k8s` folder, but change the filename to `minikube.exe`.

9. Next, download kubectl for Windows, which can communicate with Kubernetes. It is also single binary like minikube. So, download `https://storage.googleapis.com/kubernetes-release/release/v1.10.2/bin/windows/amd64/kubectl.exe` and then copy it to the `c:\k8s` folder as well.

10. Eventually, you will see two binaries in the `c:\k8s` folder, as shown in the following screenshot:

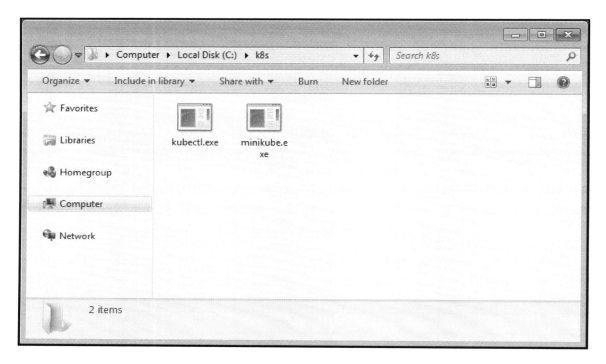

If you are running anti-virus software, it may prevent you from running `kubectl.exe` and `minikube.exe`. If so, please update your anti-virus software setting that allows running these two binaries.

How it works...

Let's get started!

1. Open Command Prompt and then type `minikube start`, as shown in the following screenshot:

```
Command Prompt

c:\>minikube start
Starting local Kubernetes v1.10.0 cluster...
Starting VM...
Downloading Minikube ISO
 150.53 MB / 150.53 MB [===============================] 100.00% 0s
Getting VM IP address...
Moving files into cluster...
Downloading kubelet v1.10.0
Downloading kubeadm v1.10.0
Finished Downloading kubeadm v1.10.0
Finished Downloading kubelet v1.10.0
Setting up certs...
Connecting to cluster...
Setting up kubeconfig...
Starting cluster components...
Kubectl is now configured to use the cluster.
Loading cached images from config file.

c:\>_
```

2. minikube downloads the Linux VM image and then sets up Kubernetes on the Linux VM; now if you open VirtualBox, you can see that the minikube guest has been registered, as illustrated in the following screenshot:

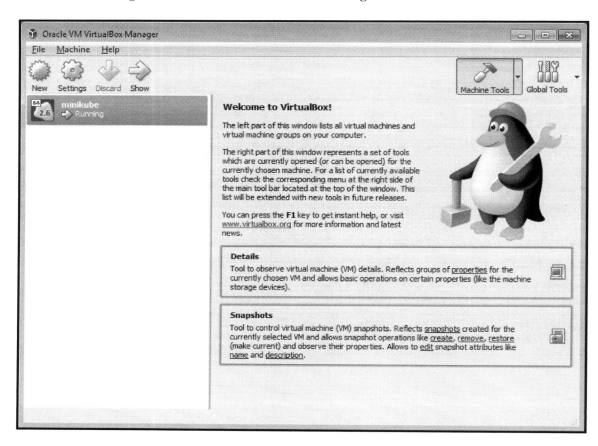

3. Wait for a few minutes to complete the setup of the Kubernetes cluster.
4. As per the following screenshot, type `kubectl version` to check the Kubernetes master version.
5. Use the `kubectl get nodes` command to check whether the Kubernetes node is ready or not:

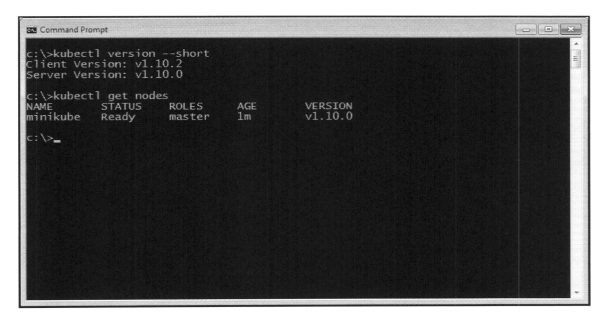

6. Now you can start to use Kubernetes on your machine! Again, Kubernetes is running on the Linux VM, as shown in the next screenshot.

7. Using `minikube ssh` allows you to access the Linux VM that runs Kubernetes:

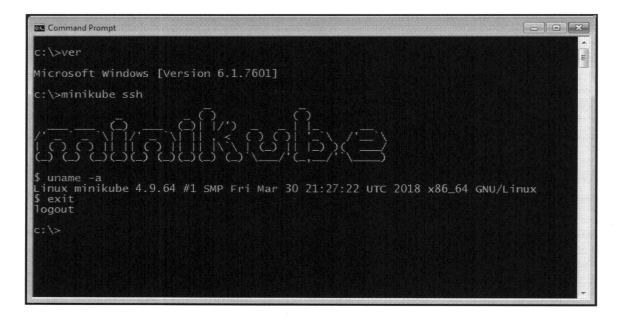

Therefore, any Linux-based Docker image is capable of running on your Windows machine.

8. Type `minikube ip` to verify which IP address the Linux VM uses and also `minikube dashboard`, to open your default web browser and navigate to the Kubernetes UI ,as shown in the following screenshot:

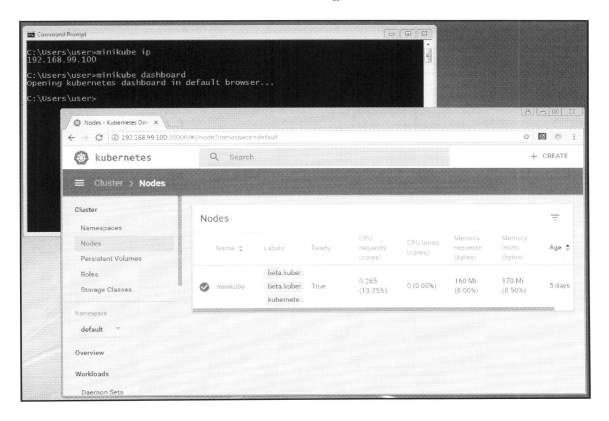

9. If you don't need to use Kubernetes anymore, type `minikube stop` or open VirtualBox to stop the Linux guest and release the resource, as shown in the following screenshot:

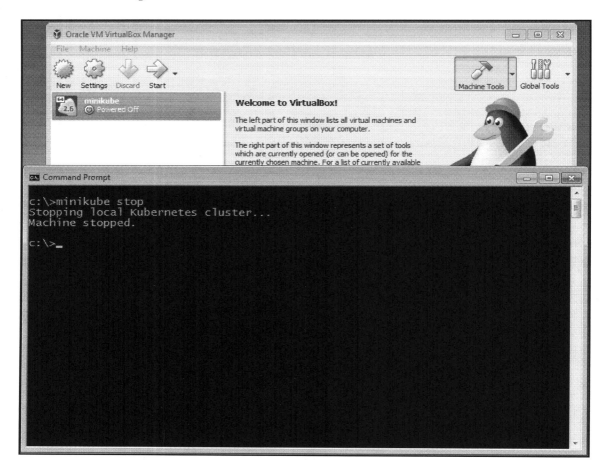

See also

This recipe describes how to set up a Kubernetes cluster on your Windows OS using minikube. It is the easiest way to start using Kubernetes. It also describes kubectl, the Kubernetes command-line interface tool, which is the entry point form which to control your Kubernetes.

Setting up the Kubernetes cluster on Linux via kubeadm

In this recipe, we are going to show how to create a Kubernetes cluster along with kubeadm (`https://github.com/kubernetes/kubeadm`) on Linux servers. Kubeadm is a command-line tool that simplifies the procedure of creating and managing a Kubernetes cluster. Kubeadm leverages the fast deployment feature of Docker, running the system services of the Kubernetes master and the etcd server as containers. When triggered by the `kubeadm` command, the container services will contact kubelet on the Kubernetes node directly; kubeadm also checks whether every component is healthy. Through the kubeadm setup steps, you can avoid having a bunch of installation and configuration commands when you build everything from scratch.

Getting ready

We will provide instructions of two types of OS:

- Ubuntu Xenial 16.04 (LTS)
- CentOS 7.4

Make sure the OS version is matched before continuing. Furthermore, the software dependency and network settings should be also verified before you proceed to thecd cd next step. Check the following items to prepare the environment:

- **Every node has a unique MAC address and product UUID**: Some plugins use the MAC address or product UUID as a unique machine ID to identify nodes (for example, `kube-dns`). If they are duplicated in the cluster, kubeadm may not work while starting the plugin:

```
// check MAC address of your NIC
$ ifconfig -a
// check the product UUID on your host
$ sudo cat /sys/class/dmi/id/product_uuid
```

- **Every node has a different hostname**: If the hostname is duplicated, the Kubernetes system may collect logs or statuses from multiple nodes into the same one.
- **Docker is installed**: As mentioned previously, the Kubernetes master will run its daemon as a container, and every node in the cluster should get Docker installed. For how to perform the Docker installation, you can follow the steps on the official website: (Ubuntu: `https://docs.docker.com/engine/installation/linux/docker-ce/ubuntu/`, and CentOS: `https://docs.docker.com/engine/installation/linux/docker-ce/centos/`) Here we have Docker CE 17.06 installed on our machines; however, only Docker versions 1.11.2 to 1.13.1, and 17.03.x are verified with Kubernetes version 1.10.
- **Network ports are available**: The Kubernetes system services need network ports for communication. The ports in the following table should now be occupied according to the role of the node:

Node role	Ports	System service
Master	6443	Kubernetes API server
	10248/10250/10255	kubelet local healthz endpoint/Kubelet API/Heapster (read-only)
	10251	kube-scheduler
	10252	kube-controller-manager
	10249/10256	kube-proxy
	2379/2380	etcd client/etcd server communication
Node	10250/10255	Kubelet API/Heapster (read-only)
	30000~32767	Port range reserved for exposing container service to outside world

- The Linux command, `netstat`, can help to check if the port is in use or not:

```
// list every listening port
$ sudo netstat -tulpn | grep LISTEN
```

- Network tool packages are installed. `ethtool` and `ebtables` are two required utilities for kubeadm. They can be download and installed by the `apt-get` or `yum` package managing tools.

How to do it...

The installation procedures for two Linux OSes, Ubuntu and CentOS, are going to be introduced separately in this recipe as they have different setups.

Package installation

Let's get the Kubernetes packages first! The repository for downloading needs to be set in the source list of the package management system. Then, we are able to get them installed easily through the command-line.

Ubuntu

To install Kubernetes packages in Ubuntu perform the following steps:

1. Some repositories are URL with HTTPS. The `apt-transport-https` package must be installed to access the HTTPS endpoint:

    ```
    $ sudo apt-get update && sudo apt-get install -y apt-transport-
    https
    ```

2. Download the public key for accessing packages on Google Cloud, and add it as follows:

    ```
    $ curl -s https://packages.cloud.google.com/apt/doc/apt-key.gpg
    | sudo apt-key add -
    OK
    ```

3. Next, add a new source list for the Kubernetes packages:

    ```
    $ sudo bash -c 'echo "deb http://apt.kubernetes.io/ kubernetes-
    xenial main" > /etc/apt/sources.list.d/kubernetes.list'
    ```

3. Finally, it is good to install the Kubernetes packages:

    ```
    // on Kubernetes master
    $ sudo apt-get update && sudo apt-get install -y kubelet
    kubeadm kubectl
    // on Kubernetes node
    $ sudo apt-get update && sudo apt-get install -y kubelet
    ```

CentOS

To install Kubernetes packages in CentOS perform the following steps:

1. As with Ubuntu, new repository information needs to be added:

```
$ sudo vim /etc/yum.repos.d/kubernetes.repo
[kubernetes]
name=Kubernetes
baseurl=https://packages.cloud.google.com/yum/repos/kubernetes-
el7-x86_64
enabled=1
gpgcheck=1
repo_gpgcheck=1
gpgkey=https://packages.cloud.google.com/yum/doc/yum-key.gpg
https://packages.cloud.google.com/yum/doc/rpm-package-key.gpg
```

2. Now, we are ready to pull the packages from the Kubernetes source base via the `yum` command:

```
// on Kubernetes master
$ sudo yum install -y kubelet kubeadm kubectl
// on Kubernetes node
$ sudo yum install -y kubelet
```

3. No matter what OS it is, check the version of the package you get!

```
// take it easy! server connection failed since there is not
server running
$ kubectl version
Client Version: version.Info{Major:"1", Minor:"10",
GitVersion:"v1.10.2",
GitCommit:"81753b10df112992bf51bbc2c2f85208aad78335",
GitTreeState:"clean", BuildDate:"2018-04-27T09:22:21Z",
GoVersion:"go1.9.3", Compiler:"gc", Platform:"linux/amd64"}
The connection to the server 192.168.122.101:6443 was refused -
did you specify the right host or port?
```

System configuration prerequisites

Before running up the whole system by kubeadm, please check that Docker is running on your machine for Kubernetes. Moreover, in order to avoid critical errors while executing kubeadm, we will show the necessary service configuration on both the system and kubelet. As well as the master, please set the following configurations on the Kubernetes nodes to get kubelet to work fine with kubeadm.

CentOS system settings

There are other additional settings in CentOS to make Kubernetes behave correctly. Be aware that, even if we are not using kubeadm to manage the Kubernetes cluster, the following setup should be considered while running kubelet:

1. Disable SELinux, since kubelet does not support SELinux completely:

```
// check the state of SELinux, if it has already been disabled,
bypass below commands
$ sestatus
```

We can `disable SELinux` through the following command, or by `modifying the configuration file`:

```
// disable SELinux through command
$   sudo setenforce 0
// or modify the configuration file
$ sudo sed -I 's/ SELINUX=enforcing/SELINUX=disabled/g'
/etc/sysconfig/selinux
```

Then we'll need to `reboot` the machine:

```
// reboot is required
$ sudo reboot
```

2. Enable the usage of iptables. To prevent some routing errors happening, add runtime parameters:

```
// enable the parameters by setting them to 1
$ sudo bash -c 'echo "net.bridge.bridge-nf-call-ip6tables = 1"
> /etc/sysctl.d/k8s.conf'
$ sudo bash -c 'echo "net.bridge.bridge-nf-call-iptables = 1"
>> /etc/sysctl.d/k8s.conf'
// reload the configuration
$ sudo sysctl --system
```

Booting up the service

Now we can start the service. First enable and then start kubelet on your Kubernetes master machine:

```
$ sudo systemctl enable kubelet && sudo systemctl start kubelet
```

While checking the status of kubelet, you may be worried to see the status displaying activating (`auto-restart`); and you may get further frustrated to see the detail logs by the `journalctl` command, as follows:

```
error: unable to load client CA file /etc/kubernetes/pki/ca.crt: open
/etc/kubernetes/pki/ca.crt: no such file or directory
```

Don't worry. kubeadm takes care of creating the certificate authorities file. It is defined in the service configuration file, `/etc/systemd/system/kubelet.service.d/10-kubeadm.conf` by argument `KUBELET_AUTHZ_ARGS`. The kubelet service won't be a healthy without this file, so keep trying to restart the daemon by itself.

Go ahead and start all the master daemons via kubeadm. It is worth noting that using kubeadm requires the root permission to achieve a service level privilege. For any sudoer, each kubeadm would go after the `sudo` command:

```
$ sudo kubeadm init
```

Find preflight checking error while firing command `kubeadm init`? Using following one to disable running swap as description.

```
$ sudo kubeadm init --ignore-preflight-errors=Swap
```

And you will see the sentence `Your Kubernetes master has initialized successfully!` showing on the screen. Congratulations! You are almost done! Just follow the information about the user environment setup below the greeting message:

```
$ mkdir -p $HOME/.kube
$ sudo cp -i /etc/kubernetes/admin.conf $HOME/.kube/config
$ sudo chown $(id -u):$(id -g) $HOME/.kube/config
```

The preceding commands ensure every Kubernetes instruction is fired by your account execute with the proper credentials and connects to the correct server portal:

```
// Your kubectl command works great now
$ kubectl version
Client Version: version.Info{Major:"1", Minor:"10", GitVersion:"v1.10.2",
GitCommit:"81753b10df112992bf51bbc2c2f85208aad78335", GitTreeState:"clean",
BuildDate:"2018-04-27T09:22:21Z", GoVersion:"go1.9.3", Compiler:"gc",
Platform:"linux/amd64"}
Server Version: version.Info{Major:"1", Minor:"10", GitVersion:"v1.10.2",
GitCommit:"81753b10df112992bf51bbc2c2f85208aad78335", GitTreeState:"clean",
BuildDate:"2018-04-27T09:10:24Z", GoVersion:"go1.9.3", Compiler:"gc",
Platform:"linux/amd64"}
```

More than that, kubelet goes into a healthy state now:

```
// check the status of kubelet
$ sudo systemctl status kubelet
...
Active: active (running) Mon 2018-04-30 18:46:58 EDT; 2min 43s ago
...
```

Network configurations for containers

After the master of the cluster is ready to handle jobs and the services are running, for the purpose of making containers accessible to each other through networking, we need to set up the network for container communication. It is even more important initially while building up a Kubernetes cluster with kubeadm, since the master daemons are all running as containers. kubeadm supports the CNI (https://github.com/containernetworking/cni). We are going to attach the CNI via a Kubernetes network add-on.

There are many third-party CNI solutions that supply secured and reliable container network environments. Calico (https://www.projectcalico.org), one CNI provide stable container networking. Calico is light and simple, but still well implemented by the CNI standard and integrated with Kubernetes:

```
$ kubectl apply -f
https://docs.projectcalico.org/v2.6/getting-started/kubernetes/installation
/hosted/kubeadm/1.6/calico.yaml
```

Here, whatever your host OS is, the command kubectl can fire any sub command for utilizing resources and managing systems. We use kubectl to apply the configuration of Calico to our new-born Kubernetes.

More advanced management of networking and Kubernetes add-ons will be discussed in Chapter 7, *Building Kubernetes on GCP*.

Getting a node involved

Let's log in to your Kubernetes node to join the group controlled by kubeadm:

1. First, enable and start the service, `kubelet`. Every Kubernetes machine should have `kubelet` running on it:

```
$ sudo systemctl enable kubelet && sudo systemctl start kubelet
```

2. After that, fire the `kubeadm` join command with an input flag token and the IP address of the master, notifying the master that it is a secured and authorized node. You can get the token on the master node via the `kubeadm` command:

```
// on master node, list the token you have in the cluster
$ sudo kubeadm token list
TOKEN                     TTL        EXPIRES
USAGES                    DESCRIPTION
EXTRA GROUPS
da3a90.9a119695a933a867   6h         2018-05-01T18:47:10-04:00
authentication,signing    The default bootstrap token generated
by 'kubeadm init'.    system:bootstrappers:kubeadm:default-node-
token
```

3. In the preceding output, if `kubeadm init` succeeds, the default token will be generated. Copy the token and paste it onto the node, and then compose the following command:

```
// The master IP is 192.168.122.101, token is
da3a90.9a119695a933a867, 6443 is the port of api server.
$ sudo kubeadm join --token da3a90.9a119695a933a867
192.168.122.101:6443 --discovery-token-unsafe-skip-ca-
verification
```

 What if you call `kubeadm token list` to list the tokens, and see they are all expired? You can create a new one manually by this command: `kubeadm token create`.

4. Please make sure that the master's firewall doesn't block any traffic to port `6443`, which is for API server communication. Once you see the words `Successfully established connection` showing on the screen, it is time to check with the master if the group got the new member:

```
// fire kubectl subcommand on master
$ kubectl get nodes
```

NAME	STATUS	ROLES	AGE	VERSION
ubuntu01	Ready	master	11h	v1.10.2
ubuntu02	Ready	<none>	26s	v1.10.2

Well done! No matter if whether your OS is Ubuntu or CentOS, kubeadm is installed and kubelet is running. You can easily go through the preceding steps to build your Kubernetes cluster.

You may be wondering about the flag `discovery-token-unsafe-skip-ca-verification` used while joining the cluster. Remember the kubelet log that says the certificate file is not found? That's it, since our Kubernetes node is brand new and clean, and has never connected with the master before. There is no certificate file to find for verification. But now, because the node has shaken hands with the master, the file exists. We may join in this way (in some situation requiring rejoining the same cluster):

```
kubeadm join --token $TOKEN $MASTER_IPADDR:6443 --discovery-token-ca-cert-hash sha256:$HASH
```

The hash value can be obtained by the `openssl` command:

```
// rejoining the same cluster
$ HASH=$(openssl x509 -pubkey -in /etc/kubernetes/pki/ca.crt | openssl rsa -pubin -outform der 2>/dev/null | openssl dgst -sha256 -hex | sed 's/^.* //')
$ sudo kubeadm join --token da3a90.9a119695a933a867 192.168.122.101:6443 --discovery-token-ca-cert-hash sha256:$HASH
```

How it works...

When kubeadm init sets up the master, there are six stages:

1. **Generating certificate files and keys for services**: Certificated files and keys are used for security management during cross-node communications. They are located in the `/etc/kubernetes/pki` directory. Take kubelet, for example. It cannot access the Kubernetes API server without passing the identity verification.
2. **Writing kubeconfig files**: The `kubeconfig` files define permissions, authentication, and configurations for kubectl actions. In this case, the Kubernetes controller manager and scheduler have related `kubeconfig` files to fulfill any API requests.

3. **Creating service daemon YAML files**: The service daemons under kubeadm's control are just like computing components running on the master. As with setting deployment configurations on disk, kubelet will make sure each daemon is active.

4. **Waiting for kubelet to be alive, running the daemons as pods**: When kubelet is alive, it will boot up the service pods described in the files under the `/etc/kubernetes/manifests` directory. Moreover, kubelet guarantees to keep them activated, restarting the pod automatically if it crashes.

5. **Setting post-configuration for the cluster**: Some cluster configurations still need to be set, such as configuring **role-based accessing control** (**RBAC**) rules, creating a namespace, and tagging the resources.

6. **Applying add-ons**: DNS and proxy services can be added along with the kubeadm system.

While the user enters kubeadm and joins the Kubernetes node, kubeadm will complete the first two stages like the master.

If you have faced a heavy and complicated set up procedure in earlier versions of Kubernetes, it is quite a relief to set up a Kubernetes cluster with kubeadm. kubeadm reduces the overhead of configuring each daemon and starting them one by one. Users can still do customization on kubelet and master services, by just modifying a familiar file, `10-kubeadm.conf` and the YAML files under `/etc/kubernetes/manifests`. Kubeadm not only helps to establish the cluster but also enhances security and availability, saving you time.

See also

We talked about how to build a Kubernetes cluster. If you're ready to run your first application on it, check the last recipe in this chapter and run the container! And for advanced management of your cluster, you can also look at `Chapter 8`, Advanced Cluster Administration, of this book:

- *Advanced settings in kubeconfig,* in `Chapter 8`, *Advanced Cluster Administration*

Setting up the Kubernetes cluster on Linux via Ansible (kubespray)

If you are familiar with configuration management, such as Puppet, Chef and Ansible, kubespray (`https://github.com/kubernetes-incubator/kubespray`) is the best choice to set up a Kubernetes cluster from scratch. It provides the Ansible playbook that supports the majority of Linux distributions and public clouds, such as AWS and GCP.

Ansible (`https://www.ansible.com`) is a Python-based SSH automation tool that can configure Linux as your desired state based on the configuration, which is called playbook. This cookbook describes how to use kubespray to set up Kubernetes on Linux.

Getting ready

As of May 2018, the latest version of kubespray is 2.5.0, which supports the following operation systems to install Kubernetes:

- RHEL/CentOS 7
- Ubuntu 16.04 LTS

 According to the kubespray documentation, it also supports CoreOS and debian distributions. However, those distributions may need some additional steps or have technical difficulties. This cookbook uses CentOS 7 and Ubuntu 16.04 LTS.

In addition, you need to install Ansible on your machine. Ansible works on Python 2.6, 2.7, and 3.5 or higher. macOS and Linux might be the best choice to install Ansible because Python is preinstalled by most of macOS and Linux distributions by default. In order to check which version of Python you have, open a Terminal and type the following command:

```
//Use capital V
$ python -V
Python 2.7.5
```

Overall, you need at least three machines, as mentioned in the following table:

Type of host	Recommended OS/Distribution
Ansible	macOS or any Linux which has Python 2.6, 2.7, or 3.5
Kubernetes master	RHEL/CentOS 7 or Ubuntu 16.04 LTS
Kubernetes node	RHEL/CentOS 7 or Ubuntu 16.04 LTS

There are some network communicating with each other, so you need to at least open a network port (for example, AWS Security Group or GCP Firewall rule) as:

- **TCP/22 (ssh)**: Ansible to Kubernetes master/node host
- **TCP/6443 (Kubernetes API server)**: Kubernetes node to master
- **Protocol 4 (IP encapsulated in IP)**: Kubernetes master and node to each other by Calico

In Protocol 4 (IP encapsulated in IP), if you are using AWS, set an ingress rule to specify `aws ec2 authorize-security-group-ingress --group-id <your SG ID> --cidr <network CIDR> --protocol 4`. In addition, if you are using GCP, set the firewall rule to specify as `cloud compute firewall-rules create allow-calico --allow 4 --network <your network name> --source-ranges <network CIDR>`.

Installing pip

The easiest way to install Ansible, is to use pip, the Python package manager. Some of newer versions of Python have `pip` already (Python 2.7.9 or later and Python 3.4 or later):

1. To confirm whether `pip` is installed or not, similar to the Python command, use –V:

```
//use capital V
$ pip -V
pip 9.0.1 from /Library/Python/2.7/site-packages (python 2.7)
```

2. On the other hand, if you see the following result, you need to install `pip`:

```
//this result shows you don't have pip yet
$ pip -V
-bash: pip: command not found
```

3. In order to install pip, download `get-pip.py` and install by using the following command:

```
//download pip install script
$ curl -LO https://bootstrap.pypa.io/get-pip.py


//run get-pip.py by privileged user (sudo)
$ sudo python get-pip.py
Collecting pip
  Downloading pip-9.0.1-py2.py3-none-any.whl (1.3MB)
    100% |###############################| 1.3MB 779kB/s
Collecting wheel
  Downloading wheel-0.30.0-py2.py3-none-any.whl (49kB)
    100% |###############################| 51kB 1.5MB/s
Installing collected packages: pip, wheel
Successfully installed pip-9.0.1 wheel-0.30.0


//now you have pip command
$ pip -V
pip 9.0.1 from /usr/lib/python2.7/site-packages (python 2.7)
```

Installing Ansible

Perform the following steps to install Ansible:

1. Once you have installed `pip`, you can install Ansible with the following command:

```
//ran by privileged user (sudo)
$ sudo pip install ansible
```

`pip` scans your Python and installs the necessary libraries for Ansible, so it may take a few minutes to complete.

2. Once you have successfully installed Ansible by `pip`, you can verify it with the following command and see output as this:

```
$ which ansible
/usr/bin/ansible

$ ansible --version
```

```
ansible 2.4.1.0
```

Installing python-netaddr

Next, according to kubespray's documentation (`https://github.com/kubernetes-incubator/kubespray#requirements`), it needs the `python-netaddr` package. This package can also be installed by pip, as shown in the following code:

```
$ sudo pip install netaddr
```

Setting up ssh public key authentication

One more thing, as mentioned previously, Ansible is actually the ssh automation tool. If you log on to host via ssh, you have to have an appropriate credential (user/password or ssh public key) to the target machines. In this case, the target machines mean the Kubernetes master and nodes.

Due to security reasons, especially in the public cloud, Kubernetes uses only the ssh public key authentication instead of ID/password authentication.

To follow the best practice, let's copy the ssh public key from your Ansible machine to the Kubernetes master/node machines:

 If you've already set up ssh public key authentication between the Ansible machine to Kubernetes candidate machines, you can skip this step.

1. In order to create an ssh public/private key pair from your Ansible machine, type the following command:

```
//with -q means, quiet output
$ ssh-keygen -q
```

2. It will ask you to set a passphrase. You may set or skip (empty) this, but you have to remember it.
3. Once you have successfully created a key pair, you can see the private key as `~/.ssh/id_rsa` and public key as `~/.ssh/id_rsa.pub`. You need to append the public key to the target machine under `~/.ssh/authorized_keys`, as shown in the following screenshot:

4. You need to copy and paste your public key to all Kubernetes master and node candidate machines.

5. To make sure your ssh public key authentication works, just ssh from the Ansible machine to the target host that won't ask for your logon password, as here:

```
//use ssh-agent to remember your private key and passphrase (if
you set)
ansible_machine$ ssh-agent bash
ansible_machine$ ssh-add
Enter passphrase for /home/saito/.ssh/id_rsa: Identity added:
/home/saito/.ssh/id_rsa (/home/saito/.ssh/id_rsa)


//logon from ansible machine to k8s machine which you copied
public key
ansible_machine$ ssh 10.128.0.2
Last login: Sun Nov  5 17:05:32 2017 from
133.172.188.35.bc.googleusercontent.com
k8s-master-1$
```

Now you are all set! Let's set up Kubernetes using kubespray (Ansible) from scratch.

How to do it...

kubespray is provided through the GitHub repository (`https://github.com/kubernetes-incubator/kubespray/tags`), as shown in the following screenshot:

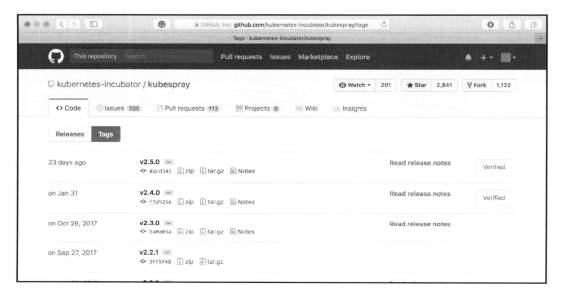

Because kubespray is an Ansible playbook, not a binary, you can download the latest version (as of May 2018, version 2.5.0 is the latest) of the `zip` or `tar.gz` to your Ansible machine directly and unarchive it with the following command:

```
//download tar.gz format
ansible_machine$ curl -LO
https://github.com/kubernetes-incubator/kubespray/archive/v2.5.0.tar.gz


//untar
ansible_machine$ tar zxvf v2.5.0.tar.gz


//it unarchives under kubespray-2.5.0 directory
ansible_machine$ ls -F
get-pip.py  kubespray-2.5.0/  v2.5.0.tar.gz


//change to kubespray-2.5.0 directory
ansible_machine$ cd kubespray-2.5.0/
```

Maintaining the Ansible inventory

In order to perform the Ansible playbook, you need to maintain your own inventory file, which contains target machine IP addresses:

1. There is a sample inventory file under the inventory directory, so you can copy it by using the following:

```
//copy sample to mycluster
ansible_machine$ cp -rfp inventory/sample inventory/mycluster

//edit hosts.ini
ansible_machine$ vi inventory/mycluster/hosts.ini
```

2. In this cookbook, we are using target machines that have the following IP addresses:
   - Kubernetes master : 10.128.0.2
   - Kubernetes node : 10.128.0.4

3. In this case, hosts.ini should be in the following format:

```
1-5 — vi inventory.cfg — 80×18
 1 my-master-1 ansible_ssh_host=10.128.0.2
 2 my-node-1 ansible_ssh_host=10.128.0.4
 3
 4
 5 [kube-master]
 6 my-master-1
 7
 8 [etcd]
 9 my-master-1
10
11 [kube-node]
12 my-master-1
13 my-node-1
14
15 [k8s-cluster:children]
16 kube-node
17 kube-master
```

4. Please change the IP address to match your environment.

Note that hostname (my-master-1 and my-node-1) will be set by the kubespray playbook based on this hosts.ini, so feel free to assign a meaningful hostname.

Running the Ansible ad hoc command to test your environment

Before running the kubespray playbook, let's check whether `hosts.ini` and Ansible itself work properly or not:

1. To do that, use the Ansible ad hoc command, using the ping module, as shown in the following screenshot:

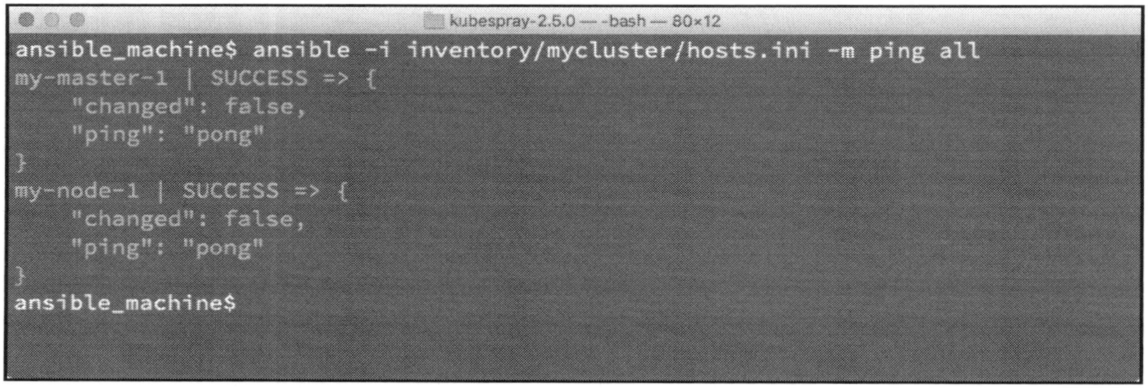

kubespray-2.5.0 — -bash — 80×12
ansible_machine$ ansible -i inventory/mycluster/hosts.ini -m ping all
my-master-1 | SUCCESS => {
"changed": false,
"ping": "pong"
}
my-node-1 | SUCCESS => {
"changed": false,
"ping": "pong"
}
ansible_machine$

2. This result indicates `SUCCESS`. But if you see the following error, probably the IP address is wrong or the target machine is down, so please the check target machine first:

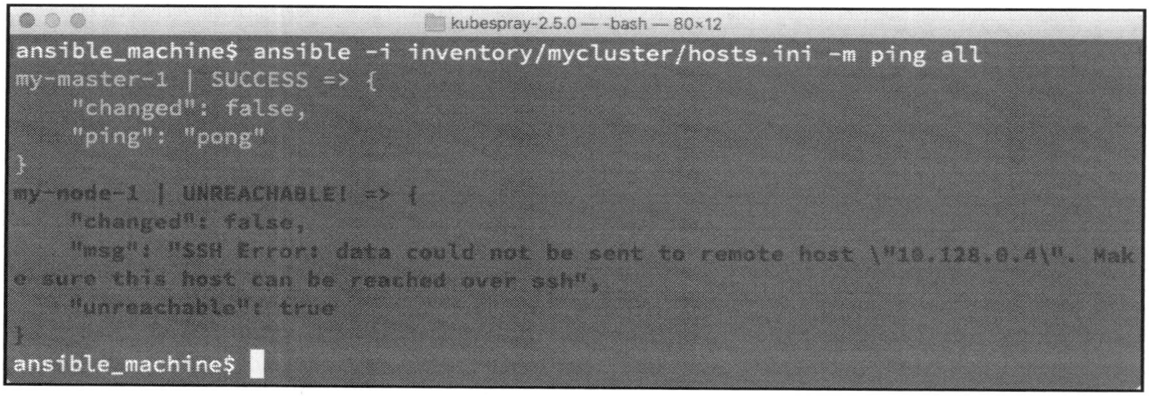

kubespray-2.5.0 — -bash — 80×12
ansible_machine$ ansible -i inventory/mycluster/hosts.ini -m ping all
my-master-1 | SUCCESS => {
"changed": false,
"ping": "pong"
}
my-node-1 | UNREACHABLE! => {
"changed": false,
"msg": "SSH Error: data could not be sent to remote host \"10.128.0.4\". Mak
e sure this host can be reached over ssh",
"unreachable": true
}
ansible_machine$

3. Next, check your authority whether you can escalate a privilege on the target machine or not. In other words, whether you can run `sudo` or not. This is because you will need to install Kubernetes, Docker, and some related binaries, and configurations that need a root privilege. To confirm that, add the −b (become) option, as shown in the following screenshot:

```
kubespray-2.5.0 — -bash — 80×12
ansible_machine$ ansible -b -i inventory/mycluster/hosts.ini -m ping all
my-master-1 | SUCCESS => {
    "changed": false,
    "ping": "pong"
}
my-node-1 | SUCCESS => {
    "changed": false,
    "ping": "pong"
}
ansible_machine$
```

4. With the −b option, it actually tries to perform sudo on the target machine. If you see SUCCESS, you are all set! Go to the *How it works...* section to run kubespray.

If you're unfortunate enough to see some errors, please refer to the following section to solve Ansible issues.

Ansible troubleshooting

The ideal situation would be to use the same Linux distribution, version, settings, and logon user. However, the environment will be different based on policy, compatibility, and other reasons. Ansible is flexible and can support many use cases to run `ssh` and `sudo`.

Need to specify a sudo password

Based on your Linux machine setting, you may see the following error when adding the −b option. In this case, you need to type your password while running the sudo command:

```
ansible_machine$ ansible -b -i inventory/mycluster/hosts.ini -m ping all
my-master-1 | FAILED! => {
    "changed": false,
    "module_stderr": "sudo: a password is required\n",
    "module_stdout": "",
    "msg": "MODULE FAILURE",
    "rc": 1
}
my-node-1 | FAILED! => {
    "changed": false,
    "module_stderr": "sudo: a password is required\n",
    "module_stdout": "",
    "msg": "MODULE FAILURE",
    "rc": 1
}
ansible_machine$
```

In this case, add −K (ask for the sudo password) and run again. It will ask for your sudo password when running the Ansible command, as shown in the following screenshot:

```
ansible_machine$ ansible -b -K -i inventory/mycluster/hosts.ini -m ping all
SUDO password:
```

> If your Linux uses the su command instead of sudo, adding --become-method=su to run the Ansible command could help. Please read the Ansible documentation for more details : http://docs.ansible.com/ansible/latest/become.html

Need to specify different ssh logon user

Sometimes you may need to ssh to target machines using a different logon user. In this case, you can append the `ansible_user` parameter to an individual host in `hosts.ini`. For example:

- Use the username `kirito` to ssh to `my-master-1`
- Use the username `asuna` to ssh to `my-node-1`

In this case, change `hosts.ini`, as shown in the following code:

```
my-master-1 ansible_ssh_host=10.128.0.2 ansible_user=kirito
my-node-1 ansible_ssh_host=10.128.0.4 ansible_user=asuna
```

Need to change ssh port

Another scenario is where you may need to run the ssh daemon on some specific port number rather than the default port number 22. Ansible also supports this scenario and uses the `ansible_port` parameter to the individual host in `hosts.ini`, as shown in the following code (in the example, the ssh daemon is running at 10022 on `my-node-1`):

```
my-master-1 ansible_ssh_host=10.128.0.2
my-node-1 ansible_ssh_host=10.128.0.4 ansible_port=10022
```

Common ansible issue

Ansible is flexible enough to support any other situations. If you need any specific parameters to customize the ssh logon for the target host, read the Ansible inventory documentation to find a specific parameter: http://docs.ansible.com/ansible/latest/intro_inventory.html

In addition, Ansible has a configuration file, `ansible.cfg`, on top of the `kubespray` directory. It defines common settings for Ansible. For example, if you are using a very long username that usually causes an Ansible error, change `ansible.cfg` to set `control_path` to solve the issue, as shown in the following code:

```
[ssh_connection]
control_path = %(directory)s/%%h-%%r
```

If you plan to set up more than 10 nodes, you may need to increase ssh simultaneous sessions. In this case, adding the `forks` parameter also requires you to increase the ssh timeout from 10 seconds to 30 seconds by adding the timeout parameter, as shown in the following code:

```
[ssh_connection]
forks = 50
timeout = 30
```

The following screenshot contains all of the preceding configurations in `ansible.cfg`:

```
ansible_machine$ cat ansible.cfg
[ssh_connection]
pipelining=True
ansible_ssh_common_args = -o ControlMaster=auto -o ControlPersist=30m -o ConnectionAttempts=100
control_path = %(directory)s/%%h-%%r
forks = 50
timeout = 30

[defaults]
host_key_checking=False
gathering = smart
fact_caching = jsonfile
fact_caching_connection = /tmp
stdout_callback = skippy
library = ./library
callback_whitelist = profile_tasks
roles_path = roles:$VIRTUAL_ENV/usr/local/share/kubespray/roles:$VIRTUAL_ENV/usr/local/share/ansible/roles
ansible_machine$
```

For more details, please visit the Ansible configuration documentation at `http://docs.ansible.com/ansible/latest/intro_configuration.html`

How it works...

Now you can start to run the kubepray playbook:

1. You've already created an inventory file as `inventory/mycluster/hosts.ini`. Other than `hosts.ini`, you need to check and update global variable configuration files at `inventory/mycluster/group_vars/all.yml`.
2. There are a lot of variables defined, but at least one variable, `bootstrap_os`, needs to be changed from `none` to your target Linux machine. If you are using RHEL/CentOS7, set `bootstrap_os` as `centos`. If you are using Ubuntu 16.04 LTS, set `bootstrap_os` as `ubuntu` as shown in the following screenshot:

```
● ○ ○                   kubespray-2.5.0 — vim inventory/mycluster/group_vars/all.yml — 80×11
  1 # Valid bootstrap options (required): ubuntu, coreos, centos, none
  2 bootstrap_os  ubuntu
  3
  4 #Directory where etcd data stored
  5 etcd_data_dir   /var/lib/etcd
  6
  7 # Directory where the binaries will be installed
  8 bin_dir  /usr/local/bin
  9
 10 ## The access_ip variable is used to define how other nodes should access
```

 You can also update other variables, such as `kube_version`, to change or install a Kubernetes version. For more details, read the documentation at `https://github.com/kubernetes-incubator/kubespray/blob/master/docs/vars.md`.

3. Finally, you can execute the playbook. Use the `ansible-playbook` command instead of the Ansible command. Ansible-playbook runs multiple Ansible modules based on tasks and roles that are defined in the playbook.

4. To run the kubespray playbook, type the ansible-playbook command with the following parameters:

```
//use -b (become), -i (inventory) and specify cluster.yml as
playbook
$ ansible-playbook -b -i inventory/mycluster/hosts.ini
cluster.yml
```

 The ansible-playbook argument parameter is the same as the Ansible command. So, if you need to use -K (ask for the `sudo` password) or --become-method=su, you need to specify for ansible-playbook as well.

5. It takes around 5 to 10 minutes to complete based on the machine spec and network bandwidth. But eventually you can see PLAY RECAP, as shown in the following screenshot, to see whether it has succeeded or not:

```
ss] ***
Tuesday 08 May 2018  15:13:01 -0700 (0:00:00.045)      0:08:39.469 **********

PLAY RECAP ********************************************************************
localhost                  : ok=2    changed=0    unreachable=0    failed=0
my-master-1                : ok=374  changed=121  unreachable=0    failed=0
my-node-1                  : ok=239  changed=71   unreachable=0    failed=0

Tuesday 08 May 2018  15:13:01 -0700 (0:00:00.037)      0:08:39.506 **********
===============================================================================
kubernetes/preinstall : Update package management cache (YUM) --------------- 34.29s
docker : ensure docker packages are installed ------------------------------- 32.01s
kubernetes/master : Master | wait for the apiserver to be running ----------- 22.72s
download : container_download | Download containers if pull is required or told to always pull (all nodes) -- 20.98s
kubernetes-apps/ansible : Kubernetes Apps | Lay Down KubeDNS Template ------- 12.86s
kubernetes/preinstall : Install packages requirements ----------------------- 11.95s
docker : Docker | pause while Docker restarts ------------------------------- 10.19s
download : container_download | Download containers if pull is required or told to always pull (all nodes) --- 9.48s
network_plugin/calico : Calico | Create calico manifests --------------------- 8.79s
kubernetes/master : Master | wait for kube-scheduler ------------------------- 6.05s
download : container_download | Download containers if pull is required or told to always pull (all nodes) --- 5.86s
kubernetes-apps/ansible : Kubernetes Apps | Start Resources ------------------ 5.56s
kubernetes/secrets : Check certs | check if a cert already exists on node ---- 5.49s
download : container_download | Download containers if pull is required or told to always pull (all nodes) --- 5.21s
download : container_download | Download containers if pull is required or told to always pull (all nodes) --- 4.16s
kubernetes-apps/network_plugin/calico : Start Calico resources -------------- 4.12s
etcd : wait for etcd up ----------------------------------------------------- 4.02s
kubernetes/node : write the kubecfg (auth) file for kubelet ------------------ 3.87s
bootstrap-os : Check presence of fastestmirror.conf ------------------------- 2.87s
docker : Docker | reload docker --------------------------------------------- 2.76s
```

6. If you see `failed=0` like in the preceding screenshot, you have been successful in setting up a Kubernetes cluster. You can ssh to the Kubernetes master machine and run the `/usr/local/bin/kubectl` command to see the status, as shown in the following screenshot:

```
kubespray-2.5.0 — saito@my-master-1:~ — ssh -A saito@35.184.93.77 — 80×15
ansible_machine$ ssh 10.128.0.2
The authenticity of host '10.128.0.2 (10.128.0.2)' can't be established.
ECDSA key fingerprint is SHA256:zv4pnlQkatt10pPuBBreAPiZdl14s/dTlrgOrY2m49s.
ECDSA key fingerprint is MD5:2a:91:5b:dd:6c:34:31:c5:fc:e7:bb:d7:4a:f7:34:bf.
Are you sure you want to continue connecting (yes/no)? yes
Warning: Permanently added '10.128.0.2' (ECDSA) to the list of known hosts.
Last login: Tue May  8 22:08:28 2018 from 209.194.91.4
[saito@my-master-1 ~]$ /usr/local/bin/kubectl get nodes
NAME            STATUS    ROLES         AGE       VERSION
my-master-1     Ready     master,node   5m        v1.10.2
my-node-1       Ready     node          5m        v1.10.2
[saito@my-master-1 ~]$ /usr/local/bin/kubectl version --short
Client Version: v1.10.2
Server Version: v1.10.2
[saito@my-master-1 ~]$
```

7. The preceding screenshot shows that you have been successful in setting up the Kubernetes version 1.10.2 master and node. You can continue to use the `kubectl` command to configure you Kubernetes cluster in the following chapters.

8. Unfortunately, if you see a failed count of more than 0, the Kubernetes cluster has probably not been set up correctly. Because failure is caused by many reasons, there is no single solution. It is recommended that you append the verbose option `-v` to see more detailed output from Ansible, as shown in the following code:

```
//use -b (become), -i (inventory) and -v (verbose)
$ ansible-playbook -v -b -i inventory/mycluster/hosts.ini
cluster.yml
```

9. If the failure is timeout, just retrying the ansible-playbook command again may solve it. Because Ansible is designed as an idempotency, if you re-perform the ansible-playbook command twice or more, Ansible still can configure correctly.

10. If the failure is change target IP address after you run ansible-playbook (for example, re-using the Ansible machine to set up another Kubernetes cluster), you need to clean up the fact cache file. It is located under /tmp directory, so you just delete this file, as shown in the following screenshot:

```
● ● ●                          🏠 saito — -bash — 80×12
$ ls /tmp/
com.apple.launchd.0oAMNFfNmM      com.apple.launchd.fBjfzMOS82
com.apple.launchd.61Imdps55v      com.apple.launchd.iHPMagpIk5
com.apple.launchd.8Incf4Cjil      com.apple.launchd.rI5b0vejWE
com.apple.launchd.KfYesGcxZE      com.apple.launchd.y2tnFHiwrO
com.apple.launchd.QtdqaYzglA      my-master-1
com.apple.launchd.XVc7C4xBVm      my-node-1
com.apple.launchd.YSQtxsh9yI      powerlog
com.apple.launchd.bIdWcoPbGO
$ rm /tmp/my-master-1 /tmp/my-node-1
$
```

See also

This section describes how to set up the Kubernetes cluster on the Linux OS using kubespray. It is the Ansible playbook that supports major Linux distribution. Ansible is simple, but due to supporting any situation and environment, you need to care about some different use cases. Especially with ssh and sudo-related configurations, you need to understand Ansible deeper to fit it with your environment.

Running your first container in Kubernetes

Congratulations! You've built your own Kubernetes cluster in the previous recipes. Now, let's get on with running your very first container, nginx (http://nginx.org/), which is an open source reverse proxy server, load balancer, and web server. Along with this recipe, you will create a simple nginx application and expose it to the outside world.

Getting ready

Before you start to run your first container in Kubernetes, it's better to check if your cluster is in a healthy mode. A checklist showing the following items would make your `kubectl` sub commands stable and successful, without unknown errors caused by background services:

1. Checking the master daemons. Check whether the Kubernetes components are running:

```
// get the components status
$ kubectl get cs
NAME                 STATUS    MESSAGE                 ERROR
controller-manager   Healthy   ok
scheduler            Healthy   ok
etcd-0               Healthy   {"health": "true"}
```

2. Check the status of the Kubernetes master:

```
// check if the master is running
$ kubectl cluster-info
Kubernetes master is running at https://192.168.122.101:6443
KubeDNS is running at
https://192.168.122.101:6443/api/v1/namespaces/kube-system/serv
ices/kube-dns/proxy

To further debug and diagnose cluster problems, use 'kubectl
cluster-info dump'.
```

3. Check whether all the nodes are ready:

```
$ kubectl get nodes
NAME       STATUS   ROLES     AGE    VERSION
ubuntu01   Ready    master    20m    v1.10.2
ubuntu02   Ready    <none>    2m     v1.10.2
```

Ideal results should look like the preceding outputs. You can successfully fire the `kubectl` command and get the response without errors. If any one of the checked items failed to meet the expectation, check out the settings in the previous recipes based on the management tool you used.

4. Check the access permission of the Docker registry, as we will use the official free image as an example. If you want to run your own application, be sure to dockerize it first! What you need to do for your custom application is to write a Dockerfile (https://docs.docker.com/engine/reference/builder/), and build and push it into the public or private Docker registry.

Test your node connectivity with the public/private Docker registry

On your node, try the Docker pull nginx command to test whether you can pull the image from the Docker Hub. If you're behind a proxy, please add HTTP_PROXY into your Docker configuration file(https://docs.docker.com/engine/admin/systemd/#httphttps-proxy). If you want to run the image from the private repository in the Docker Hub, or the image from the private Docker registry, a Kubernetes secret is required. Please check *Working with secrets*, in Chapter 2, *Working through Kubernetes Concepts, for the instructions.*

How to do it...

We will use the official Docker image of nginx as an example. The image is provided in the Docker Hub (https://store.docker.com/images/nginx), and also the Docker Store (https://hub.docker.com/_/nginx/).

Many of the official and public images are available on the Docker Hub or Docker Store so that you do not need to build them from scratch. Just pull them and set up your custom setting on top of them.

Docker Store versus Docker Hub

As you may be aware, there is a more familiar official repository, Docker Hub, which was launched for the community for sharing the based image. Compared with the Docker Hub, the Docker Store is focused on enterprise applications. It provides a place for enterprise-level Docker images, which could be free or paid for software. You may feel more confident in using a more reliable image on the Docker Store.

Running a HTTP server (nginx)

On the Kubernetes master, we can use `kubectl run` to create a certain number of containers. The Kubernetes master will then schedule the pods for the nodes to run, with general command formatting, as follows:

```
$ kubectl run <replication controller name> --image=<image name> --
replicas=<number of replicas> [--port=<exposing port>]
```

The following example will create two replicas with the name `my-first-nginx` from the nginx image and expose port `80`. We can deploy one or more containers in what is referred to as a pod. In this case, we will deploy one container per pod. Just like a normal Docker behavior, if the nginx image doesn't exist locally, it will pull it from the Docker Hub by default:

```
// run a deployment with 2 replicas for the image nginx and expose the
container port 80
$ kubectl run my-first-nginx --image=nginx --replicas=2 --port=80
deployment "my-first-nginx" created
```

The name of deployment <my-first-nginx> cannot be duplicated

The resource (pods, services, deployment, and so on) in one Kubernetes namespace cannot be duplicated. If you run the preceding command twice, the following error will pop up:

```
Error from server (AlreadyExists): deployments.extensions
"my-first-nginx" already exists
```

Let's move on and see the current status of all the pods by `kubectl get pods`. Normally the status of the pods will hold on Pending for a while, since it takes some time for the nodes to pull the image from the registry:

```
// get all pods
$ kubectl get pods
NAME                               READY   STATUS    RESTARTS   AGE
my-first-nginx-7dcd87d4bf-jp572    1/1     Running   0          7m
my-first-nginx-7dcd87d4bf-ns7h4    1/1     Running   0          7m
```

If the pod status is not running for a long time

You could always use kubectl get pods to check the current status of the pods, and kubectl describe pods $pod_name to check the detailed information in a pod. If you make a typo of the image name, you might get the `ErrImagePull` error message, and if you are pulling the images from a private repository or registry without proper credentials, you might get the `ImagePullBackOff` message. If you get the `Pending` status for a long time and check out the node capacity, make sure you don't run too many replicas that exceed the node capacity. If there are other unexpected error messages, you could either stop the pods or the entire replication controller to force the master to schedule the tasks again.

You can also check the details about the deployment to see whether all the pods are ready:

```
// check the status of your deployment
$ kubectl get deployment
NAME            DESIRED   CURRENT   UP-TO-DATE   AVAILABLE   AGE
my-first-nginx  2         2         2            2           2m
```

Exposing the port for external access

We might also want to create an external IP address for the nginx deployment. On cloud providers that support an external load balancer (such as Google compute engine), using the `LoadBalancer` type will provision a load balancer for external access. On the other hand, you can still expose the port by creating a Kubernetes service as follows, even though you're not running on platforms that support an external load balancer. We'll describe how to access this externally later:

```
// expose port 80 for replication controller named my-first-nginx
$ kubectl expose deployment my-first-nginx --port=80 --type=LoadBalancer
service "my-first-nginx" exposed
```

We can see the service status we just created:

```
// get all services
$ kubectl get service
NAME            TYPE           CLUSTER-IP      EXTERNAL-IP   PORT(S)
AGE
kubernetes      ClusterIP      10.96.0.1       <none>        443/TCP
2h
my-first-nginx  LoadBalancer   10.102.141.22   <pending>     80:31620/TCP
3m
```

You may find an additional service named `kubernetes` if the service daemon run as a container (for example, using kubeadm as a management tool). It is for exposing the REST API of the Kubernetes API server internally. The pending state of `my-first-nginx` service's external IP indicates that it is waiting for a specific public IP from cloud provider. Take a look at `Chapter 6`, *Building Kubernetes on AWS*, and `Chapter 7`, *Building Kubernetes on GCP*, for more details.

Congratulations! You just ran your first container with a Kubernetes pod and exposed port `80` with the Kubernetes service.

Stopping the application

We can stop the application using commands such as the delete deployment and service. Before this, we suggest you read through the following code first to understand more about how it works:

```
// stop deployment named my-first-nginx
$ kubectl delete deployment my-first-nginx
deployment.extensions "my-first-nginx" deleted

// stop service named my-first-nginx
$ kubectl delete service my-first-nginx
service "my-first-nginx" deleted
```

How it works...

Let's take a look at the insight of the service using describe in the `kubectl` command. We will create one Kubernetes service with the type `LoadBalancer`, which will dispatch the traffic into two endpoints, `192.168.79.9` and `192.168.79.10` with port `80`:

```
$ kubectl describe service my-first-nginx
Name:             my-first-nginx
Namespace:        default
Labels:           run=my-first-nginx
Annotations:      <none>
Selector:         run=my-first-nginx
Type:             LoadBalancer
IP:               10.103.85.175
Port:             <unset>  80/TCP
TargetPort:       80/TCP
NodePort:         <unset>  31723/TCP
Endpoints:        192.168.79.10:80,192.168.79.9:80
```

```
Session Affinity:          None
External Traffic Policy:   Cluster
Events:                    <none>
```

The port here is an abstract service port, which will allow any other resources to access the service within the cluster. The nodePort will be indicating the external port to allow external access. The targetPort is the port the container allows traffic into; by default, it will be the same port.

In the following diagram, external access will access the service with nodePort. The service acts as a load balancer to dispatch the traffic to the pod using port 80. The pod will then pass through the traffic into the corresponding container using targetPort 80:

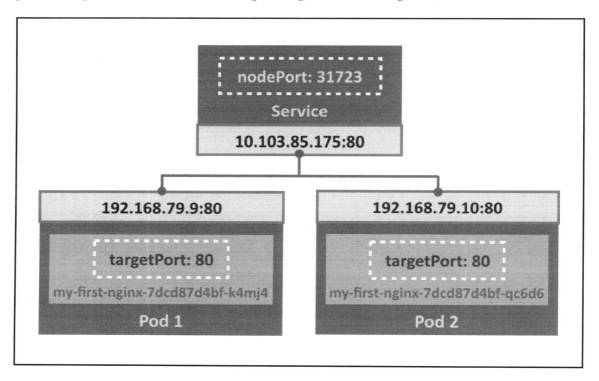

In any nodes or master, once the inter-connection network is set up, you should be able to access the nginx service using ClusterIP 192.168.61.150 with port 80:

```
// curl from service IP
$ curl 10.103.85.175:80
<!DOCTYPE html>
<html>
```

```
<head>
<title>Welcome to nginx!</title>
<style>
    body {
        width: 35em;
        margin: 0 auto;
        font-family: Tahoma, Verdana, Arial, sans-serif;
    }
</style>
</head>
<body>
<h1>Welcome to nginx!</h1>
<p>If you see this page, the nginx web server is successfully installed and
working. Further configuration is required.</p>
<p>For online documentation and support please refer to
<a href="http://nginx.org/">nginx.org</a>.<br/>
Commercial support is available at
<a href="http://nginx.com/">nginx.com</a>.</p>
<p><em>Thank you for using nginx.</em></p>
</body>
</html>
```

It will be the same result if we `curl` to the target port of the pod directly:

```
// curl from endpoint, the content is the same as previous nginx html
$ curl 192.168.79.10:80
<!DOCTYPE html>
<html>
...
```

If you'd like to try out external access, use your browser to access the external IP address. Please note that the external IP address depends on which environment you're running in.

In the Google compute engine, you could access it via a `ClusterIP` with a proper rewall rules setting:

```
$ curl http://<clusterIP>
```

In a custom environment, such as on-premise data center, you could go through the IP address of nodes to access :

```
$ curl http://<nodeIP>:<nodePort>
```

You should be able to see the following page using a web browser:

Welcome to nginx!

If you see this page, the nginx web server is successfully installed and working. Further configuration is required.

For online documentation and support please refer to nginx.org. Commercial support is available at nginx.com.

Thank you for using nginx.

See also

We have run our very first container in this section. Go ahead and read the next chapter to aquire more knowledge about Kubernetes:

- Chapter 2, *Walking through Kubernetes Concepts*

2
Walking through Kubernetes Concepts

In this chapter, we will cover the following recipes:

- Linking Pods and containers
- Managing Pods with ReplicaSets
- Deployment API
- Working with Services
- Working with Volumes
- Working with Secrets
- Working with names
- Working with Namespaces
- Working with labels and selectors

Introduction

In this chapter, we will start by creating different kinds of resources on the Kubernetes system. In order to realize your application in a microservices structure, reading the recipes in this chapter will be a good start towards understanding the concepts of the Kubernetes resources and consolidating them. After you deploy applications in Kubernetes, you can work on its scalable and efficient container management, and also fulfill the DevOps delivering procedure of microservices.

An overview of Kubernetes

Working with Kubernetes is quite easy, using either a **Command Line Interface (CLI)** or API (RESTful). This section will describe Kubernetes control by CLI. The CLI we use in this chapter is version 1.10.2.

After you install Kubernetes master, you can run a `kubectl` command as follows. It shows the kubectl and Kubernetes master versions (both the API Server and CLI are v1.10.2):

```
$ kubectl version --short
Client Version: v1.10.2
Server Version: v1.10.2
```

`kubectl` connects the Kubernetes API server using the RESTful API. By default, it attempts to access the localhost if `.kube/config` is not configured, otherwise you need to specify the API server address using the `--server` parameter. Therefore, it is recommended to use `kubectl` on the API server machine for practice.

 If you use kubectl over the network, you need to consider authentication and authorization for the API server. See `Chapter 7`, *Building Kubernetes on GCP*.

`kubectl` is the only command for Kubernetes clusters, and it controls the Kubernetes cluster manager. Find more information at `http://kubernetes.io/docs/user-guide/kubectl-overview/`. Any container, or Kubernetes cluster operation, can be performed by a `kubectl` command.

In addition, kubectl allows the inputting of information via either the command line's optional arguments or a file (use the `-f` option); it is highly recommended to use a file, because you can maintain Kubernetes configuration as code. This will be described in detail in this chapter.

Here is a typical `kubectl` command-line argument:

```
kubectl [command] [TYPE] [NAME] [flags]
```

The attributes of the preceding command are as follows:

- `command`: Specifies the operation that you want to perform on one or more resources.
- `TYPE`: Specifies the resource type. Resource types are case-sensitive and you can specify the singular, plural, or abbreviated forms.

- NAME: Specifies the name of the resource. Names are case-sensitive. If the name is omitted, details for all resources are displayed.
- flags: Specifies optional flags.

For example, if you want to launch nginx, you can use either the kubectl run command or the kubectl create -f command with the YAML file as follows:

1. Use the run command:

```
$ kubectl run my-first-nginx --image=nginx "my-first-nginx"
```

2. Use the create -f command with the YAML file:

```
$ cat nginx.yaml
apiVersion: apps/v1
kind: Deployment
metadata:
  name: my-first-nginx
  labels:
    app: nginx
spec:
  replicas: 1
  selector:
    matchLabels:
      app: nginx
  template:
    metadata:
      labels:
        app: nginx
    spec:
      containers:
      - name: nginx
        image: nginx

//specify -f (filename)
$ kubectl create -f nginx.yaml
deployment.apps "my-first-nginx" created
```

3. If you want to see the status of the Deployment, type the kubectl get command as follows:

```
$ kubectl get deployment
NAME            DESIRED   CURRENT   UP-TO-DATE   AVAILABLE
AGE
my-first-nginx  1         1         1            1
4s
```

4. If you also want the support abbreviation, type the following:

```
$ kubectl get deploy
NAME              DESIRED   CURRENT   UP-TO-DATE   AVAILABLE
AGE
my-first-nginx    1         1         1            1
38s
```

5. If you want to delete these resources, type the `kubectl delete` command as follows:

```
$ kubectl delete deploy my-first-nginx
deployment.extensions "my-first-nginx" deleted
```

6. The `kubectl` command supports many kinds of sub-commands; use the `-h` option to see the details, for example:

```
//display whole sub command options
$ kubectl -h


//display sub command "get" options
$ kubectl get -h


//display sub command "run" options
$ kubectl run -h
```

This section describes how to use the `kubectl` command to control the Kubernetes cluster. The following recipes describe how to set up Kubernetes components:

- *Setting up a Kubernetes cluster on macOS using minikube* and *Set up a Kubernetes cluster on Windows using minikube* in Chapter 1, *Building Your Own Kubernetes Cluster*
- *Setting up a Kubernetes cluster on Linux using kubeadm* in Chapter 1, *Building Your Own Kubernetes Cluster*
- *Setting up a Kubernetes cluster on Linux using kubespray (Ansible)* in Chapter 1, *Building Your Own Kubernetes Cluster*

Linking Pods and containers

The Pod is a group of one or more containers and the smallest deployable unit in Kubernetes. Pods are always co-located and co-scheduled, and run in a shared context. Each Pod is isolated by the following Linux namespaces:

- The **process ID** (**PID**) namespace
- The network namespace
- The **interprocess communication** (**IPC**) namespace
- The **unix time sharing** (**UTS**) namespace

In a pre-container world, they would have been executed on the same physical or virtual machine.

It is useful to construct your own application stack Pod (for example, web server and database) that are mixed by different Docker images.

Getting ready

You must have a Kubernetes cluster and make sure that the Kubernetes node has accessibility to the Docker Hub (`https://hub.docker.com`) in order to download Docker images.

 If you are running minikube, use `minikube ssh` to log on to the minikube VM first, then run the `docker pull` command.

You can simulate downloading a Docker image by using the `docker pull` command as follows:

```
//this step only if you are using minikube
$ minikube ssh
                          _ _
            _ _ ( ) ( )
   ___ ___  (_) ___ (_)| |/') _ _ | |_ __
 /' _ ` _ `\| |/' _ `\| || , < ( ) ( )| '_`\ /'__`\
 | ( ) ( ) || || ( ) || || |\`\ | (_) || |_) )( ___/
 (_) (_) (_)(_)(_) (_)(_)(_) (_)`\___/'(_,__/'`\____)


//run docker pull to download CentOS docker image
```

```
$ docker pull centos
Using default tag: latest
latest: Pulling from library/centos
d9aaf4d82f24: Pull complete
Digest:
sha256:4565fe2dd7f4770e825d4bd9c761a81b26e49cc9e3c9631c58cfc3188be9505a
Status: Downloaded newer image for centos:latest
```

How to do it...

The following are the steps to create a Pod has 2 containers:

1. Log on to the Kubernetes machine (no need to log on if using minikube) and prepare the following YAML file. It defines the launch nginx container and the CentOS container.

2. The nginx container opens the HTTP port (TCP/80). On the other hand, the CentOS container attempts to access the localhost:80 every three seconds using the curl command:

```
$ cat my-first-pod.yaml
apiVersion: v1
kind: Pod
metadata:
  name: my-first-pod
spec:
  containers:
  - name: my-nginx
    image: nginx
  - name: my-centos
    image: centos
    command: ["/bin/sh", "-c", "while : ;do curl
http://localhost:80/; sleep 10; done"]
```

3. Then, execute the kubectl create command to launch my-first-pod as follows:

```
$ kubectl create -f my-first-pod.yaml
pod "my-first-pod" created
```

It takes between a few seconds and a few minutes, depending on the network bandwidth of the Docker Hub and Kubernetes node's spec.

4. You can check `kubectl get pods` to see the status, as follows:

```
//still downloading Docker images (0/2)
$ kubectl get pods
NAME             READY    STATUS              RESTARTS   AGE
my-first-pod     0/2      ContainerCreating   0          14s


//my-first-pod is running (2/2)
$ kubectl get pods
NAME             READY    STATUS    RESTARTS   AGE
my-first-pod     2/2      Running   0          1m
```

Now both the nginx container (`my-nginx`) and the CentOS container (`my-centos`) are ready.

5. Let's check whether the CentOS container can access `nginx` or not. You can run the `kubectl exec` command to run bash on the CentOS container, then run the `curl` command to access the `nginx`, as follows:

```
//run bash on my-centos container
//then access to TCP/80 using curl
$ kubectl exec my-first-pod -it -c my-centos -- /bin/bash
[root@my-first-pod /]#
[root@my-first-pod /]# curl -L http://localhost:80
<!DOCTYPE html>
<html>
<head>
<title>Welcome to nginx!</title>
<style>
    body {
        width: 35em;
        margin: 0 auto;
        font-family: Tahoma, Verdana, Arial, sans-serif;
    }
</style>
</head>
<body>
<h1>Welcome to nginx!</h1>
<p>If you see this page, the nginx web server is successfully
installed and
working. Further configuration is required.</p>

<p>For online documentation and support please refer to
<a href="http://nginx.org/">nginx.org</a>.<br/>
Commercial support is available at
```

```
<a href="http://nginx.com/">nginx.com</a>.</p>

<p><em>Thank you for using nginx.</em></p>
</body>
</html>
```

As you can see, the Pod links two different containers, `nginx` and `CentOS`, into the same Linux network namespace.

How it works...

When launching a Pod, the Kubernetes scheduler dispatches to the kubelet process to handle all the operations to launch both `nginx` and `CentOS` containers on one Kubernetes node.

The following diagram illustrates these two containers and the Pod; these two containers can communicate via the localhost network, because within the Pod containers, it share the network interface:

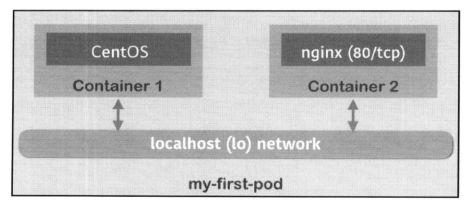

A Pod has two containers, which can communicate via localhost

If you have two or more nodes, you can check the `-o wide` option to find a node which runs a Pod:

```
//it indicates Node "minikube" runs my-first-pod
$ kubectl get pods -o wide
NAME            READY      STATUS      RESTARTS    AGE      IP          NODE
my-first-pod    2/2        Running     0           43m      172.17.0.2
minikube
```

Log in to that node, then you can check the `docker ps | grep my-first-pod` command to see the running containers as follows:

List of containers that belong to my-first-pod

You may notice that `my-first-pod` contains three containers; `centos`, `nginx`, and `pause` are running instead of two. Because each Pod we need to keep belongs to a particular Linux namespace, if both the CentOS and nginx containers die, the namespace will also destroyed. Therefore, the pause container just remains in the Pod to maintain Linux namespaces.

Let's launch a second Pod, rename it as `my-second-pod`, and run the `kubectl` create command as follows:

```
//just replace the name from my-first-pod to my-second-pod
$ cat my-first-pod.yaml | sed -e 's/my-first-pod/my-second-pod/' > my-second-pod.yaml


//metadata.name has been changed to my-second-pod
$ cat my-second-pod.yaml
apiVersion: v1
kind: Pod
metadata:
  name: my-second-pod
spec:
  containers:
```

```
  - name: my-nginx
    image: nginx
  - name: my-centos
    image: centos
    command: ["/bin/sh", "-c", "while : ;do curl
http://localhost:80/; sleep 10; done"]


//create second pod
$ kubectl create -f my-second-pod.yaml
pod "my-second-pod" created


//2 pods are running
$ kubectl get pods
NAME              READY     STATUS     RESTARTS     AGE
my-first-pod      2/2       Running    0            1h
my-second-pod     2/2       Running    0            43s
```

Now you have two Pods; each Pod has two containers, `centos` and `nginx`. So a total of four containers are running on your Kubernetes cluster as in the following diagram:

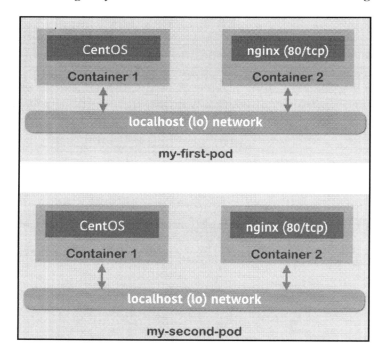

Duplicate Pod from my-first-pod to my-second-pod

If you would like to deploy more of the same Pod, consider using a Deployment (ReplicaSet) instead.

After your testing, you can run the `kubectl` delete command to delete your Pod from the Kubernetes cluster:

```
//specify --all option to delete all pods
$ kubectl delete pods --all
pod "my-first-pod" deleted
pod "my-second-pod" deleted


//pods are terminating
$ kubectl get pods
NAME             READY    STATUS        RESTARTS    AGE
my-first-pod     2/2      Terminating   0           1h
my-second-pod    2/2      Terminating   0           3m
```

See also

This recipe from this chapter described how to control Pods. They are the basic components of Kubernetes operation. The following recipes will describe the advanced operation of Pods using Deployments, Services, and so on:

- *Managing Pods with ReplicaSets*
- *Deployment API*
- *Working with Services*
- *Working with labels and selectors*

Managing Pods with ReplicaSets

A ReplicaSet is a term for API objects in Kubernetes that refer to Pod replicas. The idea is to be able to control a set of Pods' behaviors. The ReplicaSet ensures that the Pods, in the amount of a user-specified number, are running all the time. If some Pods in the ReplicaSet crash and terminate, the system will recreate Pods with the original configurations on healthy nodes automatically, and keep a certain number of processes continuously running. While changing the size of set, users can scale the application out or down easily. According to this feature, no matter whether you need replicas of Pods or not, you can always rely on ReplicaSet for auto-recovery and scalability. In this recipe, you're going to learn how to manage your Pods with ReplicaSet:

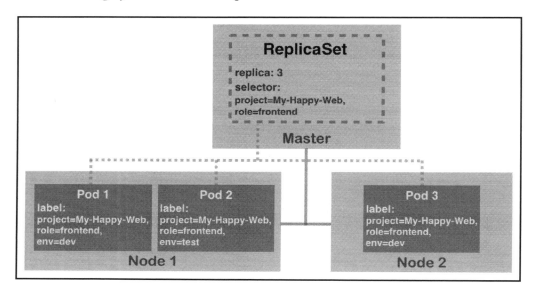

ReplicaSet and their Pods on two nodes

The ReplicaSet usually handles a tier of applications. As you can see in the preceding diagram, we launch a ReplicaSet with three Pod replicas. Some mechanism details are listed as follows:

- The **kube-controller-manager** daemon helps to maintain the resource running in its desired state. For example, the desired state of ReplicaSet in the diagram is three Pod replicas.

- The **kube-scheduler** daemon on master, the scheduler of Kubernetes, takes charge of assigning tasks to healthy nodes.
- The selector of the **ReplicaSet** is used for deciding which Pods it covers. If the key-value pairs in the Pod's label include all items in the selector of the ReplicaSet, this Pod belongs to this ReplicaSet. As you will see, the diagram shows three Pods are under the charge of the ReplicaSet. Even though Pod 2 has a different label of `env`, it is selected since the other two labels, `role` and `project`, match the ReplicaSet's selector.

> **ReplicationController? ReplicaSet?**
> For experienced Kubernetes players, you may notice ReplicaSet looks quite similar to the ReplicationController. Since version 1.2 of Kubernetes, in order to concentrate on different features, the ReplicationController's functionality has been covered by ReplicaSet and Deployment. ReplicaSet focuses on the Pod replica, keeping certain Pods running in healthy states. On the other hand, Deployment is a higher-level API, which can manage the ReplicaSet, perform application rolling updates, and expose the services. In Kubernetes v1.8.3, users can still create replication controllers. However, using Deployment with ReplicaSet is more recommended because these are up to date and have finer granularity of configuration.

Getting ready

Creating a ReplicaSet is the same as creating any Kubernetes resource; we fire the `kubectl` command on the Kubernetes master. Therefore, we ensure your Kubernetes environment is ready to accept your order. More than that, the Kubernetes node should be able to access the Docker Hub. For the demonstration in the following few pages, we would take official `nginx` docker image for example, which stores in public docker registry as well.

The evaluation of a prepared Kubernetes system
You can verify whether your Kuberenetes master is a practical one through checking the items here:

- **Check whether the daemons are running or no**t: There should be three working daemon processes on the master node: `apiserver`, `scheduler`, and `controller-manager`.
- **Check whether the command kubectl exists and is workable**: Try the command `kubectl get cs` to cover this bullet point and the first one. You can verify not only the status of components but also the feasibility of `kubectl`.
- **Check whether the nodes are ready to work**: You can check them by using the command `kubectl get nodes` to get their status.

In the case that some items listed here are invalid, please refer to Chapter 1, *Building Your Own Kubernetes Cluster,* for proper guidelines based on the installation you chose.

How to do it...

In this section, we will demonstrate the life cycle of a ReplicaSet from creation to destruction.

Creating a ReplicaSet

When trying to use the command line to launch a Kubernetes Service immediately, we usually fire `kubectl run`. However, it would creates a Deployment by default, and not only taking care of the Pod replica but also providing a container-updating mechanism. To simply create a standalone ReplicaSet, we can exploit a configuration YAML file and run it:

```
$ cat my-first-replicaset.yaml
apiVersion: extensions/v1beta1
kind: ReplicaSet
metadata:
  name: my-first-replicaset
  labels:
    version: 0.0.1
spec:
  replicas: 3
  selector:
```

```
      matchLabels:
        project: My-Happy-Web
        role: frontend
  template:
    metadata:
      labels:
        project: My-Happy-Web
        role: frontend
        env: dev
    spec:
      containers:
      - name: happy-web
        image: nginx:latest
```

The preceding file is the YAML for our first ReplicaSet. It defines a ReplicaSet named `my-first-replicaset`, which has three replicas for its Pods. Labels and the selector are the most characteristic settings of ReplicaSet. There are two sets of labels: one for ReplicaSet, the other for Pods. The first label for ReplicaSet is under the metadata of this resource, right beneath the name, which is simply used for description. However, the other label value under the template's metadata, the one for Pods, is also used for identification. ReplicaSet takes charge of the Pods which have the labels covered by its selector.

In our example configuration file, the selector of ReplicaSet looks for Pods with `project: My-Happy-Web` and `role: frontend` tags. Since we initiate Pods under control of this ReplicaSet, the Pods' labels should definitely include what selector cares. You may get following error message while creating a ReplicaSet with incorrectly labeled Pods: `` `selector` does not match template `labels` ``.

Now, let's create ReplicaSet through this file:

```
$ kubectl create -f my-first-replicaset.yaml
replicaset.extensions "my-first-replicaset" created
```

The API version of ReplicaSet in Kubernetes v1.9
While this book is under construction, Kubernetes v1.9 is released. The API version of ReplicaSet turns to a stable version `apps/v1` instead of `apps/v1beta2`. If you have an older version Kubernetes, please change the value of `apiVersion` to `apps/v1beta2`, or you can just update your Kubernetes system.

Getting the details of a ReplicaSet

After we create the ReplicaSet, the subcommands `get` and `describe` can help us to capture its information and the status of Pods. In the CLI of Kubernetes, we are able to use the abbreviation rs for resource type, instead of the full name ReplicaSet:

```
// use subcommand "get" to list all ReplicaSets
$ kubectl get rs
NAME                     DESIRED   CURRENT   READY   AGE
my-first-replicaset      3         3         3       4s
```

This result shows roughly that the Pod replicas of `my-first-replicaset` are all running successfully; currently running Pods are of the desired number and all of them are ready for serving requests.

For detailed information, check by using the subcommand `describe`:

```
// specify that we want to check ReplicaSet called my-first-replicaset
$ kubectl describe rs my-first-replicaset
Name:          my-first-replicaset
Namespace:     default
Selector:      project=My-Happy-Web,role=frontend
Labels:        version=0.0.1
Annotations:   <none>
Replicas:      3 current / 3 desired
Pods Status:   3 Running / 0 Waiting / 0 Succeeded / 0 Failed
Pod Template:
  Labels:  env=dev
           project=My-Happy-Web
           role=frontend
  Containers:
   happy-web:
    Image:          nginx:latest
    Port:           <none>
    Host Port:      <none>
    Environment:    <none>
    Mounts:         <none>
  Volumes:          <none>
Events:
  Type      Reason            Age    From                   Message
  ----      ------            ----   ----                   -------
  Normal    SuccessfulCreate  9s     replicaset-controller  Created pod: my-
first-replicaset-8hg55
  Normal    SuccessfulCreate  9s     replicaset-controller  Created pod: my-
first-replicaset-wtphz
  Normal    SuccessfulCreate  9s     replicaset-controller  Created pod: my-
first-replicaset-xcrws
```

You can see that the output lists ReplicaSet's particulars of the configuration, just like what we requested in the YAML file. Furthermore, the logs for the creation of Pods are shown as part of ReplicaSet, which confirms that the Pod replicas are successfully created and designated with unique names. You can also check Pods by name:

```
// get the description according the name of Pod, please look at the Pod
name shown on your screen, which should be different from this book.
$ kubectl describe pod my-first-replicaset-xcrws
```

Changing the configuration of a ReplicaSet

The subcommands known as `edit`, `patch`, and `replace` can help to update live Kubernetes resources. All these functionalities change the settings by way of modifying a configuration file. Here we just take `edit`, for example.

The subcommand edit lets users modify resource configuration through the editor. Try to update your ReplicaSet through the command `kubectl edit rs $REPLICASET_NAME`; you will access this resource via the default editor with a YAML configuration file:

```
// demonstrate to change the number of Pod replicas.
$ kubectl get rs
NAME                     DESIRED   CURRENT   READY    AGE
my-first-replicaset      3         3         3        2m

// get in the editor, modify the replica number, then save and leave
$ kubectl edit rs my-first-replicaset
# Please edit the object below. Lines beginning with a '#' will be ignored,
# and an empty file will abort the edit. If an error occurs while saving
this file will be
# reopened with the relevant failures.
#
apiVersion: extensions/v1beta1
kind: ReplicaSet
metadata:
  creationTimestamp: 2018-05-05T20:48:38Z
  generation: 1
  labels:
    version: 0.0.1
  name: my-first-replicaset
  namespace: default
  resourceVersion: "1255241"
  selfLink: /apis/extensions/v1beta1/namespaces/default/replicasets/my-
first-replicaset
  uid: 18330fa8-cd55-11e7-a4de-525400a9d353
spec:
```

```
replicas: 4
selector:
  matchLabels:
...
replicaset "my-first-replicaset" edited
$ kubectl get rs
NAME                    DESIRED   CURRENT   READY    AGE
my-first-replicaset     4         4         4        4m
```

In the demonstration, we succeed to add one Pod in the set, yet this is not the best practice for auto-scaling the Pod. Take a look at the *Working with configuration files* recipe in `Chapter 3`, *Playing with Containers*, for Reference, and try to change the other values.

Deleting a ReplicaSet

In order to remove the ReplicaSet from the Kubernetes system, you can rely on the subcommand `delete`. When we fire `delete` to remove the resource, it removes the target objects forcefully:

```
$ time kubectl delete rs my-first-replicaset && kubectl get pod
replicaset.extensions "my-first-replicaset" deleted
real   0m2.492s
user   0m0.188s
sys    0m0.048s
NAME                          READY   STATUS        RESTARTS   AGE
my-first-replicaset-8hg55     0/1     Terminating   0          53m
my-first-replicaset-b6kr2     1/1     Terminating   0          48m
my-first-replicaset-wtphz     0/1     Terminating   0          53m
my-first-replicaset-xcrws     1/1     Terminating   0          53m
```

We find that the response time is quite short and the effect is also instantaneous.

Removing the Pod under ReplicaSet

As we mentioned previously, it is impossible to scale down the ReplicaSet by deleting the Pod, because while a Pod is removed, the ReplicaSet is out of stable status: if the desired number of Pods is not met, and the controller manager will ask ReplicaSet to create another one. The concept is shown in the following commands:

```
// check ReplicaSet and the Pods
$ kubectl get rs,pod
NAME DESIRED CURRENT READY AGE
rs/my-first-replicaset 3 3 3 14s
NAME READY STATUS RESTARTS AGE
po/my-first-replicaset-bxf45 1/1 Running 0 14s
```

```
po/my-first-replicaset-r6wpx 1/1 Running 0 14s
po/my-first-replicaset-vt6fd 1/1 Running 0 14s

// remove certain Pod and check what happened
$ kubectl delete pod my-first-replicaset-bxf45
pod "my-first-replicaset-bxf45" deleted
$ kubectl get rs,pod
NAME DESIRED CURRENT READY AGE
rs/my-first-replicaset 3 3 3 2m
NAME READY STATUS RESTARTS AGE
po/my-first-replicaset-dvbpg 1/1 Running 0 6s
po/my-first-replicaset-r6wpx 1/1 Running 0 2m
po/my-first-replicaset-vt6fd 1/1 Running 0 2m

// check the event log as well
$ kubectl describe rs my-first-replicaset
(ignored)
:
Events:
Type Reason Age From Message
---- ------ ---- ---- -------
Normal SuccessfulCreate 2m replicaset-controller Created
pod: my-first-replicaset-bxf45
Normal SuccessfulCreate 2m replicaset-controller Created
pod: my-first-replicaset-r6wpx
Normal SuccessfulCreate 2m replicaset-controller Created
pod: my-first-replicaset-vt6fd
Normal SuccessfulCreate 37s replicaset-controller Created
pod: my-first-replicaset-dvbpg
```

You will find that although the my-first-replicaset-bxf45 Pod is removed, the my-first-replicaset-dvbpg Pod is created automatically and attached to this ReplicaSet.

How it works...

The ReplicaSet defines a set of Pods by using a Pod template and labels. As in the ideas from previous sections, the ReplicaSet only manages the Pods via their labels. It is possible that the Pod template and the configuration of the Pod are different. This also means that standalone Pods can be added into a set by using label modification.

Let's evaluate this concept of selectors and labels by creating a ReplicaSet similar to the diagram at the beginning of this recipe:

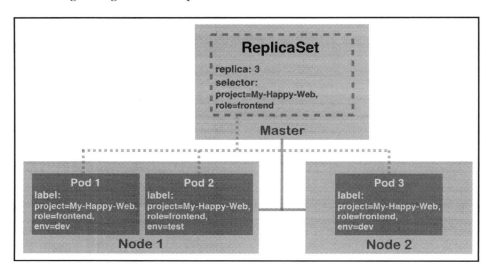

The ReplicaSet would cover Pods which have the same labels describing in its selector

First, we are going to create a CentOS Pod with the labels project: My-Happy-Web, role: frontend, and env: test:

```
// use subcommand "run" with tag restart=Never to create a Pod
$ kubectl run standalone-pod --image=centos --labels="project=My-Happy-
Web,role=frontend,env=test" --restart=Never --command sleep 3600
pod "standalone-pod" created

// check Pod along with the labels
$ kubectl get pod -L project -L role -L env
NAME             READY     STATUS     RESTARTS    AGE       PROJECT
ROLE        ENV
standalone-pod   1/1       Running    0           3m        My-Happy-Web
frontend    test
```

After adding this command, a standalone Pod runs with the labels we specified.

Next, go create your first ReplicaSet example by using the YAML file again:

```
$ kubectl create -f my-first-replicaset.yaml
replicaset.apps "my-first-replicaset" created

// check the Pod again
```

```
$ kubectl get pod -L project -L role -L env
NAME                        READY    STATUS    RESTARTS    AGE
PROJECT         ROLE        ENV
my-first-replicaset-fgdc8   1/1      Running   0           14s     My-
Happy-Web    frontend    dev
my-first-replicaset-flc9m   1/1      Running   0           14s     My-
Happy-Web    frontend    dev
standalone-pod              1/1      Running   0           6m      My-
Happy-Web    frontend    test
```

As in the preceding result, only two Pods are created. It is because the Pod standalone-pod is considered one of the sets taken by my-first-replicaset. Remember that my-first-replicaset takes care of the Pods labeled with project: My-Happy-Web and role: frontend (ignore the env tag). Go check the standalone Pod; you will find it belongs to a member of the ReplicaSet as well:

```
$ kubectl describe pod standalone-pod
Name:           standalone-pod
Namespace:      default
Node:           ubuntu02/192.168.122.102
Start Time:     Sat, 05 May 2018 16:57:14 -0400
Labels:         env=test
                project=My-Happy-Web
                role=frontend
Annotations:    <none>
Status:         Running
IP:             192.168.79.57
Controlled By:  ReplicaSet/my-first-replicaset
...
```

Similarly, once we delete the set, the standalone Pod will be removed with the group:

```
// remove the ReplicaSet and check pods immediately
$ kubectl delete rs my-first-replicaset && kubectl get pod
replicaset.extensions "my-first-replicaset" deleted
NAME                        READY    STATUS       RESTARTS    AGE
my-first-replicaset-fgdc8   0/1      Terminating  0           1m
my-first-replicaset-flc9m   0/1      Terminating  0           1m
standalone-pod              0/1      Terminating  0           7m
```

There's more...

There are multiple Kubernetes resources for Pod management. Users are encouraged to leverage various types of resources to meet different purposes. Let's comparing the resource types listed below with ReplicaSet:

- **Deployment**: In general cases, Kubernetes Deployments are used together with ReplicaSet for complete Pod management: container rolling updates, load balancing, and service exposing.
- **Job**: Sometimes, we want the Pods run as a job instead of a service. A Kubernetes job is suitable for this situation. You can consider it a ReplicaSet with the constraint of termination.
- **DaemonSet**: More than ReplicaSet, the Kubernetes DaemonSet guarantees that the specified set is running on every node in the cluster. That said, a subset of ReplicaSet on every node.

To get more idea and instruction, you can check the recipe *Ensuring flexible usage of your containers* in Chapter 3, *Playing with Containers*.

See also

Now you understand the idea of ReplicaSet. Continue to look up the following recipes in this chapter for more Kubernetes resources, which will allow you to explore the magical effects of ReplicaSet:

- *Deployment API*
- *Working with Services*
- *Working with labels an selectors*

Moreover, since you have built a simple ReplicaSet by using a configuration file, refer to more details about creating your own configuration files for Kubernetes resources:

- *Working with configuration files* section in Chapter 3, *Playing with Containers*

Deployment API

The Deployment API was introduced in Kubernetes version 1.2. It is replacing the replication controller. The functionalities of rolling-update and rollback by replication controller, it was achieved with client side (kubectl command and REST API), that kubectl need to keep connect while updating a replication controller. On the other hand, Deployments takes care of the process of rolling-update and rollback at the server side. Once that request is accepted, the client can disconnect immediately.

Therefore, the Deployments API is designed as a higher-level API to manage ReplicaSet objects. This section will explore how to use the Deployments API to manage ReplicaSets.

Getting ready

In order to create Deployment objects, as usual, use the kubectl run command or prepare the YAML/JSON file that describe Deployment configuration. This example is using the kubectl run command to create a my-nginx Deployment object:

```
//create my-nginx Deployment (specify 3 replicas and nginx version 1.11.0)
$ kubectl run my-nginx --image=nginx:1.11.0 --port=80 --replicas=3
deployment.apps "my-nginx" created


//see status of my-nginx Deployment
$ kubectl get deploy
NAME        DESIRED    CURRENT    UP-TO-DATE    AVAILABLE    AGE
my-nginx    3          3          3             3            8s


//see status of ReplicaSet
$ kubectl get rs
NAME                 DESIRED    CURRENT    READY    AGE
my-nginx-5d69b5ff7   3          3          3        11s


//see status of Pod
$ kubectl get pods
NAME                       READY    STATUS     RESTARTS    AGE
my-nginx-5d69b5ff7-9mhbc   1/1      Running    0           14s
my-nginx-5d69b5ff7-mt6z7   1/1      Running    0           14s
my-nginx-5d69b5ff7-rdl2k   1/1      Running    0           14s
```

As you can see, a Deployment object `my-nginx` creates one `ReplicaSet`, which has an identifier: `<Deployment name>-<hex decimal hash>`. And then ReplicaSet creates three Pods which have an identifier: `<ReplicaSet id>-<random id>`.

Until Kubernetes version 1.8, `<Deployment name>-<pod-template-hash value (number)>` was used as a ReplicaSet identifier instead of a hex decimal hash.

For more details, look at pull request: `https://github.com/kubernetes/kubernetes/pull/51538`.

This diagram illustrates the **Deployment**, **ReplicaSet**, and **Pod** relationship:

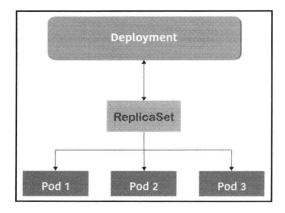

Relationship diagram for Deployments, ReplicaSets, and Pods

Because of this relationship, if you perform `delete` on a `my-nginx` Deployment object, it will also attempt to delete ReplicaSet and Pods respectively:

```
//delete my-nginx Deployment
$ kubectl delete deploy my-nginx
deployment.extensions "my-nginx" deleted


//see status of ReplicaSet
$ kubectl get rs
No resources found.


//see status of Pod, it has been terminated
$ kubectl get pods
```

NAME	READY	STATUS	RESTARTS	AGE
my-nginx-5d69b5ff7-9mhbc	0/1	Terminating	0	2m
my-nginx-5d69b5ff7-mt6z7	0/1	Terminating	0	2m
my-nginx-5d69b5ff7-rdl2k	0/1	Terminating	0	2m

This example is just a simple `create` and `delete`, that easy to understand Deployment object and ReplicaSet object 1:1 relationship at this moment. However, a Deployment object can manage many ReplicaSets to preserve as a history. So the actual relationship is 1:N, as in the following diagram:

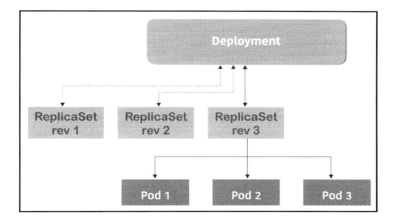

Deployments maintain ReplicaSet history

To understand the 1:N relationship, let's recreate this Deployment object again and perform to make some changes to see how Deployment manages ReplicaSet history.

How to do it...

You may run the `kubectl run` command to recreate `my-nginx`, or write a Deployments configuration file that produces the same result. This is a great opportunity to learn about the Deployment configuration file.

This example is an equivalent of `kubectl run my-nginx --image=nginx:1.11.0 --port=80 --replicas=3`:

```
$ cat deploy.yaml
apiVersion: apps/v1
kind: Deployment
metadata:
  name: my-nginx
spec:
  replicas: 3
  selector:
    matchLabels:
      run: my-nginx
  template:
    metadata:
      labels:
        run: my-nginx
    spec:
      containers:
      - name: my-nginx
        image: nginx:1.11.0
        ports:
        - containerPort: 80
```

These parameters, sorted by key and value, are described here:

Key	Value	Description
apiVersion	apps/v1	Until Kubernetes v1.8, it had been used apps/v1Beta1, v1.8 used apps/v1Beta2, then v1.9 or later use apps/v1
kind	deployment	Indicates that this is a set of Deployment configurations
metadata.name	my-nginx	Name of Deployment
spec.replicas	3	Desire to have three Pods
spec.selector.matchLabels	run:my-nginx	Control ReplicaSet/Pods which have this label
spec.template.metadata.labels	run:my-nginx	Assigns this label when creating a ReplicaSet/Pod; it must match `spec.selector.matchLabels`

spec.template.spec.containers	name: `my-nginx`
	image:
	`nginx:1.11.0`
	port:
	—
	`containerPort:80`
		ReplicaSet creates and manages Pods which have:
		• name as `my-nginx`
		• Container image as nginx version 1.11.0
		• Publish port number `80`

If you use this YAML file to create a Deployment, use the `kubectl create` command instead of `kubectl run`.

Note that, this time, you should also specify `--save-config`, which allows you to update the resource using the `kubectl apply` command in the future. In addition, specify `--record` which can store the command line history. Those two options are not mandatory to manage ReplicaSet history but help you to preserve better information:

```
//use -f to specify YAML file
$ kubectl create -f deploy.yaml --save-config --record
deployment.apps "my-nginx" created


//check my-nginx Deployment
$ kubectl get deploy
NAME       DESIRED    CURRENT    UP-TO-DATE    AVAILABLE    AGE
my-nginx   3          3          3             3            5s


$ kubectl describe deploy my-nginx
Name:                  my-nginx
Namespace:             default
CreationTimestamp:     Wed, 09 May 2018 03:40:09 +0000
Labels:                <none>
Annotations:           deployment.kubernetes.io/revision=1
                       kubectl.kubernetes.io/last-applied-
configuration={"apiVersion":"apps/v1","kind":"Deployment","metadata":{"anno
tations":{},"name":"my-
nginx","namespace":"default"},"spec":{"replicas":3,"selector":{"mat...
                       kubernetes.io/change-cause=kubectl create --
filename=deploy.yaml --save-config=true --record=true
Selector:              run=my-nginx
Replicas:              3 desired | 3 updated | 3 total | 3 available | 0
unavailable
StrategyType:          RollingUpdate
MinReadySeconds:       0
RollingUpdateStrategy: 25% max unavailable, 25% max surge
Pod Template:
  Labels:   run=my-nginx
```

```
Containers:
 my-nginx:
  Image:         nginx:1.11.0
  Port:          80/TCP
  Host Port:     0/TCP
  Environment:   <none>
  Mounts:        <none>
 Volumes:        <none>
Conditions:
 Type          Status   Reason
 ----          ------   ------
 Available     True     MinimumReplicasAvailable
 Progressing   True     NewReplicaSetAvailable
OldReplicaSets:   <none>
NewReplicaSet:    my-nginx-54bb7bbcf9 (3/3 replicas created)
Events:
 Type     Reason             Age    From                  Message
 ----     ------             ----   ----                  -------
 Normal   ScalingReplicaSet  34s    deployment-controller Scaled up replica
set my-nginx-54bb7bbcf9 to 3
```

You can see a property OldReplicaSets and NewReplicaSet in the preceding code, which are some association between Deployment and ReplicaSet.

Whenever you update a definition of a container template, for example, changing the nginx image version from 1.11.0 to 1.12.0, then Deployment my-nginx will create a new ReplicaSet. Then the property NewReplicaSet will point to the new ReplicaSet which has nginx version 1.12.0.

On the other hand, the OldReplicaSets property points to an old ReplicaSet which has nginx version 1.11.0 until new ReplicaSet is complete to setup new Pod.

These old/new ReplicaSet associations between Deployment, Kubernetes administrator can easy to achieve rollback operation in case new ReplicaSet has any issues.

In addition, Deployment can keep preserves the history of ReplicaSet which were associated with it before. Therefore, Deployment can anytime to change back (rollback) to any point of older ReplicaSet.

How it works...

As mentioned earlier, let's bump the nginx image version from 1.11.0 to 1.12.0. There are two ways to change the container image: use the kubectl set command, or update YAML then use the kubectl apply command.

Using the `kubectl set` command is quicker and there is better visibility when using the `--record` option.

On the other hand, updating YAML and using the `kubectl apply` command is better to preserve the entire Deployment YAML configuration file, which is better when using a version control system such as `git`.

Using kubectl set to update the container image

Use the `kubectl set` command allows us to overwrite the `spec.template.spec.containers[].image` property that is similar to using the `kubectl run` command to specify the image file. The following example specifies `my-nginx` deployment to set the container `my-nginx` to change the image to nginx version 1.12.0:

```
$ kubectl set image deployment my-nginx my-nginx=nginx:1.12.0 --record
deployment.apps "my-nginx" image updated


$ kubectl describe deploy my-nginx
Name:                   my-nginx
...
...
Conditions:
  Type            Status   Reason
  ----            ------   ------
  Available       True     MinimumReplicasAvailable
  Progressing     True     ReplicaSetUpdated
OldReplicaSets:   my-nginx-54bb7bbcf9 (3/3 replicas created)
NewReplicaSet:    my-nginx-77769b7666 (1/1 replicas created)
Events:
  Type     Reason             Age    From                   Message
  ----     ------             ----   ----                   -------
  Normal   ScalingReplicaSet  27s    deployment-controller  Scaled up replica
set my-nginx-54bb7bbcf9 to 3
  Normal   ScalingReplicaSet  2s     deployment-controller  Scaled up replica
set my-nginx-77769b7666 to 1
```

As you can see, `OldReplicaSets` becomes the previous `ReplicaSet` (`my-nginx-54bb7bbcf9`) and `NewReplicaSet` becomes `my-nginx-77769b7666`. Note that you can see the `OldReplicaSets` property until `NewReplicaSet` is ready, so once the new `ReplicaSet` is successfully launched, `OldReplicaSet` becomes <none>, as follows:

```
$ kubectl describe deploy my-nginx
```

```
Name:                   my-nginx
...
...
  Type             Status   Reason
  ----             ------   ------
  Available        True     MinimumReplicasAvailable
  Progressing      True     NewReplicaSetAvailable
OldReplicaSets:    <none>
NewReplicaSet:     my-nginx-77769b7666 (3/3 replicas created)
```

If you can see the `ReplicaSet` list by `kubectl get rs`, you can see two ReplicaSet, as follows:

```
$ kubectl get rs
NAME                    DESIRED   CURRENT   READY    AGE
my-nginx-54bb7bbcf9     0         0         0        3m
my-nginx-77769b7666     3         3         3        3m
```

As you can see, in the old `ReplicaSet` (`my-nginx-54bb7bbcf9`), the numbers of `DESIRED`/`CURRENT`/`READY` pods are all zero.

In addition, because the preceding example uses the `--record` option, you can see the history of the Deployment `my-nginx` rollout with the `kubectl rollout history` command, as follows:

```
$ kubectl rollout history deployment my-nginx
deployments "my-nginx"
REVISION   CHANGE-CAUSE
1          kubectl create --filename=deploy.yaml --save-config=true --
record=true
2          kubectl set image deployment/my-nginx my-nginx=nginx:1.12.0 --
record=true
```

Updating the YAML and using kubectl apply

For demo purposes, copy `deploy.yaml` to `deploy_1.12.2.yaml` and change the `nginx` version to `1.12.2`, as follows:

```
image: nginx:1.12.2
```

Then run the `kubectl apply` command with the `--record` option:

```
$ kubectl apply -f deploy_1.12.2.yaml --record
deployment.apps "my-nginx" configured
```

This will perform the same thing as the `kubectl set` image command, so you can see that the nginx image version has been bumped up to `1.12.2`; also, the `OldReplicaSets/NewReplicaSet` combination has been changed as follows:

```
$ kubectl describe deploy my-nginx
Name:                   my-nginx
...
...
Pod Template:
  Labels: run=my-nginx
  Containers:
   my-nginx:
    Image: nginx:1.12.2
...
...
Conditions:
  Type            Status   Reason
  ----            ------   ------
  Available       True     MinimumReplicasAvailable
  Progressing     True     ReplicaSetUpdated
OldReplicaSets: my-nginx-77769b7666 (3/3 replicas created)
NewReplicaSet: my-nginx-69fbc98fd4 (1/1 replicas created)
```

After a few moments, `NewReplicaSet` will be ready. Then there will be a total of three `ReplicaSets` existing on your system:

```
$ kubectl get rs
NAME                  DESIRED   CURRENT   READY   AGE
my-nginx-54bb7bbcf9   0         0         0       7m
my-nginx-69fbc98fd4   3         3         3       1m
my-nginx-77769b7666   0         0         0       6m
```

You can also see the rollout history:

```
$ kubectl rollout history deployment my-nginx
deployments "my-nginx"
REVISION   CHANGE-CAUSE
1          kubectl create --filename=deploy.yaml --save-config=true --
record=true
2          kubectl set image deployment/my-nginx my-nginx=nginx:1.12.0 --
record=true
3          kubectl apply --filename=deploy_1.12.2.yaml --record=true
```

Whenever you want to revert to a previous `ReplicaSet`, which means rolling back to the previous nginx version, you can use `kubectl rollout undo` with the `--to-revision` option. For example, if you want to roll back to revision 2 in your history (`kubectl set image deployment/my-nginx my-nginx=nginx:1.12.0 --record=true`), specify `--to-revision=2`:

```
$ kubectl rollout undo deployment my-nginx --to-revision=2
deployment.apps "my-nginx" rolled back'
```

A few moments later, Deployment will deactivate the current `ReplicaSet`, which uses the Pod template with `nginx` version `1.12.2`, and will then activate the `ReplicaSet` which uses `nginx` version `1.12`, as follows:

```
$ kubectl get rs
NAME                   DESIRED   CURRENT   READY   AGE
my-nginx-54bb7bbcf9    0         0         0       8m
my-nginx-69fbc98fd4    0         0         0       2m
my-nginx-77769b7666    3         3         3       7m
```

See also

In this section, you learned about the concept of Deployment. It is an important core feature in Kubernetes ReplicaSet life cycle management. It allows us to achieve rollout and rollback functionalities, and can integrate to CI/CD. In the following chapter you will see detailed operations of rollout and rollback:

- *Updating live containers* section in `Chapter` 3, *Playing with Containers*
- *Setting up a continuous delivery pipeline* section in `Chapter` 5, *Building Continuous Delivery Pipelines*

Working with Services

The network service is an application that receives requests and provides a solution. Clients access the service by a network connection. They don't have to know the architecture of the service or how it runs. The only thing that clients have to verify is whether the endpoint of the service can be accessed, and then follow its usage policy to get the response of the server. The Kubernetes Service has similar ideas. It is not necessary to understand every Pod before reaching their functionalities. For components outside the Kubernetes system, they just access the Kubernetes Service with an exposed network port to communicate with running Pods. It is not necessary to be aware of the containers' IPs and ports. Behind Kubernetes Services, we can fulfill a zero-downtime update for our container programs without struggling:

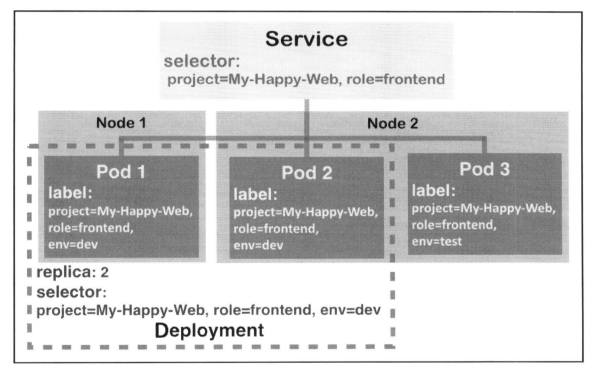

Kubernetes Service-covered Pods by labels of Pods and their selectors

The preceding diagram shows the basic structure of the **Service** and realizes the following concepts:

- As with the **Deployment**, the **Service** directs requests to Pods that have labels containing the Service's selector. In other words, the Pods selected by the **Service** are based on their labels.
- The load of requests sent to the Services will distribute to three Pods.
- The **Deployment**, along with ReplicaSet, ensures that the number of running Pods meets its desired state. It monitors the Pods for the **Service**, making sure they will be healthy for taking over duties from the **Service**.
- **Service** is an abstraction layer for grouping Pods, which allows for Pods scaling across nodes.

In this recipe, you will learn how to create Services in front of your Pods for the requests.

Getting ready

Prior to applying Kubernetes Services, it is important to verify whether all nodes in the system are running `kube-proxy`. The daemon `kube-proxy` works as a network proxy in a node. It helps to reflect Service settings, such as IPs or ports on each node, and to do network forwarding. To check if `kube-proxy` is running or not, we take a look at network connections:

```
// check by command netstat with proper tags for showing the information we
need, t:tcp, u:udp, l:listening, p:program, n:numeric address
// use root privilege for grabbing all processes
$ sudo netstat -tulpn | grep kube-proxy
tcp        0      0 127.0.0.1:10249         0.0.0.0:*               LISTEN
2326/kube-proxy
tcp6       0      0 :::31723                :::*                    LISTEN
2326/kube-proxy
tcp6       0      0 :::10256                :::*                    LISTEN
2326/kube-proxy
```

Once you see the output, the process ID `2326`, `kube-proxy`, listening on port `10249` on localhost, the node is ready for Kubernetes Services. Go ahead and verify whether all of your nodes in the Kubernetes cluster having `kube-proxy` running on them.

How to do it...

As mentioned in the previous section, the Kubernetes Service exposes Pods by selecting them through corresponding labels. However, there is another configuration we have to take care of: the network port. As the following diagram indicates, the Service and Pod have their own key-value pair labels and ports:

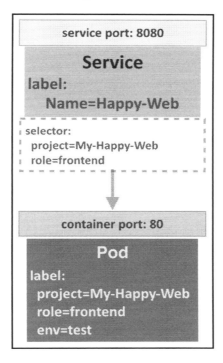

Network port mapping between Service and Pod

Therefore, setting the selector of Service and binding the service exposed port to the container port are required to be carried out while creating Services. If either of them fail to be set properly, clients won't get responses or will get connection-refused errors.

We can define and create a new Kubernetes Service through the CLI or a configuration file. Here, we are going to explain how to deploy the Services by command. The subcommands expose and describe are utilized in the following commands for various scenarios. For file-format creation, it is recommended to read the *Working with configuration files* recipe in Chapter 3, *Playing with Containers*, for a detailed discussion.

Creating a Service for different resources

You can attach a Service to a Pod, a Deployment, an endpoint outside the Kubernetes system, or even another Service. We will show you these, one by one, in this section. The creation of the Kubernetes Service looks similar to these command formats: `kubectl expose $RESOURCE_TYPE $RESOURCE_NAME [OTHER TAGS]` or `kubectl expose -f $CONFIG_FILE`. The resource types (Pod, Deployment, and Service) are supported by the subcommand `expose`. So is the configuration file, which follows the limitation type. Accordingly, for a later demonstration we will attach the newly created Service to the endpoint by the configuration file.

Creating a Service for a Pod

Kubernetes Pods covered by Service require labels, so that Service can recognize who is the one it should take charge of. In the following commands, we create a Pod with labels first, and attach a Service on it:

```
// using subcommand "run" with "never" restart policy, and without replica,
you can get a Pod
// here we create a nginx container with port 80 exposed to outside world
of Pod
$ kubectl run nginx-pod --image=nginx --port=80 --restart="Never" --
labels="project=My-Happy-Web,role=frontend,env=test"
pod "nginx-pod" created

// expose Pod "nginx-pod" with a Service officially with port 8080, target
port would be the exposed port of pod
$ kubectl expose pod nginx-pod --port=8080 --target-port=80 --name="nginx-
service"
service "nginx-service" exposed
```

You may find that, based on the preceding command, we did not assign any selector to this Service. Nonetheless, since Service `nginx-service` takes the port forwarding task of Pod `nginx-pod`, it will take the labels of the Pod as its selector. Go ahead and check the details of the Service with the subcommand `describe`:

```
// "svc" is the abbreviate of Service, for the description's resource type
$ kubectl describe svc nginx-service
Name:              nginx-service
Namespace:         default
Labels:            env=test
                   project=My-Happy-Web
                   role=frontend
Annotations:       <none>
Selector:          env=test,project=My-Happy-Web,role=frontend
```

```
Type:               ClusterIP
IP:                 10.96.107.213
Port:               <unset>   8080/TCP
TargetPort:         80/TCP
Endpoints:          192.168.79.24:80
Session Affinity:   None
Events:             <none>
```

Now you can see that, for guaranteeing the responsibility, this successfully exposed Service just copied the labels of the Pod as its selector. The value list after `Endpoints` was the IP of the Pod and its exposed port `80`. Furthermore, the Service took the Pod's labels as its own. According to this example, the Pod can be accessed through Service by surfing `10.96.107.213:8080`.

Except for the selector of Service, some parameters can be automatically configured if they are bypassed by users. One parameter is the labels of the Pod; another is the name of the Service; and the other is the exposed port of the Service. Let's take a look at how this simple set of Pod and Service can be managed:

```
// create a Pod and a Service for it
$ kubectl run nginx-no-label --image=nginx --port=80 --restart="Never" &&
kubectl expose pod nginx-no-label
pod "nginx-no-label" created
service "nginx-no-label" exposed
// take a lookat the configurations of the Service
$ kubectl describe svc nginx-no-label
Name:               nginx-no-label
Namespace:          default
Labels:             run=nginx-no-label
Annotations:        <none>
Selector:           run=nginx-no-label
Type:               ClusterIP
IP:                 10.105.96.243
Port:               <unset>   80/TCP
TargetPort:         80/TCP
Endpoints:          192.168.79.10:80
Session Affinity:   None
Events:             <none>
```

Here, we can see that the Service inherited the name, label, and port from the Pod. The selector was assigned the dummy label with the key named run and the value named as Pod's name, which is just the same dummy one of Pod `nginx-no-label`. Users should access the Service through port `80`, as well. For such simple settings, you can alternatively try the following command to create the Pods and Service at the same time:

```
// through leveraging tag "--expose", create the Service along with Pod
$ kubectl run another-nginx-no-label --image=nginx --port=80 --restart="Never" --expose
service "another-nginx-no-label" created
pod "another-nginx-no-label" created
```

Creating a Service for a Deployment with an external IP

Kubernetes Deployment is the ideal resource type for a Service. For Pods supervised by the ReplicaSet and Deployment, the Kubernetes system has a controller manager to look over the their life cycles. It is also helpful for updating the version or state of the program by binding the existing Services to another Deployment. For the following commands, we create a Deployment first, and attach a Service with an external IP:

```
// using subcommand "run" and assign 2 replicas
$ kubectl run nginx-deployment --image=nginx --port=80 --replicas=2 --labels="env=dev,project=My-Happy-Web,role=frontend"
deployment.apps "nginx-deployment" created
// explicitly indicate the selector of Service by tag "--selector", and assign the Service an external IP by tag "--external-ip"
// the IP 192.168.122.102 demonstrated here is the IP of one of the Kubernetes node in system
$ kubectl expose deployment nginx-deployment --port=8080 --target-port=80 --name="another-nginx-service" --selector="project=My-Happy-Web,role=frontend" --external-ip="192.168.122.102"
service "another-nginx-service" exposed
```

Let's go ahead and check the details of the newly created Service, another-nginx-service:

```
$ kubectl describe svc another-nginx-service
Name:           another-nginx-service
Namespace:      default
Labels:         env=dev
                project=My-Happy-Web
                role=frontend
Annotations:    <none>
Selector:       project=My-Happy-Web,role=frontend
Type:           ClusterIP
```

```
IP:                10.100.109.230
External IPs:      192.168.122.102
Port:              <unset>   8080/TCP
TargetPort:        80/TCP
Endpoints:         192.168.79.15:80,192.168.79.21:80,192.168.79.24:80
Session Affinity:  None
Events:            <none>
```

Apart from the Service IP (in the case of the preceding command, `10.100.109.230`), which can be accessed within the Kubernetes system, the Service can now be connected through an external one (`192.168.122.102`, for example) beyond the Kubernetes system. While the Kubernetes master is able to communicate with every node, in this case, we can fire a request to the Service such as the following command:

```
$ curl 192.168.122.102:8080
<!DOCTYPE html>
<html>
<head>
<title>Welcome to nginx!</title>
...
```

Creating a Service for an Endpoint without a selector

First, we are going to create an Endpoint directing the external service. A Kubernetes Endpoint is an abstraction, making components beyond Kubernetes (for instance, a database in other system) become a part of Kubernetes resources. It provides a feasible use case for a hybrid environment. To create an endpoint, an IP address, along with a port, is required. Please take a look at the following template:

```
$ cat k8s-endpoint.yaml
apiVersion: v1
kind: Endpoints
metadata:
  name: k8s-ep
subsets:
  - addresses:
      - hostname: kubernetes-io
        ip: 45.54.44.100
    ports:
      - port: 80
```

The template defines an Endpoint named `k8s-ep`, which points to the IP of the host of the official Kubernetes website (`https://kubernetes.io`). Never mind that this Endpoint forwards to a plain HTML; we just take this Endpoint as an example. As mentioned, Endpoint is not a resource supported by the Kubernetes API for exposing:

```
// Give it a try!
$ kubectl expose -f k8s-endpoint.yaml
error: cannot expose a { Endpoints}
```

In Kubernetes, an Endpoint not only represents an external service; an internal Kubernetes Service is also a Kubernetes Endpoint. You can check Endpoint resources with the command `kubectl get endpoints`. You will find that there is not a single endpoint `k8s-ep` (which you just created), but many endpoints named the same as the Services in previous pages. When a Service is created with a selector and exposes certain resources (such as a Pod, Deployment, or other Service), a corresponding Endpoint with the same name is created at the same time.

Therefore, we still can create a Service associated with the Endpoint using an identical name, as in the following template:

```
$ cat endpoint-service.yaml
apiVersion: v1
kind: Service
metadata:
  name: k8s-ep
spec:
  ports:
    - protocol: TCP
      port: 8080
      targetPort: 80
```

The relationship between the Endpoints and the Service is built up with the resource name. For the Service `k8s-ep`, we didn't indicate the selector, since it did not actually take any Pod in responsibility:

```
// go create the Service and the endpoint
$ kubectl create -f endpoint-service.yaml && kubectl create -f k8s-endpoint.yaml
service "k8s-ep" created
endpoints "k8s-ep" created
// verify the Service k8s-ep
$ kubectl describe svc k8s-ep
Name:            k8s-ep
Namespace:       default
Labels:          <none>
Annotations:     <none>
```

```
Selector:              <none>
Type:                  ClusterIP
IP:                    10.105.232.226
Port:                  <unset>  8080/TCP
TargetPort:            80/TCP
Endpoints:             45.54.44.100:80
Session Affinity:      None
Events:                <none>
```

Now you can see that the endpoint of the Service is just the one defined in `k8s-endpoint.yaml`. It is good for us to access the outside world through the Kubernetes Service! In the case earlier, we can verify the result with the following command:

```
$ curl 10.105.232.226:8080
```

Creating a Service for another Service with session affinity

While building a Service over another, we may think of multiple layers for port forwarding. In spite of redirecting traffic from one port to another, the action of exposing a Service is actually copying the setting of one Service to another. This scenario could be utilized as updating the Service setting, without causing headaches to current clients and servers:

```
// create a Service by expose an existed one
// take the one we created for Deployment for example
$ kubectl expose svc another-nginx-service --port=8081 --target-port=80 --
name=yet-another-nginx-service --session-affinity="ClientIP"
service "yet-another-nginx-service" exposed
// check the newly created Service
$ kubectl describe svc yet-another-nginx-service
Name:                  yet-another-nginx-service
Namespace:             default
Labels:                env=dev
                       project=My-Happy-Web
                       role=frontend
Annotations:           <none>
Selector:              project=My-Happy-Web,role=frontend
Type:                  ClusterIP
IP:                    10.110.218.136
Port:                  <unset>  8081/TCP
TargetPort:            80/TCP
Endpoints:             192.168.79.15:80,192.168.79.21:80,192.168.79.24:80
Session Affinity:      ClientIP
Events:                <none>
```

Here we are! We successfully exposed another Service with similar settings to the Service `another-nginx-service`. The commands and output can be summarized as follows:

- **A new Service name is required**: Although we can copy the configurations from another Service, the name of the resource type should always be unique. When exposing a Service without the tag `--name`, you will get the error message: `Error from server (AlreadyExists): services "another-nginx-service" already exists.`
- **Adding or updating the configuration is workable**: We are able to add a new configuration, like adding session affinity; or we can update the port of the Service, like here, where we change to open port `8081` instead of `8080`.
- **Avoid changing target port**: Because the target port is along with the IP of the Pods, once the Service exposing changes the target port, the newly copied Service cannot forward traffic to the same endpoints. In the preceding example, since the new target port is defined, we should point out the container port again. It prevented the new Service from using the target port as the container port and turned out a misleading transaction.

With session affinity, the list of description tags session affinity as `ClientIP`. For the current Kubernetes version, the client IP is the only option for session affinity. It takes the action as a hash function: with the same IP address, the request will always send to the identical Pod. However, this could be a problem if there is a load balancer or ingress controller in front of the Kubernetes Service: the requests would be considered to come from the same source, and the traffic forwarded to a single Pod. Users have to handle this issue on their own, for example, by building an HA proxy server instead of using the Kubernetes Service.

Deleting a Service

If you go through every command in this section, there are definitely some demonstrated Kubernetes Services (we counted six of them) that should be removed. To delete a Service, the same as with any other Kubernetes resource, you can remove the Service with the name or the configuration file through the subcommand `delete`. When you try to remove the Service and the Endpoint at the same time, the following situation will happen:

```
// the resource abbreviation of endpoint is "ep", separate different
resource types by comma
$ kubectl delete svc,ep k8s-ep
service "k8s-ep" deleted
Error from server (NotFound): endpoints "k8s-ep" not found
```

This is because a Service is also a Kubernetes Endpoint. That's why, although we created the Service and the endpoint separately, once they are considered to work as a unit, the Endpoint is going to be removed when the Service is removed. Thus, the error message expresses that there is no endpoint called `k8s-ep`, since it was already removed with the Service deletion.

How it works...

On the network protocol stack, the Kubernetes Service relies on the transport layer, working together with the **overlay network** and `kube-proxy`. The overlay network of Kubernetes builds up a cluster network by allocating a subnet lease out of a pre-configured address space and storing the network configuration in `etcd`; on the other hand, `kube-proxy` helps to forward traffic from the endpoints of Services to the Pods through `iptables` settings.

Proxy-mode and Service `kube-proxy` currently has three modes with different implementation methods: `userspace`, `iptables`, and `ipvs`. The modes affect how the requests of clients reach to certain Pods through the Kubernete Service:

- `userspace`: `kube-proxy` opens a random port, called a proxy port, for each Service on the local node, then updates the `iptables` rules, which capture any request sent to the Service and forward it to the proxy port. In the end, any message sent to the proxy port will be passed to the Pods covered by the Service. It is less efficient, since the traffic is required to go to `kube-proxy` for routing to the Pod.
- `iptables`: As with the `userspace` mode, there are also required `iptables` rules for redirecting the client traffic. But there is no proxy port as mediator. Faster but need to take care the liveness of Pod. By default, there is no way for a request to retry another Pod if the target one fails. To avoid accessing the unhealthy Pod, health-checking Pods and updating `iptables` in time is necessary.

- ipvs: ipvs is the beta feature in Kubernetes v1.9. In this mode, kube-proxy builds up the interface called netlink between the Service and its backend set. The ipvs mode takes care of the downside in both userspace and iptables; it is even faster, since the routing rules stored a hash table structure in the kernel space, and even reliable that kube-proxy keeps checking the consistency of netlinks. ipvs even provides multiple load balancing options.

The system picks the optimal and stable one as the default setting for kube-proxy. Currently, it is the mode iptables.

When a Pod tries to communicate with a Service, it can find the Service through environment variables or a DNS host lookup. Let's give it a try in the following scenario of accessing a service in a Pod:

```
// run a Pod first, and ask it to be alive 600 seconds
$ kubectl run my-1st-centos --image=centos --restart=Never sleep 600
pod "my-1st-centos" created
// run a Deployment of nginx and its Service exposing port 8080 for nginx
$ kubectl run my-nginx --image=nginx --port=80
deployment.apps "my-nginx" created
$ kubectl expose deployment my-nginx --port=8080 --target-port=80 --name="my-nginx-service"
service "my-nginx-service" exposed
// run another pod
$ kubectl run my-2nd-centos --image=centos --restart=Never sleep 600
pod "my-2nd-centos" created
//Go check the environment variables on both pods.
$ kubectl exec my-1st-centos -- /bin/sh -c export
$ kubectl exec my-2nd-centos -- /bin/sh -c export
```

You will find that the Pod my-2nd-centos comes out with additional variables showing information for the Service my-nginx-service, as follows:

```
export MY_NGINX_SERVICE_PORT="tcp://10.104.218.20:8080"
export MY_NGINX_SERVICE_PORT_8080_TCP="tcp://10.104.218.20:8080"
export MY_NGINX_SERVICE_PORT_8080_TCP_ADDR="10.104.218.20"
export MY_NGINX_SERVICE_PORT_8080_TCP_PORT="8080"
export MY_NGINX_SERVICE_PORT_8080_TCP_PROTO="tcp"
export MY_NGINX_SERVICE_SERVICE_HOST="10.104.218.20"
export MY_NGINX_SERVICE_SERVICE_PORT="8080"
```

This is because the system failed to do a real-time update for Services; only the Pods created subsequently can be applied to accessing the Service through environment variables. With this ordering-dependent constraint, pay attention to running your Kubernetes resources in a proper sequence if they have to interact with each other in this way. The keys of the environment variables representing the Service host are formed as <SERVICE NAME>_SERVICE_HOST, and the Service port is like <SERVICE NAME>_SERVICE_PORT. In the preceding example, the dash in the name is also transferred to the underscore:

```
// For my-2nd-centos, getting information of Service by environment
variables
$ kubectl exec my-2nd-centos -- /bin/sh -c 'curl
$MY_NGINX_SERVICE_SERVICE_HOST:$MY_NGINX_SERVICE_SERVICE_PORT'
<!DOCTYPE html>
<html>
<head>
<title>Welcome to nginx!</title>
...
```

Nevertheless, if the kube-dns add-on is installed, which is a DNS server in the Kubernetes system, any Pod in the same Namespace can access the Service, no matter when the Service was created. The hostname of the Service would be formed as <SERVICE NAME>.<NAMESPACE>.svc.cluster.local. cluster.local is the default cluster domain defined in booting kube-dns:

```
// go accessing my-nginx-service by A record provided by kube-dns
$ kubectl exec my-1st-centos -- /bin/sh -c 'curl my-nginx-
service.default.svc.cluster.local:8080'
$ kubectl exec my-2nd-centos -- /bin/sh -c 'curl my-nginx-
service.default.svc.cluster.local:8080'
```

There's more...

The Kubernetes Service has four types: ClusterIP, NodePort, LoadBalancer, and ExternalName. In the *How to do it...* section in this recipe, we only demonstrate the default type, ClusterIP. The type ClusterIP indicates that the Kubernetes Service is assigned a unique virtual IP in the overlay network, which also means the identity in this Kubernetes cluster. ClusterIP guarantees that the Service is accessible internally.

The following diagram expresses the availability coverage of the types, and their entry points:

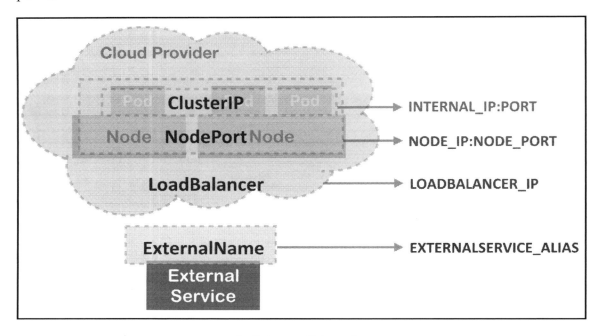

Four Service types and their entry points

For the `NodePort` type, it covers the `ClusterIP`'s features, has a peer-accessible virtual IP, and also allows the user to expose Services on each node with the same port. The type `LoadBalancer` is on the top of the other two types. The `LoadBalancer` Service would be exposed internally and on the node. More than that, if your cloud provider supports external load balancing servers, you can bind the load balancer IP to the Service, and this will become another exposing point. On the other hand, the type `ExternalName` is used for the endpoint out of your Kubernetes system. It is similar to the Endpoint we created with the configuration file in a previous section; moreover, a single `ExternalName` Service can provide this feature.

We can use the subcommand `create` to create Services in different types:

```
// create a NodePort Service
// the tag "tcp" is for indicating port configuration:
SERVICE_PORT:TARGET_PORT
$ kubectl create service nodeport my-nginx --tcp=8080:80
service "my-nginx" created
```

```
$ kubectl describe svc my-nginx
Name:                    my-nginx
Namespace:               default
Labels:                  app=my-nginx
Annotations:             <none>
Selector:                app=my-nginx
Type:                    NodePort
IP:                      10.105.106.134
Port:                    8080-80   8080/TCP
TargetPort:              80/TCP
NodePort:                8080-80   31336/TCP
Endpoints:               <none>
Session Affinity:        None
External Traffic Policy: Cluster
Events:                  <none>
```

In this example of the NodePort Service, you can see that it still has the virtual IP (10.105.106.134) in the cluster, and can be accessed through port 31336 of any Kubernetes node:

```
// run an nginx Deployment with the label as NodePort Service my-nginx's
selector
$ kubectl run test-nodeport --image=nginx --labels="app=my-nginx"
deployment.apps "test-nodeport" created
// check the Kubernetes node with Service port on the node
$ curl ubuntu02:31336
<!DOCTYPE html>
<html>
<head>
<title>Welcome to nginx!</title>
...
```

In the case here, we demonstrate creating an ExternalName Service which exposes the CNAME kubernetes.io:

```
$ kubectl create service externalname k8s-website --external-name
kubernetes.io
service "k8s-website" created
// create a CentOS Pod for testing the Service availability
$ kubectl run my-centos --image=centos --restart=Never sleep 600
pod "my-centos" created
//now you can check the Service by Service's DNS name
$ kubectl exec -it my-centos -- /bin/sh -c 'curl k8s-
website.default.svc.cluster.local '
//Check all the Services we created in this section
//ExternalName Service has no cluster IP as defined
$ kubectl get svc
```

NAME		TYPE	CLUSTER-IP	EXTERNAL-IP
PORT(S)	AGE			
k8s-website		ExternalName	**<none>**	kubernetes.io
<none>	31m			
kubernetes		ClusterIP	10.96.0.1	<none>
443/TCP	14d			
my-nginx		NodePort	10.105.106.134	<none>
8080:31336/TCP	1h			

Yet, we cannot build an `ExternalName` Service in CLI with the subcommand `expose`, because `expose` works on exposing the Kubernetes resources, while the `ExternalName` Service is for the resources in the outside world. Then, it is also reasonable that the `ExternalName` Service doesn't need to be defined with the selector.

Using the subcommand "create" to create Services
While using the subcommand `create` on Service creation, the command line would look like this: `kubectl create service <SERVICE TYPE> <SERVICE NAME> [OPTIONS]`. And we can put the Service types at `<SERVICE TYPE>`, such as `clusterip`, `nodeport`, `loadbalancer`, and `externalname`. With this method, we cannot specify the selector of the Service. As with the `NodePort` Service we created in that section, only a default selector, `app: my-nginx`, is created, and we have to assign this label to a later created Deployment `test-nodeport`. Except for the type `ExternalName`, Service types can be created with the subcommand `expose` with the tag `type`. Try to create the `NodePort` service with `kubectl expose` for existing resources!

See also

To get the best practices of Kubernetes Services, the following recipes in `Chapter 2`, *Walking though Kubernetes Concepts*, are suggested reading:

- *Deployment API*
- *Working with Secrets*
- *Working with labels and selectors*

There is more advanced knowledge to make your service more functional and flexible. Stay tuned:

- *Forwarding container ports* section in `Chapter 3`, *Playing with Containers*
- *Ensuring flexible usage of your containers* section in `Chapter 3`, *Playing with Containers*

Working with volumes

Files in a container are ephemeral. When the container is terminated, the files are gone. Docker has introduced data volumes to help us persist data (`https://docs.docker.com/engine/admin/volumes/volumes`). However, when it comes to multiple hosts, as a container cluster, it is hard to manage volumes across all the containers and hosts for file sharing or provisioning volume dynamically. Kubernetes introduces volume, which lives with a Pod across a container life cycle. It supports various types of volumes, including popular network disk solutions and storage services in different public clouds. Here are a few:

Volume type	Storage provider
`emptyDir`	Localhost
`hostPath`	Localhost
`glusterfs`	GlusterFS cluster
`downwardAPI`	Kubernetes Pod information
`nfs`	NFS server
`awsElasticBlockStore`	Amazon Web Service Amazon Elastic Block Store
`gcePersistentDisk`	Google Compute Engine persistent disk
`azureDisk`	Azure disk storage
`projected`	Kubernetes resources; currently supports `secret`, `downwardAPI`, and `configMap`
`secret`	Kubernetes Secret resource
`vSphereVolume`	vSphere VMDK volume
`gitRepo`	Git repository

Getting ready

Storage providers are required when you start to use volume in Kubernetes, except for `emptyDir`, which will be erased when the Pod is removed. For other storage providers, folders, servers, or clusters have to be built before using them in the Pod definition. Dynamic provisioning was promoted to stable in Kubernetes version 1.6, which allows you to provision storage based on the supported cloud provider.

In this section, we'll walk through the details of `emptyDir`, `hostPath`, `nfs`, `glusterfs`, `downwardAPI`, and `gitRepo`. `Secret`, which is used to store credentials, will be introduced in the next section. `Projected`, on the other hand, is a way one could group other volume resources under one single mount point. As it only supports `secret`, `downwardAPI`, and `configMap`, we'll be introducing this in the Secret section, as well. The rest of the volume types have similar Kubernetes syntax, just with different backend volume implementations.

How to do it...

Volumes are defined in the volumes section of the pod definition with unique names. Each type of volume has a different configuration to be set. Once you define the volumes, you can mount them in the `volumeMounts` section in the container specs. `volumeMounts.name` and `volumeMounts.mountPath` are required, which indicate the name of the volumes you defined and the mount path inside the container, respectively.

We'll use the Kubernetes configuration file with the YAML format to create a Pod with volumes in the following examples.

emptyDir

`emptyDir` is the simplest volume type, which will create an empty volume for containers in the same Pod to share. When the Pod is removed, the files in `emptyDir` will be erased, as well. `emptyDir` is created when a Pod is created. In the following configuration file, we'll create a Pod running Ubuntu with commands to sleep for `3600` seconds. As you can see, one volume is defined in the volumes section with name data, and the volumes will be mounted under the `/data-mount` path in the Ubuntu container:

```
// configuration file of emptyDir volume
# cat 2-6-1_emptyDir.yaml
apiVersion: v1
kind: Pod
metadata:
```

```
      name: ubuntu
      labels:
        name: ubuntu
    spec:
      containers:
        - image: ubuntu
          command:
            - sleep
            - "3600"
          imagePullPolicy: IfNotPresent
          name: ubuntu
          volumeMounts:
            - mountPath: /data-mount
              name: data
          volumes:
            - name: data
              emptyDir: {}
// create pod by configuration file emptyDir.yaml
# kubectl create -f 2-6-1_emptyDir.yaml
pod "ubuntu" created
```

Check which node the Pod is running on

By using the `kubectl describe pod <Pod name> | grep Node` command, you can check which node the Pod is running on.

After the Pod is running, you can use `docker inspect <container ID>` on the target node and you can see the detailed mount points inside your container:

```
    "Mounts": [
        ...
    {
                "Type": "bind",
                "Source": "/var/lib/kubelet/pods/98c7c676-
e9bd-11e7-9e8d-080027ac331c/volumes/kubernetes.io~empty-dir/data",
                "Destination": "/data-mount",
                "Mode": "",
                "RW": true,
                "Propagation": "rprivate"
            }
        ...
    ]
```

Kubernetes mounts `/var/lib/kubelet/pods/<id>/volumes/kubernetes.io~empty-dir/<volumeMount name>` to `/data-mount` for the Pod to use. If you create a Pod with more than one container, all of them will mount the same destination `/data-mount` with the same source. The default mount propagation is `rprivate`, which means any mount points on the host are invisible in the container, and vice versa.

`emptyDir` could be mounted as `tmpfs` by setting `emptyDir.medium` as `Memory`.

Taking the previous configuration file `2-6-1_emptyDir_mem.yaml` as an example, it would be as follows:

```
volumes:
    -
      name: data
      emptyDir:
        medium: Memory
```

We could verify whether it's successfully mounted with the `kubectl exec <pod_name> <commands>` command. We'll run the `df` command in this container:

```
# kubectl exec ubuntu df
Filesystem 1K-blocks Used Available Use% Mounted on
...
tmpfs 1024036 0 1024036 0% /data-mount
...
```

Note that `tmpfs` is stored in memory instead of in the filesystem. No file will be created, and it'll be flushed in every reboot. In addition, it is constrained by memory limits in Kubernetes. For more information about container resource constraint, refer to *Working with Namespace* in this chapter.

If you have more than one container inside a Pod, the `Kubectl exec` command will be `kubectl exec <pod_name> <container_name> <commands>`.

hostPath

hostPath acts as data volume in Docker. The local folder on a node listed in hostPath will be mounted into the Pod. Since the Pod can run on any nodes, read/write functions happening in the volume could explicitly exist in the node on which the Pod is running. In Kubernetes, however, the Pod should not be node-aware. Please note that the configuration and files might be different on different nodes when using hostPath. Therefore, the same Pod, created by the same command or configuration file, might act differently on different nodes.

By using hostPath, you're able to read and write the files between containers and localhost disks of nodes. What we need for volume definition is for hostPath.path to specify the target mounted folder on the node:

```
apiVersion: v1
# cat 2-6-2_hostPath.yaml
kind: Pod
metadata:
  name: ubuntu
spec:
  containers:
    -
      image: ubuntu
      command:
        - sleep
        - "3600"
      imagePullPolicy: IfNotPresent
      name: ubuntu
      volumeMounts:
        -
          mountPath: /data-mount
          name: data
  volumes:
    -
      name: data
      hostPath:
        path: /tmp/data
```

Using docker inspect to check the volume details, you will see the volume on the host is mounted in the /data-mount destination:

```
"Mounts": [
        {
            "Type": "bind",
            "Source": "/tmp/data",
            "Destination": "/data-mount",
```

```
                    "Mode": "",
                    "RW": true,
                    "Propagation": "rprivate"
            },
                            ...
    ]
```

If we run `kubectl exec ubuntu touch /data-mount/sample`, we should be able to see one empty file, named `sample under /tmp/data`, on the host.

NFS

You can mount an **network filesystem (NFS)** to your Pod as `nfs volume`. Multiple Pods can mount and share the files in the same `nfs volume`. The data stored into `nfs volume` will be persistent across the Pod lifetime. You have to create your own NFS server before using `nfs volume`, and make sure the `nfs-utils` package is installed on Kubernetes minions.

 Check whether your NFS server works before you go. You should check out the `/etc/exports` file with a proper sharing parameter and directory, and use the `mount -t nfs <nfs server>:<share name> <local mounted point>` command to check whether it could be mounted locally.

The configuration file of the volume type with NFS is similar to others, but `nfs.server` and `nfs.path` are required in the volume definition to specify NFS server information and the path mounted from. `nfs.readOnly` is an optional field for specifying whether the volume is read-only or not (the default is `false`):

```
# configuration file of nfs volume
$ cat 2-6-3_nfs.yaml
apiVersion: v1
kind: Pod
metadata:
  name: nfs
spec:
  containers:
    -
      name: nfs
      image: ubuntu
      volumeMounts:
          - name: nfs
            mountPath: "/data-mount"
  volumes:
```

```
  - name: nfs
    nfs:
      server: <your nfs server>
      path: "/"
```

After you run `kubectl create -f 2-6-3_nfs.yaml`, you can describe your Pod with `kubectl describe <pod name>` to check the mounting status. If it's mounted successfully, it should show conditions. Ready as true and the target `nfs` you mount:

```
Conditions:
  Type Status
  Ready True
Volumes:
  nfs:
    Type: NFS (an NFS mount that lasts the lifetime of a pod)
    Server: <your nfs server>
    Path: /
    ReadOnly: false
```

If we inspect the container with the `docker` command, we can see the volume information in the `Mounts` section:

```
"Mounts": [
 {
         "Source":
"/var/lib/kubelet/pods/<id>/volumes/kubernetes.io~nfs/nfs",
         "Destination": "/data-mount",
         "Mode": "",
         "RW": true
     },
                       . . .
     ]
```

Actually, Kubernetes just mounts your `<nfs server>:<share name>` into `/var/lib/kubelet/pods/<id>/volumes/kubernetes.io~nfs/nfs`, and then mounts it into the container as the destination in `/data-mount`. You could also use `kubectl exec` to touch the file, to test whether it's perfectly mounted.

glusterfs

GlusterFS (`https://www.gluster.org`) is a scalable, network-attached storage filesystem. The `glusterfs` volume type allows you to mount GlusterFS volume into your Pod. Just like NFS volume, the data in `glusterfs` volume is persistent across the Pod lifetime. If the Pod is terminated, the data is still accessible in `glusterfs` volume. You should build the GlusterFS system before using `glusterfs` volume.

 Check whether `glusterfs` works before you go. By using `glusterfs` volume information on GlusterFS servers, you can see currently available volumes. By using `mount -t glusterfs <glusterfs server>:/<volume name> <local mounted point>` on local, you can check whether the GlusterFS system can be successfully mounted.

Since the volume replica in GlusterFS must be greater than 1, let's assume we have two replicas in the servers `gfs1` and `gfs2`, and the volume name is `gvol`.

First, we need to create an endpoint acting as a bridge for `gfs1` and `gfs2`:

```
$ cat 2-6-4_gfs-endpoint.yaml
kind: Endpoints
apiVersion: v1
metadata:
  name: glusterfs-cluster
subsets:
  -
    addresses:
      -
        ip: <gfs1 server ip>
    ports:
      -
        port: 1
  -
    addresses:
      -
        ip: <gfs2 server ip>
    ports:
      -
        port: 1

# create endpoints
$ kubectl create -f 2-6-4_gfs-endpoint.yaml
```

Then, we can use `kubectl get endpoints` to check the endpoint was created properly:

```
$kubectl get endpoints
NAME ENDPOINTS AGE
glusterfs-cluster <gfs1>:1,<gfs2>:1 12m
```

After that, we should be able to create the Pod with `glusterfs` volume by `glusterfs.yaml`. The parameters of the `glusterfs` volume definition are `glusterfs.endpoints`, which specify the endpoint name we just created, and `glusterfs.path`, which is the volume name `gvol`. `glusterfs.readOnly` is used to set whether the volume is mounted in read-only mode:

```
$ cat 2-6-4_glusterfs.yaml
apiVersion: v1
kind: Pod
metadata:
  name: ubuntu
spec:
  containers:
    -
      image: ubuntu
      command:
        - sleep
        - "3600"
      imagePullPolicy: IfNotPresent
      name: ubuntu
      volumeMounts:
        -
          mountPath: /data-mount
          name: data
  volumes:
    -
      name: data
      glusterfs:
        endpoints: glusterfs-cluster
        path: gvol
```

Let's check the volume setting with `kubectl describle`:

```
Volumes:
  data:
    Type: Glusterfs (a Glusterfs mount on the host that shares a pod's
lifetime)
    EndpointsName: glusterfs-cluster
    Path: gvol
    ReadOnly: false
```

Using `docker inspect`, you should be able to see that the mounted source is `/var/lib/kubelet/pods/<id>/volumes/kubernetes.io~glusterfs/data` to the destination `/data-mount`.

downwardAPI

`downwardAPI` volume is used to expose Pod information into a container. The definition of `downwardAPI` is a list of items. An item contains a path and `fieldRef`. Kubernetes will dump the specified metadata listed in `fieldRef` to a file named `path` under `mountPath` and mount the `<volume name>` into the destination you specified. Currently supported metadata for `downwardAPI` volume includes:

Field path	Scope	Definition
spec.nodeName	Pod	The node that the Pod is running on
spec.serviceAccountName	Pod	The service account associating with the current Pod
metadata.name	Pod	The name of the Pod
metadata.namespace	Pod	The Namespace that the Pod belongs to
metadata.annotations	Pod	The annotations of the Pod
metadata.labels	Pod	The labels of the Pod
status.podIP	Pod	The ip of the Pod
limits.cpu	Container	The CPU limits of the container
requests.cpu	Container	The CPU requests of the container
limits.memory	Container	The memory limits of the container
requests.memory	Container	The memory requests of the container
limits.ephemeral-storage	Container	The ephemeral storage limits of the container
requests.ephemeral-storage	Container	The ephemeral storage requests of the container

We use `fieldRef.fieldPath` if the scope is with a Pod; `resourceFieldRef` is used when the scope is with a container. For example, the following configuration file could expose `metadata.labels` in `/data-mount` volume in an Ubuntu container:

```
// pod scope example
# cat 2-6-5_downward_api.yaml
apiVersion: v1
kind: Pod
metadata:
  name: downwardapi
```

```
    labels:
      env: demo
spec:
  containers:
    -
      name: downwardapi
      image: ubuntu
      command:
        - sleep
        - "3600"
      volumeMounts:
          - name: podinfo
            mountPath: "/data-mount"
  volumes:
    - name: podinfo
      downwardAPI:
        items:
          - path: metadata
            fieldRef:
              fieldPath: metadata.labels
```

By describing the pod, we could check that the volume is mounted successfully to /data-mount, and metadata.labels is pointed to the metadata file:

```
// describe the pod
# kubectl describe pod downwardapi
...
    Mounts:
      /data-mount from podinfo (rw)
...
Volumes:
  podinfo:
    Type: DownwardAPI (a volume populated by information about the pod)
    Items:
      metadata.labels -> metadata
```

We could check the file inside the container with kubectl exec downwardapi cat /data-mount/metadata, and you should be able to see env="example" presents.

If it's in the container scope, we'll have to specify the container name:

```
# cat 2-6-5_downward_api_container.yaml
apiVersion: v1
kind: Pod
metadata:
  name: downwardapi-container
spec:
```

```
containers:
  -
    name: downwardapi
    image: ubuntu
    command:
      - sleep
      - "3600"
    volumeMounts:
      - name: podinfo
        mountPath: "/data-mount"
volumes:
  - name: podinfo
    downwardAPI:
      items:
        - path: "cpu_limit"
          resourceFieldRef:
            containerName: downwardapi
            resource: limits.cpu
```

We could use the `docker inspect <container_name>` command inside a node to check the implementation:

```
{
        "Source":
"/var/lib/kubelet/pods/<id>/volumes/kubernetes.io~downward-api/<volume
name>",
        "Destination": "/data-mount",
        "Mode": "",
        "RW": true
}
```

Kubernetes exposes `pod` information in source volume, and mounts it to `/data-mount`.

For the IP of the Pod, using environment variable to propagate in Pod spec would be must easier:

```
spec:
  containers:
    - name: envsample-pod-info
      env:
        - name: MY_POD_IP
          valueFrom:
            fieldRef:
              fieldPath: status.podIP
```

The sample folder in the Kubernetes GitHub (`https://kubernetes.io/docs/tasks/`
`inject-data-application/downward-api-volume-expose-pod-information`) contains
more examples for both environment variables and `downwardAPI` volume.

gitRepo

`gitRepo` is a convenient volume type that clones your existing Git repository into a
container:

```
// an example of how to use gitRepo volume type
# cat 2-6-6_gitRepo.yaml
apiVersion: v1
kind: Pod
metadata:
  name: gitrepo
spec:
  containers:
  - image: ubuntu
    name: ubuntu
    command:
      - sleep
      - "3600"
    volumeMounts:
    - mountPath: /app
      name: app-git
  volumes:
  - name: app-git
    gitRepo:
      repository:
"https://github.com/kubernetes-cookbook/second-edition.git"
      revision: "9d8e845e2f55a5c65da01ac4235da6d88ef6bcd0"

# kubectl create -f 2-6-6_gitRepo.yaml
pod "gitrepo" created
```

In the preceding example, the volume plugin mounts an empty directory and runs the git
clone `<gitRepo.repolist>` to clone the repository into it. Then the Ubuntu container will
be able to access it.

There's more...

In the previous cases, the user needs to know the details of the storage provider. Kubernetes provides `PersistentVolumes` and `PersistentVolumeClaim` to abstract the details of the storage provider and storage consumer.

PersistentVolumes

An illustration of `PersistentVolume` is shown in the following graph. First, the administrator provisions the specification of a `PersistentVolume`. Then the consumer requests for storage with `PersistentVolumeClaim`. Finally, the Pod mounts the volume with the reference of `PersistentVolumeClaim`:

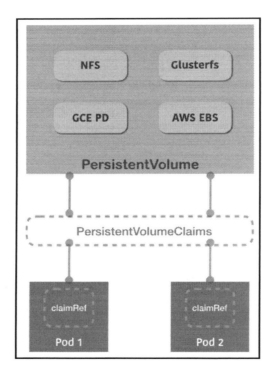

PersistentVolumeClaims is an abstract layer to decouple volumes for a Pod and physical volume resource

Here is an example using `NFS`. The administrator needs to provision and allocate `PersistentVolume` first:

```
# example of PV with NFS
```

```
$ cat 2-6-7_pv.yaml
  apiVersion: "v1"
  kind: "PersistentVolume"
  metadata:
    name: "pvnfs01"
  spec:
    capacity:
      storage: "3Gi"
    accessModes:
      - "ReadWriteOnce"
    nfs:
      path: "/"
      server: "<your nfs server>"
    persistentVolumeReclaimPolicy: "Recycle"

# create the pv
$ kubectl create -f 2-6-7_pv.yaml
persistentvolume "pvnfs01" created
```

We can see that there are three parameters here: capacity, accessModes, and
persistentVolumeReclaimPolicy. capacity is the size of this PersistentVolume.
Now, accessModes is based on the capability of the storage provider and can be set to a
specific mode during provision. For example, NFS supports multiple readers and writers
simultaneously—then we can specify the accessModes as one of ReadWriteOnce,
ReadOnlyMany, or ReadWriteMany. Now, persistentVolumeReclaimPolicy is used to
define the behavior when PersistentVolume is released. The currently supported policy
is retain and recycle for nfs and hostPath. You have to clean the volume by yourself in
retain mode; on the other hand, Kubernetes will scrub the volume in recycle mode.

PV is a resource like a node. We could use kubectl get pv to see current provisioned
PVs:

```
# list current PVs
$ kubectl get pv
NAME LABELS CAPACITY ACCESSMODES STATUS CLAIM REASON AGE
pvnfs01 <none> 3Gi RWO Bound default/pvclaim01 37m
```

Next, we will need to bind PersistentVolume with PersistentVolumeClaim in order to
mount it as volume into the pod:

```
# example of PersistentVolumeClaim
$ cat claim.yaml
apiVersion: "v1"
kind: "PersistentVolumeClaim"
metadata:
  name: "pvclaim01"
```

```
spec:
  accessModes:
    - ReadWriteOnce
  resources:
    requests:
      storage: 1Gi

# create the claim
$ kubectl create -f claim.yaml
persistentvolumeclaim "pvclaim01" created

# list the PersistentVolumeClaim (pvc)
$ kubectl get pvc
NAME LABELS STATUS VOLUME CAPACITY ACCESSMODES AGE
pvclaim01 <none> Bound pvnfs01 3Gi RWO 59m
```

The constraints of `accessModes` and storage can be set in `PersistentVolumeClaim`. If the claim is bound successfully, its status will turn to `Bound`; on the other hand, if the status is `Unbound`, it means there is no PV currently matching the requests.

Then we are able to mount the PV as volume with the reference of `PersistentVolumeClaim`:

```
# example of mounting into Pod
$ cat nginx.yaml
apiVersion: v1
kind: Pod
metadata:
  name: nginx
  labels:
    project: pilot
    environment: staging
    tier: frontend
spec:
  containers:
    -
      image: nginx
      imagePullPolicy: IfNotPresent
      name: nginx
      volumeMounts:
      - name: pv
        mountPath: "/usr/share/nginx/html"
      ports:
      - containerPort: 80
  volumes:
    - name: pv
      persistentVolumeClaim:
```

```
        claimName: "pvclaim01"

# create the pod
$ kubectl create -f nginx.yaml
pod "nginx" created
```

It will be similar syntax to other volume types. Just add the `claimName` of `persistentVolumeClaim` in the volume definition. We are all set! Let's check the details to see whether we mounted it successfully:

```
# check the details of a pod
$ kubectl describe pod nginx
...
Volumes:
  pv:
    Type: PersistentVolumeClaim (a reference to a PersistentVolumeClaim in
the same namespace)
    ClaimName: pvclaim01
    ReadOnly: false
...
```

We can see we have a volume mounted in the Pod `nginx` with the type `pv pvclaim01`. Use `docker inspect` to see how it is mounted:

```
"Mounts": [
        {
            "Source":
"/var/lib/kubelet/pods/<id>/volumes/kubernetes.io~nfs/pvnfs01",
            "Destination": "/usr/share/nginx/html",
            "Mode": "",
            "RW": true
        },
                ...
    ]
```

Kubernetes mounts `/var/lib/kubelet/pods/<id>/volumes/kubernetes.io~nfs/<persistentvolume name>` into the destination in the Pod.

Using storage classes

In the cloud world, people provision storage or data volume dynamically. While PersistentVolumeClaim is based on existing static PersistentVolume that is provisioned by administrators, it might be really beneficial if the cloud volume could be requested dynamically when it needs to be. Storage classes are designed to resolve this problem. To make storage classes available in your cluster, three conditions need to be met. First, the DefaultStorageClass admission controller has to be enabled (refer to Chapter 7, *Building Kubernetes on GCP*). Then PersistentVolumeClaim needs to request a storage class. The last condition is trivial; administrators have to configure a storage class in order to make dynamic provisioning work:

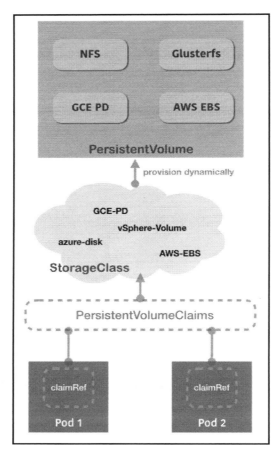

StorageClass dynamically allocates a PV and associates it with a PVC

The default storage classes are various, basically based on your underlying cloud provider. Storage classes are the abstract way to define underlying storage providers. They have different syntax based on different types of providers. Default storage classes can be changed, but cannot be deleted. The default storage class has an annotation `storageclass.beta.kubernetes.io/is-default-class=true` on. Removing that annotation can disable the dynamic provisioning. Moving the annotation to another storage class can switch the default storage class. If no storage classes have that annotation, dynamic provisioning will not be triggered when there is a new `PersistentVolumeClaim`.

gcePersistentDisk

`gcePersistentDisk` volume mounts a **Google Compute Engine (GCE) Persistent Disk (PD)** into a Pod. If you provision it statically, you'll have to create it first with the `gcloud` command or in the GCE console. The following is an example:

```
# cat 2-6-8_gce/static_mount.yaml
apiVersion: v1
kind: Pod
metadata:
  name: gce-pd-pod
spec:
  containers:
  - image: nginx
    name: gce-pd-example
    volumeMounts:
    - mountPath: /mount-path
      name: gce-pd
      ports:
        - containerPort: 80
  volumes:
  - name: gce-pd
    gcePersistentDisk:
      pdName: example
      fsType: ext4
```

Alternatively, and more cost-effectively, we could use dynamic provisioning. Then we don't need to provision PD beforehand. For enabling dynamic provisioning, the `DefaultStorageClass` admission controller has to be enabled on the API server. In some Kubernetes environments, it has been enabled by default, such as in GCE. We could explicitly disable it by setting the `storageClassName: ""` in `Pod/Deployment/ReplicaSet` configuration file.

Next, we'll introduce how to create a non-default `StorageClass`:

```
// list storageclasses (sc)
# kubectl get sc
NAME PROVISIONER
standard (default) kubernetes.io/gce-pd
```

We can see we have a default storage class named `standard`. If that's the desired provider, then you don't need to create your own storage classes. In the following example, we'll create a new storage class named `example`:

```
// gce storage class
# cat 2-6-8_gce/storageclass.yaml
kind: StorageClass
apiVersion: storage.k8s.io/v1
metadata:
  name: example
provisioner: kubernetes.io/gce-pd
parameters:
  type: pd-standard
  zones: us-central1-a
// create storage class
# kubectl create -f storageclass.yaml
    storageclass "example" created

// check current storage classes
# kubectl get sc
NAME PROVISIONER
example kubernetes.io/gce-pd
    standard (default) kubernetes.io/gce-pd
```

For the type, you can specify any storage type that GCE supports, such as `pd-ssd`. You can specify zones by changing zone parameters, too. Next, we'll add a `PersistentVolumeClaim` for using this storage class:

```
# 2-6-8_gce/pvc.yaml
apiVersion: v1
kind: PersistentVolumeClaim
metadata:
  name: gce-example
spec:
  accessModes:
    - ReadWriteOnce
  storageClassName: example
  resources:
    requests:
      storage: 5Gi
```

```
// create pvc
# kubectl create -f pvc.yaml
persistentvolumeclaim "gce-example" created

// check pvc status
# kubectl get pvc
NAME STATUS VOLUME CAPACITY ACCESS MODES STORAGECLASS AGE
gce-example Bound pvc-d04218e3-ede5-11e7-aef7-42010a8001f4 5Gi RWO example
1h
```

This configuration file will create a PVC by specifying the storage class named `example`. A PV will be created by the claim. When a PVC is in `Bound` status, Kubernetes will always bind that PV to the matching PVC. Then, let's have a Pod using this PVC:

```
# cat 2-6-8_gce/pod.yaml
kind: Pod
apiVersion: v1
metadata:
  name: gce-pd-pod
spec:
  volumes:
    - name: gce-pd
      persistentVolumeClaim:
       claimName: gce-example
  containers:
    - name: gce-pd-example
      image: nginx
      ports:
        - containerPort: 80
      volumeMounts:
        - mountPath: /mount-path
          name: gce-pd

// create a pod
# kubectl create -f pod.yaml
pod "gce-pd-pod" created

// check the volume setting in pod
# kubectl describe pod gce-pd-pod
...
Containers:
  gce-pd-example:
    Container ID:
    Mounts:
      /mount-path from gce-pd (rw)
...
Volumes:
```

```
gce-pd:
  Type: PersistentVolumeClaim (a reference to a PersistentVolumeClaim in
the same namespace)
  ClaimName: gce-example
  ReadOnly: false
```

We can see that `gce-pd` is mounted under `/mount-path`. Let's see if the volume has been provisioned dynamically.

Alternatively, you could use `gcloud compute disks list`. `gcloud` in a command-line tool in GCE.

awsElasticBlockStore

`awsElasticBlockStore` volume mounts an **Amazon Web Service Elastic Block Store (AWS EBS)** volume. It's a service that provides persistent block storage for Amazon EC2. Just like the GCE persistent disk, we can provision it statically or dynamically.

To provision it statically, administrators have to create an EBS volume by the AWS console or AWS CLI beforehand. The following is an example of how to mount an existing EBS volume to the containers in a Deployment:

```
// example of how we used pre-created EBS volume.
# cat 2-6-8_aws/static_mount.yaml
kind: Deployment
apiVersion: apps/v1
metadata:
  name: aws-ebs-deployment
spec:
  replicas: 2
  selector:
    matchLabels:
      run: nginx
  template:
    metadata:
      labels:
        run: nginx
    spec:
      volumes:
        - name: aws-ebs
          awsElasticBlockStore:
            volumeID: <ebs volume ID>
            fsType: ext4
      containers:
      - name: aws-ebs-example
        image: nginx
```

```
ports:
  - containerPort: 80
volumeMounts:
  - mountPath: /mount-path
    name: aws-ebs
```

To provision it dynamically, on the other hand, just like how we demonstrated in the GCE persistent disk, we first create a non-default storage class; you're free to use a default storage class as well. Here, our environment is provisioned by kops (https://github.com/ kubernetes/kops; for more information, please refer to Chapter 6, *Building Kubernetes on AWS*). The environment has been bound with the required IAM policies, such as ec2:AttachVolume, ec2:CreateVolume, ec2:DetachVolume, and ec2:DeleteVolume. If you provision it from scratch, be sure that you have required policies attaching to the masters:

```
// declare a storage class
# cat 2-6-8_aws/storageclass.yaml
kind: StorageClass
apiVersion: storage.k8s.io/v1
metadata:
  name: example-ebs
provisioner: kubernetes.io/aws-ebs
parameters:
  type: io1
  zones: us-east-1a

// create storage class
# kubectl create -f storageclass.yaml
storageclass "example-ebs" created

// check if example-ebs sc is created
# kubectl get sc
NAME PROVISIONER
default kubernetes.io/aws-ebs
example-ebs kubernetes.io/aws-ebs
gp2 (default) kubernetes.io/aws-ebs
```

Next, we create a PVC with the storage class name we just created:

```
// declare a PVC
# cat 2-6-8_aws/pvc.yaml
apiVersion: v1
kind: PersistentVolumeClaim
metadata:
  name: aws-example
spec:
  accessModes:
```

```
        - ReadWriteOnce
    storageClassName: example-ebs
    resources:
      requests:
        storage: 5Gi
```

```
// create a PVC
# kubectl create -f pvc.yaml
persistentvolumeclaim "aws-example" created
```

```
// check if PVC has been created
# kubectl get pvc
NAME STATUS VOLUME CAPACITY ACCESS MODES STORAGECLASS AGE
aws-example Bound pvc-d1cddc08-ee31-11e7-8582-022bb4c3719e 5Gi RWO example-
ebs 5s
```

When Kubernetes receives the request of `PersistentVolumeClaim`, it'll try to allocate a new `PersistentVolume`, or bind to an existing PV, if possible:

```
// check if a PV is created by a PVC.
# kubectl get pv
NAME CAPACITY ACCESS MODES RECLAIM POLICY STATUS CLAIM STORAGECLASS REASON
AGE
pvc-d1cddc08-ee31-11e7-8582-022bb4c3719e 5Gi RWO Delete Bound default/aws-
example example-ebs 36m
```

We can check the corresponding PV in the AWS console, as well.

At the end, we create a Deployment with this volume by specifying `persistentVolumeClaim` in the spec:

```
// create a deployment
# cat 2-6-8_aws/deployment.yaml
kind: Deployment
apiVersion: apps/v1
metadata:
  name: aws-ebs-deployment
spec:
  replicas: 2
  selector:
    matchLabels:
      run: nginx
  template:
    metadata:
      labels:
        run: nginx
    spec:
```

```
volumes:
- name: aws-ebs
  persistentVolumeClaim:
    claimName: aws-example
containers:
- name: aws-ebs-example
  image: nginx
  ports:
    - containerPort: 80
  volumeMounts:
    - mountPath: /mount-path
      name: aws-ebs
```

By specifying `claimName` as `aws-example`, it'll then use the EBS volume we just create by PVC, which is requested to AWS dynamically. If we take a look at the Pod description with `kubectl describe pod <pod_name>`, we can see the details of the volumes:

```
// kubectl describe pod <pod_name>
# kubectl describe pod aws-ebs-deployment-68bdc6f546-246s7
Containers:
  aws-ebs-example:
    ...
    Mounts:
      /mount-path from aws-ebs (rw)
Volumes:
  aws-ebs:
    Type: AWSElasticBlockStore (a Persistent Disk resource in AWS)
    VolumeID: vol-0fccc3b0af8c17727
    FSType: ext4
    Partition: 0
    ReadOnly: false
...
```

EBS volume `vol-0fccc3b0af8c17727` is mounted under `/mount-path` inside the container.

If the volume was dynamically provisioned, the default reclaim policy is set to `delete`. Set it to `retain` if you want to keep them, even if a PVC is deleted.

The StorageObjectInUseProtection admission controller

 A PVC might be deleted accidentally by user even if it's used by a Pod. In Kubernetes v1.10, a new admission controller is added to prevent this from happening. `kubernetes.io/pv-protection` or `kubernetes.io/pvc-protection` finalizer will be added into PV or PVC by `StorageObjectInUseProtection` admission controller. Then when object deletion request is sent, admission controller will do pre-delete check and see if there is any Pod are using it. This will prevent data loss.

See also

Volumes can be mounted on the Pods by declaring in Pods or ReplicaSet spec. Check out the following recipes to jog your memory:

- *Working with Pods* section in `Chapter 2`, *Walking through Kubernetes Concepts*
- *Working with replica sets* section in `Chapter 2`, *Walking through Kubernetes Concepts*
- *Working with Secrets* section in `Chapter 2`, *Walking through Kubernetes Concepts*
- *Setting resource in nodes* section in `Chapter 8`, *Advanced Cluster Administration*
- *Authentication and authorization* section in `Chapter 8`, *Advanced Cluster Administration*

Working with Secrets

Kubernetes Secrets manage information in key-value formats with the value encoded. It can be a password, access key, or token. With Secrets, users don't have to expose sensitive data in the configuration file. Secrets can reduce the risk of credential leaks and make our resource configurations more organized.

Currently, there are three types of Secrets:

- Generic/Opaque: https://en.wikipedia.org/wiki/Opaque_data_type
- Docker registry
- TLS

Generic/Opaque is the default type that we're using in our application. Docker registry is used to store the credential of a private Docker registry. TLS Secret is used to store the CA certificate bundle for cluster administration.

Kubernetes creates built-in Secrets for the credentials that using to access API server.

Getting ready

Before using Secrets, we have to keep in mind that Secret should be always created before dependent Pods, so dependent Pods can reference it properly. In addition, Secrets have a 1 MB size limitation. It works properly for defining a bunch of information in a single Secret. However, Secret is not designed for storing large amounts of data. For configuration data, consider using `ConfigMaps`. For large amounts of non-sensitive data, consider using volumes instead.

How to do it...

In the following example, we'll walk through how to create a Generic/Opaque Secret and use it in your Pods by assuming that we have an access token that needs to be used inside a Pod.

Creating a Secret

There are two ways to create a Secret. The first one is with `kubectl create secret` in the command line, and the other one is with direct resource creation in the configuration file.

Working with kubectl create command line

By using `kubectl create secret` command line, you can create a Secret from a file, directory, or literal value. With this method, you don't need to encode the Secret by yourself. Kubernetes will do that for you:

From a file

1. If a file is the source of Secret, we'll have to create a text file which contains our sensitive data first:

```
// assume we have a sensitive credential named access token.
# cat 2-7-1_access-token
9S!g0U61699r
```

2. Next, we could use `kubectl create secret` in the command line to create the Secret. The syntax is:

```
Kubectl create secret <secret-type> --from-file <file1> (--
from-file <file2> ...)
```

3. In our case, we use generic Secret type, since the access token is neither the Docker registry image pull Secrets nor TLS information:

```
# kubectl create secret generic access-token --from-file
2-7-1_access-token
secret "access-token" created
```

4. You can check the detailed Secret information with the `kubectl get secret` command:

```
// get the detailed information for a Secret.
# kubectl get secret access-token -o yaml
apiVersion: v1
data:
  2-7-1_access-token: OVMhZzBVNjE2OTlyCg==
kind: Secret
metadata:
  creationTimestamp: 2018-01-01T20:26:24Z
  name: access-token
  namespace: default
  resourceVersion: "127883"
  selfLink: /api/v1/namespaces/default/secrets/access-token
  uid: 0987ec7d-ef32-11e7-ac53-080027ac331c
type: Opaque
```

5. You can use the `base64` command (https://linux.die.net/man/1/base64) in Linux to decode the encoded Secret:

```
// decode encoded Secret
# echo "OVMhZzBVNjE2OTlyCg==" | base64 --decode
9S!g0U61699r
```

From a directory

Creating a Secret from a directory is similar to creating from a file, using the same command, but with `directory`. Kubernetes will iterate all the files inside that directory and create a Secret for you:

```
// show directory structure
# tree
.
├── 2-7-1_access-token-dir
│   └── 2-7-1_access-token

// create Secrets from a directory
# kubectl create secret generic access-token --from-file 2-7-1_access-token-dir/
secret "access-token" created
```

You can check the Secret with the `kubectl get secret access-token -o yaml` command again and see if they're identical to the ones from the file.

From a literal value

Kubernetes supports creating a Secret with a single command line, as well:

```
// create a Secret via plain text in command line
# kubectl create secret generic access-token --from-literal=2-7-1_access-token=9S\!g0U61699r
secret "access-token" created
```

Then we can use the `get secret` command to check if they're identical to the previous method:

```
// check the details of a Secret
# kubectl get secret access-token -o yaml
apiVersion: v1
data:
  2-7-1_access-token: OVMhZzBVNjE2OTlyCg==
kind: Secret
metadata:
  creationTimestamp: 2018-01-01T21:44:32Z
  name: access-token
  ...
type: Opaque
```

Via configuration file

A Secret can also be created directly through the configuration file; however, you'll have to encode the Secret manually. Just use the kind of Secret:

```
// encode Secret manually
# echo '9S!g0U61699r' | base64
OVMhZzBVNjE2OTlyCg==

// create a Secret via configuration file, put encoded Secret into the file
# cat 2-7-1_secret.yaml
apiVersion: v1
kind: Secret
metadata:
  name: access-token
type: Opaque
data:
  2-7-1_access-token: OVMhZzBVNjE2OTlyCg==

// create the resource
# kubectl create -f 2-7-1_secret.yaml
secret "access-token" created
```

Using Secrets in Pods

To use Secrets inside Pods, we can choose to expose them in environment variables or mount the Secrets as volumes.

By environment variables

In terms of accessing Secrets inside a Pod, add `env section` inside the container spec as follows:

```
// using access-token Secret inside a Pod
# cat 2-7-2_env.yaml
apiVersion: v1
kind: Pod
metadata:
  name: secret-example-env
spec:
  containers:
  - name: ubuntu
    image: ubuntu
    command: ["/bin/sh", "-c", "while : ;do echo $ACCESS_TOKEN; sleep 10;
done"]
```

```
    env:
        - name: ACCESS_TOKEN
          valueFrom:
            secretKeyRef:
              name: access-token
              key: 2-7-1_access-token
// create a pod
# kubectl create -f 2-7-2_env.yaml
pod "secret-example-env" created
```

In the preceding example, we expose `2-7-1_access-token` key in access-token Secret as `ACCESS_TOKEN` environment variable, and print it out through a while infinite loop. Check the `stdout via kubectl` log command:

```
// check stdout logs
# kubectl logs -f secret-example-env
9S!g0U61699r
```

Note that the environment variable was exposed during Pod creation. If a new value of Secret is pushed, you'll have to re-launch/rolling-update a Pod or Deployment to reflect that.

If we describe the `secret-example-env` Pod, we can see that an environment variable was set to a Secret:

```
# kubectl describe pods secret-example-env
Name: secret-example-env
...
Environment:
    ACCESS_TOKEN: <set to the key '2-7-1_access-token' in secret 'access-token'>
```

By volumes

A Secret can be also mounted as volume by using the Secret type of the volume. The following is an example of how to use it:

```
// example of using Secret volume
# cat 2-7-3_volumes.yaml
apiVersion: v1
kind: Pod
metadata:
  name: secret-example-volume
spec:
  containers:
```

```
   - name: ubuntu
     image: ubuntu
     command: ["/bin/sh", "-c", "while : ;do cat /secret/token; sleep 10;
done"]
     volumeMounts:
       - name: secret-volume
         mountPath: /secret
         readOnly: true
   volumes:
     - name: secret-volume
       secret:
         secretName: access-token
         items:
         - key: 2-7-1_access-token
           path: token

// create the Pod
kubectl create -f 2-7-3_volumes.yaml
pod "secret-example-volume" created
```

The preceding example will mount secret-volume into the /secret mount point inside the Pod. /secret will contain a file with the name token, which contains our access token. If we check the Pod details, it'll show that we mounted a read-only Secret volume:

```
// check the Pod details
# kubectl describe pods secret-example-volume
Name: secret-example-volume
...
Containers:
  ubuntu:
    ...
    Mounts:
      /secret from secret-volume (ro)
      ...
Volumes:
  secret-volume:
    Type: Secret (a volume populated by a Secret)
    SecretName: access-token
    Optional: false
...
```

If we check the stdout, it'll show the Pod can properly retrieve the expected value:

```
# kubectl logs -f secret-example-volume
9S!g0U61699r
```

The same as with the environment variable, the files in the mounted volume are created upon Pod creation time. It won't change dynamically when the Secret value is updated after the Pod creation time.

Deleting a Secret

To delete a Secret, simply use the `kubectl delete secret` command:

```
# kubectl delete secret access-token
secret "access-token" deleted
```

If a Secret is deleted when a Secret volume is attached, it'll show an error message whenever the volume reference disappears:

```
# kubectl describe pods secret-example-volume
...
Events:
  Warning FailedMount 53s (x8 over 1m) kubelet, minikube MountVolume.SetUp
failed for volume "secret-volume" : secrets "access-token" not found
```

How it works...

In order to reduce the risk of leaking the Secrets' content, Secret is not landed to the disk. Instead, kubelet creates a `tmpfs` filesystem on the node to store the Secret. The Kubernetes API server pushes the Secret to the node on which the demanded container is running. The data will be flashed when the container is destroyed.

There's more...

Secrets hold small amounts of sensitive data. For application configuration, consider using `ConfigMaps` to hold non-sensitive information.

Using ConfigMaps

Here is an example of using `ConfigMaps`:

```
# cat configmap/2-7-4_configmap.yaml
apiVersion: v1
kind: ConfigMap
metadata:
```

```
    name: config-example
data:
  app.properties: |
    name=kubernetes-cookbook
    port=443

// create configmap
# kubectl create -f configmap/2-7-4_configmap.yaml
configmap "config-example" created
```

Similar to Secret, `ConfigMaps` can be retrieved with environment variables or volumes:

```
# cat configmap/2-7-4_env.yaml
apiVersion: v1
kind: Pod
metadata:
  name: configmap-env
spec:
  containers:
    - name: configmap
      image: ubuntu
      command: ["/bin/sh", "-c", "while : ;do echo $APP_NAME; sleep 10;
done"]
      env:
        - name: APP_NAME
          valueFrom:
            configMapKeyRef:
              name: config-example
              key: app.properties

// create the pod
#kubectl create -f configmap/2-7-4_env.yaml
pod "configmap-env" created
```

Alternatively, you can use `ConfigMaps` volume to retrieve the configuration information:

```
// using configmap in a pod
# cat configmap/2-7-4_volumes.yaml
apiVersion: v1
kind: Pod
metadata:
  name: configmap-volume
spec:
  containers:
    - name: configmap
      image: ubuntu
      command: ["/bin/sh", "-c", "while : ;do cat
/src/app/config/app.properties; sleep 10; done"]
```

```
    volumeMounts:
    - name: config-volume
      mountPath: /src/app/config
  volumes:
    - name: config-volume
      configMap:
        name: config-example
```

Mounting Secrets and ConfigMap in the same volume

Projected volume is a way to group multiple volume sources into the same mount point.
Currently, it supports Secrets, ConfigMap, and downwardAPI.

The following is an example of how we group the examples of Secrets and
ConfigMaps that we used in this chapter:

```
// using projected volume
# cat 2-7-5_projected_volume.yaml
apiVersion: v1
kind: Pod
metadata:
  name: projected-volume-example
spec:
  containers:
  - name: container-tes
    image: ubuntu
    command: ["/bin/sh", "-c", "while : ;do cat /projected-volume/configmap
&& cat /projected-volume/token; sleep 10; done"]
    volumeMounts:
    - name: projected-volume
      mountPath: "/projected-volume"
  volumes:
  - name: projected-volume
    projected:
      sources:
      - secret:
          name: access-token
          items:
            - key: 2-7-1_access-token
              path: token
      - configMap:
          name: config-example
          items:
            - key: app.properties
              path: configmap
```

```
// create projected volume
# kubectl create -f 2-7-5_projected_volume.yaml
pod "projected-volume-example" created
```

Let's check `stdout` to see if it works properly:

```
# kubectl logs -f projected-volume-example
name=kubernetes-cookbook
port=443
9S!gOU61699r
```

See also

- *Working with Volumes* section in `Chapter 2`, *Walking through Kubernetes Concepts*
- The *Working with configuration files* section in `Chapter 3`, *Playing with Containers*
- The *Moving monolithic to microservices* and *Working with the private Docker registry* sections in `Chapter 5`, *Building Continuous Delivery Pipeline*
- The *Advanced settings in kubeconfig* section in `Chapter 7`, *Building Kubernetes on GCP*

Working with names

When you create any Kubernetes object, such as a Pod, Deployment, and Service, you can assign a name to it. The names in Kubernetes are spatially unique, which means you cannot assign the same name in the Pods.

Getting ready

Kubernetes allows us to assign a name with the following restrictions:

- Up to 253 characters
- Lowercase of alphabet and numeric characters
- May contain special characters in the middle, but only dashs (-) and dots (.)

How to do it...

For assigning a name to the Pod, follow the following steps:

1. The following example is the Pod YAML configuration that assigns the Pod name as `my-pod` to the container name as `my-container`; you can successfully create it as follows:

```
# cat my-pod.yaml
apiVersion: v1
kind: Pod
metadata:
  name: my-pod
spec:
  containers:
  - name: my-container
    image: nginx


# kubectl create -f my-pod.yaml
pod "my-pod" created


# kubectl get pods
NAME       READY     STATUS     RESTARTS    AGE
my-pod     0/1       Running    0           4s
```

2. You can use the `kubectl describe` command to see the container named `my-container` as follows:

```
$ kubectl describe pod my-pod
Name:           my-pod
Namespace:      default
Node:           minikube/192.168.64.12
Start Time:     Sat, 16 Dec 2017 10:53:38 -0800
Labels:         <none>
Annotations:    <none>
Status:         Running
IP:             172.17.0.3
Containers:
  my-container:
    Container ID:
docker://fcf36d0a96a49c5a08eb6de1ef27ca761b4ca1c6b4a3a4312df836cb8e0a5304
    Image:          nginx
    Image ID:       docker-
pullable://nginx@sha256:2ffc60a51c9d658594b63ef5acfac9d92f4e1550f633a3a16d8
```

```
98925c4e7f5a7
    Port:              <none>
    State:             Running
      Started:         Sat, 16 Dec 2017 10:54:43 -0800
    Ready:             True
    Restart Count:     0
    Environment:       <none>
    Mounts:
      /var/run/secrets/kubernetes.io/serviceaccount from default-token-
lmd62 (ro)
Conditions:
  Type            Status
  Initialized     True
  Ready           True
  PodScheduled    True
Volumes:
  default-token-lmd62:
    Type:          Secret (a volume populated by a Secret)
    SecretName:    default-token-lmd62
    Optional:      false
QoS Class:         BestEffort
Node-Selectors:    <none>
Tolerations:       <none>
Events:
  Type    Reason               Age    From              Message
  ----    ------               ----   ----              -------
  Normal  Scheduled            1m     default-scheduler Successfully
assigned my-pod to minikube
  Normal  SuccessfulMountVolume 1m    kubelet, minikube MountVolume.SetUp
succeeded for volume "default-token-lmd62"
  Normal  Pulling              1m     kubelet, minikube pulling image
"nginx"
  Normal  Pulled               50s    kubelet, minikube Successfully
pulled image "nginx"
  Normal  Created              50s    kubelet, minikube Created container
  Normal  Started              50s    kubelet, minikube Started container
```

3. On the other hand, the following example contains two containers, but assigns the same name, `my-container`; therefore, the `kubectl create` command returns an error and can't create the Pod:

```
//delete previous Pod
$ kubectl delete pod --all
pod "my-pod" deleted


$ cat duplicate.yaml
```

```
apiVersion: v1
kind: Pod
metadata:
  name: my-pod
spec:
  containers:
  - name: my-container
    image: nginx
  - name: my-container
    image: centos
    command: ["/bin/sh", "-c", "while : ;do curl
http://localhost:80/; sleep 3; done"]


$ kubectl create -f duplicate.yaml
The Pod "my-pod" is invalid: spec.containers[1].name: Duplicate
value: "my-container"
```

You can add the `--validate` flag.
For example, the command `kubectl create -f duplicate.yaml --validate` uses a schema to validate the input before sending it.

In another example, the YAML contains a ReplicationController and Service, both of which are using the same name, `my-nginx`, but it is successfully created because the Deployment and Service are different objects:

```
$ cat my-nginx.yaml
apiVersion: apps/v1
kind: Deployment
metadata:
  name: my-nginx
spec:
  replicas: 3
  selector:
    matchLabels:
      run: my-label
  template:
    metadata:
      labels:
        run: my-label
    spec:
      containers:
      - name: my-container
        image: nginx
        ports:
```

```
        - containerPort: 80
---
apiVersion: v1
kind: Service
metadata:
  name: my-nginx
spec:
  ports:
    - protocol: TCP
      port: 80
  type: NodePort
  selector:
    run: my-label


//create Deployment and Service
$ kubectl create -f my-nginx.yaml
deployment.apps "my-nginx" created
service "my-nginx" created


//Deployment "my-nginx" is created
$ kubectl get deploy
NAME         DESIRED    CURRENT    UP-TO-DATE    AVAILABLE    AGE
my-nginx     3          3          3             3            1m

//Service "my-nginx" is also created
$ kubectl get svc
NAME TYPE CLUSTER-IP EXTERNAL-IP PORT(S) AGE
kubernetes ClusterIP 10.0.0.1 <none> 443/TCP 13d
my-nginx NodePort 10.0.0.246 <none> 80:31168/TCP 1m
```

How it works...

A name is just a unique identifier, and all naming conventions are good; however, it is recommended to look up and identify the container image. For example:

- memcached-pod1
- haproxy.us-west
- my-project1.mysql

On the other hand, the following examples do not work because of Kubernetes restrictions:

- `Memcache-pod1` (contains uppercase)
- `haproxy.us_west` (contains underscore)
- `my-project1.mysql.` (dot in the last)

Note that Kubernetes supports a label that allows assigning a `key=value` style identifier. It also allows duplication. Therefore, if you want to assign something like the following information, use a label instead:

- Environment (for example: staging, production)
- Version (for example: v1.2)
- Application role (for example: frontend, worker)

In addition, Kubernetes also supports names that have different Namespaces. This means that you can use the same name in different Namespaces (for example: `nginx`). Therefore, if you want to assign just an application name, use Namespaces instead.

See also

This section from the chapter described how to assign and find the name of objects. This is just a basic methodology, but Kubernetes has more powerful naming tools, such as Namespace and selectors, to manage clusters:

- *Working with Pods*
- *Deployment API*
- *Working with Services*
- *Working with Namespaces*
- *Working with labels and selectors*

Working with Namespaces

In a Kubernetes cluster, the name of a resource is a unique identifier within a Namespace. Using a Kubernetes Namespace could separate user spaces for different environments in the same cluster. It gives you the flexibility of creating an isolated environment and partitioning resources to different projects and teams. You may consider Namespace as a virtual cluster. Pods, Services, and Deployments are contained in a certain Namespace. Some low-level resources, such as nodes and `persistentVolumes`, do not belong to any Namespace.

Before we dig into the resource Namespace, let's understand `kubeconfig` and some keywords first:

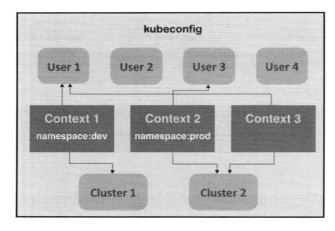

The relationship of kubeconfig components

`kubeconfig` is used to call the file which configures the access permission of Kubernetes clusters. As the original configuration of the system, Kubernetes takes `$HOME/.kube/config` as a `kubeconfig` file. Some concepts that are illustrated by the preceding diagram are as follows:

- **kubeconfig defines user, cluster, and context**: `kubeconfig` lists multiple users for defining authentication, and multiple clusters for indicating the Kubernetes API server. Also, the context in `kubeconfig` is the combination of a user and a cluster: accessing a certain Kubernetes cluster with what kind of authentication.
- **Users and clusters are sharable between contexts**: In the previous diagram, both **Context 1** and **Context 3** take **User 1** as their user content. However, each context can only have a single user and single cluster definition.

- **Namespace can be attached to context**: Every context can be assigned to an existing Namespace. If there are none, like **Context 3**, it is along with the default Namespace, named `default`, as well.
- **The current context is the default environment for client**: We may have several contexts in `kubeconfig`, but only one for the current context. The current context and the Namespace attached on it will construct the default computing environment for users.

Now you will get the idea that, as Namespace works with `kubeconfig`, users can easily switch default resources for usage by switching the current context in `kubeconfig`. Nevertheless, users can still start any resource in a different Namespace with a specified one. In this recipe, you will learn how to create your own Namespace and how to work with it.

Getting ready

By default, Kubernetes has created a Namespace named `default`. All the objects created without specifying Namespaces will be put into the `default` Namespace. Kubernetes will also create another initial Namespace called `kube-system` for locating Kubernetes system objects, such as an add-on or overlay network. Try to list all the Namespaces:

```
// check all Namespaces, "ns" is the resource abbreviation of Namespace
$ kubectl get ns
NAME           STATUS    AGE
default        Active    15d
kube-public    Active    15d
kube-system    Active    15d
```

You may find an additional Namespace, `kube-public`, listed at the initial stage. It is designed for presenting some public configurations for even users without permission to access the Kubernetes system. Both of the provisioning tools, minikube and kubeadm, will create it while booting the system up.

The name of a Namespace must be a DNS label and follow the following rules:

- At most, 63 characters
- Matching regex [a-z0-9]([-a-z0-9]*[a-z0-9])

How to do it...

In this section, we will demonstrate how to create a Namespace, change the default Namespace, and delete the Namespace.

Creating a Namespace

For creating a Namespace, following are the steps:

1. After deciding on our desired name for Namespace, let's create it with a configuration file:

```
$ cat my-first-namespace.yaml
apiVersion: v1
kind: Namespace
metadata:
  name: my-namespace

// create the resource by subcommand "create"
$ kubectl create -f my-first-namespace.yaml
namespace "my-namespace" created
// list the namespaces again
$ kubectl get ns
NAME            STATUS     AGE
default         Active     16d
kube-public     Active     16d
kube-system     Active     16d
my-namespace    Active     6s
```

2. You can now see that we have an additional namespace called `my-namespace`. Next, let's run a Kubernetes Deployment in this new Namespace:

```
// run a Deployment with a flag specifying Namespace
$ kubectl run my-nginx --image=nginx --namespace=my-namespace
deployment.apps "my-nginx" created
```

3. While trying to check the newly created resource, we cannot easily find them as usual:

```
$ kubectl get deployment
No resources found.
```

4. Instead, the Deployment is shown with a flag related to the Namespace:

```
// list any Deployment in all Namespaces
$ kubectl get deployment --all-namespaces
NAMESPACE       NAME                        DESIRED    CURRENT
UP-TO-DATE    AVAILABLE    AGE
kube-system     calico-kube-controllers     1          1            1
1             16d
kube-system     calico-policy-controller    0          0            0
0             16d
kube-system     kube-dns                    1          1            1
1             16d
my-namespace    my-nginx                    1          1            1
1             1m

// get Deployments from my-namespace
$ kubectl get deployment --namespace=my-namespace
NAME        DESIRED    CURRENT    UP-TO-DATE    AVAILABLE    AGE
my-nginx    1          1          1             1            1m
```

Now you can find the resource that was just created.

Changing the default Namespace

As in the previous introduction, we can change the default Namespace by switching the current context in `kubeconfig` to another one:

1. First, we may check the current context with the subcommand `config`:

```
// check the current context in kubeconfig
$ kubectl config current-context
kubernetes-admin@kubernetes
```

You may feel unfamiliar with the output when checking the current context. The value of the preceding current context is defined and created by `kubeadm`. You could get `minikube` shown on screen if you leveraged `minikube` as your Kubernetes system management tool.

2. No matter what you got from checking the current context in `kubeconfig`, use the subcommand `config set-context` to create a new context:

```
// create a new context called "my-context"
// the new context is going to follow the cluster and the user
of current context, but attached with new Namespace
//This is for kubeadm environment
```

```
$ kubectl config set-context my-context --namespace=my-
namespace --cluster=kubernetes --user=kubernetes-admin
Context "my-context" created.
```

3. The preceding command is based on `kubeadm` managed Kubernetes; you may fire a similar one for `minikube`, with the names of the default cluster and user in `kubeconfig`:

```
// for minikube environemt
$ kubectl config set-context my-context --namespace=my-
namespace --cluster=minikube --user=minikube
```

4. Next, check `kubeconfig` to verify the changes:

```
//check kubectlconfig for the new context
$ kubectl config view
apiVersion: v1
clusters:
- cluster:
    certificate-authority-data: REDACTED
    server: https://192.168.122.101:6443
  name: kubernetes
contexts:
- context:
    cluster: kubernetes
    user: kubernetes-admin
  name: kubernetes-admin@kubernetes
- context:
    cluster: kubernetes
    namespace: my-namespace
    user: kubernetes-admin
  name: my-context
current-context: kubernetes-admin@kubernetes
kind: Config
preferences: {}
users:
- name: kubernetes-admin
  user:
    client-certificate-data: REDACTED
    client-key-data: REDACTED
```

When checking the configuration of `kubeconfig`, in the section of contexts, you can find a context named exactly as what we defined and which also takes our newly created Namespace.

5. Fire the following command to switch to using the new context:

```
$ kubectl config use-context my-context
Switched to context "my-context".
// check current context
$ kubectl config current-context
my-context
```

Now the current context is our customized one, which is along with the Namespace `my-namespace`.

6. Since the default Namespace is changed to `my-namespace`, it is possible that we can get the Deployment without specifying the Namespace:

```
$ kubectl get deployment
NAME        DESIRED    CURRENT    UP-TO-DATE    AVAILABLE    AGE
my-nginx    1          1          1             1            20m

//double check the namespace of resource
$ kubectl describe deployment my-nginx
Name:                    my-nginx
Namespace:               my-namespace
CreationTimestamp:       Mon, 18 Dec 2017 15:39:46 -0500
Labels:                  run=my-nginx
:
(ignored)
```

Deleting a Namespace

If you followed the previous pages for the Kubernetes resource, you may have gotten the idea that the subcommand `delete` is used to remove resources. It is workable in the case of removing a Namespace. At the same time, if we try to delete a Namespace, the resources under it will be removed, as well:

```
// first, go ahead to remove the Namespace "my-namespace"
$ kubectl delete ns my-namespace
namespace "my-namespace" deleted
// check the Deployment again, the exited "my-nginx" is terminated
$ kubectl get deployment
No resources found.

// while trying to create anything, the error message showing the default
Namespace is not existed
$ kubectl run my-alpine --image=alpine
Error from server (NotFound): namespaces "my-namespace" not found
```

To solve this issue, you may attach another Namespace to the current context, or just change your current context to the previous one:

```
// first solution: use set-context to update the Namespace
// here we just leave Namespace empty, which means to use default Namespace
$ kubectl config set-context my-context --namespace=""
Context "my-context" modified.

// second solution: switch current context to another context
// in this case, it is kubeadm environment
$ kubectl config use-context kubernetes-admin@kubernetes
Switched to context "kubernetes-admin@kubernetes".
```

How it works...

Although we discussed the Namespaces and context of kubeconfig together, they are independent objects in the Kubernetes system. The context of kubeconfig is a client concept which can only be controlled by certain users, and it makes it easier to work with Namespaces and clusters. On the other hand, Namespace is the concept of the server side, working for resource isolation in clusters, and it is able to be shared between clients.

There's more...

We not only leverage Namespace to separate our resources, but also to realize finer computing resource provisioning. By restricting the usage amount of the computing power of a Namespace, the system manager can avoid the client creating too many resources and making servers overload.

Creating a LimitRange

To set the resource limitation of each Namespace, the admission controller LimitRanger should be added in the Kubernetes API server. Do not worry about this setting if you have minikube or kubeadm as your system manager.

The admission controller in the Kubernetes API server

Admission controller is a setting in the Kubernetes API server which defines more advanced functionality in the API server. There are several functions that can be set in the admission controller. Users can add the functions when starting the API server through the configuration file or using CLI with the flag `--admission-control`. Relying on `minikube` or `kubeadm` for system management, they have their own initial settings in the admission controller:

- **Default admission controller in kubeadm**: `Initializers`, `NamespaceLifecycle`, `LimitRanger`, `ServiceAccount`, `PersistentVolumeLabel`, `DefaultStorageClass`, `DefaultTolerationSeconds`, `NodeRestriction`, `ResourceQuota`
- **Default admission controller in minikube**: `NamespaceLifecycle`, `LimitRanger`, `ServiceAccount`, `DefaultStorageClass`, `ResourceQuota`

Based on the version of your API server, there is a recommended list in an official document at `https://kubernetes.io/docs/admin/admission-controllers/#is-there-a-recommended-set-of-admission-controllers-to-use`. Check for more ideas!

A plain new Namespace has no limitation on the resource quota. At the beginning, we start a Namespace and take a look at its initial settings:

```
// create a Namespace by YAML file
$ kubectl create -f my-first-namespace.yaml
namespace "my-namespace" created

$ kubectl describe ns my-namespace
Name:          my-namespace
Labels:        <none>
Annotations:   <none>
Status:        Active

No resource quota.

No resource limits.
```

After that, we create a resource called `LimitRange` for specifying the resource limitation of a Namespace. The following is a good example of creating a limit in a Namespace:

```
$ cat my-first-limitrange.yaml
apiVersion: v1
kind: LimitRange
metadata:
  name: my-limitrange
spec:
  limits:
  - type: Pod
    max:
      cpu: 2
      memory: 1Gi
    min:
      cpu: 200m
      memory: 6Mi
  - type: Container
    default:
      cpu: 300m
      memory: 200Mi
    defaultRequest:
      cpu: 200m
      memory: 100Mi
    max:
      cpu: 2
      memory: 1Gi
    min:
      cpu: 100m
      memory: 3Mi
```

We will then limit the resources in a Pod with the values of 2 as `max` and 200m as a `min` for CPU, and 1Gi as max and 6Mi as a min for memory. For the container, the CPU is limited between 100m – 2 and the memory is between 3Mi - 1Gi. If the max is set, then you have to specify the limit in the Pod/container spec during the resource creation; if the min is set, then the request has to be specified during the Pod/container creation. The `default` and `defaultRequest` section in LimitRange is used to specify the default limit and request in the container spec.

The value of CPU limitation in LimitRange
What do the values of 2 and 200m mean in the Pod limitation in the file `my-first-limitrange.yaml`? The integer value means the number of CPU; the "m" in the value means millicpu, so 200m means 0.2 CPU (200 * 0.001). Similarly, the default CPU limitation of the container is 0.2 to 0.3, and the real limitation is 0.1 to 2.

Afterwards, we create the LimitRange in our plain Namespace and check what will happen:

```
// create the limitrange by file with the flag of Namespace
// the flag --namespace can be abbreviated to "n"
$ kubectl create -f my-first-limitrange.yaml -n my-namespace
limitrange "my-limitrange" created

// check the resource by subcommand "get"
$ kubectl get limitrange -n my-namespace
NAME            AGE
my-limitrange   23s

// check the customized Namespace
$ kubectl describe ns my-namespace
Name:          my-namespace
Labels:        <none>
Annotations:   <none>
Status:        Active

No resource quota.

Resource Limits
  Type       Resource   Min   Max  Default Request  Default Limit  Max
Limit/Request Ratio
  ----       --------   ---   ---  ---------------  -------------  ----------
------------
  Pod        cpu        200m  2    -                -              -
  Pod        memory     6Mi   1Gi  -                -              -
  Container  memory     3Mi   1Gi  100Mi            200Mi          -
  Container  cpu        100m  2    200m             300m           -
```

When you query the detail description of `my-namespace`, you will see the constraint attached to the Namespace directly. There is not any requirement to add the LimitRange. Now, all the Pods and containers created in this Namespace have to follow the resource limits listed here. If the definitions violate the rule, a validation error will be thrown accordingly:

```
// Try to request an overcommitted Pod, check the error message
$ kubectl run my-greedy-nginx --image=nginx --namespace=my-namespace --
restart=Never --requests="cpu=4"
The Pod "my-greedy-nginx" is invalid:
spec.containers[0].resources.requests: Invalid value: "4": must be less
than or equal to cpu limit
```

Deleting a LimitRange

We can delete the LimitRange resource with the subcommand `delete`. Like creating the `LimitRange`, deleting a `LimitRange` in a Namespace would remove the constraints in the Namespace automatically:

```
$ kubectl delete -f my-first-limitrange.yaml -n=my-namespace
limitrange "my-limitrange" deleted
$ kubectl describe ns my-namespace
Name:          my-namespace
Labels:        <none>
Annotations:   <none>
Status:        Active

No resource quota.

No resource limits.
```

See also

Many Kubernetes resources are able to run under a Namespace. To achieve good resource management, check out the following recipes:

- *Working with Pods*
- *Deployment API*
- *Working with names*
- *Setting resources in nodes* section in `Chapter 7`, *Building Kubernetes on GCP*

Working with labels and selectors

Labels are a set of key/value pairs, which are attached to object metadata. We could use labels to select, organize, and group objects, such as Pods, ReplicaSets, and Services. Labels are not necessarily unique. Objects could carry the same set of labels.

Label selectors are used to query objects with labels of the following types:

- Equality-based:
    - Use equal (= or ==) or not-equal (! =) operators
- Set-based:
    - Use `in` or `notin` operators

Getting ready

Before you get to setting labels in the objects, you should consider the valid naming convention of key and value.

A valid key should follow these rules:

- A name with an optional prefix, separated by a slash.
- A prefix must be a DNS subdomain, separated by dots, no longer than 253 characters.
- A name must be less than 63 characters with the combination of [a-z0-9A-Z] and dashes, underscores, and dots. Note that symbols are illegal if put at the beginning and the end.

A valid value should follow the following rules:

- A name must be less than 63 characters with the combination of [a-z0-9A-Z] and dashes, underscores, and dots. Note that symbols are illegal if put at the beginning and the end.

You should also consider the purpose, too. For example, there are two projects, `pilot` and `poc`. Also, those projects are under different environments, such as `develop` and `production`. In addition, some contain multiple tiers, such as `frontend`, `cache`, and `backend`. We can make our labels key and value pair combination like follows:

```
labels:
  project: pilot
  environment: develop
  tier: frontend
```

How to do it...

1. Let's try to create several Pods with the previous labels to distinguish different projects, environments, and tiers, as follows:

YAML Filename	Pod Image	Project	Environment	Tier
pilot-dev.yaml	nginx	pilot	develop	frontend
pilot-dev.yaml	memcached			cache
pilot-prod.yaml	nginx		production	frontend
pilot-prod.yaml	memcached			cache

poc-dev.yaml	httpd	poc	develop	frontend
poc-dev.yaml	memcached			cache

2. For convenience, we will prepare three YAML files that contain two Pods each, with a `YAML separator` `---` between Pods:

- `pilot-dev.yaml`:

```
apiVersion: v1
kind: Pod
metadata:
  name: pilot.dev.nginx
  labels:
    project: pilot
    environment: develop
    tier: frontend
spec:
  containers:
    - name: nginx
      image: nginx
---
apiVersion: v1
kind: Pod
metadata:
  name: pilot.dev.memcached
  labels:
    project: pilot
    environment: develop
    tier: cache
spec:
  containers:
    - name: memcached
      image: memcached
```

- `pilot-prod.yaml`:

```
apiVersion: v1
kind: Pod
metadata:
  name: pilot.prod.nginx
  labels:
    project: pilot
    environment: production
    tier: frontend
spec:
  containers:
    - name : nginx
```

```
        image: nginx
---
apiVersion: v1
kind: Pod
metadata:
  name: pilot.prod.memcached
  labels:
    project: pilot
    environment: production
    tier: cache
spec:
  containers:
    - name: memcached
      image: memcached
```

- poc-dev.yaml:

```
apiVersion: v1
kind: Pod
metadata:
  name: poc.dev.httpd
  labels:
    project: poc
    environment: develop
    tier: frontend
spec:
  containers:
    - name: httpd
      image: httpd
---
apiVersion: v1
kind: Pod
metadata:
  name: poc.dev.memcached
  labels:
    project: poc
    environment: develop
    tier: cache
spec:
  containers:
    - name: memcached
      image: memcached
```

3. Create those six Pods with the `kubectl create` command, as follows, to see how labels are defined:

```
$ kubectl create -f pilot-dev.yaml
pod "pilot.dev.nginx" created
pod "pilot.dev.memcached" created


$ kubectl create -f pilot-prod.yaml
pod "pilot.prod.nginx" created
pod "pilot.prod.memcached" created


$ kubectl create -f poc-dev.yaml
pod "poc.dev.httpd" created
pod "poc.dev.memcached" created
```

4. Run `kubectl describe <Pod name>` to check labels, as follows. It looks good, so let's use the label selector to query these Pods by different criteria:

```
$ kubectl describe pod poc.dev.memcache
Name: poc.dev.memcached
Namespace: default
Node: minikube/192.168.99.100
Start Time: Sun, 17 Dec 2017 17:23:15 -0800
Labels: environment=develop
        project=poc
        tier=cache
Annotations: <none>
Status: Running
...
```

How it works...

As mentioned earlier in this section, there are two types of label selectors: either equality-based or set-based. Those types have different operators to specify criteria.

Equality-based label selector

The equality-based selector can specify equal or not equal, and also uses commas to add more criteria. Use the -l or --selector option to specify these criteria to filter the name of the object; for example:

- Query Pods which belong to the pilot project:

```
$ kubectl get pods -l "project=pilot"
NAME READY STATUS RESTARTS AGE
pilot.dev.memcached 1/1 Running 0 21m
pilot.dev.nginx 1/1 Running 0 21m
pilot.prod.memcached 1/1 Running 0 21m
pilot.prod.nginx 1/1 Running 0 21m
```

- Query Pods which belong to the frontend tier:

```
$ kubectl get pods -l "tier=frontend"
NAME READY STATUS RESTARTS AGE
pilot.dev.nginx 1/1 Running 0 21m
pilot.prod.nginx 1/1 Running 0 21m
poc.dev.httpd 1/1 Running 0 21m
```

- Query Pods which belong to the frontend tier AND the under develop environment:

```
$ kubectl get pods -l "tier=frontend,environment=develop"
NAME READY STATUS RESTARTS AGE
pilot.dev.nginx 1/1 Running 0 22m
poc.dev.httpd 1/1 Running 0 21m
```

- Query Pods which belong to the frontend tier and NOT the under develop environment:

```
$ kubectl get pods -l "tier=frontend,environment!=develop"
NAME READY STATUS RESTARTS AGE
pilot.prod.nginx 1/1 Running 0 29m
```

Set-based label selector

With the set-based selector, you can use either the `in` or `notin` operator, which is similar to the `SQL IN` clause that can specify multiple keywords, as in the following examples:

- Query `Pods` which belong to the `pilot` project:

```
$ kubectl get pods -l "project in (pilot)"
NAME READY STATUS RESTARTS AGE
pilot.dev.memcached 1/1 Running 0 36m
pilot.dev.nginx 1/1 Running 0 36m
pilot.prod.memcached 1/1 Running 0 36m
pilot.prod.nginx 1/1 Running 0 36m
```

- Query `Pods` which belong to the pilot project and `frontend` tier:

```
$ kubectl get pods -l "project in (pilot), tier in (frontend)"
NAME READY STATUS RESTARTS AGE
pilot.dev.nginx 1/1 Running 0 37m
pilot.prod.nginx 1/1 Running 0 37m
```

- Query `Pods` which belong to the pilot project and either the `frontend` or `cache` tier:

```
$ kubectl get pods -l "project in (pilot), tier in (frontend,cache)"
NAME READY STATUS RESTARTS AGE
pilot.dev.memcached 1/1 Running 0 37m
pilot.dev.nginx 1/1 Running 0 37m
pilot.prod.memcached 1/1 Running 0 37m
pilot.prod.nginx 1/1 Running 0 37m
```

- Query `Pods` which belong to the pilot project and not the `frontend` or `backend` tier (note, we didn't create the `backend` tier object):

```
$ kubectl get pods -l "project in (pilot), tier notin (frontend, backend)"
NAME READY STATUS RESTARTS AGE
pilot.dev.memcached 1/1 Running 0 50m
pilot.prod.memcached 1/1 Running 0 50m
```

As you can see in the preceding examples for both the equality-based and set-based label selector, equality-based is simpler and set-based is more expressive. Note that you can mix both operator as follows:

- Query Pods which do not belong to the pilot project and develop environment:

```
$ kubectl get pods -l "project notin (pilot),
environment=develop"
NAME READY STATUS RESTARTS AGE
poc.dev.httpd 1/1 Running 0 2m
poc.dev.memcached 1/1 Running 0 2m
```

So, you can use the most efficient way to filter out the Kubernetes objects. In addition, you can also use either or both types of selectors to configure the Kubernetes Service, Deployments, and so on. However, some objects support the equality-based selector and some objects support both. So, let's take a look at how to define it.

There's more...

Label selectors are useful to not only list an object, but also to specify the Kubernetes Service and Deployment to bind objects.

Linking Service to Pods or ReplicaSets using label selectors

As of Kubernetes version 1.9, Service only supports the equality-based selector to bind to Pods or ReplicaSet.

Let's create one Service that binds to `nginx`, which belongs to the production environment and the pilot project. Remember that `nginx` also belongs to the frontend tier:

```
//check your selector filter is correct or not
$ kubectl get pods -l 'environment=production,project=pilot,tier=frontend'
NAME READY STATUS RESTARTS AGE
pilot.prod.nginx 1/1 Running 0 19m


//create Service yaml that specify selector
$ cat pilot-nginx-svc.yaml
apiVersion: v1
kind: Service
metadata:
```

```
    name: pilot-nginx-svc
spec:
  type: NodePort
  ports:
    - protocol: TCP
      port: 80
  selector:
    project: pilot
    environment: production
    tier: frontend


//create pilot-nginx-svc
$ kubectl create -f pilot-nginx-svc.yaml
service "pilot-nginx-svc" created
```

Here is the equivalent, where you can use the `kubectl expose` command to specify the label selector:

```
$ kubectl expose pod pilot.prod.nginx --name=pilot-nginx-svc2 --
type=NodePort --port=80 --
selector="project=pilot,environment=develop,tier=frontend"
service "pilot-nginx-svc2" exposed
```

Based on your Kubernetes environment, if you are using minikube, it is easier to check your Service with `minikube service <Service name>`, as in the following screenshot. If you are not using minikube, access to any Kubernetes node and assigned Service port number. For the following screenshot, it would be `<node ip>:31981` or `<node ip>:31820`:

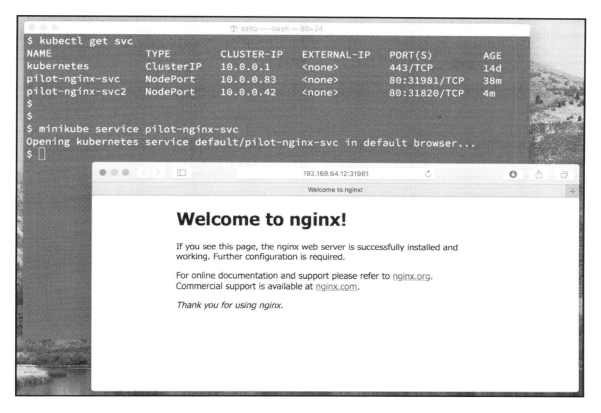

Access to Service which is running on minikube

Linking Deployment to ReplicaSet using the set-based selector

Deployment supports not only the equality-based selector, but also the set-based selector, to specify ReplicaSet. To do that, you can write spec.selector.matchExpressions[] to specify the key and in/notin operator. For example, if you want to specify project in (poc), environment in (staging), tier notn (backend,cache), then matchExpressions would be as follows:

```
$ cat deploy_set_selector.yaml
apiVersion: apps/v1
kind: Deployment
metadata:
  name: my-nginx
```

```
spec:
  replicas: 3
  selector:
    matchExpressions:
      - {key: project, operator: In, values: [poc]}
      - {key: environment, operator: In, values: [staging]}
      - {key: tier, operator: NotIn, values: [backend,cache]}
  template:
    metadata:
      labels:
        project: poc
        environment: staging
        tier: frontend
    spec:
      containers:
      - name: my-nginx
        image: nginx
        ports:
        - containerPort: 80
```

As you can see, the YAML array is represented as –, and the map object as { }, to specify the key, operator, and values. Note that values would also be an array, so use the square bracket [] to specify one or more values.

One thing you need to aware of is one label, called the `pod-template-hash` label, which is created by Deployment. When you create a Deployment, it will also create a `ReplicaSet` object. At this time, Deployment will also assign the `pod-template-hash` label to the `ReplicaSet`. Let's see how it works:

```
$ kubectl create -f deploy_set_selector.yaml
deployment.apps "my-nginx" created

$ kubectl get rs
NAME                   DESIRED   CURRENT   READY   AGE
my-nginx2-764d7cfff    3         3         3       19s

$ kubectl describe rs my-nginx2-764d7cfff
Name:           my-nginx2-764d7cfff
Namespace:      default
Selector:       environment in (staging),pod-template-
hash=320837999,project in (poc),tier notin (backend,cache)
...
...
Pod Template:
  Labels:  environment=staging
           pod-template-hash=320837999
```

```
            project=poc
            tier=frontend
   . . .
   . . .
```

As you can see, the `ReplicaSet my-nginx2-764d7cfff` has an equality-based selector, as `pod-template-hash=320837999` is appended to the Selector and Pod template. It will be used to generate a `ReplicaSet` and Pod name with a particular hash function (for example, `my-nginx2-764d7cfff`).

See also

In this section, you learned how flexible it is to assign a label to your Kubernetes object. In addition, equality-based and set-based selectors allow us to filter out an object by label. Selector is important that loosely couple an object such as Service and ReplicaSet/Pod as well as Deployment and ReplicaSet.

The following sections will also use labels and the concept of selectors to utilize container management:

- *Updating live containers* section in `Chapter 3`, *Playing with Containers*
- *Managing the Kubernetes cluster on GKE* section in `Chapter 7`, *Building Kubernetes on GCP*

3
Playing with Containers

In this chapter, we will cover the following topics:

- Scaling your containers
- Updating live containers
- Forwarding container ports
- Ensuring flexible usage of your containers
- Submitting Jobs on Kubernetes
- Working with configuration files

Introduction

When talking about container management, you need to know some of the differences compared to application package management, such as rpm/dpkg, because you can run multiple containers on the same machine. You also need to care about network port conflicts. This chapter covers how to update, scale, and launch a container application using Kubernetes.

Scaling your containers

Scaling up and down the application or service based on predefined criteria is a common way to utilize the most compute resources in most efficient way. In Kubernetes, you can scale up and down manually or use a **Horizontal Pod Autoscaler** (**HPA**) to do autoscaling. In this section, we'll describe how to perform both operations.

Getting ready

Prepare the following YAML file, which is a simple Deployment that launches two nginx containers. Also, a NodePort service with TCP—30080 exposed:

```
# cat 3-1-1_deployment.yaml
apiVersion: apps/v1
kind: Deployment
metadata:
  name: my-nginx
spec:
  replicas: 2
  selector:
    matchLabels:
      service : nginx
  template:
    metadata:
      labels:
        service : nginx
    spec:
      containers:
        - name: my-container
          image: nginx
---
apiVersion: v1
kind: Service
metadata:
  name: my-nginx
spec:
  ports:
    - protocol: TCP
      port: 80
      nodePort: 30080
  type: NodePort
  selector:
    service: nginx
```

 NodePort will bind to all the Kubernetes nodes (port range: 30000 to 32767); therefore, make sure NodePort is not used by other processes.

Let's use `kubectl` to create the resources used by the preceding configuration file:

```
// create deployment and service
# kubectl create -f 3-1-1_deployment.yaml
deployment "my-nginx" created
service "my-nginx" created
```

After a few seconds, we should see that the `pods` are scheduled and up and running:

```
# kubectl get pods
NAME READY STATUS RESTARTS AGE
my-nginx-6484b5fc4c-9v7dc 1/1 Running 0 7s
my-nginx-6484b5fc4c-krd7p 1/1 Running 0 7s
```

The service is up, too:

```
# kubectl get services
NAME TYPE CLUSTER-IP EXTERNAL-IP PORT(S) AGE
kubernetes ClusterIP 10.96.0.1 <none> 443/TCP 20d
my-nginx NodePort 10.105.9.153 <none> 80:30080/TCP 59s
```

How to do it...

Assume our services are expected to have a traffic spike at a certain of time. As a DevOps, you might want to scale it up manually, and scale it down after the peak time. In Kubernetes, we can use the `kubectl scale` command to do so. Alternatively, we could leverage a HPA to scale up and down automatically based on compute resource conditions or custom metrics.

Let's see how to do it manually and automatically in Kubernetes.

Scale up and down manually with the kubectl scale command

Assume that today we'd like to scale our `nginx` Pods from two to four:

```
// kubectl scale --replicas=<expected_replica_num> deployment
<deployment_name>
# kubectl scale --replicas=4 deployment my-nginx
deployment "my-nginx" scaled
```

Let's check how many `pods` we have now:

```
# kubectl get pods
NAME READY STATUS RESTARTS AGE
my-nginx-6484b5fc4c-9v7dc 1/1 Running 0 1m
my-nginx-6484b5fc4c-krd7p 1/1 Running 0 1m
my-nginx-6484b5fc4c-nsvzt 0/1 ContainerCreating 0 2s
my-nginx-6484b5fc4c-v68dr 1/1 Running 0 2s
```

We could find two more Pods are scheduled. One is already running and another one is creating. Eventually, we will have four Pods up and running if we have enough compute resources.

> Kubectl scale (also kubectl autoscale!) supports **Replication Controller (RC)** and **Replica Set (RS)**, too. However, deployment is the recommended way to deploy Pods.

We could also scale down with the same `kubectl` command, just by setting the `replicas` parameter lower:

```
// kubectl scale --replicas=<expected_replica_num> deployment
<deployment_name>
# kubectl scale --replicas=2 deployment my-nginx
deployment "my-nginx" scaled
```

Now, we'll see two Pods are scheduled to be terminated:

```
# kubectl get pods
NAME READY STATUS RESTARTS AGE
my-nginx-6484b5fc4c-9v7dc 1/1 Running 0 1m
my-nginx-6484b5fc4c-krd7p 1/1 Running 0 1m
my-nginx-6484b5fc4c-nsvzt 0/1 Terminating 0 23s
my-nginx-6484b5fc4c-v68dr 0/1 Terminating 0 23s
```

There is an option, `--current-replicas`, which specifies the expected current replicas. If it doesn't match, Kubernetes doesn't perform the scale function as follows:

```
// adding --current-replicas to precheck the condistion for scaling.
# kubectl scale --current-replicas=3 --replicas=4 deployment my-nginx
error: Expected replicas to be 3, was 2
```

Horizontal Pod Autoscaler (HPA)

An HPA queries the source of metrics periodically and determines whether scaling is required by a controller based on the metrics it gets. There are two types of metrics that could be fetched; one is from Heapster (`https://github.com/kubernetes/heapster`), another is from RESTful client access. In the following example, we'll show you how to use Heapster to monitor Pods and expose the metrics to an HPA.

First, Heapster has to be deployed in the cluster:

 If you're running minikube, use the `minikube addons enable heapster` command to enable heapster in your cluster. Note that `minikube logs | grep heapster` command could also be used to check the logs of heapster.

```
// at the time we're writing this book, the latest configuration file of
heapster in kops is 1.7.0. Check out
https://github.com/kubernetes/kops/tree/master/addons/monitoring-standalone
for the latest version when you use it.
# kubectl create -f
https://raw.githubusercontent.com/kubernetes/kops/master/addons/monitoring-
standalone/v1.7.0.yaml
deployment "heapster" created
service "heapster" created
serviceaccount "heapster" created
clusterrolebinding "heapster" created
rolebinding "heapster-binding" created
```

Check if the `heapster` pods are up and running:

```
# kubectl get pods --all-namespaces | grep heapster
kube-system heapster-56d577b559-dnjvn 2/2 Running 0 26m
kube-system heapster-v1.4.3-6947497b4-jrczl 3/3 Running 0 5d
```

Assuming we continue right after the *Getting Ready* section, we will have two `my-nginx` Pods running in our cluster:

```
# kubectl get pods
NAME READY STATUS RESTARTS AGE
my-nginx-6484b5fc4c-9v7dc 1/1 Running 0 40m
my-nginx-6484b5fc4c-krd7p 1/1 Running 0 40m
```

Then, we can use the `kubectl autoscale` command to deploy an HPA:

```
# kubectl autoscale deployment my-nginx --cpu-percent=50 --min=2 --max=5
deployment "my-nginx" autoscaled
```

```
# cat 3-1-2_hpa.yaml
apiVersion: autoscaling/v1
kind: HorizontalPodAutoscaler
metadata:
  name: my-nginx
spec:
  scaleTargetRef:
    kind: Deployment
    name: my-nginx
  minReplicas: 2
  maxReplicas: 5
  targetCPUUtilizationPercentage: 50
```

To check if it's running as expected:

```
// check horizontal pod autoscaler (HPA)
# kubectl get hpa
NAME REFERENCE TARGETS MINPODS MAXPODS REPLICAS AGE
my-nginx Deployment/my-nginx <unknown> / 50% 2 5 0 3s
```

We find the target shows as unknown and replicas are 0. Why is this? the runs as a control loop, at a default interval of 30 seconds. There might be a delay before it reflects the real metrics.

 The default sync period of an HPA can be altered by changing the following parameter in control manager: `--horizontal-pod-autoscaler-sync-period`.

After waiting a couple of seconds, we will find the current metrics are there now. The number showed in the target column presents (`current / target`). It means the load is currently `0%`, and scale target is `50%`:

```
# kubectl get hpa
NAME REFERENCE TARGETS MINPODS MAXPODS REPLICAS AGE
my-nginx Deployment/my-nginx 0% / 50% 2 5 2 48m

// check details of a hpa
# kubectl describe hpa my-nginx
Name: my-nginx
Namespace: default
Labels: <none>
Annotations: <none>
CreationTimestamp: Mon, 15 Jan 2018 22:48:28 -0500
Reference: Deployment/my-nginx
Metrics: ( current / target )
  resource cpu on pods (as a percentage of request): 0% (0) / 50%
```

```
Min replicas: 2
Max replicas: 5
```

To test if HPA can scale the Pod properly, we'll manually generate some loads to `my-nginx`
service:

```
// generate the load
# kubectl run -it --rm --restart=Never <pod_name> --image=busybox -- sh -c
"while true; do wget -O - -q http://my-nginx; done"
```

In the preceding command, we ran a `busybox` image which allowed us to run a simple
command on it. We used the `-c` parameter to specify the default command, which is an
infinite loop, to query `my-nginx` service.

After about one minute, you can see that the current value is changing:

```
// check current value – it's 43% now. not exceeding scaling condition yet.
# kubectl get hpa
NAME REFERENCE TARGETS MINPODS MAXPODS REPLICAS AGE
my-nginx Deployment/my-nginx 43% / 50% 2 5 2 56m
```

With the same command, we can run more loads with different Pod names repeatedly.
Finally, we see that the condition has been met. It's scaling up to 3 replicas, and up to 4
replicas afterwards:

```
# kubectl get hpa
NAME REFERENCE TARGETS MINPODS MAXPODS REPLICAS AGE
my-nginx Deployment/my-nginx 73% / 50% 2 5 3 1h

# kubectl get hpa
NAME REFERENCE TARGETS MINPODS MAXPODS REPLICAS AGE
my-nginx Deployment/my-nginx 87% / 50% 2 5 4 15m
Keeping observing it and deleting some busybox we deployed. It will
eventually cool down and scale down without manual operation involved.
# kubectl get hpa
NAME REFERENCE TARGETS MINPODS MAXPODS REPLICAS AGE
my-nginx Deployment/my-nginx 40% / 50% 2 5 2 27m
```

We can see that HPA just scaled our Pods from 4 to 2.

How it works...

Note that cAdvisor acts as a container resource utilization monitoring service, which is running inside kubelet on each node. The CPU utilizations we just monitored are collected by cAdvisor and aggregated by Heapster. Heapster is a service running in the cluster that monitors and aggregates the metrics. It queries the metrics from each cAdvisor. When HPA is deployed, the controller will keep observing the metrics which are reported by Heapster, and scale up and down accordingly. An illustration of the process is as follows:

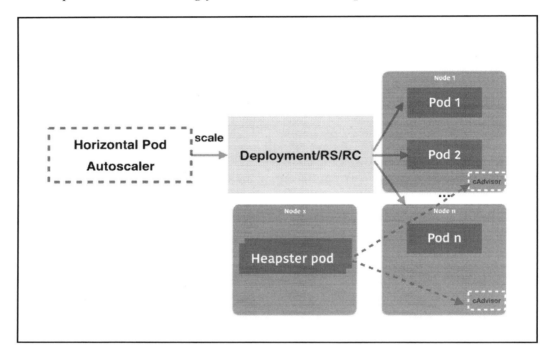

Based on the specified metrics, HPA determines whether scaling is required

There is more...

Alternatively, you could use custom metrics, such as Pod metrics or object metrics, to determine if it's time to scale up or down. Kubernetes also supports multiple metrics. HPA will consider each metric sequentially. Check out https://kubernetes.io/docs/tasks/run-application/horizontal-pod-autoscale for more examples.

See also

This recipe described how to change the number of Pods using the scaling option of the deployment. It is useful to scale up and scale down your application quickly. To know more about how to update your container, refer to the following recipes:

- *Updating live containers* in `Chapter 3`, *Playing with Containers*
- *Ensuring flexible usage of your containers* in `Chapter 3`, *Playing with Containers*

Updating live containers

For the benefit of containers, we can easily publish new programs by executing the latest image, and reduce the headache of environment setup. But, what about publishing the program on running containers? While managing a container natively, we have to stop the running containers prior to booting up new ones with the latest images and the same configurations. There are some simple and efficient methods for updating your program in the Kubernetes system. One is called rolling-update, which means Deployment can update its Pods without downtime to clients. The other method is called *recreate*, which just terminates all Pods then create a new set. We will demonstrate how these solutions are applied in this recipe.

Rolling-update in Docker swarm

To achieve zero downtime application updating, there is a similar managing function in Docker swarm. In Docker swarm, you can leverage the command docker service update with the flag `--update-delay`, `--update-parallelism` and `--update-failure-action`. Check the official website for more details about Docker swarm's rolling-update: `https://docs.docker.com/engine/swarm/swarm-tutorial/rolling-update/`.

Getting ready

For a later demonstration, we are going to update `nginx` Pods . Please make sure all Kubernetes nodes and components are working healthily:

```
// check components
$ kubectl get cs
// check nodes
$ kubectl get node
```

Furthermore, to well understand the relationship between ReplicaSet and Deployment, please check *Deployment API* section in `Chapter 2`, *Walking through Kubernetes Concepts*.

To illustrate the updating of the containers in Kubernetes system, we will create a Deployment, change its configurations of application, and then check how the updating mechanism handles it. Let's get all our resources ready:

```
// create a simple nginx Deployment with specified labels
$ kubectl run simple-nginx --image=nginx --port=80 --replicas=5 --
labels="project=My-Happy-Web,role=frontend,env=test"
deployment.apps "simple-nginx" created
```

This Deployment is created with 5 replicas. It is good for us to discover the updating procedure with multiple numbers of Pods:

```
// expose the Deployment, and named the service "nginx-service"
$ kubectl expose deployment simple-nginx --port=8080 --target-port=80 --
name="nginx-service"
service "nginx-service" exposed
// For minikube environment only, since Kubernetes is installed in a VM,
add Service type as NodePort for accessing outside the VM.
$ kubectl expose deployment simple-nginx --port=8080 --target-port=80 --
name="nginx-service" --type=NodePort
service "nginx-service" exposed
```

Attaching a Service on the Deployment will help to simulate the real experience of clients.

How to do it...

At the beginning, take a look at the Deployment you just created and its ReplicaSet by executing the following code block:

```
$ kubectl describe deployment simple-nginx
Name:                   simple-nginx
Namespace:              default
CreationTimestamp:      Fri, 04 May 2018 12:14:21 -0400
Labels:                 env=test
                        project=My-Happy-Web
                        role=frontend
Annotations:            deployment.kubernetes.io/revision=1
Selector:               env=test,project=My-Happy-Web,role=frontend
Replicas:               5 desired | 5 updated | 5 total | 5 available | 0
unavailable
StrategyType:           RollingUpdate
MinReadySeconds:        0
```

```
RollingUpdateStrategy:  1 max unavailable, 1 max surge
Pod Template:
  Labels:   env=test
            project=My-Happy-Web
            role=frontend
  Containers:
   simple-nginx:
    Image:        nginx
    Port:         80/TCP
    Environment:  <none>
    Mounts:       <none>
  Volumes:        <none>
Conditions:
  Type            Status  Reason
  ----            ------  ------
  Available       True    MinimumReplicasAvailable
  Progressing     True    NewReplicaSetAvailable
OldReplicaSets:   <none>
NewReplicaSet:    simple-nginx-585f6cddcd (5/5 replicas created)
Events:
  Type    Reason          Age    From              Message
  ----    ------          ----   ----              -------
  Normal  ScalingReplicaSet  1h   deployment-controller  Scaled up replica
set simple-nginx-585f6cddcd to 5
// rs is the abbreviated resource key of replicaset
$ kubectl get rs
NAME                         DESIRED   CURRENT   READY   AGE
simple-nginx-585f6cddcd      5         5         5       1h
```

Based on the preceding output, we know that the default updating strategy of deployment is rolling-update. Also, there is a single ReplicaSet named `<Deployment Name>-<hex decimal hash>` that is created along with the Deployment.

Next, check the content of the current Service endpoint for the sake of verifying our update later:

```
// record the cluster IP of Service "nginx-service"
$ export SERVICE_URL=$(kubectl get svc | grep nginx-service | awk '{print
$3}'):8080

// For minikube environment only, record the VM host IP and port for the
service
$ export SERVICE_URL=$(minikube service nginx-service --url)
$ curl $SERVICE_URL | grep "title"
<title>Welcome to nginx!</title>
```

We will get the welcome message in the title of the HTML response with the original `nginx` image.

Deployment update strategy – rolling-update

The following will introduce the subcommands `edit` and `set`, for the purpose of updating the containers under Deployment:

1. First, let's update the Pods in Deployment with a new command:

```
// get into editor mode with the command below
// the flag "--record" is for recording the update
// add the command argument as below and save the change
$ kubectl edit deployment simple-nginx --record
spec:
  replicas: 5
  ...
  template:
    ...
    spec:
      containers:
      - image: nginx
        command:
          - sh
          - -c
          - echo "Happy Programming with Kubernetes!" >
/usr/share/nginx/html/index.html && service nginx stop && nginx
-g "daemon off;"
        imagePullPolicy: Always
        ...
deployment.extensions "simple-nginx" edited
```

We are not only doing the update; we record this change as well. With the flag `--record`, we keep the command line as a tag in revision.

2. After editing the Deployment, check the status of rolling-update with the subcommand `rollout` right away:

```
// you may see different output on your screen, but definitely
has the last line showing update successfully
$ kubectl rollout status deployment simple-nginx
Waiting for rollout to finish: 4 out of 5 new replicas have
been updated...
Waiting for rollout to finish: 4 out of 5 new replicas have
been updated...
```

```
Waiting for rollout to finish: 4 out of 5 new replicas have
been updated...
Waiting for rollout to finish: 4 out of 5 new replicas have
been updated...
Waiting for rollout to finish: 1 old replicas are pending
termination...
Waiting for rollout to finish: 1 old replicas are pending
termination...
Waiting for rollout to finish: 1 old replicas are pending
termination...
Waiting for rollout to finish: 4 of 5 updated replicas are
available...
deployment "simple-nginx" successfully rolled out
```

It is possible that you get several `Waiting for` ... lines, as shown in the
preceding code. They are the standard output showing the status of the update.

3. For whole updating procedures, check the details of the Deployment to list its
events:

```
// describe the Deployment again
$ kubectl describe deployment simple-nginx
Name:                   simple-nginx
...
Events:
  Type      Reason            Age    From
Message
  ----      ------            ----   ----
--
  Normal    ScalingReplicaSet 1h     deployment-controller
Scaled up replica set simple-nginx-585f6cddcd to 5
  Normal    ScalingReplicaSet 1h     deployment-controller
Scaled up replica set simple-nginx-694f94f77d to 1
  Normal    ScalingReplicaSet 1h     deployment-controller
Scaled down replica set simple-nginx-585f6cddcd to 4
  Normal    ScalingReplicaSet 1h     deployment-controller
Scaled up replica set simple-nginx-694f94f77d to 2
  Normal    ScalingReplicaSet 1h     deployment-controller
Scaled down replica set simple-nginx-585f6cddcd to 3
  Normal    ScalingReplicaSet 1h     deployment-controller
Scaled up replica set simple-nginx-694f94f77d to 3
  Normal    ScalingReplicaSet 1h     deployment-controller
Scaled down replica set simple-nginx-585f6cddcd to 2
  Normal    ScalingReplicaSet 1h     deployment-controller
Scaled up replica set simple-nginx-694f94f77d to 4
  Normal    ScalingReplicaSet 1h     deployment-controller
Scaled down replica set simple-nginx-585f6cddcd to
```

```
  Normal  ScalingReplicaSet  1h   deployment-controller
Scaled up replica set simple-nginx-694f94f77d to 5
  Normal  ScalingReplicaSet  1h   deployment-controller
(combined from similar events): Scaled down replica set simple-
nginx-585f6cddcd to 0
```

As you see, a new `replica set simple-nginx-694f94f77d` is created in the Deployment `simple-nginx`. Each time the new ReplicaSet scales one Pod up successfully, the old ReplicaSet will scale one Pod down. The scaling process finishes at the moment that the new ReplicaSet meets the original desired Pod number (as said, 5 Pods), and the old ReplicaSet has zero Pods.

4. Go ahead and check the new ReplicaSet and existing Service for this update:

```
// look at the new ReplicaSet in detail, you will find it
copied the labels of the old one
$ kubectl describe rs simple-nginx-694f94f77d
Name:           simple-nginx-694f94f77d
Namespace:      default
Selector:       env=test,pod-template-
hash=2509509338,project=My-Happy-Web,role=frontend
Labels:         env=test
                pod-template-hash=2509509338
                project=My-Happy-Web
                role=frontend
...
// send request to the same endpoint of Service.
$ curl $SERVICE_URL
Happy Programming with Kubernetes!
```

5. Let's make another update! This time, use the subcommand `set` to modify a specific configuration of a Pod.

6. To set a new image to certain containers in a Deployment, the subcommand format would look like this: `kubectl set image deployment <Deployment name> <Container name>=<image name>`:

```
// change the image version with the subcommand "set"
// when describing the deployment, we can know that the
container name is the same as the name of the Deployment
// record this change as well
$ kubectl set image deployment simple-nginx simple-
nginx=nginx:stable --record
deployment.apps "simple-nginx" image updated
```

What else could the subcommand "set" help to configure?

The subcommand set helps to define the configuration of the application. Until version 1.9, CLI with set could assign or update the following resources:

Subcommand after set	Acting resource	Updating item
env	Pod	Environment variables
image	Pod	Container image
resources	Pod	Computing resource requirement or limitation
selector	Any resource	Selector
serviceaccount	Any resource	ServiceAccount
subject	RoleBinding or ClusterRoleBinding	User, group, or ServiceAccount

7. Now, check if the update has finished and whether the image is changed:

```
// check update status by rollout
$ kubectl rollout status deployment simple-nginx
...
deployment "simple-nginx" successfully rolled out
// check the image of Pod in simple-nginx
$ kubectl describe deployment simple-nginx
Name:              simple-nginx
...
Pod Template:
  Labels:   env=test
            project=My-Happy-Web
            role=frontend
  Containers:
   simple-nginx:
    Image:   nginx:stable
    Port:    80/TCP
    Host Port:  0/TCP
...
```

8. You can also check out the ReplicaSets. There should be another one taking responsibility of the Pods for Deployment:

```
$ kubectl get rs
NAME                        DESIRED   CURRENT   READY   AGE
simple-nginx-585f6cddcd     0         0         0       1h
simple-nginx-694f94f77d     0         0         0       1h
simple-nginx-b549cc75c      5         5         5       1h
```

Rollback the update

Kubernetes system records every update for Deployment:

1. We can list all of the revisions with the subcommand `rollout`:

```
// check the rollout history
$ kubectl rollout history deployment simple-nginx
deployments "simple-nginx"
REVISION   CHANGE-CAUSE
1          <none>
2          kubectl edit deployment simple-nginx --record=true
3          kubectl set image deployment simple-nginx simple-
nginx=nginx:stable --record=true
```

You will get three revisions, as in the preceding lines, for the Deployment `simple-nginx`. For Kubernetes Deployment, each revision has a matched `ReplicaSet` and represents a stage of running an update command. The first revision is the initial state of `simple-nginx`. Although there is no command tag for indication, Kubernetes takes its creation as its first version. However, you could still record the command when you create the Deployment.

2. Add the flag `--record` after the subcommand `create` or `run`.

3. With the revisions, we can easily resume the change, which means rolling back the update. Use the following commands to rollback to previous revisions:

```
// let's jump back to initial Deployment!
// with flag --to-revision, we can specify which revision for
rollback processing
$ kubectl rollout undo deployment simple-nginx --to-revision=1
deployment.apps "simple-nginx"
// check if the rollback update is finished
$ kubectl rollout status deployment simple-nginx
...
deployment "simple-nginx" successfully rolled out
// take a look at ReplicaSets, you will find that the old
ReplicaSet takes charge of the business now
$ kubectl get rs
NAME                      DESIRED   CURRENT   READY   AGE
simple-nginx-585f6cddcd   5         5         5       4h
simple-nginx-694f94f77d   0         0         0       4h
simple-nginx-b549cc75c    0         0         0       3h
// go ahead and check the nginx webpage or the details of
Deployment
$ curl $SERVICE_URL
$ kubectl describe deployment simple-nginx
```

4. Without specifying the revision number, the rollback process will simply jump back to previous version:

```
// just go back to previous status
$ kubectl rollout undo deployment simple-nginx
deployment.apps "simple-nginx"
// look at the ReplicaSets agin, now the latest one takes the
job again
$ kubectl get rs
NAME                        DESIRED   CURRENT   READY   AGE
simple-nginx-585f6cddcd     0         0         0       4h
simple-nginx-694f94f77d     0         0         0       4h
simple-nginx-b549cc75c      5         5         5       4h
```

Deployment update strategy – recreate

Next, we are going to introduce the other update strategy, `recreate`, for Deployment. Although there is no subcommand or flag to create a recreate-strategy deployment, users could fulfill this creation by overriding the default element with the specified configuration:

```
// create a new Deployment, and override the update strategy.
$ kubectl run recreate-nginx --image=nginx --port=80 --replicas=5 --
overrides='{"apiVersion": "apps/v1", "spec": {"strategy": {"type":
"Recreate"}}}'
deployment.apps "recreate-nginx" created
// verify our new Deployment
$ kubectl describe deployment recreate-nginx
Name:              recreate-nginx
Namespace:         default
CreationTimestamp: Sat, 05 May 2018 18:17:07 -0400
Labels:            run=recreate-nginx
Annotations:       deployment.kubernetes.io/revision=1
Selector:          run=recreate-nginx
Replicas:          5 desired | 5 updated | 5 total | 0 available | 5
unavailable
StrategyType:      Recreate
...
```

In our understanding, the `recreate` mode is good for an application under development. With `recreate`, Kubernetes just scales the current ReplicaSet down to zero Pods, and creates a new ReplicaSet with the full desired number of Pods. Therefore, recreate has a shorter total updating time than rolling-update because it scales ReplicaSets up or down simply, once for all. Since a developing Deployment doesn't need to take care of any user experience, it is acceptable to have downtime while updating and enjoy faster updates:

```
// try to update recreate-strategy Deployment
$ kubectl set image deployment recreate-nginx recreate-nginx=nginx:stable
deployment.apps "recreate-nginx" image updated
// check both the rollout status and the events of Deployment
$ kubectl rollout status deployment recreate-nginx
$ kubectl describe deployment recreate-nginx
...
Events:
  Type    Reason            Age    From                   Message
  ----    ------            ----   ----                   -------
  Normal  ScalingReplicaSet 3h     deployment-controller  Scaled up replica
set recreate-nginx-9d5b69986 to 5
  Normal  ScalingReplicaSet 2h     deployment-controller  Scaled down
replica set recreate-nginx-9d5b69986 to 0
  Normal  ScalingReplicaSet 2h     deployment-controller  Scaled up replica
set recreate-nginx-674d7f9c7f to 5
```

How it works...

Rolling-update works on the units of the ReplicaSet in a Deployment. The effect is to create a new ReplicaSet to replace the old one. Then, the new ReplicaSet is scaling up to meet the desired numbers, while the old ReplicaSet is scaling down to terminate all the Pods in it. The Pods in the new ReplicaSet are attached to the original labels. Therefore, if any service exposes this Deployment, it will take over the newly created Pods directly.

An experienced Kubernetes user may know that the resource ReplicationController can be rolling-update as well. So, what are the differences of rolling-update between ReplicationController and deployment? The scaling processing uses the combination of ReplicationController and a client such as `kubectl`. A new ReplicationController will be created to replace the previous one. Clients don't feel any interruption since the service is in front of ReplicationController while doing replacement. However, it is hard for developers to roll back to previous ReplicationControllers (they have been removed), because there is no built-in mechanism that records the history of updates.

In addition, rolling-update might fail if the client connection is disconnected while rolling-update is working. Most important of all, Deployment with ReplicaSet is the most recommended deploying resource than ReplicationController or standalone ReplicaSet.

While paying close attention to the history of update in deployment, be aware that it is not always listed in sequence. The algorithm of adding revisions could be clarified as the following bullet points show:

- Take the number of last revision as *N*
- When a new rollout update comes, it would be *N+1*
- Roll back to a specific revision number *X*, *X* would be removed and it would become *N+1*
- Roll back to the previous version, which means *N-1*, then *N-1* would be removed and it would become *N+1*

With this revision management, no stale and overlapped updates occupy the rollout history.

There's more...

Taking Deployment update into consideration is a good step towards building a CI/CD (continuous integration and continuous delivery) pipeline. For a more common usage, developers don't exploit command lines to update the Deployment. They may prefer to fire some API calls from CI/CD platform, or update from a previous configuration file. Here comes an example working with the subcommand `apply`:

```
// A simple nginx Kubernetes configuration file
$ cat my-update-nginx.yaml
apiVersion: apps/v1
kind: Deployment
metadata:
  name: my-update-nginx
spec:
  replicas: 5
  selector:
    matchLabels:
      run: simple-nginx
  template:
    metadata:
      labels:
        run: simple-nginx
    spec:
      containers:
```

```
- name: simple-nginx
  image: nginx
  ports:
  - containerPort: 80
```

```
// create the Deployment by file and recording the command in the revision
tag
$ kubectl create -f my-update-nginx.yaml --record
deployment.apps "my-update-nginx" created
```

As a demonstration, modifying the container image from nginx to nginx:stable (you may check the code bundle my-update-nginx-updated.yaml for the modification). Then, we can use the changed file to update with the subcommand apply:

```
$ kubectl apply -f my-update-nginx-updated.yaml --record
Warning: kubectl apply should be used on resource created by either kubectl
create --save-config or kubectl apply
deployment.apps "my-update-nginx" configured
// check the update revisions and status
$ kubectl rollout history deployment my-update-nginx
deployments "my-update-nginx"
REVISION    CHANGE-CAUSE
1           kubectl create --filename=my-update-nginx.yaml --record=true
2           kubectl apply --filename=my-update-nginx-updated.yaml --
record=true
$ kubectl rollout status deployment my-update-nginx
deployment "my-update-nginx" successfully rolled out
```

Now, you can learn another way to update your Deployment.

Digging deeper into rolling-update on Deployment, there are some parameters we may leverage when doing updates:

- minReadySeconds: After a Pod is considered to be ready, the system still waits for a period of time for going on to the next step. This time slot is the minimum ready seconds, which will be helpful when waiting for the application to complete post-configuration.
- maxUnavailable: The maximum number of Pods that can be unavailable during updating. The value could be a percentage (the default is 25%) or an integer. If the value of maxSurge is 0, which means no tolerance of the number of Pods over the desired number, the value of maxUnavailable cannot be 0.

- `maxSurge`: The maximum number of Pods that can be created over the desired number of ReplicaSet during updating. The value could be a percentage (the default is 25%) or an integer. If the value of `maxUnavailable` is 0, which means the number of serving Pods should always meet the desired number, the value of `maxSurge` cannot be 0.

Based on the configuration file `my-update-nginx-advanced.yaml` in the code bundle, try playing with these parameters by yourself and see if you can feel the ideas at work.

See also

You could continue studying the following recipes to learn more ideas about deploying Kubernetes resources efficiently:

- Scaling your containers
- Working with configuration files
- The *Moving monolithic to microservices, Integrating with Jenkins, Working with the private Docker registry*, and *Setting up the Continuous Delivery Pipeline* recipes in `Chapter 5`, *Building a Continuous Delivery Pipeline*

Forwarding container ports

In previous chapters, you have learned how to work with the Kubernetes Services to forward the container port internally and externally. Now, it's time to take it a step further to see how it works.

There are four networking models in Kubernetes, and we'll explore the details in the following sections:

- Container-to-container communications
- Pod-to-pod communications
- Pod-to-service communications
- External-to-internal communications

Getting ready

Before we go digging into Kubernetes networking, let's study the networking of Docker to understand the basic concept. Each container will have a network namespace with its own routing table and routing policy. By default, the network bridge docker0 connects the physical network interface and virtual network interfaces of containers, and the virtual network interface is the bidirectional cable for the container network namespace and the host one. As a result, there is a pair of virtual network interfaces for a single container: the Ethernet interface (**eth0**) on the container and the virtual Ethernet interface (**veth-**) on the host.

The network structure can be expressed as in the following image:

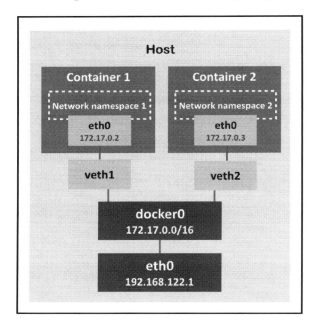

Container network interfaces on host

 What is a network namespace?
A network namespace is the technique provided by Linux kernel. With this feature, the operating system can fulfill network virtualization by separating the network capability into independent resources. Each network namespace has its own iptable setup and network devices.

How to do it...

A Pod contains one or more containers, which run on the same host. Each Pod has their own IP address on an overlay network; all the containers inside a Pod see each other as on the same host. Containers inside a Pod will be created, deployed, and deleted almost at the same time. We will illustrate four communication models between container, Pod, and Service.

Container-to-container communication

In this scenario, we would focus on the communications between containers within single Pod:

1. Let's create two containers in one Pod: a nginx web application and a CentOS, which checks port 80 on localhost:

```
// configuration file of creating two containers within a pod
$ cat two-container-pod.yaml
apiVersion: v1
kind: Pod
metadata:
  name: two-container
spec:
  containers:
    - name: web
      image: nginx
      ports:
        - containerPort: 80
          hostPort: 80
    - name: centos
      image: centos
      command: ["/bin/sh", "-c", "while : ;do curl
http://localhost:80/; sleep 30; done"]

// create the pod
$ kubectl create -f two-container-pod.yaml
pod "two-container" created
// check the status of the newly-created Pod
$ kubectl get pod two-container
NAME            READY     STATUS     RESTARTS    AGE
two-container   2/2       Running    0           5s
```

We see the count in the READY column becomes 2/2, since there are two containers inside this Pod.

2. Using the `kubectl describe` command, we may see the details of the Pod:

```
$ kubectl describe pod two-container
Name:          two-container
Namespace:     default
Node:          ubuntu02/192.168.122.102
Start Time:    Sat, 05 May 2018 18:28:22 -0400
Labels:        <none>
Annotations:   <none>
Status:        Running
IP:            192.168.79.198
Containers:
  web:
    Container ID:
docker://e832d294f176f643d604445096439d485d94780faf60eab7ae5d38
49cbf15d75
...
  centos:
    Container ID:
docker://9e35275934c1acdcfac4017963dc046f9517a8c1fc972df56ca37e
69d7389a72
...
```

We can see that the Pod is run on node ubuntu02 and that its IP is 192.168.79.198.

3. Also, we may find that the Centos container can access the `nginx` on localhost:

```
$ kubectl logs two-container centos | grep "title"
<title>Welcome to nginx!</title>
...
```

4. Let's log in to node ubuntu02 to check the network setting of these two containers:

```
// list containers of the Pod
$ docker ps | grep "two-container"
9e35275934c1          centos
"/bin/sh -c 'while..."   11 hours ago       Up 11 hours
k8s_centos_two-container_default_113e727f-f440-11e7-
ac3f-525400a9d353_0
e832d294f176          nginx
"nginx -g 'daemon ..."   11 hours ago       Up 11 hours
k8s_web_two-container_default_113e727f-f440-11e7-
```

```
ac3f-525400a9d353_0
9b3e9caf5149        gcr.io/google_containers/pause-amd64:3.1
"/pause"                 11 hours ago        Up 11 hours
k8s_POD_two-container_default_113e727f-f440-11e7-
ac3f-525400a9d353_0
```

Now, we know that the two containers created are 9e35275934c1 and
e832d294f176. On the other hand, there is another container, 9b3e9caf5149,
that is created by Kubernetes with the Docker image
gcr.io/google_containers/pause-amd64. We will introduce it later.
Thereafter, we may get a detailed inspection of the containers with the command
docker inspect, and by adding the command jq (https://stedolan.github.
io/jq/) as a pipeline, we can parse the output information to show network
settings only.

5. Taking a look at both containers covered in the same Pod:

```
// inspect the nginx container, and use jq to parse it
$ docker inspect e832d294f176 | jq '.[]| {NetworkMode:
.HostConfig.NetworkMode, NetworkSettings: .NetworkSettings}'
{
  "NetworkMode":
"container:9b3e9caf5149ffb0ec14c1ffc36f94b2dd55b223d0d20e4d48c4
e33228103723",
  "NetworkSettings": {
    "Bridge": "",
    "SandboxID": "",
    "HairpinMode": false,
    "LinkLocalIPv6Address": "",
    "LinkLocalIPv6PrefixLen": 0,
    "Ports": {},
    "SandboxKey": "",
    "SecondaryIPAddresses": null,
    "SecondaryIPv6Addresses": null,
    "EndpointID": "",
    "Gateway": "",
    "GlobalIPv6Address": "",
    "GlobalIPv6PrefixLen": 0,
    "IPAddress": "",
    "IPPrefixLen": 0,
    "IPv6Gateway": "",
    "MacAddress": "",
    "Networks": {}
  }
}
// then inspect the centos one
```

```
$ docker inspect 9e35275934c1 | jq '.[]| {NetworkMode:
.HostConfig.NetworkMode, NetworkSettings: .NetworkSettings}'
{
  "NetworkMode":
"container:9b3e9caf5149ffb0ec14c1ffc36f94b2dd55b223d0d20e4d48c4
e33228103723",
  ...
```

We can see that both containers have identical network settings; the network mode is set to mapped container mode, leaving the other configurations cleaned. The network bridge container is `container:9b3e9caf5149ffb0ec14c1ffc36f94b2dd55b223d0d20e4d48c4e33228103 723`. What is this container? It is the one created by Kubernetes, container ID `9b3e9caf5149`, with the image `gcr.io/google_containers/pause-amd64`.

What does the container "pause" do?

Just as its name suggests, this container does nothing but "pause". However, it preserves the network settings, and the Linux network namespace, for the Pod. Anytime the container shutdowns and restarts, the network configuration will still be the same and not need to be recreated, because the "pause" container holds it. You can check its code and Dockerfile at `https://github.com/kubernetes/kubernetes/tree/master/build/pause` for more information.

The "pause" container is a network container, which is created when a Pod

is created and used to handle the route of the Pod network. Then, two containers will share the network namespace with pause; that's why they see each other as localhost.

Create a network container in Docker

In Docker, you can easily make a container into a network container, sharing its network namespace with another container. Use the command line: `$ docker run --network=container:<CONTAINER_ID or CONTAINER_NAME> [other options]`. Then, you will be able to start a container which uses the network namespace of the assigned container.

Pod-to-Pod communication

As mentioned, containers in a Pod share the same network namespace. And a Pod is the basic computing unit in Kubernetes. Kubernetes assigns an IP to a Pod in its world. Every Pod can see every other with the virtual IP in Kubernetes network. While talking about the communication between Pods , we can separate into two scenarios: Pods that communicate within a node, or Pods that communicate across nodes. For Pods in single node, since they have separate IPs, their transmissions can be held by bridge, same as containers in a Docker node. However, for communication between Pods across nodes, how would be the package routing work while Pod doesn't have the host information (the host IP)?

Kubernetes uses the CNI to handle cluster networking. CNI is a framework for managing connective containers, for assigning or deleting the network resource on a container. While Kubernetes takes CNI as a plugin, users can choose the implementation of CNI on demand. Commonly, there are the following types of CNI:

- **Overlay**: With the technique of packet encapsulation. Every data is wrapped with host IP, so it is routable in the internet. An example is flannel (`https://github.com/coreos/flannel`).
- **L3 gateway**: Transmission between containers pass to a gateway node first. The gateway will maintain the routing table to map the container subnet and host IP. An example is Project Calico (`https://www.projectcalico.org/`).
- **L2 adjacency**: Happening on L2 switching. In Ethernet, two nodes have adjacency if the package can be transmitted directly from source to destination, without passing by other nodes. An example is Cisco ACI (`https://www.cisco.com/c/en/us/td/docs/switches/datacenter/aci/apic/sw/kb/b_Kubernetes_Integration_with_ACI.html`).

There are pros and cons to every type of CNI. The former type within the bullet points has better scalability but bad performance, while the latter one has a shorter latency but requires complex and customized setup. Some CNIs cover all three types in different modes, for example, Contiv (`https://github.com/contiv/netplugin`). You can get more information about CNI while checking its spec at: `https://github.com/containernetworking/cni`. Additionally, look at the CNI list on official website of Kubernetes to try out these CNIs: `https://kubernetes.io/docs/concepts/cluster-administration/networking/#how-to-achieve-this`.

After introducing the basic knowledge of the packet transaction between Pods , we will continue to bring you a Kubernetes API, `NetworkPolicy`, which provides advanced management between the communication of Pods .

Working with NetworkPolicy

As a resource of Kubernetes, NetworkPolicy uses label selectors to configure the firewall of Pods from infrastructure level. Without a specified NetworkPolicy, any Pod in the same cluster can communicate with each other by default. On the other hand, once a NetworkPolicy with rules is attached to a Pod, either it is for ingress or egress, or both, and all traffic that doesn't follow the rules will be blocked.

Before demonstrating how to build a NetworkPolicy, we should make sure the network plugin in Kubernetes cluster supports it. There are several CNIs that support NetworkPolicy: Calico, Contive, Romana (`https://github.com/romana/kube`), Weave Net (`https://github.com/weaveworks/weave`), Trireme (`https://github.com/aporeto-inc/trireme-kubernetes`), and others.

Enable CNI with NetworkPolicy support as network plugin in minikube

While working on minikube, users will not need to attach a CNI specifically, since it is designed as a single local Kubernetes node. However, to enable the functionality of NetworkPolicy, it is necessary to start a NetworkPolicy-supported CNI. Be careful, as, while you configure the minikube with CNI, the configuration options and procedures could be quite different to various CNI implementations. The following steps show you how to start minikube with CNI, Calico:

1. We take this issue `https://github.com/projectcalico/calico/issues/1013#issuecomment-325689943` as reference for these building steps.
2. The minikube used here is the latest version, 0.24.1.
3. Reboot your minikube: `minikube start --network-plugin=cni \`
`--host-only-cidr 172.17.17.1/24 \`
`--extra-config=kubelet.PodCIDR=192.168.0.0/16 \`
`--extra-config=proxy.ClusterCIDR=192.168.0.0/16 \`
`--extra-config=controller-manager.ClusterCIDR=192.168.0.0/16`.
4. Create Calico with the configuration file "minikube-calico.yaml" from the code bundle `kubectl create -f minikue-calico.yaml`.

To illustrate the functionality of NetworkPolicy, we are going to create a Pod and expose it as a service, then attach a NetworkPolicy on the Pod to see what happens:

```
// start a pod of our favourite example, nginx
$ kubectl run nginx-pod --image=nginx --port=80 --restart=Never
pod "nginx-pod" created
//expose the pod as a service listening on port 8080
$ kubectl expose pod nginx-pod --port=8080 --target-port=80
service "nginx-pod" exposed
// check the service IP
$ kubectl get svc
NAME         TYPE        CLUSTER-IP       EXTERNAL-IP    PORT(S)     AGE
kubernetes   ClusterIP   10.96.0.1        <none>         443/TCP     1h
nginx-pod    ClusterIP   10.102.153.182   <none>         8080/TCP    1m
```

Now, we can go ahead and check the Pod's connection from a simple Deployment, `busybox`, using the command `wget` with `--spider` flag to verify the existence of endpoint:

```
// check the accessibility of the service
// create busybox and open standard input and independent terminal by flag
"i" and "t", similar to docker command
$ kubectl run busybox -it --image=busybox /bin/sh
If you don't see a command prompt, try pressing enter.
/ # wget --spider 10.102.153.182:8080
Connecting to 10.102.153.182:8080 (10.102.153.182:8080)
```

As shown in the preceding result, we know that the `nginx` service can be accessed without any constraints. Later, let's run a `NetworkPolicy` that restricts that only the Pod tagging `<test: inbound>` can access `nginx` service:

```
// a configuration file defining NetworkPolicy of pod nginx-pod
$ cat networkpolicy.yaml
kind: NetworkPolicy
apiVersion: networking.k8s.io/v1
metadata:
  name: nginx-networkpolicy
spec:
  podSelector:
    matchLabels:
      run: nginx-pod
  ingress:
    - from:
      - podSelector:
          matchLabels:
            test: inbound
```

As you can see, in the spec of NeworkPolicy, it is configured to apply to Pods with the label `<run: nginx-pod>`, which is the one we have on the `pod nginx-pod`. Also, a rule of ingress is attached in the policy, which indicates that only Pods with a specific label can access `nginx-pod`:

```
// create the NetworkPolicy
$ kubectl create -f networkpolicy.yaml
networkpolicy.networking.k8s.io "nginx-networkpolicy" created
// check the details of NetworkPolicy
$ kubectl describe networkpolicy nginx-networkpolicy
Name:         nginx-networkpolicy
Namespace:    default
Created on:   2018-05-05 18:36:56 -0400 EDT
Labels:       <none>
Annotations:  <none>
```

```
Spec:
  PodSelector:        run=nginx-pod
  Allowing ingress traffic:
    To Port: <any> (traffic allowed to all ports)
    From PodSelector: test=inbound
  Allowing egress traffic:
    <none> (Selected pods are isolated for egress connectivity)
  Policy Types: Ingress
```

Great, everything is looking just like what we expected. Next, check the same service endpoint on our previous `busybox` Pod:

```
// if you turned off the terminal, resume it with the subcommand attach
$ kubectl attach busybox-598b87455b-s2mfq -c busybox -i -t
// we add flag to specify timeout interval, otherwise it will just keep
hanging on wget
/ # wget --spider 10.102.153.182:8080 --timeout=3
wget: download timed out
```

As expected again, now we cannot access the `nginx-pod` service after NetworkPolicy is attached. The `nginx-pod` can only be touched by Pod labelled with `<test: inbound>`:

```
// verify the connection by yourself with new busybox
$ kubectl run busybox-labelled --labels="test=inbound" -it --image=busybox
/bin/sh
```

 Catch up with the concept of label and selector in the recipe *Working with labels and selectors* in `Chapter 2`, *Walking through Kubernetes Concepts*.

In this case, you have learned how to create a NetworkPolicy with ingress restriction by Pod selector. Still, there are other settings you may like to build on your Pod:

- **Egress restriction**: Egress rules can be applied by `.spec.egress`, which has similar settings to ingress.
- **Port restriction**: Each ingress and egress rule can point out what port, and with what kind of port protocol, is to be accepted or blocked. Port configuration can be applied through `.spec.ingress.ports` or `.spec.egress.ports`.
- **Namespace selector**: We can also make limitations on certain Namespaces. For example, Pods for the system daemon might only allow access to others in the Namespace `kube-system`. Namespace selector can be applied with `.spec.ingress.from.namespaceSelector` or `.spec.egress.to.namespaceSelector`.

- **IP block**: A more customized configuration is to set rules on certain CIDR ranges, which come out as similar ideas to what we work with iptables. We may utilize this configuration through `.spec.ingress.from.ipBlock` or `.spec.egress.to.ipBlock`.

It is recommended to check more details in the API document: `https://kubernetes.io/docs/reference/generated/kubernetes-api/v1.10/#networkpolicyspec-v1-networking`. Furthermore, we would like to show you some more interesting setups to fulfill general situations:

- **Apply to all Pod**: A NetworkPolicy can be easily pushed to every Pod by setting `.spec.podSelector` with an empty value.
- **Allow all traffic**: We may allow all incoming traffic by assigning `.spec.ingress` with empty value, an empty array; accordingly, outgoing traffic could be set without any restriction by assigning `.spec.egress` with empty value.
- **Deny all traffic**: We may deny all incoming or outgoing traffic by simply indicating the type of NetworkPolicy without setting any rule. The type of the NetworkPolicy can be set at `.spec.policyTypes`. At the same time, do not set `.spec.ingress` or `.spec.egress`.

Go check the code bundle for the example files `networkpolicy-allow-all.yaml` and `networkpolicy-deny-all.yaml`.

Pod-to-Service communication

In the ordinary course of events, Pods can be stopped accidentally. Then, the IP of the Pod can be changed. When we expose the port for a Pod or a Deployment, we create a Kubernetes Service that acts as a proxy or a load balancer. Kubernetes would create a virtual IP, which receives the request from clients and proxies the traffic to the Pods in a service. Let's review how to do this:

1. First, we would create a Deployment and expose it to a Service:

```
$ cat nodeport-deployment.yaml
apiVersion: apps/v1
kind: Deployment
metadata:
  name: nodeport-deploy
spec:
  replicas: 2
  selector:
```

```
        matchLabels:
          app: nginx
      template:
        metadata:
          labels:
            app: nginx
        spec:
          containers:
          - name: my-nginx
            image: nginx
---
apiVersion: v1
kind: Service
metadata:
  name: nodeport-svc
spec:
  type: NodePort
  selector:
    app: nginx
  ports:
    - protocol: TCP
      port: 8080
      targetPort: 80
$ kubectl create -f nodeport-deployment.yaml
deployment.apps "nodeport-deploy" created
service "nodeport-svc" created
```

2. At this moment, check the details of the Service with the subcommand
   describe:

```
$ kubectl describe service nodeport-svc
Name:                    nodeport-svc
Namespace:               default
Labels:                  <none>
Annotations:             <none>
Selector:                app=nginx
Type:                    NodePort
IP:                      10.101.160.245
Port:                    <unset>  8080/TCP
TargetPort:              80/TCP
NodePort:                <unset>  30615/TCP
Endpoints:               192.168.80.5:80,192.168.80.6:80
Session Affinity:        None
External Traffic Policy: Cluster
Events:                  <none>
```

The virtual IP of the Service is `10.101.160.245`, which exposes the port `8080`. The Service would then dispatch the traffic into the two endpoints `192.168.80.5:80` and `192.168.80.6:80`. Moreover, because the Service is created in `NodePort` type, clients can access this Service on every Kubernetes node at `<NODE_IP>:30615`. As with our understanding of the recipe *Working with Services* in `Chapter 2`, *Walking through Kubernetes Concepts*, it is the Kubernetes daemon `kube-proxy` that helps to maintain and update routing policy on every node.

3. Continue on, checking the `iptable` on any Kubernetes node:

 Attention! If you are in minikube environment, you should jump into the node with the command `minikube ssh`.

```
// Take a look at following marked "Chain"
$ sudo iptables -t nat -nL
...
Chain KUBE-NODEPORTS (1 references)
target       prot opt source                destination
KUBE-MARK-MASQ  tcp  --  0.0.0.0/0              0.0.0.0/0
/* default/nodeport-svc: */ tcp dpt:30615
KUBE-SVC-GFPAJ7EGCNM4QF4H  tcp  --  0.0.0.0/0
0.0.0.0/0              /* default/nodeport-svc: */ tcp dpt:30615
...
Chain KUBE-SEP-DIS6NYZTQKZ5ALQS (1 references)
target       prot opt source                destination
KUBE-MARK-MASQ  all  --  192.168.80.6           0.0.0.0/0
/* default/nodeport-svc: */
DNAT         tcp  --  0.0.0.0/0              0.0.0.0/0
/* default/nodeport-svc: */ tcp to:192.168.80.6:80
...
Chain KUBE-SEP-TC6HXYYMMLGUSFNZ (1 references)
target       prot opt source                destination
KUBE-MARK-MASQ  all  --  192.168.80.5           0.0.0.0/0
/* default/nodeport-svc: */
DNAT         tcp  --  0.0.0.0/0              0.0.0.0/0
/* default/nodeport-svc: */ tcp to:192.168.80.5:80
Chain KUBE-SERVICES (2 references)
target       prot opt source                destination
...
KUBE-SVC-GFPAJ7EGCNM4QF4H  tcp  --  0.0.0.0/0
10.101.160.245          /* default/nodeport-svc: cluster IP */ tcp
dpt:8080
```

```
...
KUBE-NODEPORTS  all  --  0.0.0.0/0              0.0.0.0/0
/* kubernetes service nodeports; NOTE: this must be the last
rule in this chain */ ADDRTYPE match dst-type LOCAL
...
Chain KUBE-SVC-GFPAJ7EGCNM4QF4H (2 references)
target      prot opt source              destination
KUBE-SEP-TC6HXYYMMLGUSFNZ  all  --  0.0.0.0/0
0.0.0.0/0            /* default/nodeport-svc: */ statistic mode
random probability 0.50000000000
KUBE-SEP-DIS6NYZTQKZ5ALQS  all  --  0.0.0.0/0
0.0.0.0/0            /* default/nodeport-svc: */
...
```

There will be a lot of rules showing out. To focus on policies related to the Service
nodeport-svc, go through the following steps for checking them all. The output on your
screen may not be listed in the expected order:

1. Find targets under chain KUBE-NODEPORTS with the comment mentioned
   nodeport-svc. One target will be named with the prefix KUBE-SVC-. In the
   preceding output, it is the one named KUBE-SVC-GFPAJ7EGCNM4QF4H. Along
   with the other target KUBE-MARK-MASQ, they work on passing traffics at port
   30615 to the Service.

2. Find a specific target named KUBE-SVC-XXX under Chain KUBE-SERVICES. In
   this case, it is the target named KUBE-SVC-GFPAJ7EGCNM4QF4H, ruled as
   allowing traffics from "everywhere" to the endpoint of nodeport-svc,
   10.160.245:8080.

3. Find targets under the specific Chain KUBE-SVC-XXX. In this case, it is Chain
   KUBE-SVC-GFPAJ7EGCNM4QF4H. Under the Service chain, you will have number
   of targets based on the according Pods with the prefix KUBE-SEP-. In the
   preceding output, they are KUBE-SEP-TC6HXYYMMLGUSFNZ and KUBE-SEP-
   DIS6NYZTQKZ5ALQS.

4. Find targets under specific Chain KUBE-SEP-YYY. In this case, the two chains
   required to take a look are Chain KUBE-SEP-TC6HXYYMMLGUSFNZ and Chain
   KUBE-SEP-DIS6NYZTQKZ5ALQS. Each of them covers two targets, KUBE-MARK-
   MASQ and DNAT, for incoming and outgoing traffics between "everywhere" to the
   endpoint of Pod, 192.168.80.5:80 or 192.168.80.6:80.

One key point here is that the Service target KUBE-SVC-GFPAJ7EGCNM4QF4H exposing its cluster IP to outside world will dispatch the traffic to chain KUBE-SEP-TC6HXYYMMLGUSFNZ and KUBE-SEP-DIS6NYZTQKZ5ALQS with a statistic mode random probability of 0.5. Both chains have DNAT targets that work on changing the destination IP of the packets to the private subnet one, the one of a specific Pod.

External-to-internal communication

To publish applications in Kubernetes, we can leverage either Kubernetes Service, with type NodePort or LoadBalancer, or Kubernetes Ingress. For NodePort service, as introduced in previous section, the port number of the node will be a pair with the Service. Like the following diagram, port 30361 on both node 1 and node 2 points to Service A, which dispatch the traffics to Pod1 and a Pod with static probability.

LoadBalancer Service, as you may have learned from the recipe *Working with Services* in Chapter 2, *Walking through Kubernetes Concepts*, includes the configurations of NodePort. Moreover, a LoadBalancer Service can work with an external load balancer, providing users with the functionality to integrate load balancing procedures between cloud infrastructure and Kubernetes resource, such as the settings healthCheckNodePort and externalTrafficPolicy. **Service B** in the following image is a LoadBalancer Service. Internally, **Service B** works the same as **Service A**, relying on **iptables** to redirect packets to Pod; Externally, cloud load balancer doesn't realize Pod or container, it only dispatches the traffic by the number of nodes. No matter which node is chosen to get the request, it would still be able to pass packets to the right Pod:

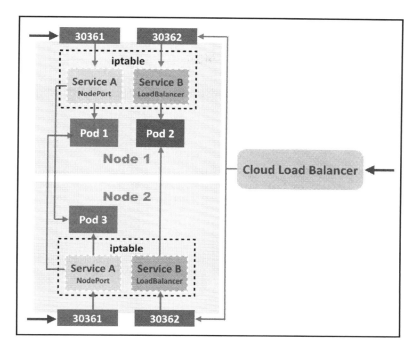

Kubernetes Services with type NodePort and type LoadBalancer

Working with Ingress

Walking through the journey of Kubernetes networking, users get the idea that each Pod and Service has its private IP and corresponding port to listen on request. In practice, developers may deliver the endpoint of service, the private IP or Kubernetes DNS name, for internal clients; or, developers may expose Services externally by type of NodePort or LoadBalancer. Although the endpoint of Service is more stable than Pod, the Services are offered separately, and clients should record the IPs without much meaning to them. In this section, we will introduce Ingress, a resource that makes your Services work as a group. More than that, we could easily pack our service union as an API server while we set Ingress rules to recognize the different URLs, and then ingress controller works for passing the request to specific Services based on the rules.

Before we try on Kubernetes Ingress, we should create an ingress controller in cluster. Different from other controllers in `kube-controller-manager` (`https://kubernetes.io/docs/reference/generated/kube-controller-manager/`), ingress controller is run by custom implementation instead of working as a daemon. In the latest Kubernetes version, 1.10, nginx ingress controller is the most stable one and also generally supports many platforms. Check the official documents for the details of deployment: `https://github.com/kubernetes/ingress-nginx/blob/master/README.md`. We will only demonstrate our example on minikube; please see the following information box for the setup of the ingress controller.

Enable Ingress functionality in minikube
Ingress in minikube is an add-on function. Follow these steps to start this feature in your environment:

1. Check if the add-on ingress is enabled or not: Fire the command `minikube addons list` on your terminal. If it is not enabled, means it shows `ingress: disabled`, you should keep follow below steps.
2. Enable ingress: Enter the command `minikube addons enable ingress`, you will see an output like `ingress was successfully enabled`.
3. Check the add-on list again to verify that the last step does work. We expect that the field ingress shows as `enabled`.

Here comes an example to demonstrate how to work with Ingress. We would run up two Deployments and their Services, and an additional Ingress to expose them as a union. In the beginning, we would add a new hostname in the host file of Kubernetes master. It is a simple way for our demonstration. If you work on the production environment, a general use case is that the hostname should be added as a record in the DNS server:

```
// add a dummy hostname in local host file
$ sudo sh -c "echo `minikube ip` happy.k8s.io >> /etc/hosts"
```

Our first Kubernetes Deployment and Service would be `echoserver`, a dummy Service showing server and request information. For the other pair of Deployment and Service, we would reuse the NodePort Service example from the previous section:

```
$ cat echoserver.yaml
apiVersion: apps/v1
kind: Deployment
metadata:
  name: echoserver-deploy
```

```
spec:
  replicas: 2
  selector:
    matchLabels:
      app: echo
  template:
    metadata:
      labels:
        app: echo
    spec:
      containers:
        - name: my-echo
          image: gcr.io/google_containers/echoserver:1.8
---
apiVersion: v1
kind: Service
metadata:
  name: echoserver-svc
spec:
  selector:
    app: echo
  ports:
    - protocol: TCP
      port: 8080
      targetPort: 8080
```

Go ahead and create both set of resources through configuration files:

```
$ kubectl create -f echoserver.yaml
deployment.apps "echoserver-deploy" created
service "echoserver-svc" created
$ kubectl create -f nodeport-deployment.yaml
deployment.apps "nodeport-deploy" created
service "nodeport-svc" created
```

Our first Ingress makes two Services that listen at the separate URLs /nginx and /echoserver, with the hostname happy.k8s.io, the dummy one we added in the local host file. We use annotation rewrite-target to guarantee that traffic redirection starts from root, /. Otherwise, the client may get page not found because of surfing the wrong path. More annotations we may play with are listed at https://github.com/kubernetes/ingress-nginx/blob/master/docs/user-guide/nginx-configuration/annotations.md:

```
$ cat ingress.yaml
apiVersion: extensions/v1beta1
kind: Ingress
metadata:
  name: happy-ingress
```

```
    annotations:
      nginx.ingress.kubernetes.io/rewrite-target:
spec:
  rules:
    - host: happy.k8s.io
      http:
        paths:
          - path: /nginx
            backend:
              serviceName: nodeport-svc
              servicePort: 8080
          - path: /echoserver
            backend:
              serviceName: echoserver-svc
              servicePort: 8080
```

Then, just create the Ingress and check its information right away:

```
$ kubectl create -f ingress.yaml
ingress.extensions "happy-ingress" created
// "ing" is the abbreviation of "ingress"
$ kubectl describe ing happy-ingress
Name:           happy-ingress
Namespace:      default
Address:
Default backend: default-http-backend:80 (172.17.0.3:8080)
Rules:
  Host          Path  Backends
  ----          ----  --------
  happy.k8s.io
                /nginx        nodeport-svc:8080 (<none>)
                /echoserver   echoserver-svc:8080 (<none>)
Annotations:
  nginx.ingress.kubernetes.io/rewrite-target
Events:
  Type    Reason  Age   From               Message
  ----    ------  ----  ----               -------
  Normal  CREATE  14s   ingress-controller  Ingress default/happy-ingress
```

You may find that there is no IP address in the field of description. It will be attached after the first DNS lookup:

```
// verify the URL set in ingress rules
$ curl http://happy.k8s.io/nginx
...
<title>Welcome to nginx!</title>
...
$ curl http://happy.k8s.io/echoserver
```

```
Hostname: echoserver-deploy-5598f5796f-d8cr4
Pod Information:
    -no pod information available-
Server values:
    server_version=nginx: 1.13.3 - lua: 10008
...
// the IP address would be added after connection
$ kubectl get ing
NAME            HOSTS           ADDRESS         PORTS     AGE
happy-ingress   happy.k8s.io    192.168.64.4    80        1m
```

Although working with Ingress is not as straightforward as other resources, as you have to start an ingress controller implementation by yourself, it still makes our application exposed and flexible. There are many network features coming that are more stable and user friendly. Keep up with the latest updates and have fun!

There's more...

In the last part of external-to-internal communication, we learned about Kubernetes Ingress, the resource that makes services work as a union and dispatches requests to target services. Does any similar idea jump into your mind? It sounds like a microservice, the application structure with several loosely coupled services. A complicated application would be distributed to multiple lighter services. Each service is developed independently while all of them can cover original functions. Numerous working units, such as Pods in Kubernetes, run volatile and can be dynamically scheduled on Services by the system controller. However, such a multi-layered structure increases the complexity of networking and also suffers potential overhead costs.

External load balancers are not aware the existence of Pods; they only balance the workload to hosts. A host without any served Pod running would then redirect the loading to other hosts. This situation comes out of a user's expectation for fair load balancing. Moreover, a Pod may crash accidentally, in which case it is difficult to do failover and complete the request. To make up the shortcomings, the idea of a service mesh focus on the networking management of microservice was born, dedicated to delivering more reliable and performant communications on orchestration like Kubernetes:

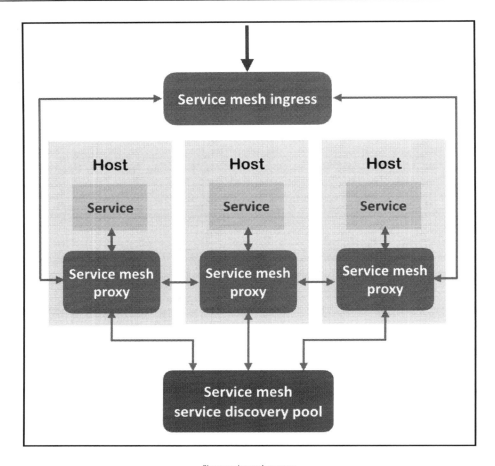

Simpe service mesh structure

The preceding diagram illustrates the main components in a service mesh. They work together to achieve features as follows:

- **Service mesh ingress**: Using applied Ingress rules to decide which Service should handle the incoming requests. It could also be a proxy that is able to check the runtime policies.
- **Service mesh proxy**: Proxies on every node not only direct the packets, but can also be used as an advisory agent reporting the overall status of the Services.
- **Service mesh service discovery pool**: Serving the central management for mesh and pushing controls over proxies. Its responsibility includes procedures of network capability, authentication, failover, and load balancing.

Although well-known service mesh implementations such as Linkerd (`https://linkerd.io`) and Istio (`https://istio.io`) are not mature enough for production usage, the idea of service mesh is not ignorable.

See also

Kubernetes forwards ports based on the overlay network. In this chapter, we also run Pods and Services with nginx. Reviewing the previous sections will help you to understand more about how to manipulate it. Also, look at the following recipes:

- The *Creating an overlay network* and *Running your first container in Kubernetes* recipes in `Chapter 1`, *Building Your Own Kubernetes Cluster*
- The *Working with Pods* and *Working with Services* recipes in `Chapter 2`, *Walking through Kubernetes Concepts*
- The *Moving monolithic to microservices* recipe in `Chapter 5`, *Building Continuous Delivery Pipelines*

Ensuring flexible usage of your containers

Pod, in Kubernetes, means a set of containers, which is also the smallest computing unit. You may have know about the basic usage of Pod in the previous recipes. Pods are usually managed by deployments and exposed by services; they work as applications with this scenario.

In this recipe, we will discuss two new features: **DaemonSets** and **StatefulSets**. These two features can manage Pods with more specific purpose.

Getting ready

What are **Daemon-like Pod** and **Stateful Pod**? The regular Pods in Kubernetes will determine and dispatch to particular Kubernetes nodes based on current node resource usage and your configuration.

However, a **Daemon-like Pod** will be created in each node. For example, if you have three nodes, three daemon-like Pods will be created and deployed to each node. Whenever a new node is added, DaemonSets Pod will be deployed to the new node automatically. Therefore, it will be useful to use node level monitoring or log correction.

On the other hand, a **Stateful Pod** will stick to some resources such as network identifier (Pod name and DNS) and **persistent volume (PV)**. This also guarantees an order during deployment of multiple Pods and during rolling update. For example, if you deploy a Pod named `my-pod`, and set the scale to **4**, then Pod name will be assigned as `my-pod-0`, `my-pod-1`, `my-pod-2`, and `my-pod-3`. Not only Pod name but also DNS and persistent volume are preserved. For example, when `my-pod-2` is recreated due to resource shortages or application crash, those names and volumes are taken over by a new Pod which is also named `my-pod-2`. It is useful for some cluster based applications such as HDFS and ElasticSearch.

In this recipe, we will demonstrate how to use DaemonSets and StatefulSet; however, to have a better understanding, it should use multiple Kubernetes Nodes environment. To do this, minikube is not ideal, so instead, use either kubeadm/kubespray to create a multiple Node environment.

Using kubeadm or kubespray to set up Kubernetes cluster was described in Chapter 1, *Build Your Own Kubernetes Cluster*.

To confirm whether that has 2 or more nodes, type `kubectl get nodes` as follows to check how many nodes you have:

```
//this result indicates you have 2 nodes
$ kubectl get nodes
NAME         STATUS    ROLES          AGE    VERSION
node1        Ready     master,node    6h     v1.10.2
node2        Ready     node           6h     v1.10.2
```

In addition, if you want to execute the StatefulSet recipe later in this chapter, you need a StorageClass to set up a dynamic provisioning environment. It was described in *Working with volumes* section in Chapter 2, *Walking through Kubernetes Concepts*. It is recommended to use public cloud such as AWS and GCP with a CloudProvider; this will be described in Chapter 6, *Building Kubernetes on AWS* and Chapter 7, *Building Kubernetes on GCP*, as well.

To check whether `StorageClass` is configured or not, use `kubectl get sc`:

```
//in Google Kubernetes Engine Environment
$ kubectl get sc
NAME                PROVISIONER
standard (default)  kubernetes.io/gce-pd
```

How to do it...

There is no CLI for us to create DaemonSets or StatefulSets. Therefore, we will build these two resource types by writing all the configurations in a YAML file.

Pod as DaemonSets

If a Kubernetes DaemonSet is created, the defined Pod will be deployed in every single node. It is guaranteed that the running containers occupy equal resources in each node. In this scenario, the container usually works as the daemon process.

For example, the following template has an Ubuntu image container that keeps checking its memory usage half a minute at a time:

1. To build it as a DaemonSet, execute the following code block:

```
$ cat daemonset-free.yaml
apiVersion: apps/v1
kind: DaemonSet
metadata:
  name: ram-check
spec:
  selector:
    matchLabels:
      name: checkRam
  template:
    metadata:
      labels:
        name: checkRam
    spec:
      containers:
      - name: ubuntu-free
        image: ubuntu
        command: ["/bin/bash","-c","while true; do free; sleep
30; done"]
      restartPolicy: Always
```

As the Job, the selector could be ignored, but it takes the values of the labels. We will always configure the restart policy of the DaemonSet as `Always`, which makes sure that every node has a Pod running.

2. The abbreviation of the `daemonset` is `ds` in `kubectl` command, use this shorter one in the CLI for convenience:

```
$ kubectl create -f daemonset-free.yaml
daemonset.apps "ram-check" created

$ kubectl get ds
NAME          DESIRED    CURRENT    READY      UP-TO-DATE
AVAILABLE     NODE SELECTOR    AGE
ram-check     2          2          2          2              2
<none>             5m
```

3. Here, we have two Pods running in separated nodes. They can still be recognized in the channel of the `pod`:

```
$ kubectl get pods -o wide
NAME              READY     STATUS     RESTARTS     AGE          IP
NODE
ram-check-6ldng   1/1       Running    0            9m
10.233.102.130    node1
ram-check-ddpdb   1/1       Running    0            9m
10.233.75.4       node2
```

4. It is good for you to evaluate the result using the subcommand `kubectl logs`:

```
$ kubectl logs ram-check-6ldng
              total        used        free        shared
buff/cache    available
Mem:          3623848      790144      329076      9128
2504628       2416976
Swap:         0            0           0
              total        used        free        shared
buff/cache    available
Mem:          3623848      786304      328028      9160
2509516       2420524
Swap:         0            0           0
              total        used        free        shared
buff/cache    available
Mem:          3623848      786344      323332      9160
2514172       2415944
Swap:         0            0           0
  .
  .
```

Whenever, you add a Kubernetes node onto your existing cluster, DaemonSets will recognize and deploy a Pod automatically.

5. Let's check again current status of DaemonSets, there are two Pods that have been deployed due to having two nodes as follows:

```
$ kubectl get ds
NAME          DESIRED   CURRENT   READY   UP-TO-DATE
AVAILABLE   NODE SELECTOR   AGE
ram-check     2         2         2       2               2
<none>        14m

$ kubectl get nodes
NAME     STATUS   ROLES         AGE   VERSION
node1    Ready    master,node   6h    v1.10.2
node2    Ready    node          6h    v1.10.2
```

6. So, now we are adding one more node onto the cluster through either `kubespray` or `kubeadm`, based on your setup:

```
$ kubectl get nodes
NAME     STATUS   ROLES         AGE   VERSION
node1    Ready    master,node   6h    v1.10.2
node2    Ready    node          6h    v1.10.2
node3    Ready    node          3m    v1.10.2
```

7. A few moments later, without any operation, the DaemonSet's size become 3 automatically, which aligns to the number of nodes:

```
$ kubectl get ds
NAME          DESIRED   CURRENT   READY   UP-TO-DATE
AVAILABLE   NODE SELECTOR   AGE
ram-check     3         3         3       3               3
<none>        18m


$ kubectl get pods -o wide
NAME               READY   STATUS    RESTARTS   AGE        IP
NODE
ram-check-6ldng    1/1     Running   0          18m
10.233.102.130     node1
ram-check-ddpdb    1/1     Running   0          18m
10.233.75.4        node2
ram-check-dpdmt    1/1     Running   0          3m
10.233.71.0        node3
```

Running a stateful Pod

Let's see another use case. We used Deployments/ReplicaSets to replicate the Pods. It scales well and is easy to maintain and Kubernetes assigns a DNS to the Pod using the Pod's IP address, such as `<Pod IP address>.<namespace>.pod.cluster.local`.

The following example demonstrates how the Pod DNS will be assigned:

```
$ kubectl run apache2 --image=httpd --replicas=3
deployment "apache2" created


//one of Pod has an IP address as 10.52.1.8
$ kubectl get pods -o wide
NAME                        READY     STATUS     RESTARTS    AGE          IP
NODE
apache2-55c684c66b-7m5zq    1/1       Running    0           5s
10.52.1.8    gke-chap7-default-pool-64212da9-z96q
apache2-55c684c66b-cjkcz    1/1       Running    0           1m
10.52.0.7    gke-chap7-default-pool-64212da9-8gzm
apache2-55c684c66b-v78tq    1/1       Running    0           1m
10.52.2.5    gke-chap7-default-pool-64212da9-bbs6


//another Pod can reach to 10-52-1-8.default.pod.cluster.local
$ kubectl exec apache2-55c684c66b-cjkcz -- ping -c 2
10-52-1-8.default.pod.cluster.local
PING 10-52-1-8.default.pod.cluster.local (10.52.1.8): 56 data bytes
64 bytes from 10.52.1.8: icmp_seq=0 ttl=62 time=1.642 ms
64 bytes from 10.52.1.8: icmp_seq=1 ttl=62 time=0.322 ms
--- 10-52-1-8.default.pod.cluster.local ping statistics ---
2 packets transmitted, 2 packets received, 0% packet loss
round-trip min/avg/max/stddev = 0.322/0.982/1.642/0.660 ms
```

However, this DNS entry is not guaranteed to stay in use for this Pod, because the Pod might crash due to an application error or node resource shortage. In such a case, the IP address will possibly be changed:

```
$ kubectl delete pod apache2-55c684c66b-7m5zq
pod "apache2-55c684c66b-7m5zq" deleted


//Pod IP address has been changed to 10.52.0.7
$ kubectl get pods -o wide
NAME                        READY     STATUS        RESTARTS    AGE          IP
NODE
apache2-55c684c66b-7m5zq    0/1       Terminating   0           1m
```

```
<none>       gke-chap7-default-pool-64212da9-z96q
apache2-55c684c66b-cjkcz   1/1        Running       0       2m
10.52.0.7   gke-chap7-default-pool-64212da9-8gzm
apache2-55c684c66b-l9vqt   1/1        Running       0       7s
10.52.1.9   gke-chap7-default-pool-64212da9-z96q
apache2-55c684c66b-v78tq   1/1        Running       0       2m
10.52.2.5   gke-chap7-default-pool-64212da9-bbs6


//DNS entry also changed
$ kubectl exec apache2-55c684c66b-cjkcz -- ping -c 2
10-52-1-8.default.pod.cluster.local
PING 10-52-1-8.default.pod.cluster.local (10.52.1.8): 56 data bytes
92 bytes from gke-chap7-default-pool-64212da9-z96q.c.kubernetes-
cookbook.internal (192.168.2.4): Destination Host Unreachable
92 bytes from gke-chap7-default-pool-64212da9-z96q.c.kubernetes-
cookbook.internal (192.168.2.4): Destination Host Unreachable
--- 10-52-1-8.default.pod.cluster.local ping statistics ---
2 packets transmitted, 0 packets received, 100% packet loss
```

For some applications, this will cause an issue; for example, if you manage a cluster application that needs to be managed by DNS or IP address. As of the current Kubernetes implementation, IP addresses can't be preserved for Pods . How about we use Kubernetes Service? Service preserves a DNS name. Unfortunately, it's not realistic to create the same amount of service with Pod. In the previous case, create three Services that bind to three Pods one to one.

Kubernetes has a solution for this kind of use case that uses StatefulSet. It preserves not only the DNS but also the persistent volume to keep a bind to the same Pod. Even if Pod is crashed, StatefulSet guarantees the binding of the same DNS and persistent volume to the new Pod. Note that the IP address is not preserved due to the current Kubernetes implementation.

To demonstrate, use **Hadoop Distributed File System (HDFS)** to launch one NameNode and three DataNodes. To perform this, use a Docker image from https://hub.docker.com/r/uhopper/hadoop/ that has NameNode and DataNode images. In addition, borrow the YAML configuration files namenode.yaml and datanode.yaml from https://gist.github.com/polvi/34ef498a967de563dc4252a7bfb7d582 and change a little bit:

1. Let's launch a Service and StatefulSet for namenode and datanode:

```
//create NameNode
$ kubectl create -f
https://raw.githubusercontent.com/kubernetes-cookbook/second-ed
ition/master/chapter3/3-4/namenode.yaml
```

```
service "hdfs-namenode-svc" created
statefulset "hdfs-namenode" created

$ kubectl get statefulset
NAME            DESIRED   CURRENT    AGE
hdfs-namenode   1         1          19s

$ kubectl get pods
NAME              READY    STATUS     RESTARTS    AGE
hdfs-namenode-0   1/1      Running    0           26s


//create DataNodes
$ kubectl create -f
https://raw.githubusercontent.com/kubernetes-cookbook/second-ed
ition/master/chapter3/3-4/datanode.yaml
statefulset "hdfs-datanode" created

$ kubectl get statefulset
NAME            DESIRED   CURRENT    AGE
hdfs-datanode   3         3          50s
hdfs-namenode   1         1          5m

$ kubectl get pods
NAME              READY    STATUS     RESTARTS    AGE
hdfs-datanode-0   1/1      Running    0           9m
hdfs-datanode-1   1/1      Running    0           9m
hdfs-datanode-2   1/1      Running    0           9m
hdfs-namenode-0   1/1      Running    0           9m
```

As you can see, the Pod naming convention is `<StatefulSet-name>`-`<sequence number>`. For example, NameNode Pod's name is `hdfs-namenode-0`. Also DataNode Pod's names are `hdfs-datanode-0`, `hdfs-datanode-1` and `hdfs-datanode-2`.

In addition, both NameNode and DataNode have a service that is configured as Headless mode (by `spec.clusterIP: None`). Therefore, you can access these Pods using DNS as `<pod-name>.<service-name>.<namespace>.svc.cluster.local`. In this case, this NameNode DNS entry could be `hdfs-namenode-0.hdfs-namenode-svc.default.svc.cluster.local`.

2. Let's check what NameNode Pod's IP address is, you can get this using `kubectl get pods -o wide` as follows:

```
//Pod hdfs-namenode-0 has an IP address as 10.52.2.8
$ kubectl get pods hdfs-namenode-0 -o wide
NAME                 READY     STATUS      RESTARTS    AGE        IP
NODE
hdfs-namenode-0      1/1       Running     0           9m
10.52.2.8    gke-chapter3-default-pool-97d2e17c-0dr5
```

3. Next, log in (run `/bin/bash`) to one of the DataNodes using `kubectl exec` to resolve this DNS name and check whether the IP address is `10.52.2.8` or not:

```
$ kubectl exec hdfs-datanode-1 -it -- /bin/bash
root@hdfs-datanode-1:/#
root@hdfs-datanode-1:/# ping -c 1 hdfs-namenode-0.hdfs-
namenode-svc.default.svc.cluster.local
PING hdfs-namenode-0.hdfs-namenode-
svc.default.svc.cluster.local (10.52.2.8): 56 data bytes
...
...
```

Looks all good! For demonstration purposes, let's access the HDFS web console to see DataNode's status.

4. To do that, use `kubectl port-forward` to access to the NameNode web port (tcp/50070):

```
//check the status by HDFS web console
$ kubectl port-forward hdfs-namenode-0 :50070
Forwarding from 127.0.0.1:60107 -> 50070
```

5. The preceding result indicates that your local machine TCP port `60107` (you result will vary) has been forwarded to NameNode Pod TCP port `50070`. Therefore, use a web browser to access `http://127.0.0.1:60107/` as follows:

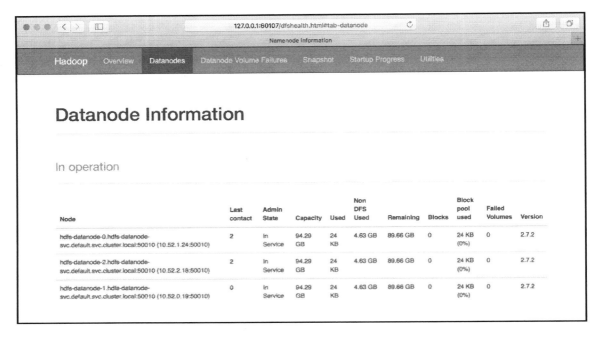

HDFS Web console shows three DataNodes

As you may see, three DataNodes have been registered to NameNode successfully. The DataNodes are also using the Headless Service so that same name convention assigns DNS names for DataNode as well.

How it works...

DaemonSets and StatefulSets; both concepts are similar but behave differently, especially when Pod is crashed. Let's take a look at how it works.

Pod recovery by DaemonSets

DaemonSets keep monitoring every Kubernetes node, so when one of the Pods crashes, DaemonSets recreates it on the same Kubernetes node.

To simulate this, go back to the DaemonSets example and use `kubectl delete pods` to delete an existing Pod from `node1` manually, as follows:

```
$ kubectl delete pod ram-check-6ldng
pod "ram-check-6ldng" deleted

$ kubectl get pods -o wide
NAME                 READY     STATUS        RESTARTS    AGE       IP
NODE
ram-check-6ldng      1/1       Terminating   0           29m
10.233.102.132       node1
ram-check-ddpdb      1/1       Running       0           29m       10.233.75.5
node2
ram-check-dpdmt      1/1       Running       0           13m       10.233.71.0
node3

$ kubectl get pods -o wide
NAME                 READY     STATUS      RESTARTS    AGE       IP
NODE
ram-check-ddpdb      1/1       Running     0           30m       10.233.75.5
node2
ram-check-dh5hq      1/1       Running     0           24s       10.233.102.135
node1
ram-check-dpdmt      1/1       Running     0           14m       10.233.71.0
node3
```

As you can see, a new Pod has been created automatically to recover the Pod in `node1`. Note that the Pod name has been changed from `ram-check-6ldng` to `ram-check-dh5hq`—it has been assigned a random suffix name. In this use case, Pod name doesn't matter, because we don't use hostname or DNS to manage this application.

Pod recovery by StatefulSet

StatefulSet behaves differently to DaemonSet during Pod recreation. In StatefulSet managed Pods, the Pod name is always consisted to assign an ordered number such as `hdfs-datanode-0`, `hdfs-datanode-1` and `hdfs-datanode-2`, and if you delete one of them, a new Pod will take over the same Pod name.

To simulate this, let's delete one DataNode (`hdfs-datanode-1`) to see how StatefulSet recreates a Pod:

```
$ kubectl get pods
NAME                 READY     STATUS       RESTARTS     AGE
hdfs-datanode-0      1/1       Running      0            3m
hdfs-datanode-1      1/1       Running      0            2m
hdfs-datanode-2      1/1       Running      0            2m
hdfs-namenode-0      1/1       Running      0            23m

//delete DataNode-1
$ kubectl delete pod hdfs-datanode-1
pod "hdfs-datanode-1" deleted

//DataNode-1 is Terminating
$ kubectl get pods
NAME                 READY     STATUS       RESTARTS     AGE
hdfs-datanode-0      1/1       Running      0            3m
hdfs-datanode-1      1/1       Terminating  0            3m
hdfs-datanode-2      1/1       Running      0            2m
hdfs-namenode-0      1/1       Running      0            23m

//DataNode-1 is recreating automatically by statefulset
$ kubectl get pods
NAME                 READY     STATUS              RESTARTS     AGE
hdfs-datanode-0      1/1       Running             0            4m
hdfs-datanode-1      0/1       ContainerCreating   0            16s
hdfs-datanode-2      1/1       Running             0            3m
hdfs-namenode-0      1/1       Running             0            24m

//DataNode-1 is recovered
$ kubectl get pods
NAME                 READY     STATUS       RESTARTS     AGE
hdfs-datanode-0      1/1       Running      0            4m
hdfs-datanode-1      1/1       Running      0            22s
hdfs-datanode-2      1/1       Running      0            3m
hdfs-namenode-0      1/1       Running      0            24m
```

As you see, the same Pod name (`hdfs-datanode-1`) has been assigned. Approximately after 10 minutes (due to HDFS's heart beat interval), HDFS web console shows that the old Pod has been marked as dead and the new Pod has the in service state, shown as follows:

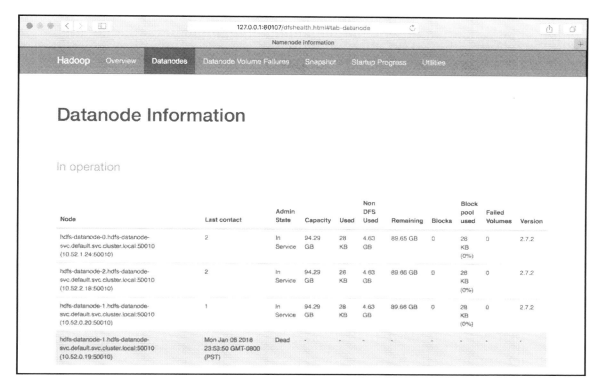

Status when one DataNode is dead

Note that this is not a perfect ideal case for HDFS, because DataNode-1 lost data and expects to re-sync from other DataNodes. If the data size is bigger, it may take a long time to complete re-sync.

Fortunately, StatefulSets has an capability that preserve a persistent volume while replacing a Pod. Let's see how HDFS DataNode can preserve data during Pod recreation.

There's more...

StatefulSet with persistent volume; it requires a `StorageClass` that provisions a volume dynamically. Because each Pod is created by StatefulSets, it will create a **persistent volume claim (PVC)** with a different identifier. If your StatefulSets specify a static name of PVC, there will be trouble if multiple Pods try to attach the same PVC.

If you have `StorageClass` on your cluster, update `datanode.yaml` to add `spec.volumeClaimTemplates` as follows:

```
$ curl
https://raw.githubusercontent.com/kubernetes-cookbook/second-edition/master
/chapter3/3-4/datanode-pv.yaml
...
  volumeClaimTemplates:
  - metadata:
      name: hdfs-data
    spec:
      accessModes: [ "ReadWriteOnce" ]
      resources:
        requests:
          storage: 10Gi
```

This tells Kubernetes to create a PVC and PV when a new Pod is created by StatefulSet. So, that Pod template (`spec.template.spec.containers.volumeMounts`) should specify `hdfs-data`, as follows:

```
$ curl
https://raw.githubusercontent.com/kubernetes-cookbook/second-edition/master
/chapter3/3-4/datanode-pv.yaml
...
          volumeMounts:
          - mountPath: /hadoop/dfs/data
            name: hdfs-data
```

Let's recreate HDFS cluster again:

```
//delete DataNodes
$ kubectl delete -f
https://raw.githubusercontent.com/kubernetes-cookbook/second-edition/master
/chapter3/3-4/datanode.yaml
service "hdfs-datanode-svc" deleted
statefulset "hdfs-datanode" deleted

//delete NameNode
$ kubectl delete -f
https://raw.githubusercontent.com/kubernetes-cookbook/second-edition/master
/chapter3/3-4/namenode.yaml
service "hdfs-namenode-svc" deleted
statefulset "hdfs-namenode" deleted


//create NameNode again
$ kubectl create -f
```

```
https://raw.githubusercontent.com/kubernetes-cookbook/second-edition/master
/chapter3/3-4/namenode.yaml
service "hdfs-namenode-svc" created
statefulset "hdfs-namenode" created

//create DataNode which uses Persistent Volume (datanode-pv.yaml)
$ kubectl create -f
https://raw.githubusercontent.com/kubernetes-cookbook/second-edition/master
/chapter3/3-4/datanode-pv.yaml
service "hdfs-datanode-svc" created
statefulset "hdfs-datanode" created

//3 PVC has been created automatically
$ kubectl get pvc
NAME STATUS VOLUME CAPACITY ACCESS MODES STORAGECLASS AGE
hdfs-data-hdfs-datanode-0 Bound pvc-bc79975d-f5bd-11e7-ac7a-42010a8a00ef
10Gi RWO standard 53s
hdfs-data-hdfs-datanode-1 Bound pvc-c753a336-f5bd-11e7-ac7a-42010a8a00ef
10Gi RWO standard 35s
hdfs-data-hdfs-datanode-2 Bound pvc-d1e10587-f5bd-11e7-ac7a-42010a8a00ef
10Gi RWO standard 17s
```

To demonstrate, use `kubectl exec` to access the NameNode, then copy some dummy files to HDFS:

```
$ kubectl exec -it hdfs-namenode-0 -- /bin/bash
root@hdfs-namenode-0:/# hadoop fs -put /lib/x86_64-linux-gnu/* /
root@hdfs-namenode-0:/# exit
command terminated with exit code 255

//delete DataNode-1
$ kubectl delete pod hdfs-datanode-1
pod "hdfs-datanode-1" deleted
```

At this moment, DataNode-1 is restarting, as shown in the following image. However, the data directory of DataNode-1 is kept by PVC as hdfs-data-hdfs-datanode-1. The new Pod hdfs-datanode-1 will take over this PVC again:

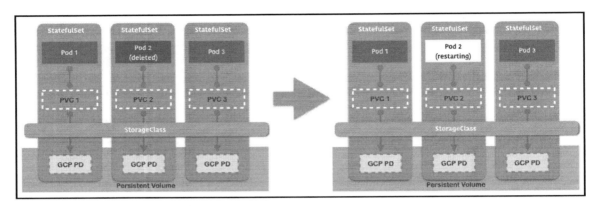

StatefulSet keeps PVC/PV while restarting

Therefore, when you access HDFS after hdfs-datanode-1 has recovered, you don't see any data loss or re-sync processes:

```
$ kubectl exec -it hdfs-namenode-0 -- /bin/bash
root@hdfs-namenode-0:/# hdfs fsck /
Connecting to namenode via
http://hdfs-namenode-0.hdfs-namenode-svc.default.svc.cluster.local:50070/fs
ck?ugi=root&path=%2F
FSCK started by root (auth:SIMPLE) from /10.52.1.13 for path / at Wed Jan
10 04:32:30 UTC 2018
.................................................................................
.......................
...................................................................Status:
HEALTHY
 Total size: 22045160 B
 Total dirs: 2
 Total files: 165
 Total symlinks: 0
 Total blocks (validated): 165 (avg. block size 133607 B)
 Minimally replicated blocks: 165 (100.0 %)
 Over-replicated blocks: 0 (0.0 %)
 Under-replicated blocks: 0 (0.0 %)
 Mis-replicated blocks: 0 (0.0 %)
 Default replication factor: 3
 Average block replication: 3.0
 Corrupt blocks: 0
```

```
 Missing replicas: 0 (0.0 %)
 Number of data-nodes: 3
 Number of racks: 1
FSCK ended at Wed Jan 10 04:32:30 UTC 2018 in 85 milliseconds


The filesystem under path '/' is HEALTHY
```

As you see, the Pod and PV pair is fully managed by StatefulSets. It is convenient if you want to scale more HDFS DataNode using just the `kubectl scale` command to make it double or hundreds—whatever you need:

```
//make double size of HDFS DataNodes
$ kubectl scale statefulset hdfs-datanode --replicas=6
statefulset "hdfs-datanode" scaled

$ kubectl get pods
NAME READY STATUS RESTARTS AGE
hdfs-datanode-0 1/1 Running 0 20m
hdfs-datanode-1 1/1 Running 0 13m
hdfs-datanode-2 1/1 Running 0 20m
hdfs-datanode-3 1/1 Running 0 56s
hdfs-datanode-4 1/1 Running 0 38s
hdfs-datanode-5 1/1 Running 0 21s
hdfs-namenode-0 1/1 Running 0 21m

$ kubectl get pvc
NAME STATUS VOLUME CAPACITY ACCESS MODES STORAGECLASS AGE
hdfs-data-hdfs-datanode-0 Bound pvc-bc79975d-f5bd-11e7-ac7a-42010a8a00ef
10Gi RWO standard 21m
hdfs-data-hdfs-datanode-1 Bound pvc-c753a336-f5bd-11e7-ac7a-42010a8a00ef
10Gi RWO standard 21m
hdfs-data-hdfs-datanode-2 Bound pvc-d1e10587-f5bd-11e7-ac7a-42010a8a00ef
10Gi RWO standard 21m
hdfs-data-hdfs-datanode-3 Bound pvc-888b6e0d-f5c0-11e7-ac7a-42010a8a00ef
10Gi RWO standard 1m
hdfs-data-hdfs-datanode-4 Bound pvc-932e6148-f5c0-11e7-ac7a-42010a8a00ef
10Gi RWO standard 1m
hdfs-data-hdfs-datanode-5 Bound pvc-9dd71bf5-f5c0-11e7-ac7a-42010a8a00ef
10Gi RWO standard 1m
```

 You can also use PV to NameNode to persist metadata. However, `kubectl` scale does not work well due to HDFS architecture. In order to have high availability or scale out HDFS NameNode, please visit the HDFS Federation document at : `https://hadoop.apache.org/docs/stable/hadoop-project-dist/hadoop-hdfs/Federation.html`.

See also

In this recipe, we went deeply into Kubernetes Pod management through DaemonSets and StatefulSet. It manages Pod in a particular way, such as Pod per node and consistent Pod names. It is useful when the Deployments/ReplicaSets stateless Pod management style can't cover your application use cases. For further information, consider the following:

- The *Working with Pods* recipe in Chapter 2, *Walking through Kubernetes Concepts*
- Working with configuration files

Submitting Jobs on Kubernetes

Your container application is designed not only for daemon processes such as nginx, but also for some batch Jobs which eventually exit when the task is complete. Kubernetes supports this scenario; you can submit a container as a Job and Kubernetes will dispatch to an appropriate node and execute your Job.

In this recipe, we will discuss two new features: **Jobs** and **CronJob**. These two features can make another usage of Pods to utilize your resources.

Getting ready

Since Kubernetes version 1.2, Kubernetes Jobs has been introduced as a stable feature (apiVersion: batch/v1). In addition, CronJob is a beta feature (apiVersion: batch/v1beta1) as of Kubernetes version 1.10.

Both work well on **minikube,** which was introduced at Chapter 1, *Building Your Own Kubernetes Cluster.* Therefore, this recipe will use minikube version 0.24.1.

How to do it...

When submitting a Job to Kubernetes, you have three types of Job that you can define:

- Single Job
- Repeat Job
- Parallel Job

Pod as a single Job

A Job-like Pod is suitable for testing your containers, which can be used for unit test or integration test; alternatively, it can be used for batch programs:

1. In the following example, we will write a Job template to check the packages installed in image Ubuntu:

```
$ cat job-dpkg.yaml
apiVersion: batch/v1
kind: Job
metadata:
  name: package-check
spec:
  template:
    spec:
      containers:
      - name: package-check
        image: ubuntu
        command: ["dpkg-query", "-l"]
      restartPolicy: Never
```

Note that restart policy for Pods created in a Job should be set to `Never` or `OnFailure`, since a Job goes to termination once it is completed successfully.

2. Now, you are ready to create a `job` using your template:

```
$ kubectl create -f job-dpkg.yaml
job.batch "package-check" created
```

3. After creating a `job` object, it is possible to verify the status of both the Pod and Job:

```
$ kubectl get jobs
NAME            DESIRED   SUCCESSFUL   AGE
package-check   1         1            26s
```

4. This result indicates that Job is already done, executed (by `SUCCESSFUL = 1`) in `26` seconds. In this case, Pod has already disappeared:

```
$ kubectl get pods
No resources found, use --show-all to see completed objects.
```

5. As you can see, the `kubectl` command hints to us that we can use `--show-all` or `-a` option to find the completed Pod, as follows:

```
$ kubectl get pods --show-all
NAME                    READY   STATUS      RESTARTS   AGE
package-check-hmjxj     0/1     Completed   0          3m
```

Here you go. So why does the `Completed` Pod object remain? Because you may want to see the result after your program has ended. You will find that a Pod is booting up for handling this task. This Pod is going to be stopped very soon at the end of the process.

6. Use the subcommand `kubectl logs` to get the result:

```
$ kubectl logs package-check-hmjxj
Desired=Unknown/Install/Remove/Purge/Hold
| Status=Not/Inst/Conf-files/Unpacked/halF-conf/Half-inst/trig-
aWait/Trig-pend
|/ Err?=(none)/Reinst-required (Status,Err: uppercase=bad)
||/ Name                    Version
Architecture Description
+++-=================================-===================================-
============-
=====================================================================
=======
ii   adduser                3.113+nmu3ubuntu4                  all
add and remove users and groups
ii   apt                    1.2.24
amd64         commandline package manager
ii   base-files             9.4ubuntu4.5
amd64         Debian base system miscellaneous files
ii   base-passwd            3.5.39
amd64         Debian base system master password and group files
ii   bash                   4.3-14ubuntu1.2
amd64         GNU Bourne Again SHell
.
.
.
```

7. Please go ahead and check the `job package-check` using the subcommand `kubectl describe`; the confirmation for Pod completion and other messages are shown as system information:

```
$ kubectl describe job package-check
Name:          package-check
Namespace:     default
```

```
Selector:          controller-uid=9dfd1857-f5d1-11e7-8233-
ae782244bd54
Labels:            controller-uid=9dfd1857-f5d1-11e7-8233-
ae782244bd54

                   job-name=package-check
Annotations:       <none>
Parallelism:       1
Completions:       1
Start Time:        Tue, 09 Jan 2018 22:43:50 -0800
Pods Statuses:     0 Running / 1 Succeeded / 0 Failed
.
.
.
```

8. Later, to remove the `job` you just created, delete it with the name. This also removes the completed Pod as well:

```
$ kubectl delete jobs package-check
job.batch "package-check" deleted

$ kubectl get pods --show-all
No resources found.
```

Create a repeatable Job

Users can also decide the number of tasks that should be finished in a single Job. It is helpful to solve some random and sampling problems. Let's try it on the same template in the previous example:

1. Add the `spec.completions` item to indicate the Pod number:

```
$ cat job-dpkg-repeat.yaml
apiVersion: batch/v1
kind: Job
metadata:
  name: package-check
spec:
  completions: 3
  template:
    spec:
      containers:
      - name: package-check
        image: ubuntu
        command: ["dpkg-query", "-l"]
      restartPolicy: Never
```

2. After creating this Job, check how the Pod looks with the subcommand `kubectl describe`:

```
$ kubectl create -f job-dpkg-repeat.yaml
job.batch "package-check" created

$ kubectl describe jobs package-check
Name:           package-check
Namespace:      default
...
...
Annotations:    <none>
Parallelism:    1
Completions:    3
Start Time:     Tue, 09 Jan 2018 22:58:09 -0800
Pods Statuses:  0 Running / 3 Succeeded / 0 Failed
...
...
Events:
  Type     Reason           Age   From             Message
  ----     ------           ----  ----             -------
  Normal   SuccessfulCreate 42s   job-controller   Created pod:
package-check-f72wk
  Normal   SuccessfulCreate 32s   job-controller   Created pod:
package-check-2mnw8
  Normal   SuccessfulCreate 27s   job-controller   Created pod:
package-check-whbr6
```

As you can see, three Pods are created to complete this Job. This is useful if you need to run your program repeatedly at particular times. However, as you may have noticed from the Age column in preceding result, these Pods ran sequentially, one by one. This means that the 2nd Job was started after the 1st Job was completed, and the 3rd Job was started after the 2nd Job was completed.

Create a parallel Job

If your batch Job doesn't have a state or dependency between Jobs, you may consider submitting Jobs in parallel. Similar to the `spec.completions` parameter, the Job template has a `spec.parallelism` parameter to specify how many Jobs you want to run in parallel:

1. Re-use a repeatable Job but change it to specify `spec.parallelism: 3` as follows:

```
$ cat job-dpkg-parallel.yaml
apiVersion: batch/v1
```

```
kind: Job
metadata:
  name: package-check
spec:
  parallelism: 3
  template:
    spec:
      containers:
      - name: package-check
        image: ubuntu
        command: ["dpkg-query", "-l"]
      restartPolicy: Never
```

2. The result is similar to `spec.completions=3`, which made 3 Pods to run your application:

```
$ kubectl get pods --show-all
NAME                   READY   STATUS      RESTARTS   AGE
package-check-5jhr8    0/1     Completed   0          1m
package-check-5zlmx    0/1     Completed   0          1m
package-check-glkpc    0/1     Completed   0          1m
```

3. However, if you see an `Age` column through the `kubectl describe` command, it indicates that 3 Pods ran at the same time:

```
$ kubectl describe jobs package-check
Name:           package-check
Namespace:      default
Selector:       controller-uid=de41164e-f5d6-11e7-8233-
ae782244bd54
Labels:         controller-uid=de41164e-f5d6-11e7-8233-
ae782244bd54

                job-name=package-check
Annotations:    <none>
Parallelism:    3
Completions:    <unset>
...
Events:
  Type    Reason           Age   From            Message
  ----    ------           ----  ----            -------
  Normal  SuccessfulCreate 24s   job-controller  Created pod:
package-check-5jhr8
  Normal  SuccessfulCreate 24s   job-controller  Created pod:
package-check-glkpc
  Normal  SuccessfulCreate 24s   job-controller  Created pod:
package-check-5zlmx
```

In this setting, Kubernetes can dispatch to an available node to run your application and that easily scale your Jobs. It is useful if you want to run something like a worker application to distribute a bunch of Pods to different nodes.

Schedule to run Job using CronJob

If you are familiar with **UNIX CronJob** or **Java Quartz** (`http://www.quartz-scheduler.org`), Kubernetes CronJob is a very straightforward tool that you can define a particular timing to run your Kubernetes Job repeatedly.

The scheduling format is very simple; it specifies the following five items:

- Minutes (0 – 59)
- Hours (0 – 23)
- Day of Month (1 – 31)
- Month (1 – 12)
- Day of week (0: Sunday – 6: Saturday)

For example, if you want to run your Job only at 9:00am on November 12th, every year, to send a birthday greeting to me :-), the schedule format could be `0 9 12 11 *`.

You may also use slash (/) to specify a step value; a `run every 5 minutes` interval for the previous Job example would have the following schedule format: `*/5 * * * *`.

In addition, there is an optional parameter, `spec.concurrencyPolicy`, that you can specify a behavior if the previous Job is not finished but the next Job schedule is approaching, to determine how the next Job runs. You can set either:

- **Allow**: Allow execution of the next Job
- **Forbid**: Skip execution of the next Job
- **Replace**: Delete the current Job, then execute the next Job

If you set as `Allow`, there might be a potential risk of accumulating some unfinished Jobs in the Kubernetes cluster. Therefore, during the testing phase, you should set either `Forbid` or `Replace` to monitor Job execution and completion:

```
$ cat cron-job.yaml
apiVersion: batch/v1beta1
kind: CronJob
metadata:
  name: package-check
```

```
spec:
  schedule: "*/5 * * * *"
  concurrencyPolicy: "Forbid"
  jobTemplate:
    spec:
      template:
        spec:
          containers:
          - name: package-check
            image: ubuntu
            command: ["dpkg-query", "-l"]
          restartPolicy: Never

//create CronJob
$ kubectl create -f cron-job.yaml
cronjob.batch "package-check" created


$ kubectl get cronjob
NAME            SCHEDULE       SUSPEND     ACTIVE     LAST SCHEDULE     AGE
package-check   */5 * * * *    False       0          <none>
```

After a few moments, the Job will be triggered by your desired timing—in this case, every 5 minutes. You may then see the Job entry through the `kubectl get jobs` and `kubectl get pods -a` commands, as follows:

```
//around 9 minutes later, 2 jobs have been submitted already
$ kubectl get jobs
NAME                         DESIRED     SUCCESSFUL     AGE
package-check-1515571800     1           1              7m
package-check-1515572100     1           1              2m


//correspond Pod are remain and find by -a option
$ kubectl get pods -a
NAME                              READY     STATUS        RESTARTS     AGE
package-check-1515571800-jbzbr    0/1       Completed     0            7m
package-check-1515572100-bp5fz    0/1       Completed     0            2m
```

CronJob will keep remaining until you delete; this means that, every 5 minutes, CronJob will create a new Job entry and related Pods will also keep getting created. This will impact the consumption of Kubernetes resources. Therefore, by default, CronJob will keep up to 3 successful Jobs (by `spec.successfulJobsHistoryLimit`) and one failed Job (by `spec.failedJobsHistoryLimit`). You can change these parameters based on your requirements.

Overall, CronJob supplement allows Jobs to automatically to run in your application with the desired timing. You can utilize CronJob to run some report generation Jobs, daily or weekly batch Jobs, and so on.

How it works...

Although Jobs and CronJob are the special utilities of Pods, the Kubernetes system has different management systems between them and Pods.

For Job, its selector cannot point to an existing pod. It is a bad idea to take a Pod controlled by the deployment/ReplicaSets as a Job. The deployment/ReplicaSets have a desired number of Pods running, which is against Job's ideal situation: Pods should be deleted once they finish their tasks. The Pod in the Deployments/ReplicaSets won't reach the state of end.

See also

In this recipe, we executed Jobs and CronJob, demonstrating another usage of Kubernetes Pod that has a completion state. Even once a Pod is completed, Kubernetes can preserve the logs and Pod object so that you can retrieve the result easily. For further information, consider:

- The *Working with Pods* recipe in `Chapter 2`, *Walking through Kubernetes Concepts*
- *Working with configuration files*

Working with configuration files

Kubernetes supports two different file formats, *YAML* and *JSON*. Each format can describe the same function of Kubernetes.

Getting ready

Before we study how to write a Kubernetes configuration file, learning how to write a correct template format is important. We can learn the standard format of both YAML and JSON from their official websites.

YAML

The YAML format is very simple, with few syntax rules; therefore, it is easy to read and write, even for users. To know more about YAML, you can refer to the following website link: `http://www.yaml.org/spec/1.2/spec.html`. The following example uses the YAML format to set up the `nginx` Pod:

```
$ cat nginx-pod.yaml
apiVersion: v1
kind: Pod
metadata:
  name: my-nginx
  labels:
    env: dev
spec:
  containers:
  - name: my-nginx
    image: nginx
    ports:
    - containerPort: 80
```

JSON

The JSON format is also simple and easy to read for users, but more program-friendly. Because it has data types (number, string, Boolean, and object), it is popular to exchange the data between systems. Technically, YAML is a superset of JSON, so JSON is a valid YAML, but not the other way around. To know more about JSON, you can refer to the following website link: `http://json.org/`.

The following example of the Pod is the same as the preceding YAML format, but using the JSON format:

```
$ cat nginx-pod.json
{
  "apiVersion": "v1",
  "kind": "Pod",
  "metadata": {
      "name": "my-nginx",
      "labels": {
              "env": "dev"
      }
  },
  "spec": {
    "containers": [
      {
```

```
        "name": "my-nginx",
        "image": "nginx",
        "ports": [
          {
            "containerPort": 80
          }
        ]
      }
    ]
  }
}
```

How to do it...

Kubernetes has a schema that is defined using a verify configuration format; schema can be generated after the first instance of running the subcommand `create` with a configuration file. The cached schema will be stored under the
`.kube/cache/discovery/<SERVICE_IP>_<PORT>`, based on the version of API server you run:

```
// create the resource by either YAML or JSON file introduced before
$ kubectl create -f nginx-pod.yaml
// or
$ kubectl create -f nginx-pod.json
// as an example of v1.10.0, the content of schema directory may look like
following
// you would have different endpoint of server
ll ~/.kube/cache/discovery/192.168.99.100_8443/
total 76
drwxr-xr-x 18 nosus nosus 4096 May 6 10:10 ./
drwxr-xr-x 4 nosus nosus 4096 May 6 10:00 ../
drwxr-xr-x 3 nosus nosus 4096 May 6 10:00 admissionregistration.k8s.io/
drwxr-xr-x 3 nosus nosus 4096 May 6 10:00 apiextensions.k8s.io/
drwxr-xr-x 4 nosus nosus 4096 May 6 10:00 apiregistration.k8s.io/
drwxr-xr-x 5 nosus nosus 4096 May 6 10:00 apps/
drwxr-xr-x 4 nosus nosus 4096 May 6 10:00 authentication.k8s.io/
drwxr-xr-x 4 nosus nosus 4096 May 6 10:00 authorization.k8s.io/
drwxr-xr-x 4 nosus nosus 4096 May 6 10:00 autoscaling/
drwxr-xr-x 4 nosus nosus 4096 May 6 10:00 batch/
drwxr-xr-x 3 nosus nosus 4096 May 6 10:00 certificates.k8s.io/
drwxr-xr-x 3 nosus nosus 4096 May 6 10:00 events.k8s.io/
drwxr-xr-x 3 nosus nosus 4096 May 6 10:00 extensions/
drwxr-xr-x 3 nosus nosus 4096 May 6 10:00 networking.k8s.io/
drwxr-xr-x 3 nosus nosus 4096 May 6 10:00 policy/
drwxr-xr-x 4 nosus nosus 4096 May 6 10:00 rbac.authorization.k8s.io/
```

```
-rwxr-xr-x 1 nosus nosus 3898 May 6 10:10 servergroups.json*
drwxr-xr-x 4 nosus nosus 4096 May 6 10:00 storage.k8s.io/
drwxr-xr-x 2 nosus nosus 4096 May 6 10:10 v1/
```

Each directory listed represents an API category. You will see a file named
`serverresources.json` under the last layer of each directory, which clearly defines every
resource covered by this API category. However, there are some alternative and easier
ways to check the schema. From the website of Kubernetes, we can get any details of how
to write a configuration file of specific resources. Go ahead and check the official API
documentation of the latest version: `https://kubernetes.io/docs/reference/generated/kubernetes-api/v1.10/`. In the webpage, there are three panels: from left to right, they are
the resource list, description, and the input and output of HTTP requests or the command
kubectl. Taking Deployment as an example, you may click **Deployment v1 app** at the
resource list, the leftmost panel, and the following screenshot will show up:

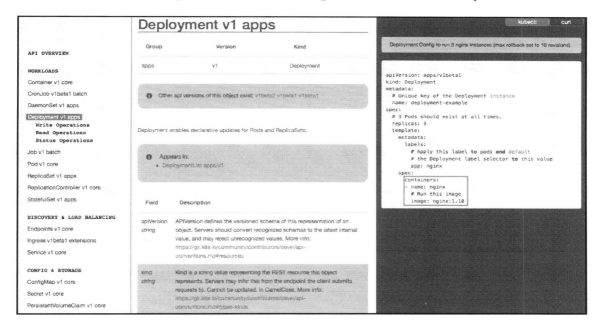

Documentation of Kubernetes Deployment API

But, how do we know the details of setting the container part at the marked place on the preceding image? In the field part of object description, there are two values. The first one, like **apiVersion**, means the name, and the second one, like **string**, is the type. Type could be integer, string, array, or the other resource object. Therefore, for searching the containers configuration of deployment, we need to know the structure of layers of objects. First, according to the example configuration file on web page, the layer of objects to containers is `spec.template.spec.containers`. So, start by clicking the hyperlink **spec DeploymentSpec** under Deployment's fields, which is the type of resource object, and go searching hierarchically. Finally, you can find the details listed on this page: `https://kubernetes.io/docs/reference/generated/kubernetes-api/v1.10/#container-v1-core`.

Solution for tracing the configuration of containers of Deployment
Here comes the solution for the preceding example:

- Click **spec DeploymentSpec**
- Click **template PodTemplateSpec**
- Click **spec PodSpec**
- Click **containers Container array**

Now you got it!

Taking a careful look at the definition of container configuration. The following are some common descriptions you should pay attention to:

- **Type**: The user should always set the corresponding type for an item.
- **Optional or not**: Some items are indicated as optional, which means not necessary, and can be applied as a default value, or not set if you don't specify it.
- **Cannot be updated**: If the item is indicated as failed to be updated, it is fixed when the resource is created. You need to recreate a new one instead of updating it.
- **Read-only**: Some of the items are indicated as `read-only`, such as UID. Kubernetes generates these items. If you specify this in the configuration file, it will be ignored.

Another method for checking the schema is through swagger UI. Kubernetes uses swagger (`https://swagger.io/`) and OpenAPI (`https://www.openapis.org`) to generate the REST API. Nevertheless, the web console for swagger is by default disabled in the API server. To enable the swagger UI of your own Kubernetes API server, just add the flag `--enable-swagger-ui=ture` when you start the API server. Then, by accessing the endpoint `https://<KUBERNETES_MASTER>:<API_SERVER_PORT>/swagger-ui`, you can successfully browse the API document through the web console:

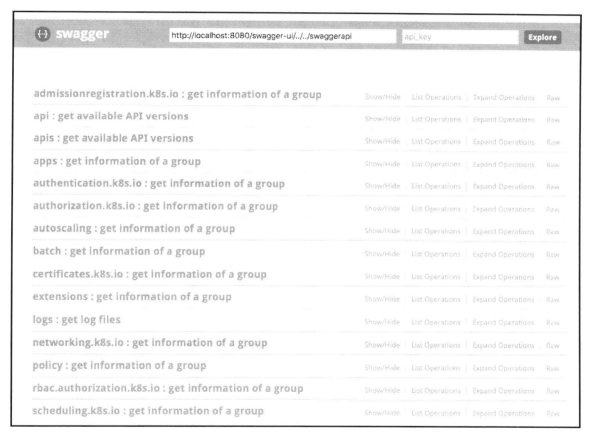

The swagger web console of Kubernetes API

How it works...

Let's introduce some necessary items in configuration files for creating Pod, Deployment, and Service.

Pod

Item	Type	Example
apiVersion	String	v1
kind	String	Pod
metadata.name	String	my-nginx-pod
spec	v1.PodSpec	
v1.PodSpec.containers	Array[v1.Container]	
v1.Container.name	String	my-nginx
v1.Container.image	String	nginx

Deployment

Item	Type	Example
apiVersion	String	apps/v1beta1
kind	String	Deployment
metadata.name	String	my-nginx-deploy
spec	v1.DeploymentSpec	
v1.DeploymentSpec.template	v1.PodTemplateSpec	
v1.PodTemplateSpec.metadata.labels	Map of string	env: test
v1.PodTemplateSpec.spec	v1.PodSpec	my-nginx
v1.PodSpec.containers	Array[v1.Container]	As same as Pod

Service

Item	Type	Example
apiVersion	String	v1
kind	String	Service
metadata.name	String	my-nginx-svc
spec	v1.ServiceSpec	
v1.ServiceSpec.selector	Map of string	env: test

`v1.ServiceSpec.ports`	Array[`v1.ServicePort`]	
`v1.ServicePort.protocol`	String	TCP
`v1.ServicePort.port`	Integer	80

Please check the code bundle file `minimal-conf-resource.yaml` to find these three resources with minimal configuration.

See also

This recipe described how to find and understand a configuration syntax. Kubernetes has some detailed options to define containers and components. For more details, the following recipes will describe how to define Pods, Deployments, and Services:

- The *Working with Pods, Deployment API,* and *Working with Services* recipes in `Chapter 2`, *Walking through Kubernetes Concepts*

4
Building High-Availability Clusters

In this chapter, we will cover the following recipes:

- Clustering etcd
- Building multiple masters

Introduction

Avoiding a single point of failure is a concept we need to always keep in mind. In this chapter, you will learn how to build components in Kubernetes with high availability. We will also go through the steps to build a three-node etcd cluster and masters with multinodes.

Clustering etcd

etcd stores network information and states in Kubernetes. Any data loss could be crucial. Clustering etcd is strongly recommended in a production environment. etcd comes with support for clustering; a cluster of N members can tolerate up to $(N-1)/2$ failures. Typically, there are three mechanisms for creating an etcd cluster. They are as follows:

- Static
- etcd discovery
- DNS discovery

Static is a simple way to bootstrap an etcd cluster if we have all etcd members provisioned before starting. However, it's more common if we use an existing etcd cluster to bootstrap a new member. Then, the discovery method comes into play. The discovery service uses an existing cluster to bootstrap itself. It allows a new member in an etcd cluster to find other existing members. In this recipe, we will discuss how to bootstrap an etcd cluster via static and etcd discovery manually.

We learned how to use kubeadm and kubespray in Chapter 1, *Building Your Own Kubernetes Cluster*. At the time of writing, HA work in kubeadm is still in progress. Regularly backing up your etcd node is recommended in the official documentation. The other tool we introduced, kubespray, on the other hand, supports multi-nodes etcd natively. In this chapter, we'll also describe how to configure etcd in kubespray.

Getting ready

Before we learn a more flexible way to set up an etcd cluster, we should know etcd comes with two major versions so far, which are v2 and v3. etcd3 is a newer version that aims to be more stable, efficient, and reliable. Here is a simple comparison to introduce the major differences in their implementation:

	etcd2	etcd3
Protocol	http	gRPC
Key expiration	TTL mechanism	Leases
Watchers	Long polling over HTTP	Via a bidirectional gRPC stream

etcd3 aims to be the next generation of etcd2 . etcd3 supports the gRPC protocol by default. gRPC uses HTTP2, which allows multiple RPC streams over a TCP connection. In etcd2, however, a HTTP request must establish a connection in every request it makes. For dealing with key expiration, in etcd2, a TTL attaches to a key; the client should periodically refresh the keys to see if any keys have expired. This will establish lots of connections.

In etcd3, the lease concept was introduced. A lease can attach multiple keys; when a lease expires, it'll delete all attached keys. For the watcher, the etcd2 client creates long polling over HTTP—this means a TCP connection is opened per watch. However, etcd3 uses bidirectional gRPC stream implementation, which allows multiple steams to share the same connection.

Although etcd3 is preferred. However, some deployments still use etcd2. We'll still introduce how to use those tools to achieve clustering, since data migration in etcd is well-documented and smooth. For more information, please refer to the upgrade migration steps at `https://coreos.com/blog/migrating-applications-etcd-v3.html`.

Before we start building an etcd cluster, we have to decide how many members we need. How big the etcd cluster should be really depends on the environment you want to create. In the production environment, at least three members are recommended. Then, the cluster can tolerate at least one permanent failure. In this recipe, we will use three members as an example of a development environment:

Name/hostname	IP address
ip-172-31-3-80	172.31.3.80
ip-172-31-14-133	172.31.14.133
ip-172-31-13-239	172.31.13.239

Secondly, the etcd service requires `port 2379` (4001 for legacy uses) for etcd client communication and `port 2380` for peer communication. These ports have to be exposed in your environment.

How to do it...

There are plenty of ways to provision an etcd cluster. Normally, you'll use kubespray, kops (in AWS), or other provisioning tools.

Here, we'll simply show you how to perform a manual install. It's fairly easy as well:

```
// etcd installation script
$ cat install-etcd.sh
ETCD_VER=v3.3.0

# ${DOWNLOAD_URL} could be ${GOOGLE_URL} or ${GITHUB_URL}
GOOGLE_URL=https://storage.googleapis.com/etcd
GITHUB_URL=https://github.com/coreos/etcd/releases/download
DOWNLOAD_URL=${GOOGLE_URL}

# delete tmp files
rm -f /tmp/etcd-${ETCD_VER}-linux-amd64.tar.gz
rm -rf /tmp/etcd && rm -rf /etc/etcd && mkdir -p /etc/etcd

curl -L ${DOWNLOAD_URL}/${ETCD_VER}/etcd-${ETCD_VER}-linux-amd64.tar.gz -o
/tmp/etcd-${ETCD_VER}-linux-amd64.tar.gz
tar xzvf /tmp/etcd-${ETCD_VER}-linux-amd64.tar.gz -C /etc/etcd --strip-
```

```
components=1
rm -f /tmp/etcd-${ETCD_VER}-linux-amd64.tar.gz

# check etcd version
/etc/etcd/etcd --version
```

This script will put `etcd` binary under `/etc/etcd` folder. You're free to put them in different place. We'll need `sudo` in order to put them under `/etc` in this case:

```
// install etcd on linux
# sudo sh install-etcd.sh
...
etcd Version: 3.3.0
Git SHA: c23606781
Go Version: go1.9.3
Go OS/Arch: linux/amd64
```

The version we're using now is 3.3.0. After we check the `etcd` binary work on your machine, we can attach it to the default `$PATH` as follows. Then we don't need to include the`/etc/etcd` path every time we execute the `etcd` command:

```
$ export PATH=/etc/etcd:$PATH
$ export ETCDCTL_API=3
```

You also can put it into your `.bashrc` or `.bash_profile` to let it set by default.

After we have at least three etcd servers provisioned, it's time to make them pair together.

Static mechanism

A static mechanism is the easiest way to set up a cluster. However, the IP address of every member should be known beforehand. This means that if you bootstrap an etcd cluster in a cloud provider environment, the static mechanism might not be so practical. Therefore, etcd also provides a discovery mechanism to bootstrap itself from the existing cluster.

To make etcd communications secure, etcd supports TLS channels to encrypt the communication between peers, and also clients and servers. Each member needs to have a unique key pair. In this section, we'll show you how to use automatically generated certificates to build a cluster.

 In CoreOs GitHub, there is a handy tool we can use to generate self-signed certificates (https://github.com/coreos/etcd/tree/v3.2.15/hack/tls-setup) . After cloning the repo, we have to modify a configuration file under config/req-csr.json. Here is an example:

```
// sample config, put under $repo/config/req-csr.json
$ cat config/req-csr.json
{
  "CN": "etcd",
  "hosts": [
    "172.31.3.80",
    "172.31.14.133",
    "172.31.13.239"
  ],
  "key": {
    "algo": "ecdsa",
    "size": 384
  },
  "names": [
    {
      "O": "autogenerated",
      "OU": "etcd cluster",
      "L": "the internet"
    }
  ]
}
```

In the next step we'll need to have Go (https://golang.org/) installed and set up $GOPATH:

```
$ export GOPATH=$HOME/go
$ make
```

Then the certs will be generated under ./certs/.

First, we'll have to set a bootstrap configuration to declare what members will be inside the cluster:

```
// set as environment variables, or alternatively, passing by --initial-
cluster and --initial-cluster-state parameters inside launch command.
#
ETCD_INITIAL_CLUSTER="etcd0=http://172.31.3.80:2380,etcd1=http://172.31.14.
133:2380,etcd2=http://172.31.13.239:2380"
ETCD_INITIAL_CLUSTER_STATE=new
```

In all three nodes, we'll have to launch the etcd server separately:

```
// first node: 172.31.3.80
# etcd --name etcd0 --initial-advertise-peer-urls https://172.31.3.80:2380
\
  --listen-peer-urls https://172.31.3.80:2380 \
  --listen-client-urls https://172.31.3.80:2379,https://127.0.0.1:2379 \
  --advertise-client-urls https://172.31.3.80:2379 \
  --initial-cluster-token etcd-cluster-1 \
  --initial-cluster
etcd0=https://172.31.3.80:2380,etcd1=https://172.31.14.133:2380,etcd2=https
://172.31.13.239:2380 \
  --initial-cluster-state new \
  --auto-tls \
  --peer-auto-tls
```

Then, you'll see the following output:

```
2018-02-06 22:15:20.508687 I | etcdmain: etcd Version: 3.3.0
2018-02-06 22:15:20.508726 I | etcdmain: Git SHA: c23606781
2018-02-06 22:15:20.508794 I | etcdmain: Go Version: go1.9.3
2018-02-06 22:15:20.508824 I | etcdmain: Go OS/Arch: linux/amd64
...
2018-02-06 22:15:21.439067 N | etcdserver/membership: set the initial
cluster version to 3.0
2018-02-06 22:15:21.439134 I | etcdserver/api: enabled capabilities for
version 3.0
```

Let's wake up the second etcd service:

```
// second node: 172.31.14.133
$ etcd --name etcd1 --initial-advertise-peer-urls
```

```
https://172.31.14.133:2380 \
  --listen-peer-urls https://172.31.14.133:2380 \
  --listen-client-urls https://172.31.14.133:2379,https://127.0.0.1:2379 \
  --advertise-client-urls https://172.31.14.133:2379 \
  --initial-cluster-token etcd-cluster-1 \
  --initial-cluster
etcd0=https://172.31.3.80:2380,etcd1=https://172.31.14.133:2380,etcd2=https
://172.31.13.239:2380 \
  --initial-cluster-state new \
  --auto-tls \
  --peer-auto-tls
```

You'll see similar logs in the console:

```
2018-02-06 22:15:20.646320 I | etcdserver: starting member ce7c9e3024722f01
in cluster a7e82f7083dba2c1
2018-02-06 22:15:20.646384 I | raft: ce7c9e3024722f01 became follower at
term 0
2018-02-06 22:15:20.646397 I | raft: newRaft ce7c9e3024722f01 [peers: [],
term: 0, commit: 0, applied: 0, lastindex: 0, lastterm: 0]
2018-02-06 22:15:20.646403 I | raft: ce7c9e3024722f01 became follower at
term 1
...
2018-02-06 22:15:20.675928 I | rafthttp: starting peer 25654e0e7ea045f8...
2018-02-06 22:15:20.676024 I | rafthttp: started HTTP pipelining with peer
25654e0e7ea045f8
2018-02-06 22:15:20.678515 I | rafthttp: started streaming with peer
25654e0e7ea045f8 (writer)
2018-02-06 22:15:20.678717 I | rafthttp: started streaming with peer
25654e0e7ea045f8 (writer)
```

It starts pairing with our previous node (25654e0e7ea045f8). Let's trigger the following
command in the third node:

```
// third node: 172.31.13.239
$ etcd --name etcd2 --initial-advertise-peer-urls
https://172.31.13.239:2380 \
  --listen-peer-urls https://172.31.13.239:2380 \
  --listen-client-urls https://172.31.13.239:2379,https://127.0.0.1:2379 \
  --advertise-client-urls https://172.31.13.239:2379 \
  --initial-cluster-token etcd-cluster-1 \
  --initial-cluster
etcd0=https://172.31.3.80:2380,etcd1=https://172.31.14.133:2380,etcd2=https
://172.31.13.239:2380 \
  --initial-cluster-state new \
  --auto-tls \
  --peer-auto-tls
```

```
// in node2 console, it listens and receives new member (4834416c2c1e751e)
added.
2018-02-06 22:15:20.679548 I | rafthttp: starting peer 4834416c2c1e751e...
2018-02-06 22:15:20.679642 I | rafthttp: started HTTP pipelining with peer
4834416c2c1e751e
2018-02-06 22:15:20.679923 I | rafthttp: started streaming with peer
25654e0e7ea045f8 (stream Message reader)
2018-02-06 22:15:20.680190 I | rafthttp: started streaming with peer
25654e0e7ea045f8 (stream MsgApp v2 reader)
2018-02-06 22:15:20.680364 I | rafthttp: started streaming with peer
4834416c2c1e751e (writer)
2018-02-06 22:15:20.681880 I | rafthttp: started peer 4834416c2c1e751e
2018-02-06 22:15:20.681909 I | rafthttp: added peer 4834416c2c1e751e
After all nodes are in, it'll start to elect the leader inside the cluster,
we could find it in the logs:
2018-02-06 22:15:21.334985 I | raft: raft.node: ce7c9e3024722f01 elected
leader 4834416c2c1e751e at term 27
...
2018-02-06 22:17:21.510271 N | etcdserver/membership: updated the cluster
version from 3.0 to 3.3
2018-02-06 22:17:21.510343 I | etcdserver/api: enabled capabilities for
version 3.3
```

And the cluster is set. We should check to see if it works properly:

```
$ etcdctl cluster-health
member 25654e0e7ea045f8is healthy: got healthy result from
http://172.31.3.80:2379
member ce7c9e3024722f01 is healthy: got healthy result from
http://172.31.14.133:2379
member 4834416c2c1e751e is healthy: got healthy result from
http://172.31.13.239:2379
```

Discovery mechanism

Discovery provides a more flexible way to create a cluster. It doesn't need to know other peer IPs beforehand. It uses an existing etcd cluster to bootstrap one. In this section, we'll demonstrate how to leverage that to launch a three-node etcd cluster:

1. Firstly, we'll need to have an existing cluster with three-node configuration. Luckily, the etcd official website provides a discovery service (https://discovery.etcd.io/new?size=n); n will be the number of nodes in your etcd cluster, which is ready to use:

   ```
   // get a request URL
   ```

```
# curl -w "n" 'https://discovery.etcd.io/new?size=3'
https://discovery.etcd.io/f6a3fb54b3fd1bb02e26a89fd40df0e8
```

2. Then we are able to use the URL to bootstrap a cluster easily. The command line is pretty much the same as in the static mechanism. What we need to do is change —initial-cluster to –discovery, which is used to specify the discovery service URL:

```
// in node1, 127.0.0.1 is used for internal client listeneretcd
-name ip-172-31-3-80 -initial-advertise-peer-urls
http://172.31.3.80:2380   -listen-peer-urls
http://172.31.3.80:2380   -listen-client-urls
http://172.31.3.80:2379,http://127.0.0.1:2379  -advertise-
client-urls http://172.31.3.80:2379  -discovery
https://discovery.etcd.io/f6a3fb54b3fd1bb02e26a89fd40df0e8

// in node2, 127.0.0.1 is used for internal client listener
etcd -name ip-172-31-14-133 -initial-advertise-peer-urls
http://172.31.14.133:2380   -listen-peer-urls
http://172.31.14.133:2380   -listen-client-urls
http://172.31.14.133:2379,http://127.0.0.1:2379  -advertise-
client-urls http://172.31.14.133:2379  -discovery
https://discovery.etcd.io/f6a3fb54b3fd1bb02e26a89fd40df0e8

// in node3, 127.0.0.1 is used for internal client listener
etcd -name ip-172-31-13-239 -initial-advertise-peer-urls
http://172.31.13.239:2380   -listen-peer-urls
http://172.31.13.239:2380   -listen-client-urls
http://172.31.13.239:2379,http://127.0.0.1:2379  -advertise-
client-urls http://172.31.13.239:2379  -discovery
https://discovery.etcd.io/f6a3fb54b3fd1bb02e26a89fd40df0e8
```

3. Let's take a closer look at node1's log:

```
2018-02-10 04:58:03.819963 I | etcdmain: etcd Version: 3.3.0
...
2018-02-10 04:58:03.820400 I | embed: listening for peers on
http://172.31.3.80:2380
2018-02-10 04:58:03.820427 I | embed: listening for client
requests on
127.0.0.1:2379
2018-02-10 04:58:03.820444 I | embed: listening for client
requests on 172.31.3.80:2379
2018-02-10 04:58:03.947753 N | discovery: found self
f60c98e749d41d1b in the cluster
2018-02-10 04:58:03.947771 N | discovery: found 1 peer(s),
waiting for 2 more
```

```
2018-02-10 04:58:22.289571 N | discovery: found peer
6645fe871c820573 in the cluster
2018-02-10 04:58:22.289628 N | discovery: found 2 peer(s),
waiting for 1 more
2018-02-10 04:58:36.907165 N | discovery: found peer
1ce61c15bdbb20b2 in the cluster
2018-02-10 04:58:36.907192 N | discovery: found 3 needed
peer(s)
...
2018-02-10 04:58:36.931319 I | etcdserver/membership: added
member 1ce61c15bdbb20b2 [http://172.31.13.239:2380] to cluster
29c0e2579c2f9563
2018-02-10 04:58:36.931422 I | etcdserver/membership: added
member 6645fe871c820573 [http://172.31.14.133:2380] to cluster
29c0e2579c2f9563
2018-02-10 04:58:36.931494 I | etcdserver/membership: added
member f60c98e749d41d1b [http://172.31.3.80:2380] to cluster
29c0e2579c2f9563
2018-02-10 04:58:37.116189 I | raft: f60c98e749d41d1b became
leader at term 2
```

We can see that the first node waited for the other two members to join, and added member to cluster, became the leader in the election at term 2:

4. If you check the other server's log, you might find a clue to the effect that some members voted for the current leader:

```
// in node 2
2018-02-10 04:58:37.118601 I | raft: raft.node:
6645fe871c820573 elected leader f60c98e749d41d1b at term 2
```

5. We can also use member lists to check the current leader:

```
# etcdctl member list
1ce61c15bdbb20b2: name=ip-172-31-13-239
peerURLs=http://172.31.13.239:2380
clientURLs=http://172.31.13.239:2379 isLeader=false
6645fe871c820573: name=ip-172-31-14-133
peerURLs=http://172.31.14.133:2380
clientURLs=http://172.31.14.133:2379 isLeader=false
f60c98e749d41d1b: name=ip-172-31-3-80
peerURLs=http://172.31.3.80:2380
clientURLs=http://172.31.3.80:2379 isLeader=true
```

6. Then we can confirm the current leader is `172.31.3.80`. We can also use `etcdctl` to check cluster health:

```
# etcdctl cluster-health
member 1ce61c15bdbb20b2 is healthy: got healthy result from
http://172.31.13.239:2379
member 6645fe871c820573 is healthy: got healthy result from
http://172.31.14.133:2379
member f60c98e749d41d1b is healthy: got healthy result from
http://172.31.3.80:2379
cluster is healthy
```

7. If we remove the current leader by `etcdctl` command:

```
# etcdctl member remove f60c98e749d41d1b
```

8. We may find that the current leader has been changed:

```
# etcdctl member list
1ce61c15bdbb20b2: name=ip-172-31-13-239
peerURLs=http://172.31.13.239:2380
clientURLs=http://172.31.13.239:2379 isLeader=false
6645fe871c820573: name=ip-172-31-14-133
peerURLs=http://172.31.14.133:2380
clientURLs=http://172.31.14.133:2379 isLeader=true
```

By using `etcd` discovery, we can set up a cluster painlessly `etcd` also provides lots of APIs for us to use. We can leverage it to check cluster statistics:

9. For example, use `/stats/leader` to check the current cluster view:

```
# curl http://127.0.0.1:2379/v2/stats/leader
{"leader":"6645fe871c820573","followers":{"1ce61c15bdbb20b2":{"
latency":{"current":0.002463,"average":0.0038775,"standardDevia
tion":0.001414499999999997,"minimum":0.002463,"maximum":0.0052
92},"counts":{"fail":0,"success":2}}}}
```

For more information about APIs, check out the official API document: `https://coreos.com/etcd/docs/latest/v2/api.html`.

Building a cluster in EC2
CoreOS builds CloudFormation in AWS to help you bootstrap your cluster in AWS dynamically. What we have to do is just launch a CloudFormation template and set the parameters, and we're good to go. The resources in the template contain AutoScaling settings and network ingress (security group). Note that these etcds are running on CoreOS. To log in to the server, firstly you'll have to set your keypair name in the KeyPair parameter, then use the command `ssh -i $your_keypair core@$ip` to log in to the server.

kubeadm

If you're using kubeadm (`https://github.com/kubernetes/kubeadm`) to bootstrap your Kubernetes cluster, unfortunately, at the time of writing, HA support is still in progress (v.1.10). The cluster is created as a single master with a single etcd configured. You'll have to back up etcd regularly to secure your data. Refer to the kubeadm limitations at the official Kubernetes website for more information (`https://kubernetes.io/docs/setup/independent/create-cluster-kubeadm/#limitations`).

kubespray

On the other hand, if you're using kubespray to provision your servers, kubespray supports multi-node etcd natively. What you need to do is add multiple nodes in the etcd section in the configuration file (`inventory.cfg`):

```
# cat inventory/inventory.cfg
my-master-1 ansible_ssh_host=<master_ip>
my-node-1 ansible_ssh_host=<node_ip>
my-etcd-1 ansible_ssh_host=<etcd1_ip>
my-etcd-2 ansible_ssh_host=<etcd2_ip>
my-etcd-3 ansible_ssh_host=<etcd3_ip>

[kube-master]
my-master-1

[etcd]
my-etcd-1
my-etcd-2
my-etcd-3

[kube-node]
my-master-1
```

```
my-node-1
```

Then you are good to provision a cluster with three-node etcd:

```
// provision a cluster
$ ansible-playbook -b -i inventory/inventory.cfg cluster.yml
```

After the ansible playbook is launched, it will configure the role, create the user, check if all certs have already been generated in the first master, and generate and distribute the certs. At the end of the deployment, ansible will check if every component is in a healthy state.

Kops

Kops is the most efficient way to create Kubernetes clusters in AWS. Via the kops configuration file, you can easily launch a custom cluster on the cloud. To build an etcd multi-node cluster, you could use the following section inside the kops configuration file:

```
etcdClusters:
  - etcdMembers:
    - instanceGroup: my-master-us-east-1a
      name: my-etcd-1
    - instanceGroup: my-master-us-east-1b
      name: my-etcd-2
    - instanceGroup: my-master-us-east-1c
      name: my-etcd-3
```

Normally, an instanceGroup means an auto-scaling group. You'll have to declare a related `intanceGroup my-master-us-east-1x` in the configuration file as well. We'll learn more about it in `Chapter 6`, *Building Kubernetes on AWS*. By default, kops still uses etcd2 at the time this book is being written; you could add a version key inside the kops configuration file, such as **version: 3.3.0**, under each `instanceGroup`.

See also

- *Setting up Kubernetes clusters on Linux by using kubespray* in `Chapter 1`, *Building Your Own Kubernetes Cluster*
- *The Building multiple masters* section of this chapter
- `Chapter 6`, *Building Kubernetes on AWS*
- *Working with etcd logs* in `Chapter 9`, *Logging and Monitoring*

Building multiple masters

The master node serves as a kernel component in the Kubernetes system. Its duties include the following:

1. Pushing and pulling information from etcd servers
2. Acting as the portal for requests
3. Assigning tasks to nodes
4. Monitoring the running tasks

Three major daemons enable the master to fulfill the preceding duties; the following diagram indicates the activities of the aforementioned bullet points:

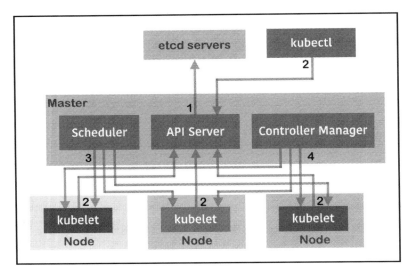

The interaction between the Kubernetes master and other components

As you can see, the master is the communicator between workers and clients. Therefore, it will be a problem if the master crashes. A multiple-master Kubernetes system is not only fault tolerant, but also workload-balanced. It would not be an issue if one of them crashed, since other masters would still handle the jobs. We call this infrastructure design *high availability*, abbreviated to HA. In order to support HA structures, there will no longer be only one API server for accessing datastores and handling requests. Several API servers in separated master nodes would help to solve tasks simultaneously and shorten the response time.

Getting ready

There are some brief ideas you should understand about building a multiple-master system:

- Add a load balancer server in front of the masters. The load balancer will become the new endpoint accessed by nodes and clients.
- Every master runs its own API server.
- Only one scheduler and one controller manager are eligible to work in the system, which can avoid conflicting directions from different daemons while managing containers. To achieve this setup, we enable the `--leader-elect` flag in the scheduler and controller manager. Only the one getting the lease can take duties.

In this recipe, we are going to build a two-master system via *kubeadm*, which has similar methods while scaling more masters. Users may also use other tools to build up HA Kubernetes clusters. Our target is to illustrate the general concepts.

Before starting, in addition to master nodes, you should prepare other necessary components in the systems:

- Two Linux hosts, which will be set up as master nodes later. These machines should be configured as kubeadm masters. Please refer to the *Setting up Kubernetes clusters on Linux by kubeadm recipe* in `Chapter 1`, *Building Your Own Kubernetes Cluster*. You should finish the *Package installation and System configuring prerequisites* parts on both hosts.
- A LoadBalancer for masters. It would be much easier if you worked on the public cloud, that's said EL*B* of AWS and Load balancing of GCE.
- An etcd cluster. Please check the *Clustering etcd* recipe in this chapter.

How to do it...

We will use a configuration file to run kubeadm for customized daemon execution. Please follow the next sections to make multiple master nodes as a group.

Setting up the first master

First, we are going to set up a master, ready for the HA environment. Like the initial step, running a cluster by using kubeadm, it is important to enable and start kubelet on the master at the beginning. It can then take daemons running as pods in the `kube-system` namespace:

```
// you are now in the terminal of host for first master
$ sudo systemctl enable kubelet && sudo systemctl start kubelet
```

Next, let's start the master services with the custom kubeadm configuration file:

```
$ cat custom-init-1st.conf
apiVersion: kubeadm.k8s.io/v1alpha1
kind: MasterConfiguration
api:
  advertiseAddress: "<FIRST_MASTER_IP>"
etcd:
  endpoints:
  - "<ETCD_CLUSTER_ENDPOINT>"
apiServerCertSANs:
- "<FIRST_MASTER_IP>"
- "<SECOND_MASTER_IP>"
- "<LOAD_BALANCER_IP>"
- "127.0.0.1"
token: "<CUSTOM_TOKEN: [a-z0-9]{6}.[a-z0-9]{16}>"
tokenTTL: "0"
apiServerExtraArgs:
  endpoint-reconciler-type: "lease"
```

This configuration file has multiple values required to match your environment settings. The IP ones are straightforward. Be aware that you are now setting the first master; the `<FIRST_MASTER_IP>` variable will be the physical IP of your current location. `<ETCD_CLUSTER_ENDPOINT>` will be in a format like `"http://<IP>:<PORT>"`, which will be the load balancer of the etcd cluster. `<CUSTOM_TOKEN>` should be valid in the specified format (for example, `123456.aaaabbbbccccdddd`). After you allocate all variables aligning to your system, you can run it now:

```
$ sudo kubeadm init --config=custom-init-1st.conf
```

 You may get the Swap is not supported error message. Add an additional `--ignore-preflight-errors=Swap` flag with `kubeadm init` to avoid this interruption.

Make sure to update in both files of the masters.

We need to complete client functionality via the following commands:

```
$ mkdir -p $HOME/.kube
$ sudo cp -i /etc/kubernetes/admin.conf $HOME/.kube/config
$ sudo chown $(id -u):$(id -g) $HOME/.kube/config
```

Like when running a single master cluster via kubeadm, without a container network interface the add-on `kube-dns` will always have a pending status. We will use CNI Calico for our demonstration. It is fine to apply the other CNI which is suitable to kubeadm:

```
$ kubectl apply -f
https://docs.projectcalico.org/v2.6/getting-started/kubernetes/installation
/hosted/kubeadm/1.6/calico.yaml
```

Now it is OK for you to add more master nodes.

Setting up the other master with existing certifications

Similar to the last session, let's start and enable `kubelet` first:

```
// now you're in the second master
$ sudo systemctl enable kubelet && sudo systemctl start kubelet
```

After we have set up the first master, we should share newly generated certificates and keys with the whole system. It makes sure that the masters are secured in the same manner:

```
$ sudo scp -r root@$FIRST_MASTER_IP:/etc/kubernetes/pki/*
/etc/kubernetes/pki/
```

You will have found that several files such as certificates or keys are copied to the `/etc/kubernetes/pki/` directly, where they can only be accessed by the root. However, we are going to remove the files `apiserver.crt` and `apiserver.key`. It is because these files should be generated in line with the hostname and IP of the second master, but the shared client certificate `ca.crt` is also involved in the generating process:

```
$ sudo rm /etc/kubernetes/pki/apiserver.*
```

Next, before we fire the master initialization command, please change the API advertise address in the configuration file for the second master. It should be the IP of the second master, your current host. The configuration file of the second master is quite similar to the first master's.

The difference is that we should indicate the information of `etcd` server and avoid creating a new set of them:

```
// Please modify the change by your case
$ cat custom-init-2nd.conf
apiVersion: kubeadm.k8s.io/v1alpha1
kind: MasterConfiguration
api:
  advertiseAddress: "<SECOND_MASTER_IP>"
...
```

Go ahead and fire the `kubeadm init` command, record the `kubeadm join` command shown in the last line of the `init` command to add the node later, and enable the client API permission:

```
$ sudo kubeadm init --config custom-init-2nd.conf
// copy the "kubeadm join" command showing in the output
$ mkdir -p $HOME/.kube
$ sudo cp -i /etc/kubernetes/admin.conf $HOME/.kube/config
$ sudo chown $(id -u):$(id -g) $HOME/.kube/config
```

Then, check the current nodes; you will find there are two master :

```
$ kubectl get nodes
NAME       STATUS   ROLES    AGE   VERSION
master01   Ready    master   8m    v1.10.2
master02   Ready    master   1m    v1.10.2
```

Adding nodes in a HA cluster

Once the masters are ready, you can add nodes into the system. This node should be finished with the prerequisite configuration as a worker node in the kubeadm cluster. And, in the beginning, you should start kubelet as the master ones:

```
// now you're in the second master
$ sudo systemctl enable kubelet && sudo systemctl start kubelet
```

After that, you can go ahead and push the join command you copied. However, please change the master IP to the load balancer one:

```
// your join command should look similar to following one
$ sudo kubeadm join --token <CUSTOM_TOKEN> <LOAD_BALANCER_IP>:6443 --
discovery-token-ca-cert-hash sha256:<HEX_STRING>
```

You can then jump to the first master or second master to check the nodes' status:

```
// you can see the node is added
$ kubectl get nodes
NAME        STATUS    ROLES     AGE      VERSION
master01    Ready     master    4h       v1.10.2
master02    Ready     master    3h       v1.10.2
node01      Ready     <none>    22s      v1.10.2
```

How it works...

To verify our HA cluster, take a look at the pods in the namespace kube-system:

```
$ kubectl get pod -n kube-system
NAME                                           READY    STATUS     RESTARTS
AGE
calico-etcd-6bnrk                              1/1      Running    0          1d
calico-etcd-p7lpv                              1/1      Running    0          1d
calico-kube-controllers-d554689d5-qjht2        1/1      Running    0          1d
calico-node-2r2zs                              2/2      Running    0          1d
calico-node-97fjk                              2/2      Running    0          1d
calico-node-t5518                              2/2      Running    0          1d
kube-apiserver-master01                        1/1      Running    0          1d
kube-apiserver-master02                        1/1      Running    0          1d
kube-controller-manager-master01               1/1      Running    0          1d
kube-controller-manager-master02               1/1      Running    0          1d
kube-dns-6f4fd4bdf-xbfvp                       3/3      Running    0          1d
kube-proxy-8jk69                               1/1      Running    0          1d
kube-proxy-qbt7q                               1/1      Running    0          1d
kube-proxy-rkxwp                               1/1      Running    0          1d
kube-scheduler-master01                        1/1      Running    0          1d
kube-scheduler-master02                        1/1      Running    0          1d
```

These pods are working as system daemons: Kubernetes system services such as the API server, Kubernetes add-ons such as the DNS server, and CNI ones; here we used Calico. But wait! As you take a closer look at the pods, you may be curious about why the controller manager and scheduler runs on both masters. Isn't there just single one in the HA cluster?

As we understood in the previous section, we should avoid running multiple controller managers and multiple schedulers in the Kubernetes system. This is because they may try to take over requests at the same time, which not only creates conflict but is also a waste of computing power. Actually, while booting up the whole system by using kubeadm, the controller manager and scheduler are started with the `leader-elect` flag enabled by default:

```
// check flag leader-elect on master node
$ sudo cat /etc/kubernetes/manifests/kube-controller-manager.yaml
apiVersion: v1
kind: Pod
metadata:
  annotations:
    scheduler.alpha.kubernetes.io/critical-pod: ""
  creationTimestamp: null
  labels:
    component: kube-controller-manager
    tier: control-plane
  name: kube-controller-manager
  namespace: kube-system
spec:
  containers:
  - command:
    - kube-controller-manager
...
    - --leader-elect=true
...
```

You may find that the scheduler has also been set with `leader-elect`. Nevertheless, why is there still more than one pod? The truth is, one of the pods with the same role is idle. We can get detailed information by looking at system endpoints:

```
// ep is the abbreviation of resource type "endpoints"
$ kubectl get ep -n kube-system
NAME                       ENDPOINTS                                      AGE
calico-etcd                192.168.122.201:6666,192.168.122.202:6666      1d
kube-controller-manager    <none>                                         1d
kube-dns                   192.168.241.67:53,192.168.241.67:53            1d
kube-scheduler             <none>                                         1d

// check endpoint of controller-manager with YAML output format
$ kubectl get ep kube-controller-manager -n kube-system -o yaml
apiVersion: v1
kind: Endpoints
metadata:
  annotations:
```

```
    control-plane.alpha.kubernetes.io/leader:
'{"holderIdentity":"master01_bf4e22f7-4f56-11e8-
aee3-52540048ed9b","leaseDurationSeconds":15,"acquireTime":"2018-05-04T04:5
1:11Z","renewTime":"2018-05-04T05:28:34Z","leaderTransitions":0}'
    creationTimestamp: 2018-05-04T04:51:11Z
    name: kube-controller-manager
    namespace: kube-system
    resourceVersion: "3717"
    selfLink: /api/v1/namespaces/kube-system/endpoints/kube-controller-
manager
    uid: 5e2717b0-0609-11e8-b36f-52540048ed9b
```

Take the endpoint for `kube-controller-manager`, for example: there is no virtual IP of a pod or service attached to it (the same as `kube-scheduler`). If we dig deeper into this endpoint, we find that the endpoint for `kube-controller-manager` relies on `annotations` to record lease information; it also relies on `resourceVersion` for pod mapping and to pass traffic. According to the annotation of the `kube-controller-manager` endpoint, it is our first master that took control. Let's check the controller manager on both masters:

```
// your pod should be named as kube-controller-manager-<HOSTNAME OF MASTER>
$ kubectl logs kube-controller-manager-master01 -n kube-system | grep
"leader"
I0504 04:51:03.015151 1 leaderelection.go:175] attempting to acquire leader
lease kube-system/kube-controller-manager...
...
I0504 04:51:11.627737 1 event.go:218]
Event(v1.ObjectReference{Kind:"Endpoints", Namespace:"kube-system",
Name:"kube-controller-manager", UID:"5e2717b0-0609-11e8-b36f-52540048ed9b",
APIVersion:"v1", ResourceVersion:"187", FieldPath:""}): type: 'Normal'
reason: 'LeaderElection' master01_bf4e22f7-4f56-11e8-aee3-52540048ed9b
became leader
```

As you can see, only one master works as a leader and handles the requests, while the other one persists, acquires the lease, and does nothing.

For a further test, we are trying to remove our current leader pod, to see what happens. While deleting the deployment of system pods by a `kubectl` request, a kubeadm Kubernetes would create a new one since it's guaranteed to boot up any application under the/etc/kubernetes/manifests directory. Therefore, avoid the automatic recovery by kubeadm, we remove the configuration file out of the manifest directory instead. It makes the downtime long enough to give away the leadership:

```
// jump into the master node of leader
// temporary move the configuration file out of kubeadm's control
```

```
$ sudo mv /etc/kubernetes/manifests/kube-controller-manager.yaml ./
// check the endpoint
$ kubectl get ep kube-controller-manager -n kube-system -o yaml
apiVersion: v1
kind: Endpoints
metadata:
  annotations:
    control-plane.alpha.kubernetes.io/leader:
'{"holderIdentity":"master02_4faf95c7-4f5b-11e8-
bda3-525400b06612","leaseDurationSeconds":15,"acquireTime":"2018-05-04T05:3
7:03Z","renewTime":"2018-05-04T05:37:47Z","leaderTransitions":1}'
  creationTimestamp: 2018-05-04T04:51:11Z
  name: kube-controller-manager
  namespace: kube-system
  resourceVersion: "4485"
  selfLink: /api/v1/namespaces/kube-system/endpoints/kube-controller-
manager
  uid: 5e2717b0-0609-11e8-b36f-52540048ed9b
subsets: null
```

The /etc/kubernetes/manifests directory is defined in kubelet by --pod-manifest-path flag. Check /etc/systemd/system/kubelet.service.d/10-kubeadm.conf, which is the system daemon configuration file for kubelet, and the help messages of kubelet for more details.

Now, it is the other node's turn to wake up its controller manager and put it to work. Once you put back the configuration file for the controller manager, you find the old leader is now waiting for the lease:

```
$ kubectl logs kube-controller-manager-master01 -n kube-system
I0504 05:40:10.218946 1 controllermanager.go:116] Version: v1.10.2
W0504 05:40:10.219688 1 authentication.go:55] Authentication is disabled
I0504 05:40:10.219702 1 insecure_serving.go:44] Serving insecurely on
127.0.0.1:10252
I0504 05:40:10.219965 1 leaderelection.go:175] attempting to acquire leader
lease kube-system/kube-controller-manager...
```

See also

Before you read this recipe, you should have mastered the basic concept of single master installation by kubeadm. Refer to the related recipes mentioned here to get an idea for how to build a multiple-master system automatically:

- *Setting up a Kubernetes cluster on Linux by kubeadm* in `Chapter 1`, *Building Your Own Kubernetes Cluster*
- Clustering etcd

Building Continuous Delivery Pipelines

5

In this chapter, we will cover the following recipes:

- Moving monolithic to microservices
- Working with the private Docker registry
- Integrating with Jenkins

Introduction

Kubernetes is a perfect match for applications featuring the microservices architecture. However, most of the old applications are built in the monolithic style. We will give you an idea about how to move from the monolithic to the microservices world. As for microservices, deployment will become a burden if you are doing it manually. We will learn how to build up our own continuous delivery pipeline by coordinating Jenkins, the Docker registry, and Kubernetes.

Moving monolithic to microservices

Typically, application architecture is the monolithic design that contains a **Model-View-Controller** (**MVC**) and every component within a single, big binary. A monolithic design has some benefits, such as less latency within components, being all in one straightforward package, and being easy to deploy and test.

However, a monolithic design has some downsides because the binary will be getting bigger and bigger. You always need to take care of the side effects when adding or modifying the code, therefore making release cycles longer.

Containers and Kubernetes give more flexibility when using microservices for your application. The microservices architecture is very simple and can be divided into some modules or some service classes together with MVC:

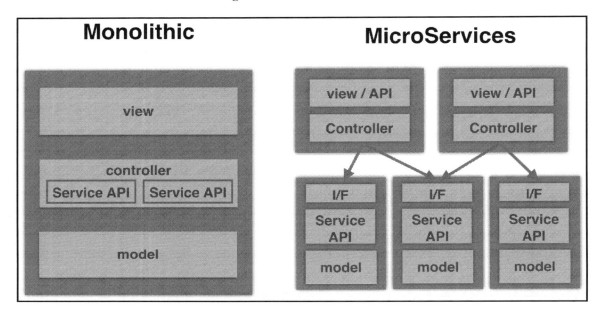

Monolithic and microservices design

Each microservice provides a **Remote Procedure Call** (**RPC**) using RESTful or some standard network APIs to other microservices. The benefit is that each microservice is independent. There are minimal side effects when adding or modifying the code. Release the cycle independently, so it perfectly ties in with the Agile software development methodology and allows for the reuse of these microservices to construct another application that builds the microservices ecosystem.

Getting ready

Prepare the simple microservices program. In order to push and pull your microservices, please register to Docker hub (https://hub.docker.com/) to create your free Docker ID in advance.

If you push the Docker image to Docker hub, it will be public; anyone can pull your image. Therefore, don't put any confidential information into the image.

Once you successfully log in to your Docker ID, you will be redirected to your **Dashboard** page as follows:

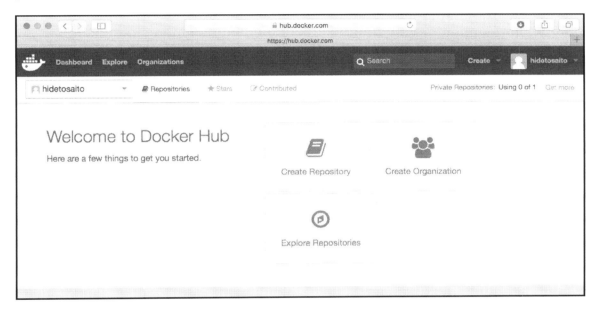

After logging in to Docker hub

How to do it...

Prepare both microservices and the frontend WebUI as a Docker image. Then, deploy them using the Kubernetes replication controller and service.

Microservices

Build a microservice which provides a simple math function by using following steps:

1. Here is the simple microservice using Python Flask (http://flask.pocoo.org/):

```
$ cat entry.py
from flask import Flask, request
app = Flask(__name__)

@app.route("/")
def hello():
    return "Hello World!"

@app.route("/power/<int:base>/<int:index>")
def power(base, index):
    return "%d" % (base ** index)

@app.route("/addition/<int:x>/<int:y>")
def add(x, y):
    return "%d" % (x+y)

@app.route("/substraction/<int:x>/<int:y>")
def substract(x, y):
    return "%d" % (x-y)

if __name__ == "__main__":
    app.run(host='0.0.0.0')
```

2. Prepare a Dockerfile as follows in order to build the Docker image:

```
$ cat Dockerfile
FROM ubuntu:14.04

# Update packages
RUN apt-get update -y

# Install Python Setuptools
RUN apt-get install -y python-setuptools git telnet curl

# Install pip
RUN easy_install pip

# Bundle app source
ADD . /src
WORKDIR /src
```

```
# Add and install Python modules
RUN pip install Flask

# Expose
EXPOSE 5000

# Run
CMD ["python", "entry.py"]
```

3. Then, use the `docker build` command to build the Docker image as follows:

```
//name as "your_docker_hub_id/my-calc"
$ sudo docker build -t hidetosaito/my-calc .
Sending build context to Docker daemon 3.072 kB
Step 1 : FROM ubuntu:14.04
 ---> 6cc0fc2a5ee3
Step 2 : RUN apt-get update -y
 ---> Using cache


(snip)


Step 8 : EXPOSE 5000
 ---> Running in 7c52f4bfe373
 ---> 28f79bb7481f
Removing intermediate container 7c52f4bfe373
Step 9 : CMD python entry.py
 ---> Running in 86b39c727572
 ---> 20ae465bf036
Removing intermediate container 86b39c727572
Successfully built 20ae465bf036


//verity your image
$ sudo docker images
REPOSITORY            TAG            IMAGE ID
CREATED               VIRTUAL SIZE
hidetosaito/my-calc   latest         20ae465bf036
19 seconds ago        284 MB
ubuntu                14.04          6cc0fc2a5ee3      3
weeks ago             187.9 MB
```

4. Then, use the `docker login` command to log in to Docker hub:

```
//type your username, password and e-mail address in Docker hub
$ sudo docker login
Username: hidetosaito
```

```
Password:
Email: hideto.saito@yahoo.com
WARNING: login credentials saved in /home/ec2-
user/.docker/config.json
Login Succeeded
```

5. Finally, use the `docker push` command to register to your Docker hub repository as follows:

```
//push to your docker index
$ sudo docker push hidetosaito/my-calc
The push refers to a repository [docker.io/hidetosaito/my-calc]
(len: 1)
20ae465bf036: Pushed

(snip)

92ec6d044cb3: Pushed
latest: digest:
sha256:203b81c5a238e228c154e0b53a58e60e6eb3d1563293483ce58f4835
1031a474 size: 19151
```

6. Upon access to Docker hub, you can see your microservice in the repository:

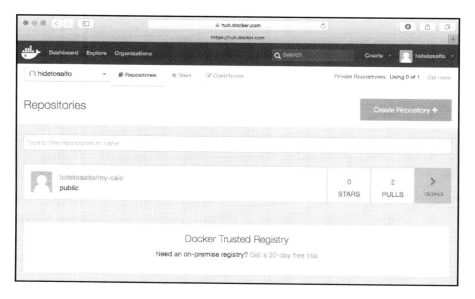

Your microservice Docker image on Docker hub

Frontend WebUI

Build WebUI that uses preceding microservice by following steps:

1. Here is the simple frontend WebUI that also uses Python `Flask`:

```
$ cat entry.py
import os
import httplib
from flask import Flask, request, render_template

app = Flask(__name__)

@app.route("/")
def index():
    return render_template('index.html')


@app.route("/add", methods=['POST'])
def add():
    #
    # from POST parameters
    #
    x = int(request.form['x'])
    y = int(request.form['y'])

    #
    # from Kubernetes Service(environment variables)
    #
    my_calc_host = os.environ['MY_CALC_SERVICE_SERVICE_HOST']
    my_calc_port = os.environ['MY_CALC_SERVICE_SERVICE_PORT']

    #
    # REST call to MicroService(my-calc)
    #
    client = httplib.HTTPConnection(my_calc_host, my_calc_port)
    client.request("GET", "/addition/%d/%d" % (x, y))
    response = client.getresponse()
    result = response.read()
    return render_template('index.html', add_x=x, add_y=y,
add_result=result)

if __name__ == "__main__":
    app.debug = True
    app.run(host='0.0.0.0')
```

Kubernetes service generates the Kubernetes service name and port number as an environment variable to the other pods. Therefore, the environment variable's name and the Kubernetes service name must be consistent. In this scenario, the `my-calc` service name must be `my-calc-service`.

2. The frontend WebUI uses the `Flask` HTML template; it is similar to PHP and JSP in that `entry.py` will pass the parameter to the template (`index.html`) to render the HTML:

```
$ cat templates/index.html
<html>
    <body>
    <div>
        <form method="post" action="/add">
            <input type="text" name="x" size="2"/>
            <input type="text" name="y" size="2"/>
            <input type="submit" value="addition"/>
        </form>
        {% if add_result %}
        <p>Answer : {{ add_x }} + {{ add_y }} = {{ add_result
}}</p>
        {% endif %}
    </div>
    </body>
</html>
```

3. `Dockerfile` is exactly the same as the microservice `my-calc`. So, eventually, the file structure will be as follows. Note that `index.html` is a jinja2 template file; therefore, put it under the `/templates` directory:

```
/Dockerfile
/entry.py
/templates/index.html
```

4. Then, build a Docker image and push to Docker hub as follows:

In order to push your image to Docker hub, you need to log in using the Docker login command. It is needed only once; the system checks `~/.docker/config.json` to read from there.

```
//build frontend Webui image
$ sudo docker build -t hidetosaito/my-frontend .
```

```
//login to docker hub
$ sudo docker login

//push frontend webui image
$ sudo docker push hidetosaito/my-frontend
```

5. Upon access to Docker hub, you can see your WebUI application in the repository:

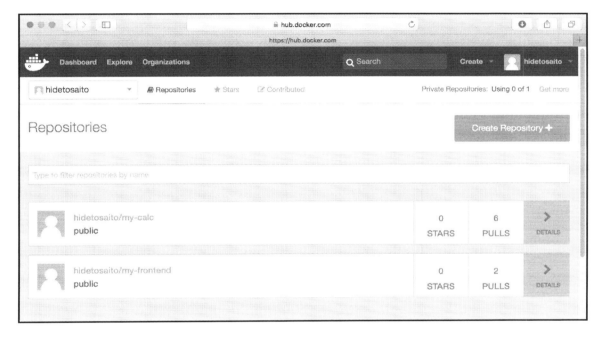

Microservices and frontend WebUI image on Docker Hub

How it works...

Let's prepare two YAML configurations to launch a microservice container and frontend WebUI container using Kubernetes.

Microservices

Microservices (`my-calc`) uses the Kubernetes deployment and service, but it needs to communicate to other pods only. In other words, there's no need to expose it to the outside Kubernetes network. Therefore, the service type is set as `ClusterIP`:

```
$ cat my-calc.yaml
apiVersion: apps/v1
kind: Deployment
metadata:
  name: my-calc-deploy
spec:
  replicas: 2
  selector:
    matchLabels:
      run: my-calc
  template:
    metadata:
      labels:
        run: my-calc
    spec:
      containers:
      - name: my-calc
        image: hidetosaito/my-calc
---
apiVersion: v1
kind: Service
metadata:
  name: my-calc-service
spec:
  ports:
    - protocol: TCP
      port: 5000
  type: ClusterIP
  selector:
    run: my-calc
```

Use the `kubectl` command to load the `my-calc` pods as follows:

```
$ kubectl create -f my-calc.yaml
deployment.apps "my-calc-deploy" created
service "my-calc-service" created
```

Frontend WebUI

Frontend WebUI also uses the deployment and service, but it exposes the port (TCP port 30080) in order to access it from an external web browser:

```
$ cat my-frontend.yaml
apiVersion: apps/v1
kind: Deployment
metadata:
  name: my-frontend-deploy
spec:
  replicas: 2
  selector:
    matchLabels:
      run: my-frontend
  template:
    metadata:
      labels:
        run: my-frontend
    spec:
      containers:
      - name: my-frontend
        image: hidetosaito/my-frontend
---
apiVersion: v1
kind: Service
metadata:
  name: my-frontend-service
spec:
  ports:
    - protocol: TCP
      port: 5000
      nodePort: 30080
  type: NodePort
  selector:
    run: my-frontend


$ kubectl create -f my-frontend.yaml
deployment.apps "my-frontend-deploy" created
service "my-frontend-service" created
```

Let's try to access `my-frontend-service` using a web browser. You can access any Kubernetes node's IP address; specify the port number 30080. If you are using minikube, simply type `minikube service my-frontend-service` to access. Then you can see the `my-frontend` application as follows:

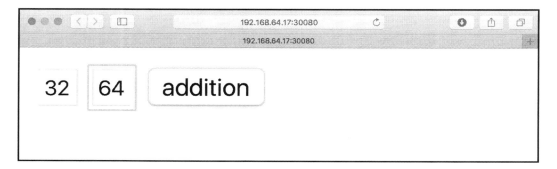

Access to the frontend WebUI

When you click on the **addition** button, it will forward a parameter to microservices (`my-calc`). Microservices compute the addition (yes, just an addition!) and then return the result back to the frontend WebUI as follows:

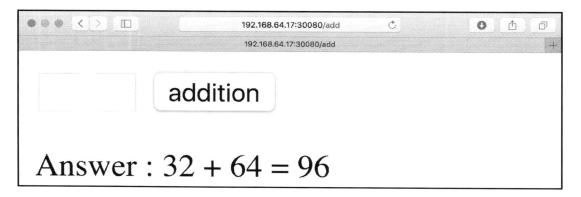

Getting a result from microservices and rendering the HTML

So now, it is easy to scale the pod for the frontend WebUI and microservices independently. For example, scale WebUI pod from 2 to 8 and microservice pod from 2 to 16, as shown:

```
$ kubectl get deploy
NAME                DESIRED   CURRENT   UP-TO-DATE   AVAILABLE   AGE
my-calc-deploy      2         2         2            2           30m
my-frontend-deploy  2         2         2            2           28m
```

```
$ kubectl scale deploy my-frontend-deploy --replicas=8
deployment "my-frontend-deploy" scaled

$ kubectl scale deploy my-calc-deploy --replicas=16
deployment "my-calc-deploy" scaled

$ kubectl get deploy
NAME                    DESIRED    CURRENT    UP-TO-DATE    AVAILABLE    AGE
my-calc-deploy          16         16         16            16           31m
my-frontend-deploy      8          8          8             8            29m
```

Also, if there's a need to fix some bugs, for example, if there's a frontend need to validate the input parameter to check whether it is numeric or a string (yes, if you type string and then submit, it will show an error!), it will not affect the build and deploy the cycle against microservices:

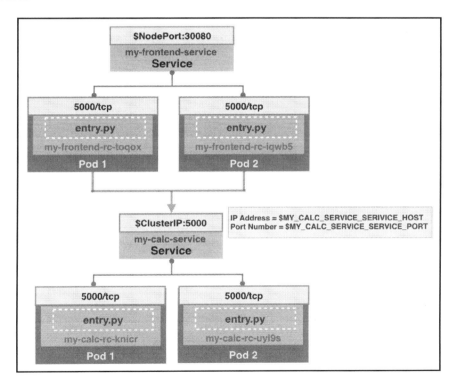

Frontend and microservice pods and services

In addition, if you want to add another microservice, for example, subtraction microservices, you may need to create another Docker image and deploy with another deployments and service, so it will be independent from the current microservices. Then, you can keep accumulating your own microservice ecosystem to reuse in another application.

Working with the private Docker registry

Once you start to build your microservice application via Docker, you'll need to have a Docker registry to put your container image in. Docker hub offers you free public repositories, however, in some cases you might want to make your image private due to business needs or organization policy.

Docker hub offers the **private repository**, which only allows authenticated users to push and pull your images, and is not visible to other users. However, there is only one quota (repository) for a free plan. You may pay to increase the number of private repositories, but if you adopt the microservices architecture, you will need a large number of private repositories:

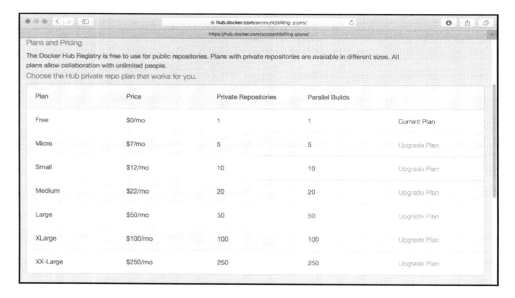

Docker hub private repositories price list

Docker hub with a paid plan is the easiest way to set up your private registry, but there are some other ways to set up your own private Docker registry, which the unlimited Docker image quota locates inside your network. In addition, you can also use other cloud-provided registry services to manage your private registry.

Getting ready

In this recipe, we will show you three different ways to set up your own private registries:

- Using Kubernetes to run a private registry image (`https://hub.docker.com/_/registry/`)
- Using Amazon elastic container registry (`https://aws.amazon.com/ecr/`)
- Using Google container registry (`https://cloud.google.com/container-registry/`)

When using a Kubernetes to set up a private registry, you may use your own Kubernetes cluster on the private or public cloud, which allows you to have full control and utilize most of your physical resources.

On the other hand, when using a public cloud-provided service, such as AWS or GCP, you can be relieved of the management of servers and storage. Whatever you need, those public clouds provide you with elastic resources. We'll just have to set the credentials to Kubernetes and let the nodes know. The following recipes will go through these three different options.

Using Kubernetes to run a Docker registry server

If you want to launch a private registry server using Kubernetes, you need your own Kubernetes cluster. You will have set up your own Kubernetes while exploring this book. If you haven't done yet, please read `Chapter 1`, *Building Your Own Kubernetes Cluster*, to choose the easiest way.

Please note that Docker registry will store some of your Docker images. You must have a `PersistentVolume` to manage your storage via Kubernetes. In addition, we should expect that multiple pods will read and write to the same `PersistentVolume` due to scalability. Therefore, you must have the **ReadWriteMany** (**RWX**) access mode of `PersistentVolume`, such as GlusterFS or NFS.

Details of `PersistentVolume` are described in the *Working with volumes* section in `Chapter 2`, *Walking through Kubernetes Concepts*. Let's create a `PersistentVolume` that uses NFS and the name `pvnfs01` to allocate `100` GB:

```
//my NFS server(10.138.0.5) shares /nfs directory
$ showmount -e 10.138.0.5
Export list for 10.138.0.5:
/nfs *


//please change spec.nfs.path and spec.nfs.server to yours
$ cat pv_nfs.yaml
apiVersion: "v1"
kind: "PersistentVolume"
metadata:
  name: pvnfs01
spec:
  capacity:
    storage: "100Gi"
  accessModes:
    - "ReadWriteMany"
  nfs:
    path: "/nfs"
    server: "10.138.0.5"


$ kubectl create -f pv_nfs.yaml
persistentvolume "pvnfs01" created

$ kubectl get pv
NAME      CAPACITY ACCESS MODES RECLAIM POLICY STATUS    CLAIM STORAGECLASS
REASON AGE
pvnfs01 100Gi     RWX          Retain         Available
5s
```

> If you can't prepare RWX `PersistentVolume`, you may still be able to set up Docker registry by Kubernetes, but you can launch only one pod (replicas: one). As an alternative, you may use AWS S3 or GCP PD as private registry backend storage; please visit `https://docs.docker.com/registry/configuration/` to learn how to configure backend storage for your registry.

Next, create `PersistentVolumeClaim` that decouples NFS `PersistentVolume` and pod configuration. Let's create one `PersistentVolumeClaim` named `pvc-1`. Make sure `accessModes` is `ReadWriteMany` and that `STATUS` became `Bound` after creation:

```
$ cat pvc-1.yml
apiVersion: v1
kind: PersistentVolumeClaim
metadata:
    name: pvc-1
spec:
  storageClassName: ""
  accessModes:
    - ReadWriteMany
  resources:
    requests:
      storage: 100Gi

$ kubectl create -f pvc-1.yml
persistentvolumeclaim "pvc-1" created

$ kubectl get pvc
NAME STATUS VOLUME CAPACITY ACCESS MODES STORAGECLASS AGE
pvc-1 Bound pvnfs01 100Gi RWX 5s
```

This is enough to set up your private registry. It has some prerequisites; alternatively, using the public cloud is much simpler.

Using Amazon elastic container registry

Amazon **elastic container registry (ECR)** was introduced as a part of Amazon **elastic container service (ECS)**. This recipe won't touch on ECS itself; instead, just use ECR as a private registry.

In order to use Amazon ECR, you have to have an AWS account and install AWS CLI on your machine. It will be described in more detail in Chapter 6, *Building Kubernetes on AWS*. You'll have to create an IAM user with `ACCESS KEY ID` and `SECRET ACCESS KEY`, and associated `AmazonEC2ContainerRegistryFullAccess` policies, which allow full administrator access to Amazon ECR:

```
{
  "Version": "2012-10-17",
  "Statement": [
    {
      "Effect": "Allow",
      "Action": [
```

```
        "ecr:*"
      ],
      "Resource": "*"
    }
  ]
}
```

Then configure the default settings in AWS CLI via the `aws configure` command:

```
$ aws configure
AWS Access Key ID [None]: <Your AWS ACCESS KEY ID>
AWS Secret Access Key [None]: <Your AWS SECRET ACCESS KEY>
Default region name [None]: us-east-1
Default output format [None]:
```

Then we can start to play with Amazon ECR.

Using Google cloud registry

Google container registry (`https://cloud.google.com/container-registry/`) is a part of the GCP. Similar to AWS, having a GCP account is required, as well as Cloud SDK (`https://cloud.google.com/sdk/`), which is the command-line interface in GCP. More details about GCP will be described in `Chapter 7`, *Building Kubernetes on GCP*.

On GCP, we'll just need to create a project and enable billing and the container registry API for our project. Otherwise, any operation in `gcloud` will display an error:

```
$ gcloud container images list
ERROR: (gcloud.container.images.list) Bad status during token exchange: 403
```

In order to enable billing and container registry API, visit the GCP web console (`https://console.cloud.google.com`), navigate to the billing page and container registry page, then just enable those. Once activation is done, you can use the `gcloud container` command:

```
$ gcloud container images list
Listed 0 items.
```

Now we can start to use Google container registry.

How to do it...

We have set up the preparation steps. Let's see how to configure your private registry step by step.

Launching a private registry server using Kubernetes

In order to launch a private registry, it is necessary to configure these files in order to configure a private registry with appropriate security settings:

- SSL certificate
- HTTP secret
- HTTP basic authentication file

Creating a self-signed SSL certificate

There is a pitfall—people tend to set up a plain HTTP (disable TLS) registry without authentication in the beginning. Then it also needs to configure a Docker client (Kubernetes node) to allow an insecure registry and so on. It is a bad practice that requires many steps to set up an insecure environment.

The best practice is always using the official SSL certificate that is issued by the certificate authority. However, a self-signed certificate is always handy, especially in the testing phase. An official certificate can wait until we have FQDN defined. Therefore, this recipe will show you how to use OpenSSL to create a self-signed SSL certificate via the following steps:

1. Create a `secrets` directory:

    ```
    $ mkdir secrets
    ```

2. Run the `openssl` command to specify the options to generate a certificate (`domain.crt`) and a private key (`domain.key`) under the **secrets** directory. Note that you may type `.` to skip to input location and email info:

    ```
    $ openssl req -newkey rsa:4096 -nodes -sha256 -keyout
    secrets/domain.key -x509 -days 365 -out secrets/domain.crt
    Generating a 4096 bit RSA private key
    ...........................................++
    ............................................................++
    writing new private key to 'secrets/domain.key'
    -----
    You are about to be asked to enter information that will be
    incorporated
    into your certificate request.
    What you are about to enter is what is called a Distinguished
    Name or a DN.
    There are quite a few fields but you can leave some blank
    For some fields there will be a default value,
    ```

```
If you enter '.', the field will be left blank.
-----
Country Name (2 letter code) []:us
State or Province Name (full name) []:California
Locality Name (eg, city) []:Cupertino
Organization Name (eg, company) []:packtpub
Organizational Unit Name (eg, section) []:chapter5
Common Name (eg, fully qualified host name) []:.
Email Address []:.
```

3. Check whether both certificate and private keys are generated under the `secrets` directory:

```
$ ls secrets/
domain.crt domain.key
```

Creating HTTP secret

Regarding HTTP secret, it will be randomly generated by the private registry instance upon startup by default. However, it is a problem if you run multiple pods, because each pod may have a different HTTP secret that occur an error when Docker client push or pull the image. So we explicitly state that all pods will use the same HTTP secret, via the following steps:

1. Use the `openssl` command to create a `http.secret` file under the `secrets` directory:

```
//create 8 byte random HEX string by OpenSSL
$ openssl rand -hex -out secrets/http.secret 8
```

2. Check the `secrets` directory, which has three files now:

```
$ ls secrets/
domain.crt domain.key http.secret
```

Creating the HTTP basic authentication file

Finally, regarding the HTTP basic authentication file, if you set up a private registry, authentication is needed when you interact with the Docker registry. You'll have to do `docker login` to get a token when pushing and pulling images. In order to create an HTTP basic authentication file, use the `htpasswd` command that is provided by Apache2 as this is easiest. Let's create a HTTP basic authentication file via the following steps:

1. Run Docker with Apache2 Docker image (`httpd`) to run the `htpasswd` command with the `bcrypt` (`-B`) option and generate a basic authentication file (`registry_passwd`) under the `secrets` directory:

```
//set user=user01, passwd=my-super-secure-password
$ docker run -i httpd /bin/bash -c 'echo my-super-secure-
password | /usr/local/apache2/bin/htpasswd -nBi user01' >
secrets/registry_passwd
```

2. Check the `secrets` directory so that now you have four files:

```
$ ls secrets/
domain.crt domain.key http.secret registry_passwd
```

Creating a Kubernetes secret to store security files

There are four files. We use **Kubernetes Secret** so that all pods can access it via an environment variable or mount a volume and access as a file. For more details about secrets, please refer to the *Working with secrets* section in Chapter 2, *Walking through Kubernetes Concepts*. You can use the `kubectl` command to load these four files to store to the Kubernetes secret via the following steps:

1. Run the `kubectl create` command with the `--from-file` parameter to specify the secrets directory:

```
$ kubectl create secret generic registry-secrets --from-file
secrets/
secret "registry-secrets" created
```

2. Check the status via the `kubectl describe` command:

```
$ kubectl describe secret registry-secrets
Name:          registry-secrets
Namespace:     default
Labels:        <none>
Annotations:   <none>
Type:   Opaque
Data
====
domain.key:       3243 bytes
http.secret:      17 bytes
registry_passwd:  69 bytes
domain.crt:       1899 bytes
```

Configuring a private registry to load a Kubernetes secret

On the other hand, the private registry itself supports reading the HTTP secret as an environment variable in string format. It also can support specifying the file path for the SSL certificate and HTTP basic authentication file as environment variables:

Environment variable name	Description	Sample value

REGISTRY_HTTP_SECRET	HTTP secret string	valueFrom:
		  secretKeyRef:
		      name:
		registry-secrets
		      key:
		http.secret

REGISTRY_HTTP_TLS_CERTIFICATE	File path for certificate (domain.crt)	/mnt/domain.crt
REGISTRY_HTTP_TLS_KEY	File path for private key (domain.key)	/mnt/domain.key
REGISTRY_AUTH_HTPASSWD_REALM	The realm in which the registry server authenticates	basic-realm
REGISTRY_AUTH_HTPASSWD_PATH	File path for htpasswd file (registry_passwd)	/mnt/registry_passwd
REGISTRY_HTTP_HOST	Specify one of Kubernetes node IP and nodePort	10.138.0.3:30500

Ideally, you should have a load balancer and set up a Kubernetes Service type as LoadBalancer. And then REGISTRY_HTTP_HOST could be the load balancer IP and port number. For simplicity, we'll just use NodePort in this recipe. For more information about LoadBalancer, refer to the *Working with services* section in Chapter 2, *Walking through Kubernetes Concepts*, and the *Forwarding container ports* section in Chapter 3, *Playing with Containers*.

We'll conduct a deployment to a Kubernetes YAML file for creating a registry, and include the preceding variables inside it, so the registry pods can use them. Now we have PersistentVolumeClaim as pvc-1 that supplies the container image store, and mounts SSL certificate files (domain.crt and domain.key) and an HTTP basic authentication file (registry_passwd) via Secret registry-secrets. As well as reading the HTTP Secret string as an environment variable by Secret registry-secrets. The entire YAML configuration is as follows:

```
$ cat private_registry.yaml
apiVersion: apps/v1
kind: Deployment
metadata:
  name: my-private-registry
spec:
  replicas: 1
  selector:
    matchLabels:
      run: my-registry
  template:
    metadata:
      labels:
        run: my-registry
    spec:
      containers:
      - name: my-registry
        image: registry
        env:
          - name: REGISTRY_HTTP_HOST
            value: 10.138.0.3:30500
          - name: REGISTRY_HTTP_SECRET
            valueFrom:
              secretKeyRef:
                name: registry-secrets
                key: http.secret
          - name: REGISTRY_HTTP_TLS_CERTIFICATE
            value: /mnt/domain.crt
          - name: REGISTRY_HTTP_TLS_KEY
            value: /mnt/domain.key
          - name: REGISTRY_AUTH_HTPASSWD_REALM
            value: basic-realm
          - name: REGISTRY_AUTH_HTPASSWD_PATH
            value: /mnt/registry_passwd
        ports:
        - containerPort: 5000
        volumeMounts:
          - mountPath: /var/lib/registry
            name: registry-storage
          - mountPath: /mnt
            name: certs
      volumes:
      - name: registry-storage
        persistentVolumeClaim:
          claimName: "pvc-1"
      - name: certs
        secret:
          secretName: registry-secrets
```

```
              items:
              - key: domain.key
                path: domain.key
              - key: domain.crt
                path: domain.crt
              - key: registry_passwd
                path: registry_passwd
      ---
apiVersion: v1
kind: Service
metadata:
  name: private-registry-svc
spec:
  ports:
    - protocol: TCP
      port: 5000
      nodePort: 30500
  type: NodePort
  selector:
      run: my-registry


$ kubectl create -f private_registry.yaml
deployment.apps "my-private-registry" created
service "private-registry-svc" created


//can scale to multiple Pod (if you have RWX PV set)
$ kubectl scale deploy my-private-registry --replicas=3
deployment "my-private-registry" scaled


$ kubectl get deploy
NAME                     DESIRED   CURRENT   UP-TO-DATE   AVAILABLE   AGE
my-private-registry      3         3         3            3           2m
```

Now your own private registry is ready to use!

Create a repository on the AWS elastic container registry

In order to push a container image to Amazon ECR, you need to create a repository beforehand. Unlike Docker hub or private registry, Amazon ECR doesn't create a repository automatically when it is the first time to push the image. Therefore, if you want to push three container images, you have to create three repositories in advance:

It is simple to type the `aws ecr create-repository` command to specify the repository name:

```
$ aws ecr create-repository --repository-name my-nginx
{
    "repository": {
        "registryId": "************",
        "repositoryName": "my-nginx",
        "repositoryArn": "arn:aws:ecr:us-east-1:************:repository/my-
nginx",
        "createdAt": 1516608220.0,
        "repositoryUri": "************.dkr.ecr.us-east-1.amazonaws.com/my-
nginx"
    }
}
```

That's it! You need to remember the `repositoryUri` (in the previous case, `************.dkr.ecr.us-east-1.amazonaws.com/my-nginx`) that will be used as the private image URL.

 The previous URL is masked as an ID as `************`. It is tied with your AWS account ID.

On the other hand, if you see something like the following error message, your IAM user doesn't have the permission of the `CreateRepository` operation. In this case, you need to attach an IAM policy from `AmazonEC2ContainerRegistryFullAccess`:

```
$ aws ecr create-repository --repository-name chapter5
An error occurred (AccessDeniedException) when calling the CreateRepository
operation: User: arn:aws:iam::************:user/ecr-user is not authorized
to perform: ecr:CreateRepository on resource: *
```

Determining your repository URL on Google container registry

In order to push a container image to Google container registry, there is an important consideration regarding the repository URL. First of all, there are several Google container registry region hosts available:

- `gcr.io` (currently USA region)
- `us.gcr.io` (USA region)

- `eu.gcr.io` (Europe region)
- `asia.gcr.io` (Asia region)

 Note that these region hosts are network latency purpose, doesn't mean to restrict to a particular region. They are still accessible worldwide.

Second of all, while you tag the container image, you also need to specify your `project-id` on which you've enabled billing and API. Therefore, the entire repository URL could be:

```
<gcr region>/<project-id>/<image name>:tag
```

In my case, I used the region USA default, the project ID is `kubernetes-cookbook`, and the image name is `my-nginx`; therefore, my repository URL is:

```
gcr.io/kubernetes-cookbook/my-nginx:latest
```

Other than that, Google container registry is ready to use now!

How it works...

When you start to use private registry with Kubernetes, you must configure a credential properly. Amazon ECR and Google cloud registry need special consideration. Let's configure a credential for private registry, Amazon ECR and Google cloud registry.

Push and pull an image from your private registry

Now you can push your container image to your private registry. Because we have set up an HTTP basic authentication, you need to do `docker login` first. Otherwise you get a `no basic auth credentials` error:

```
//just tag nginx to your own private image
$ docker tag nginx 10.138.0.3:30500/my-nginx

//will be failed when push without login information. using complete image
name with private registry as prefix
$ docker push 10.138.0.3:30500/my-nginx
The push refers to a repository [10.138.0.3:30500/my-nginx]
a103d141fc98: Preparing
73e2bd445514: Preparing
2ec5c0a4cb57: Preparing
```

```
no basic auth credentials
```

Therefore, you need `docker login` to specify the username and password, which you set onto the `registry_passwd` file:

```
//docker login
$ docker login 10.138.0.3:30500
Username: user01
Password:
Login Succeeded

//successfully to push
$ docker push 10.138.0.3:30500/my-nginx
The push refers to a repository [10.138.0.3:30500/my-nginx]
a103d141fc98: Pushed
73e2bd445514: Pushed
2ec5c0a4cb57: Pushed
latest: digest:
sha256:926b086e1234b6ae9a11589c4cece66b267890d24d1da388c96dd8795b2ffcfb
size: 948
```

On the other hand, as for pulling an image from a private registry, Kubernetes nodes also needs to have a credential for your private registry. But using the `docker login` command on every node is not realistic. Instead, Kubernetes supports storing this credential as a Kubernetes secret and each node will use this credential while pulling an image.

To do that, we need to create a `docker-registry` resource that needs to specify:

- `--docker-server`: In this example, `10.138.0.3:30500`
- `--docker-username`: In this example, `user01`
- `--docker-password`: In this example, `my-super-secure-password`
- `--docker-email`: Your email address

```
//create secret named "my-private-credential"
$ kubectl create secret docker-registry my-private-credential \
> --docker-server=10.138.0.3:30500 \
> --docker-username=user01 \
> --docker-password=my-super-secure-password \
> --docker-email=hideto.saito@example.com
secret "my-private-credential" created

//successfully to created
$ kubectl get secret my-private-credential
NAME TYPE DATA AGE
```

```
my-private-credential kubernetes.io/dockerconfigjson 1 18s
```

Finally, you can pull your private image from the private registry that is specifying the `my-private-credential` secret. To do that, set `spec.imagePullSecrets` as follows:

```
$ cat private-nginx.yaml
apiVersion: v1
kind: Pod
metadata:
  name: private-nginx
spec:
  containers:
  - name: private-nginx
    image: 10.138.0.3:30500/my-nginx
  imagePullSecrets:
  - name: my-private-credential

$ kubectl create -f private-nginx.yaml
pod "private-nginx" created

//successfully to launch your Pod using private image
$ kubectl get pods private-nginx
NAME            READY     STATUS     RESTARTS    AGE
private-nginx   1/1       Running    0           10s
```

Congratulations! Now you can feel free to push your private images to your private registry run by Kubernetes. Also, pull an image from Kubernetes too. At any time, you can scale out based on client traffic.

Push and pull an image from Amazon ECR

Amazon ECR has an authentication mechanism to provide access to your private repositories. AWS CLI has a functionality to generate an access token using the `aws ecr get-login` command:

```
$ aws ecr get-login --no-include-email
```

It outputs the `docker login` command with the ID and password:

```
docker login -u AWS -p eyJwYXlsb2FkIjoiNy(very long strings)...
https://***********.dkr.ecr.us-east-1.amazonaws.com
```

Therefore, just copy and paste to your terminal to acquire a token from AWS. Then try `docker push` to upload your Docker image to ECR:

```
$ docker tag nginx ************.dkr.ecr.us-east-1.amazonaws.com/my-nginx

$ docker push ************.dkr.ecr.us-east-1.amazonaws.com/my-nginx
The push refers to repository [************.dkr.ecr.us-
east-1.amazonaws.com/my-nginx]
a103d141fc98: Pushed
73e2bd445514: Pushing 8.783MB/53.23MB
2ec5c0a4cb57: Pushing 4.333MB/55.26MB
```

On the other hand, pulling an image from ECR to Kubernetes follows exactly the same steps as the private registry that uses a Kubernetes secret to store the token:

```
$ kubectl create secret docker-registry my-ecr-secret \
> --docker-server=https://************.dkr.ecr.us-east-1.amazonaws.com \
> --docker-email=hideto.saito@example.com \
> --docker-username=AWS \
> --docker-password=eyJwYXlsb2FkIjoiS...
secret "my-ecr-secret" created


$ kubectl get secret my-ecr-secret
NAME             TYPE                                DATA      AGE
my-ecr-secret    kubernetes.io/dockerconfigjson      1         10s
```

Now, `spec.imagePullSecrets` needs to specify `my-ecr-secret`. As well as the image URL, it also specifies the ECR repository:

```
$ cat private-nginx-ecr.yaml
apiVersion: v1
kind: Pod
metadata:
  name: private-nginx-ecr
spec:
  containers:
  - name: private-nginx-ecr
    image: ************.dkr.ecr.us-east-1.amazonaws.com/my-nginx
  imagePullSecrets:
  - name: my-ecr-secret


$ kubectl create -f private-nginx-ecr.yaml
pod "private-nginx-ecr" created
```

```
$ kubectl get pods private-nginx-ecr
NAME                 READY    STATUS     RESTARTS    AGE
private-nginx-ecr    1/1      Running    0           1m
```

Note that this token is short-lived: it's valid up to 12 hours. So, 12 hours later, you need to run `aws ecr get-login` again to acquire a new token, then update the secret `my-ecr-secret`. It is absolutely not ideal to do this.

The good news is that Kubernetes supports the updating of the ECR token automatically via `CloudProvider`. However, it requires that your Kubernetes runs on an AWS environment such as EC2. In addition, the EC2 instance has to have an IAM role that is equivalent or higher than the `AmazonEC2ContainerRegistryReadOnly` policy. It will be described in `Chapter 6`, *Building Kubernetes on AWS*.

If you really want to use your Kubernetes cluster outside of AWS by pulling an image from the ECR repository, there is a challenge in that you need to update the ECR token every 12 hours. Maybe you can do this using a cron job or by adopting some automation tools.

> For more detail, please visit the AWS online document at `https://docs.aws.amazon.com/AmazonECR/latest/userguide/Registries.html`.

Push and pull an image from Google cloud registry

According to GCP documentation (`https://cloud.google.com/container-registry/docs/advanced-authentication`), there are several way to push/pull to a container registry.

Using gcloud to wrap the Docker command

The `gcloud` command has a wrapper function to run a `docker` command to push and pull. For example, if you want to push the image `gcr.io/kubernetes-cookbook/my-nginx`, use the `gcloud` command:

```
$ gcloud docker -- push gcr.io/kubernetes-cookbook/my-nginx
```

It is sufficient to push the image from your machine, however, it is not ideal if you integrate with Kubernetes. This is because it is not easy to wrap the `gcloud` command on the Kubernetes node.

Fortunately, there is a solution that creates a GCP service account and grants a permission (role) to it.

Using the GCP service account to grant a long-lived credential

We need to integrate to pull an image from the Kubernetes node, which requires a long-lived credential that can be stored to the Kubernetes secret. To do that, perform the following steps:

1. Create a GCP service account (`container-sa`):

```
$ gcloud iam service-accounts create container-sa
Created service account [container-sa].

//full name is as below
$ gcloud iam service-accounts list | grep container
container-sa@kubernetes-cookbook.iam.gserviceaccount.com
```

2. Assign `container-sa` (use full name) to the `roles/storage.admin` role:

```
$ gcloud projects add-iam-policy-binding kubernetes-cookbook \
> --member serviceAccount:container-sa@kubernetes-
cookbook.iam.gserviceaccount.com \
> --role=roles/storage.admin
```

3. Generate a key file (`container-sa.json`) for `container-sa`:

```
$ gcloud iam service-accounts keys create container-sa.json \
> --iam-account container-sa@kubernetes-
cookbook.iam.gserviceaccount.com

created key [f60a81235a1ed9fbce881639f621470cb087149c] of type
[json] as [container-sa.json] for [container-sa@kubernetes-
cookbook.iam.gserviceaccount.com]
```

4. Use `docker login` to check whether the key file is working or not:

```
//note that username must be _json_key
$ cat container-sa.json | docker login --username _json_key --
password-stdin gcr.io
Login Succeeded
```

5. Use `docker pull` to check whether you can pull from container registry or not:

```
$ docker pull gcr.io/kubernetes-cookbook/my-nginx
Using default tag: latest
latest: Pulling from kubernetes-cookbook/my-nginx
e7bb522d92ff: Pulling fs layer
6edc05228666: Pulling fs layer
...
```

Looks all fine! Now you can use the Kubernetes secret the exact same way with the private registry or AWS ECR.

6. Create a Kubernetes secret (`my-gcr-secret`) to specify `_json_key` and `container-sa.json`:

```
$ kubectl create secret docker-registry my-gcr-secret \
> --docker-server=gcr.io \
> --docker-username=_json_key \
> --docker-password=`cat container-sa.json` \
> --docker-email=hideto.saito@example.com
secret "my-gcr-secret" created
```

7. Specify `my-gcr-secret` to `imagePullSecrets` to launch a pod:

```
$ cat private-nginx-gcr.yaml
apiVersion: v1
kind: Pod
metadata:
  name: private-nginx-gcr
spec:
  containers:
  - name: private-nginx-gcr
    image: gcr.io/kubernetes-cookbook/my-nginx
  imagePullSecrets:
  - name: my-gcr-secret


$ kubectl create -f private-nginx-gcr.yaml
pod "private-nginx-gcr" created


$ kubectl get pods
NAME                READY    STATUS     RESTARTS    AGE
private-nginx-gcr   1/1      Running    0           47s
```

Congratulations! Now you can use Google container registry for your private registry that is fully managed by GCP. And Kubernetes can pull your private image from there.

Integrating with Jenkins

In software engineering, **continuous integration (CI)** (https://en.wikipedia.org/wiki/Continuous_integration) and **continuous delivery (CD)** (https://en.wikipedia.org/wiki/Continuous_delivery), abbreviated as CI/CD, have the ability to simplify the procedure of the traditional development process with continuous developing, testing, and delivering mechanisms in order to reduce the panic of serious conflict, namely, to deliver small changes one at a time and to narrow down the problems immediately, if any. Furthermore, through automatic tools, a product delivered by the CI/CD system can achieve better efficiency and shorten time-to-market.

Jenkins is one of the well-known CI systems, which can be configured as a continuous delivery system. Jenkins can pull your project codes from the source code control system, run the tests, and then deploy based on your configuration. In this recipe, we will show you how to integrate Jenkins to Kubernetes to achieve continuous delivery.

Getting ready

Before you start this recipe, prepare a Docker hub account (https://hub.docker.com) or you may use your private registry that is described in the previous section. But the important part is you must have a credential to pull and push to the registry. If you use Docker hub, make sure `docker login` with your credentials works.

Next, make sure your Kubernetes is ready. But we will use RBAC authentication for access from the Jenkins pod to the Kubernetes master API. If you use `minikube`, you need to add the `--extra-config=apiserver.Authorization.Mode=RBAC` option when starting a minikube:

```
//enable RBAC and allocate 8G memory
$ minikube start --memory=8192 --extra-
config=apiserver.Authorization.Mode=RBAC
```

Then, you can set up your own Jenkins server through Kubernetes as well; the details are in this section.

Some minikube versions have a `kube-dns` issue that can't resolve the external domain name, such as `https://github.com/` and `https://jenkins.io/`, that can't process this recipe. Replacing the `kube-dns` add-on with the `coredns` add-on could resolve the issue after launching `minikube` with the following command:

```
$ minikube addons disable kube-dns
$ minikube addons enable coredns
```

How to do it...

There are two important parts to go through in the Jenkins setup:

1. Jenkins needs to run a `docker` command to build your application to compose your container image
2. Jenkins need to communicate with the Kubernetes master to control deployment

To achieve step 1, there is a tricky part that needs something like a **Docker-in-Docker (dind)**. This is because Jenkins is run by Kubernetes as a pod (Docker container), and Jenkins also needs to invoke a `docker` command to build your application. It can be achieved by mounting `/var/run/docker.sock` from the Kubernetes node to the Jenkins pod that can communicate with Jenkins, the Kubernetes node, and the Docker daemon.

Docker-in-Docker and mounting `/var/run/docker.sock` have been described at `https://blog.docker.com/2013/09/docker-can-now-run-within-docker/` and `http://jpetazzo.github.io/2015/09/03/do-not-use-docker-in-docker-for-ci/`.

In order to achieve step 2, we will set up a Kubernetes service account and assign one `ClusterRole` so that the Jenkins service account can have a necessary privilege.

Let's do it step by step.

Setting up a custom Jenkins image

Run Jenkins by Kubernetes, we use an official image (`https://hub.docker.com/u/jenkins/`) but customize it to install the following applications on it:

- Docker CE
- kubectl binary
- Jenkins Docker plugin

To do that, prepare `Dockerfile` to maintain your own Jenkins image:

```
$ cat Dockerfile
FROM jenkins/jenkins:lts

EXPOSE 8080 50000

# install Docker CE for Debian :
https://docs.docker.com/engine/installation/linux/docker-ce/debian/
USER root
RUN apt-get update
RUN apt-get install -y sudo apt-transport-https ca-certificates curl gnupg2
software-properties-common
RUN curl -fsSL https://download.docker.com/linux/$(. /etc/os-release; echo
"$ID")/gpg | apt-key add -
RUN add-apt-repository "deb [arch=amd64]
https://download.docker.com/linux/$(. /etc/os-release; echo "$ID")
$(lsb_release -cs) stable"
RUN apt-get update && apt-get install -y docker-ce

# install kubectl binary
RUN curl -LO https://storage.googleapis.com/kubernetes-
release/release/v1.9.2/bin/linux/amd64/kubectl
RUN chmod +x ./kubectl
RUN mv ./kubectl /usr/local/bin/kubectl

# setup Jenkins plubins : https://github.com/jenkinsci/docker#script-usage
RUN /usr/local/bin/install-plugins.sh docker
```

Use `docker build` to build your Jenkins image and then `docker push` command to upload to your own registry in Docker hub, as shown:

```
//build your own Jenkins image
$ docker build -t <your-docker-hub-account>/my-jenkins .

//push to Docker Hub
$ docker push <your-docker-hub-account>/my-jenkins
```

Or, alternatively, you could upload that to your private registry or any other cloud-provided registry.

Hurray! We have our build system image ready now.

Setting up Kubernetes service account and ClusterRole

Imagine that after using Jenkins successfully to build your application container, you then use `kubectl` to update deployment to roll out a new binary. To do that, invoke a `kubectl` command from the inside of a Jenkins pod. In this scenario, we need a credential to communicate to the Kubernetes master.

Fortunately, Kubernetes supports this kind of scenario, which uses a service account. It is described in detail in Chapter 8, *Advanced Cluster Administration*. So, this recipe will use the simplest way, which uses the `default` namespace and `cluster-admin` ClusterRole.

To check whether RBAC is enabled and also if the `cluster-admin` ClusterRole exists or not, type the `kubectl get clusterrole` command:

```
$ kubectl get clusterrole cluster-admin
NAME            AGE
cluster-admin   42m
```

Next, create a service account, `jenkins-sa`, which will be used by a Jenkins pod. Prepare the following YAML configuration, and type the `kubectl create` command to create it:

```
$ cat jenkins-serviceaccount.yaml
apiVersion: v1
kind: ServiceAccount
metadata:
  name: jenkins-sa
  namespace: default


$ kubectl create -f jenkins-serviceaccount.yaml
serviceaccount "jenkins-sa" created
```

Now we can associate the `jenkins-sa` service account with a `cluster-admin` ClusterRole. Prepare a `ClusterRoleBinding` configuration and run the `kubectl create` command:

```
$ cat jenkins-cluteradmin.yaml
apiVersion: rbac.authorization.k8s.io/v1
kind: ClusterRoleBinding
```

```
metadata:
  name: jenkins-cluster-admin
roleRef:
  apiGroup: rbac.authorization.k8s.io
  kind: ClusterRole
  name: cluster-admin
subjects:
- kind: ServiceAccount
  name: jenkins-sa
  namespace: default


$ kubectl create -f jenkins-cluster-admin.yaml
clusterrolebinding.rbac.authorization.k8s.io "jenkins-cluster-admin"
created
```

In the result, if a pod is launched with the service account `jenkins-sa`, this Pod has the privilege to control a Kubernetes cluster because of the `cluster-admin ClusterRole`.

 It should create a custom `ClusterRole` that has minimal privilege for Jenkins usage. But this recipe is to focus on the Jenkins setup itself. If you want to create a custom `ClusterRole`, please go to `Chapter 8`, *Advanced Cluster Administration*.

Launching the Jenkins server via Kubernetes deployment

Based on the previous recipes, now you have:

- A custom Jenkins container image
- A service account

Finally, you can launch your custom Jenkins server on your Kubernetes cluster. Remember that we need to run a `docker` command in the Docker environment, which needs to mount `/var/run/docker.sock` from the local Kubernetes node.

In addition, we need to use a `jenkins-sa` service account to launch a Jenkins pod. It needs to specify `spec.template.spec.serviceAccountName: jenkins-sa` in the deployment configuration.

It is also recommended to have a `PersistentVolume` to preserve Jenkins home (`/var/jenkins_home`), in case a pod is restarted. We just simply use the `hostPath` `/data/jenkins-data` directory (assuming you use minikube). You may change to another path or other types of `PersistentVolume` to fit with your environment.

Overall, the deployments YAML configuration for Jenkins is as follows:

```
$ cat jenkins.yaml
apiVersion: apps/v1
kind: Deployment
...
    spec:
      serviceAccountName: jenkins-sa
      containers:
      - name: my-jenkins
        image: hidetosaito/my-jenkins
        readinessProbe:
          initialDelaySeconds: 40
          tcpSocket:
            port: 8080
        volumeMounts:
        - mountPath: /var/run/docker.sock
          name: docker-sock
        - mountPath: /var/jenkins_home
          name: jenkins-data
      volumes:
      - name: docker-sock
        hostPath:
          path: /var/run/docker.sock
      - name: jenkins-data
        hostPath:
          path: /data/jenkins-data
...


$ kubectl create -f jenkins.yaml
deployment.apps "my-jenkins" created
service "my-jenkins-service" created
```

After a few minutes, Kubernetes pulls your custom Jenkins image and runs a Jenkins pod which is capable of running a `docker` command and a `kubectl` command without any configuration due to mounting the `/var/run/docker.sock` and `jenkins-sa` service account:

```
//check Jenkins Pod status
$ kubectl get pods
```

```
NAME                          READY      STATUS      RESTARTS    AGE
my-jenkins-758b89849c-t2sm9   1/1        Running     0           17m


//access to Jenkins Pod
$ kubectl exec -it my-jenkins-758b89849c-t2sm9 -- /bin/bash


//within Jenkins Pod, you can run docker command
root@my-jenkins-758b89849c-t2sm9:/# docker pull nginx
Using default tag: latest
latest: Pulling from library/nginx
e7bb522d92ff: Pull complete
6edc05228666: Pull complete
cd866a17e81f: Pull complete
Digest:
sha256:926b086e1234b6ae9a11589c4cece66b267890d24d1da388c96dd8795b2ffcfb
Status: Downloaded newer image for nginx:latest


//within Jenkins Pod, you can run kubectl command
root@my-jenkins-758b89849c-t2sm9:/# kubectl get nodes
NAME                                      STATUS     ROLES       AGE
VERSION
gke-chapter5-default-pool-97f6cad9-19vm   Ready      <none>      1h
v1.8.6-gke.0
gke-chapter5-default-pool-97f6cad9-1qxc   Ready      <none>      1h
v1.8.6-gke.0
gke-chapter5-default-pool-97f6cad9-cglm   Ready      <none>      1h
v1.8.6-gke.0


//go back to your terminal
root@my-jenkins-758b89849c-t2sm9:/# exit
exit
```

You are all set! Now you can configure a Jenkins job to build your application, build a container, and deploy to Kubernetes.

How it works...

Now we start to configure Jenkins to build your application. However, to access the WebUI of your custom Jenkins, you need to access the Kubernetes service that binds to your Jenkins pod. It is easier to use `kubectl port-forward` to access remotely to configure Jenkins:

```
//check pod name
$ kubectl get pods
NAME                          READY    STATUS     RESTARTS   AGE
my-jenkins-cbdd6446d-ttxj5    1/1      Running    0          1m

//port forward from your machine :58080 to Jenkins :8080
$ kubectl port-forward my-jenkins-cbdd6446d-ttxj5 58080:8080
Forwarding from 127.0.0.1:58080 -> 8080
```

The initial configuration of Jenkins is done via the following steps:

1. Access the `http://127.0.0.1:58080` Jenkins WebUI; it asks you to input `initialAdminPassword`.

2. Use `kubectl exec` to acquire the `initialAdminPassword`. Then copy and paste to the Jenkins WebUI to proceed with the initial configuration to install the suggested plugin and create an admin user:

```
$ kubectl get pods
NAME                          READY    STATUS     RESTARTS   AGE
my-jenkins-cbdd6446d-ttxj5    1/1      Running    0          1m

//now you see initialAdminPassword
$ kubectl exec my-jenkins-cbdd6446d-ttxj5 -- /bin/bash -c 'cat
/var/jenkins_home/secrets/initialAdminPassword'
47e236f0bf334f838c33f80aac206c22
```

3. You will see a Jenkins top page. Then click **Manage Jenkins**, then **Configure System**:

Navigate to Jenkins configuration

4. Scroll to the bottom and find a **Cloud** section. Click **Add a new cloud** to select **Docker**:

Adding a Docker setting

5. Put **Name** as your desired name (example: `my-docker`) and specify the **Docker Host URI** and Docker domain socket as `unix:///var/run/docker.sock`:

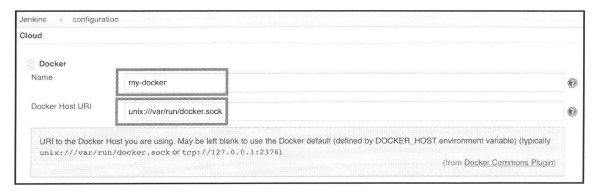

Configure Docker on Jenkins

Using Jenkins to build a Docker image

Let's configure a Jenkins job to build a sample microservice application, which was introduced in the previous recipe (`my-calc`). Perform the following steps to configure and build a Docker image:

1. On the left navigation, click **New Item**:

Navigating to create a new item

2. Put your in desired item name (example: my-calc), select **Freestyle project**, then click **OK**:

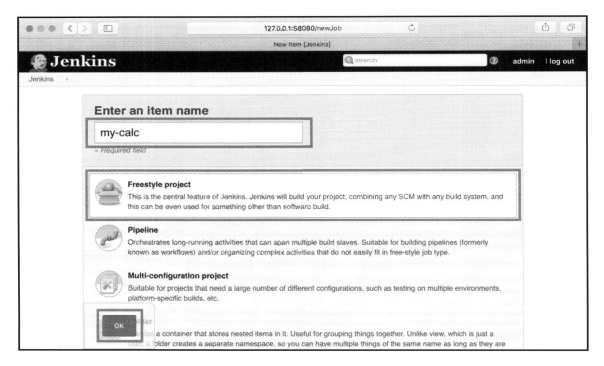

Creating a new Jenkins Job

3. In the **Source Code Management** tab, select **Git** and set the **Repository URL** as `https://github.com/kubernetes-cookbook/my-calc.git`, or you may use your own repository which has a `Dockerfile`:

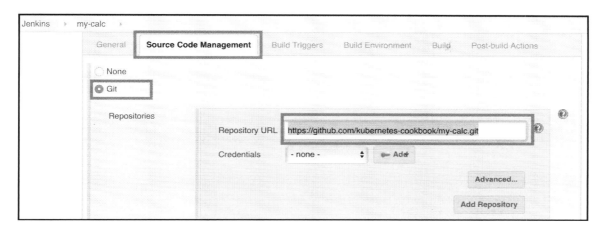

Source Code Management settings

4. On the **Build Environment** tab, click **Add build step** to add **Build / Publish Docker Image**:

Build Environment settings

5. In the **Build / Publish Docker Image** panel:
    1. Directory for `Dockerfile` as current (`.`)
    2. Choose **my-docker** in the **Cloud** that we've set up
    3. Put image as your Docker repository, but append `:${BUILD_NUMBER}` (example: `hidetosaito/my-calc:${BUILD_NUMBER}`)
    4. Enable **Push image**
    5. Click **Add** to add your Docker hub ID credential
    6. Then, click **Save**:

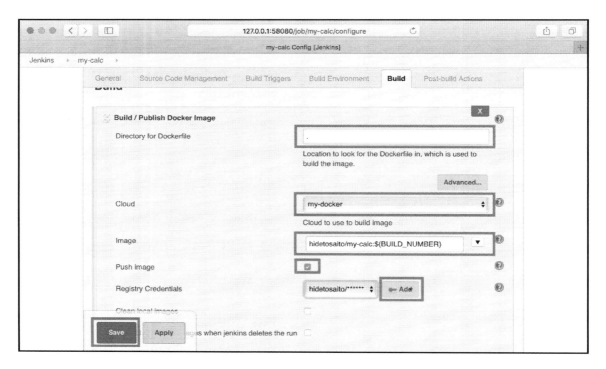

Docker build/publish settings

6. Finally, you can click **Build Now** to trigger a build; for testing purposes you can click five times to see how it works:

Trigger a build

7. Note that you can see a **Console** that knows it performs a Docker build and push:

Showing a build log

8. Access your Docker hub repository; it has been pushed five times (because of clicking on **build** five times):

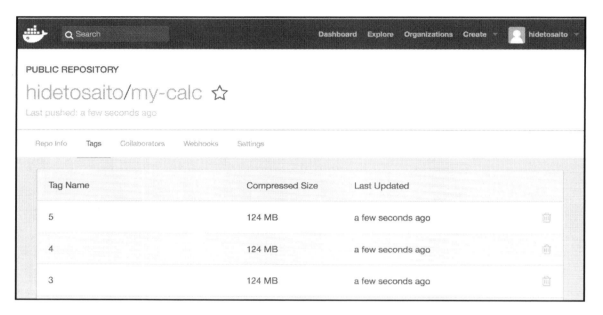

Docker hub repository

That's it! You can achieve continuous integration to build a Docker image so that when you update a source in GitHub, you can continuously build and push the latest image to your Docker hub repository by Jenkins.

Deploying the latest container image to Kubernetes

After each build, Jenkins keeps pushing your container image on your Docker hub repository at the end of the CI process. Next, update the Jenkins job configuration to use the latest image to deploy to Kubernetes, via the following steps:

1. The first time, we pre-deploy microservice application manually via `kubectl deploy --record`. Note that you may change `spec.template.spec.containers.image: hidetosaito/my-calc` to your repository:

```
$ cat my-calc.yaml
apiVersion: apps/v1
kind: Deployment
metadata:
  name: my-calc-deploy
spec:
  replicas: 2
  selector:
    matchLabels:
      run: my-calc
  template:
    metadata:
      labels:
        run: my-calc
    spec:
      containers:
      - name: my-calc
        image: hidetosaito/my-calc


//use --record to trace the history
$ kubectl create -f my-calc-deploy.yaml --record
deployment.apps "my-calc-deploy" created
```

2. Open Jenkins Job configuration; on the **Build** tab, right after the **Docker build settings**, click **Add build step** and choose **Execute shell**:

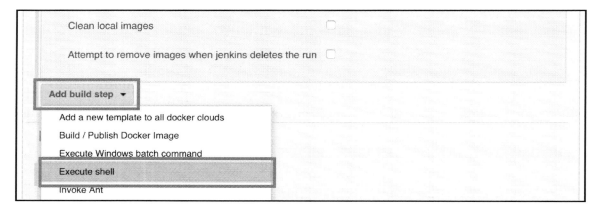

Adding a build step

3. Add this shell script and click **Save**:

```
#!/bin/sh

set +x

# These 2 are defined in Deployment YAML
DEPLOYMENT_NAME=my-calc-deploy
CONTAINER_NAME=my-calc

# change to your Docker Hub repository
REPOSITORY=hidetosaito/my-calc


echo "*********************"
echo "*** before deploy ***"
echo "*********************"
kubectl rollout history deployment $DEPLOYMENT_NAME
kubectl set image deployment $DEPLOYMENT_NAME
$CONTAINER_NAME=$REPOSITORY:$BUILD_NUMBER


echo "*******************************************"
echo "*** waiting to complete rolling update ***"
echo "*******************************************"
kubectl rollout status --watch=true deployment $DEPLOYMENT_NAME
```

```
echo "**********************"
echo "*** after deploy ***"
echo "**********************"
kubectl rollout history deployment $DEPLOYMENT_NAME
```

4. Trigger a new build; you can see that after Docker push, it runs the preceding script:

```
Jenkins  →  my-calc  →  #14

**********************
*** before deploy ***
**********************
deployments "my-calc-deploy"
REVISION    CHANGE-CAUSE
1           kubectl create --filename=my-calc.yaml --record=true
2           kubectl set image deployment my-calc-deploy my-calc=hidetosaito/my-calc:8
3           kubectl set image deployment my-calc-deploy my-calc=hidetosaito/my-calc:9
4           kubectl set image deployment my-calc-deploy my-calc=hidetosaito/my-calc:10
5           kubectl set image deployment my-calc-deploy my-calc=hidetosaito/my-calc:11
6           kubectl set image deployment my-calc-deploy my-calc=hidetosaito/my-calc:12
7           kubectl set image deployment my-calc-deploy my-calc=hidetosaito/my-calc:13

deployment "my-calc-deploy" image updated
*******************************************
*** waiting to complete rolling update ***
*******************************************
Waiting for rollout to finish: 1 out of 2 new replicas have been updated...
Waiting for rollout to finish: 1 out of 2 new replicas have been updated...
Waiting for rollout to finish: 1 out of 2 new replicas have been updated...
Waiting for rollout to finish: 1 old replicas are pending termination...
Waiting for rollout to finish: 1 old replicas are pending termination...
deployment "my-calc-deploy" successfully rolled out
**********************
*** after deploy ***
**********************
deployments "my-calc-deploy"
REVISION    CHANGE-CAUSE
1           kubectl create --filename=my-calc.yaml --record=true
2           kubectl set image deployment my-calc-deploy my-calc=hidetosaito/my-calc:8
3           kubectl set image deployment my-calc-deploy my-calc=hidetosaito/my-calc:9
4           kubectl set image deployment my-calc-deploy my-calc=hidetosaito/my-calc:10
5           kubectl set image deployment my-calc-deploy my-calc=hidetosaito/my-calc:11
6           kubectl set image deployment my-calc-deploy my-calc=hidetosaito/my-calc:12
7           kubectl set image deployment my-calc-deploy my-calc=hidetosaito/my-calc:13
8           kubectl set image deployment my-calc-deploy my-calc=hidetosaito/my-calc:14

Finished: SUCCESS
```

Kubernetes rollout result

Now you can extend continuous integration to continuous delivery! You may extend to add a unit test or integration test and roll back mechanisms onto the above script to make your CI/CD work stronger.

6
Building Kubernetes on AWS

The following recipes are covered in this chapter:

- Playing with Amazon Web Services
- Setting up Kubernetes by kops
- Using AWS as Kubernetes Cloud Provider
- Managing Kubernete cluster on AWS by kops

Introduction

Based on a recent survey of the Cloud Native Computing Foundation, CNCF, **Amazon Web Services** (**AWS**) is a dominant solution for production-level Kubernetes systems (`https://www.cncf.io/blog/2017/12/06/cloud-native-technologies-scaling-production-applications/`). In this chapter, you will learn about the cloud services of AWS, and how these services work together to deliver a robust Kubernetes system. We will also introduce how kops works, a tool for Kubernetes operation, which helps us manage the Kubernetes cluster. Let's explore the world of Kubernetes in AWS!

Playing with Amazon Web Services

Amazon Web Services (`https://aws.amazon.com`) is the most popular public cloud service. It provides the online service for Virtual Server (EC2), Software Defined Network (VPC), Object Store (S3), and so on. It is a suitable infrastructure to set up a Kubernetes cluster. We will explore AWS to understand the fundamental function of AWS.

Getting ready

First of all, you need to sign up to AWS. AWS gives a free tier that allows you to use some amount of AWS resources, free for 12 months. Go to `https://aws.amazon.com/free/` to register your information and credit card. It may take 24 hours to verify and activate your account.

Once your AWS account is activated, we need to create one **Identity and Access Management (IAM)** user, which will control your AWS infrastructure via APIs. Then, install the AWS CLI on to your computer.

Creating an IAM user

Perform the following steps to create an IAM user:

1. Go to AWS Web console `https://console.aws.amazon.com`.
2. Click on **IAM** (use the search box, which makes it easier to find):

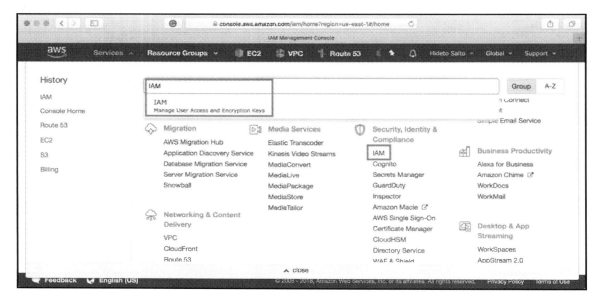

Access to IAM console

3. Click on **Users** in the left navigation and then click on **Add user**:

Creating an IAM user

4. Type **User name** chap6, then choose **Programmatic access**:

Creating chap6 user

5. Choose **Attach existing policies directly**, as shown in the following screenshot, and then select the following policies:
   - **AmazonEC2FullAccess**
   - **AmazonRoute53FullAcccess**
   - **AmazonS3FullAccess**
   - **AmazonVPCFullAccess**
   - **IAMFullAccess**

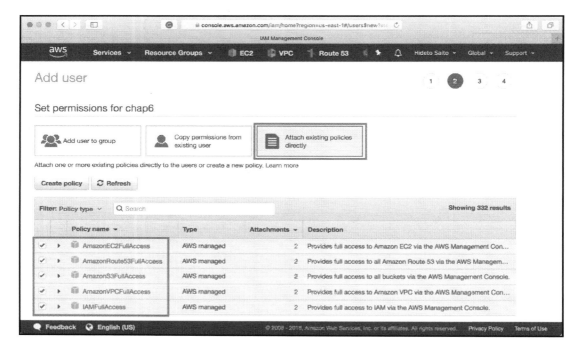

Attaching the necessary Policy

6. Eventually, it generates **Access key ID** and **Secret access key**. Copy and paste into your text editor or click on **Download .csv** to preserve to your computer:

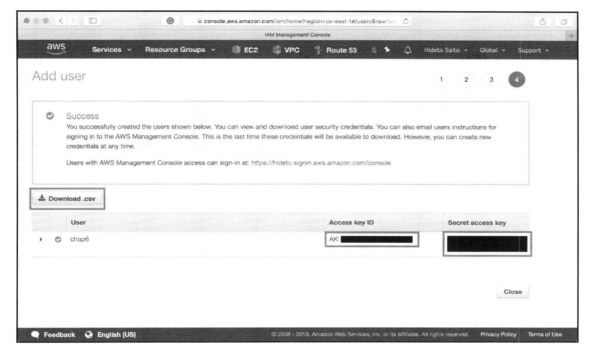

Downloading Access key ID and Secret access key

Installing AWS CLI on macOS

Install `awscli` to macOS using HomeBrew (`https://brew.sh`); this is the easiest way. HomeBrew has already been introduced in `Chapter 1`, *Building your own Kubernetes Cluster*, while installing minikube.

To install awscli by HomeBrew on your Mac, perform the following steps:

1. Type the following command to update the latest formula:

    ```
    $ brew update
    ```

2. Specify `awscli` to install:

    ```
    $ brew install awscli
    ```

3. Verify the `aws` command using the `--version` option:

```
$ aws --version
aws-cli/1.15.0 Python/3.6.5 Darwin/17.5.0 botocore/1.10.0
```

Installing AWS CLI on Windows

Install awscli on Windows; there is a Windows installer package, which is the easiest way to install awscli on to your Windows:

1. Go to AWS Command Line Interface page (`https://aws.amazon.com/cli/`).
2. Download Windows installer 64 bit (`https://s3.amazonaws.com/aws-cli/AWSCLI64.msi`) or 32 bit (`https://s3.amazonaws.com/aws-cli/AWSCLI32.msi`), based on your Windows OS.
3. Launch AWS CLI installer, and then choose the default option to proceed with the installation:

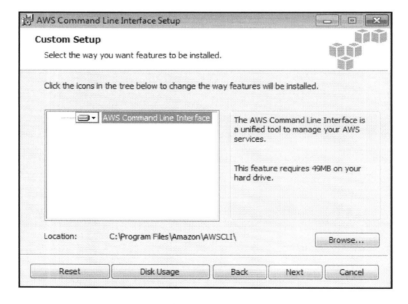

Installing AWS CLI for Windows

4. After complete installation, launch Command Prompt. Then, type the `aws` command with the `--version` option to verify:

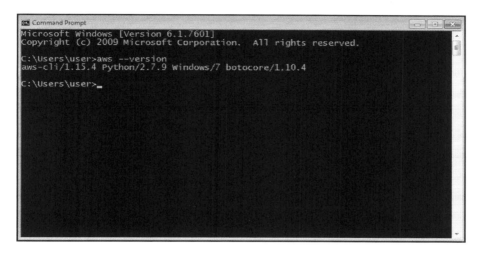

Showing aws command on Windows

How to do it...

First of all, you need to set your **AWS Access Key ID** and **AWS Secret Access Key** for awscli. We've already acquired `chap6` for the IAM user. We will use this user's Access Key ID and Secret Access Key.

1. Launch terminal (Command Prompt for Windows), and then use the `aws` command to set `Access Key ID` and `Secret Access Key`. Also, set the default region as `us-east-1`:

```
$ aws configure
AWS Access Key ID [None]: <Your Access KeyID>
AWS Secret Access Key [None]: <Your Secret Access Key>
Default region name [None]: us-east-1
Default output format [None]:
```

2. Check `chap6` IAM user using the following command:

```
$ aws iam get-user
{
    "User": {
        "Path": "/",
        "UserName": "chap6",
        "UserId": "*********************",
        "Arn": "arn:aws:iam::**************:user/chap6",
        "CreateDate": "2018-04-14T04:22:21Z"
    }
}
```

That's it! Now you can start using AWS to launch your own network and instances.

How it works...

Let's explorer AWS to launch a typical infrastructure. Using awscli to build your own VPC, Subnet, Gateway, and Security group. Then, launch the EC2 instance to understand the basic usage of AWS.

Creating VPC and Subnets

Virtual Private Cloud (VPC) is a Software-Defined Network. You can configure a virtual network on AWS. Subnets are inside of VPC that define network block (**Classless Inter Domain Routing (CIDR)**) such as `192.168.1.0/24`.

Let's create one VPC and two subnets using the following steps:

1. Create a new VPC that has `192.168.0.0/16` CIDR block (IP range: `192.168.0.0 − 192.168.255.255`). Then, capture `VpcId`:

```
$ aws ec2 create-vpc --cidr-block 192.168.0.0/16
{
    "Vpc": {
        "CidrBlock": "192.168.0.0/16",
        "DhcpOptionsId": "dopt-3d901958",
        "State": "pending",
        "VpcId": "vpc-69cfbd12",
        "InstanceTenancy": "default",
        "Ipv6CidrBlockAssociationSet": [],
        "CidrBlockAssociationSet": [
            {
```

```
                    "AssociationId": "vpc-cidr-assoc-c35411ae",
                    "CidrBlock": "192.168.0.0/16",
                    "CidrBlockState": {
                        "State": "associated"
                    }
                }
            ],
            "IsDefault": false,
            "Tags": []
        }
    }
```

2. Create the first subnet under the VPC (vpc-69cfbd12) that has
   192.168.0.0/24 CIDR block (IP range: 192.168.0.0 − 192.168.0.255) and
   specify the availability zone as us-east-1a. Then, capture SubnetId:

```
$ aws ec2 create-subnet --vpc-id vpc-69cfbd12 --cidr-block
192.168.0.0/24 --availability-zone us-east-1a
{
    "Subnet": {
        "AvailabilityZone": "us-east-1a",
        "AvailableIpAddressCount": 251,
        "CidrBlock": "192.168.0.0/24",
        "DefaultForAz": false,
        "MapPublicIpOnLaunch": false,
        "State": "pending",
        "SubnetId": "subnet-6296863f",
        "VpcId": "vpc-69cfbd12",
        "AssignIpv6AddressOnCreation": false,
        "Ipv6CidrBlockAssociationSet": []
    }
}
```

3. Create the second subnet on us-east-1b, which has 192.168.1.0/24 CIDR
   block (IP range: 192.168.1.0 − 192.168.1.255). Then, capture SubnetId:

```
$ aws ec2 create-subnet --vpc-id vpc-69cfbd12 --cidr-block
192.168.1.0/24 --availability-zone us-east-1b
{
    "Subnet": {
        "AvailabilityZone": "us-east-1b",
        "AvailableIpAddressCount": 251,
        "CidrBlock": "192.168.1.0/24",
        "DefaultForAz": false,
        "MapPublicIpOnLaunch": false,
        "State": "pending",
        "SubnetId": "subnet-ce947da9",
```

```
        "VpcId": "vpc-69cfbd12",
        "AssignIpv6AddressOnCreation": false,
        "Ipv6CidrBlockAssociationSet": []
    }
}
```

4. Check the subnet list under VPC (vpc-69cfbd12) using the following command:

```
$ aws ec2 describe-subnets --filters "Name=vpc-
id,Values=vpc-69cfbd12" --query
"Subnets[*].{Vpc:VpcId,CIDR:CidrBlock,AZ:AvailabilityZone,Id:Su
bnetId}" --output=table
------------------------------------------------------------
------
|                        DescribeSubnets
|
+-----------+----------------+------------------+----------
-----+
|    AZ     |     CIDR       |       Id         |     Vpc
|
+-----------+----------------+------------------+----------
-----+
|  us-east-1a|  192.168.0.0/24  |  subnet-6296863f  |
vpc-69cfbd12 |
|  us-east-1b|  192.168.1.0/24  |  subnet-ce947da9  |
vpc-69cfbd12 |
+-----------+----------------+------------------+----------
-----+
```

This looks good!

Internet gateway

To access your VPC network, you need to have a gateway that accesses it from the internet. **Internet Gateway (IGW)** is the one that connects the internet to your VPC.

Then, in the subnets under VPC, you can set the default route to go to IGW or not. If it routes to IGW, the subnet is classified as the public subnet. Then, you can assign the global IP address on the public subnet.

Let's configure the first subnet (`192.168.0.0/24`) as the public subnet that routes to IGW using the following steps:

1. Create IGW and capture `InternetGatewayId`:

```
$ aws ec2 create-internet-gateway
{
    "InternetGateway": {
        "Attachments": [],
        "InternetGatewayId": "igw-e50b849d",
        "Tags": []
    }
}
```

2. Attach IGW (`igw-e50b849d`) to your VPC (`vpc-69cfbd12`):

```
$ aws ec2 attach-internet-gateway --vpc-id vpc-69cfbd12 --
internet-gateway-id igw-e50b849d
```

3. Create a routing table on VPC (`vpc-69cfbd12`) and then capture `RouteTableId`:

```
$ aws ec2 create-route-table --vpc-id vpc-69cfbd12
{
    "RouteTable": {
        "Associations": [],
        "PropagatingVgws": [],
        "RouteTableId": "rtb-a9e791d5",
        "Routes": [
            {
                "DestinationCidrBlock": "192.168.0.0/16",
                "GatewayId": "local",
                "Origin": "CreateRouteTable",
                "State": "active"
            }
        ],
        "Tags": [],
        "VpcId": "vpc-69cfbd12"
    }
}
```

4. Set the default route (0.0.0.0/0) for route table (rtb-a9e791d5) as IGW (igw-e50b849d):

```
$ aws ec2 create-route --route-table-id rtb-a9e791d5 --gateway-id igw-e50b849d --destination-cidr-block 0.0.0.0/0
```

5. Associate route table (rtb-a9e791d5) to public subnet (subnet-6296863f):

```
$ aws ec2 associate-route-table --route-table-id rtb-a9e791d5 --subnet-id subnet-6296863f
```

6. Enable autoassign public IP on the public subnet (subnet-6296863f):

```
$ aws ec2 modify-subnet-attribute --subnet-id subnet-6296863f --map-public-ip-on-launch
```

NAT-GW

What happens if the subnet default route is not pointing to IGW? The subnet is classified as a private subnet with no connectivity to the internet. However, some of situation, your VM in private subnet needs to access to the Internet. For example, download some security patch.

In this case, you can setup NAT-GW. It allows you access to the internet from the private subnet. However, it allows outgoing traffic only, so you cannot assign public IP address for a private subnet. Therefore, it is suitable for backend instances, such as the database.

Let's create NAT-GW and configure a second subnet (192.168.1.0/24) as a private subnet that routes to NAT-GW using the following steps:

1. NAT-GW needs a Global IP address, so create **Elastic IP (EIP)**:

```
$ aws ec2 allocate-address
{
    "PublicIp": "18.232.18.38",
    "AllocationId": "eipalloc-bad28bb3",
    "Domain": "vpc"
}
```

2. Create NAT-GW on the public subnet (subnet-6296863f) and assign EIP (eipalloc-bad28bb3). Then, capture NatGatewayId.

Since NAT-GW needs to access the internet, it must be located on the public subnet instead of the private subnet.

Input the following command:

```
$ aws ec2 create-nat-gateway --subnet-id subnet-6296863f --
allocation-id eipalloc-bad28bb3
{
    "NatGateway": {
        "CreateTime": "2018-04-14T18:49:36.000Z",
        "NatGatewayAddresses": [
            {
                "AllocationId": "eipalloc-bad28bb3"
            }
        ],
        "NatGatewayId": "nat-0b12be42c575bba43",
        "State": "pending",
        "SubnetId": "subnet-6296863f",
        "VpcId": "vpc-69cfbd12"
    }
}
```

3. Create the route table and capture `RouteTableId`:

```
$ aws ec2 create-route-table --vpc-id vpc-69cfbd12
{
    "RouteTable": {
        "Associations": [],
        "PropagatingVgws": [],
        "RouteTableId": "rtb-70f1870c",
        "Routes": [
            {
                "DestinationCidrBlock": "192.168.0.0/16",
                "GatewayId": "local",
                "Origin": "CreateRouteTable",
                "State": "active"
            }
        ],
        "Tags": [],
        "VpcId": "vpc-69cfbd12"
    }
}
```

4. Set the default route (0.0.0.0/0) of the route table (rtb-70f1870c) to NAT-GW (nat-0b12be42c575bba43):

```
$ aws ec2 create-route --route-table-id rtb-70f1870c --nat-
gateway-id nat-0b12be42c575bba43 --destination-cidr-block
0.0.0.0/0
```

5. Associate route table (rtb-70f1870c) to private subnet (subnet-ce947da9):

```
$ aws ec2 associate-route-table --route-table-id rtb-70f1870c -
-subnet-id subnet-ce947da9
```

Security group

Before launching your Virtual Server (EC2), you need to create a Security Group that has an appropriate security rule. Now, we have two subnets, public and private. Let's set public subnet such that it allows ssh (22/tcp) and http (80/tcp) from the internet. Then, set the private subnet such that it allows ssh from the public subnet:

1. Create one security group for the public subnet on VPC (vpc-69cfbd12):

```
$ aws ec2 create-security-group --vpc-id vpc-69cfbd12 --group-
name public --description "public facing host"
{
    "GroupId": "sg-dd8a3f94"
}
```

2. Add the ssh allow rule to the public security group (sg-dd8a3f94):

```
$ aws ec2 authorize-security-group-ingress --group-id sg-
dd8a3f94 --protocol tcp --port 22 --cidr 0.0.0.0/0
```

3. Add the http allow rule to the public security group (sg-dd8a3f94):

```
$ aws ec2 authorize-security-group-ingress --group-id sg-
dd8a3f94 --protocol tcp --port 80 --cidr 0.0.0.0/0
```

4. Create a second security group for the private subnet on VPC (vpc-69cfbd12):

```
$ aws ec2 create-security-group --vpc-id vpc-69cfbd12 --group-
name private --description "private subnet host"
{
    "GroupId": "sg-a18c39e8"
}
```

5. Add an `ssh` allow rule to the private security group (`sg-a18c39e8`):

```
$ aws ec2 authorize-security-group-ingress --group-id sg-
a18c39e8 --protocol tcp --port 22 --source-group sg-dd8a3f94
```

6. Check the Security Group list using the following command:

```
$ aws ec2 describe-security-groups --filters "Name=vpc-id,
Values=vpc-69cfbd12" --query
"SecurityGroups[*].{id:GroupId,name:GroupName}" --output table
---------------------------
|   DescribeSecurityGroups  |
+--------------+----------+
|      id      |   name   |
+--------------+----------+
|  sg-2ed56067 |  default |
|  sg-a18c39e8 |  private |
|  sg-dd8a3f94 |  public  |
+--------------+----------+
```

EC2

Now you need to upload your ssh public key and then launch the EC2 instance on both the public subnet and the private subnet:

1. Upload your ssh public key (assume you have a public key that is located at `~/.ssh/id_rsa.pub`):

```
$ aws ec2 import-key-pair --key-name=chap6-key --public-key-
material "`cat ~/.ssh/id_rsa.pub`"
```

2. Launch the first EC2 instance with the following parameters:
   - Use Amazon Linux image: `ami-1853ac65` (Amazon Linux)
   - T2.nano instance type: `t2.nano`
   - Ssh key: `chap6-key`
   - Public Subnet: `subnet-6296863f`
   - Public Security Group: `sg-dd8a3f94`

```
$ aws ec2 run-instances --image-id ami-1853ac65 --instance-type
t2.nano --key-name chap6-key --security-group-ids sg-dd8a3f94 -
-subnet-id subnet-6296863f
```

3. Launch the second EC2 instance with the following parameters:
    - Use Amazon Linux image: `ami-1853ac65`
    - T2.nano instance type: `t2.nano`
    - Ssh key: `chap6-key`
    - Private subnet: `subnet-ce947da9`
    - Private Secuity Group: `sg-a18c39e8`

```
$ aws ec2 run-instances --image-id ami-1853ac65 --instance-type
t2.nano --key-name chap6-key --security-group-ids sg-a18c39e8 -
-subnet-id subnet-ce947da9
```

4. Check the status of the EC2 instances:

```
$ aws ec2 describe-instances --filters "Name=vpc-
id,Values=vpc-69cfbd12" --query
"Reservations[*].Instances[*].{id:InstanceId,PublicIP:PublicIpA
ddress,PrivateIP:PrivateIpAddress,Subnet:SubnetId}" --
output=table
-------------------------------------------------------------
----------------
|                              DescribeInstances
|
+--------------+----------------+-----------------+---------
--------------+
|   PrivateIP  |    PublicIP    |     Subnet      |
id            |
+--------------+----------------+-----------------+---------
--------------+
|  192.168.0.206|  34.228.228.140|   subnet-6296863f|
i-03a0e49d26a2dafa4    |
|  192.168.1.218|  None          |  subnet-ce947da9|
i-063080766d2f2f520    |
+--------------+----------------+-----------------+---------
--------------+
```

5. SSH (use the `-A` option to forward your authentication info) to the public EC2 host from your computer:

```
$ ssh -A ec2-user@34.228.228.140
The authenticity of host '34.228.228.140 (34.228.228.140)'
can't be established.
ECDSA key fingerprint is
SHA256:lE7hoBhHntVDvRItnasqyHRynajn2iuHJ7U3nsWySRU.
Are you sure you want to continue connecting (yes/no)? yes
Warning: Permanently added '34.228.228.140' (ECDSA) to the list
```

```
of known hosts.
       __|  __|_  )
       _|  (     /    Amazon Linux AMI
       ___|\___|___|
https://aws.amazon.com/amazon-linux-ami/2017.09-release-notes/
8 package(s) needed for security, out of 13 available
Run "sudo yum update" to apply all updates.
[ec2-user@ip-192-168-0-206 ~]$
```

6. Install and launch nginx to the public EC2 host:

```
[ec2-user@ip-192-168-0-206 ~]$ sudo yum -y install nginx
[ec2-user@ip-192-168-0-206 ~]$ sudo service nginx start
Starting nginx:                                              [ OK
]
```

7. Make sure you can access the nginx server from your machine (see the following screenshot):

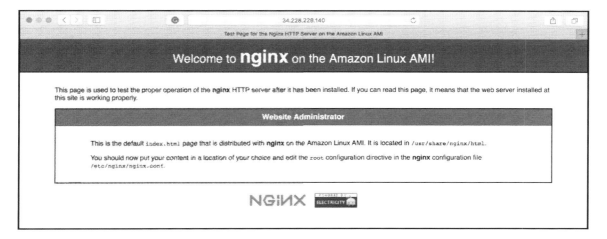

Accessing nginx web server on public host

8. SSH from the public host to the private host (you must use a private IP address):

```
$ ssh 192.168.1.218
```

9. Make sure the private host can perform yum update via NAT-GW:

```
[ec2-user@ip-192-168-1-218 ~]$ sudo yum -y update
```

Congratulations! You can set up your own infrastructure on AWS, as shown in the following diagram, which has the following:

- One VPC with CIDR `192.168.0.0/16`
- IGW
- NAT-GW
- Two Subnets
    - public subnet: `192.168.0.0/24` route to IGW
    - private subnet: 192.168.1.0/24 route to NAT-GW
- Two EC2 instances (public and private)
- Two Security Groups (allow public http/ssh and private ssh)

Now, take a look at the diagram:

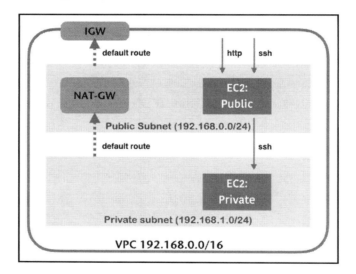

AWS components diagram

In this section, you have learned how to use AWS from scratch. We have covered its basic uses, but it is important to know while setup Kubernetes on AWS. Next, we will explore how to set up Kubernetes on AWS.

Setting up Kubernetes with kops

What is kops? It is the abbreviated term of Kubernetes Operation (`https://github.com/kubernetes/kops`). Similar to kubeadm, minikube, and kubespray, kops reduces the heavy duty of building up a Kubernetes cluster by ourselves. It helps in creation, and provides an interface to users for managing the clusters. Furthermore, kops achieves a more automatic installing procedure and delivers a production-level system. It targets to support dominate cloud platforms, such as AWS, GCE, and VMware vSphere. In this recipe, we will talk about how to run a Kubernetes cluster with kops.

Getting ready

Before our major tutorial, we will need to install kops on to your local host. It is a straightforward step for downloading the binary file and moving it to the system directory of the execution file:

```
// download the latest stable kops binary
$ curl -LO https://github.com/kubernetes/kops/releases/download/$(curl -s
https://api.github.com/repos/kubernetes/kops/releases/latest | grep
tag_name | cut -d '"' -f 4)/kops-linux-amd64
$ chmod +x kops-linux-amd64
$ sudo mv kops-linux-amd64 /usr/local/bin/kops
// verify the command is workable
$ kops version
Version 1.9.0 (git-cccd71e67)
```

Next, we have to prepare some AWS configuration on your host and required services for cluster. Refer to the following items and make sure that they are ready:

- **IAM user**: Since kops would create and build several AWS service components together for you, you must have an IAM user with kops required permissions. We've created an IAM user named **chap6** in the previous section that has the following policies with the necessary permissions for kops:
  - AmazonEC2FullAccess
  - AmazonRoute53FullAccess
  - AmazonS3FullAccess
  - IAMFullAccess
  - AmazonVPCFullAccess

Then, exposing the AWS access key ID and secret key as environment variables can make this role applied on host while firing `kops` commands:

```
$ export AWS_ACCESS_KEY_ID=${string of 20 capital character
combination}
$ export AWS_SECRET_ACCESS_KEY=${string of 40 character and
number combination}
```

- **Prepare an S3 bucket for storing cluster configuration**: In our demonstration later, the S3 bucket name will be `kubernetes-cookbook`.
- **Prepare a Route53 DNS domain for accessing points of cluster**: In our demonstration later, the domain name we use will be `k8s-cookbook.net`.

How to do it...

We can easily run up a Kubernetes cluster using a single command with parameters containing complete configurations. These parameters are described in the following table:

Parameter	Description	Value in example
`--name`	This is the name of the cluster. It will also be the domain name of the cluster's entry point. So you can utilize your Route53 DNS domain with a customized name, for example, `{your cluster name}.{your Route53 domain name}`.	`my-cluster.k8s-cookbook.net`
`--state`	This indicates the S3 bucket that stores the status of the cluster in the format `s3://{bucket name}`.	`s3://kubernetes-cookbook`
`--zones`	This is the availability zone where you need to build your cluster.	`us-east-1a`
`--cloud`	This is the cloud provider.	`aws`
`--network-cidr`	Here, kops helps to create independent CIDR range for the new VPC.	`10.0.0.0/16`

`--master-size`	This is the instance size of Kubernetes master.	`t2.large`
`--node-size`	This is the instance size of Kubernetes nodes.	`t2.medium`
`--node-count`	This is the number of nodes in the cluster.	`2`
`--network`	This is the overlay network used in this cluster.	`calico`
`--topology`	This helps you decide whether the cluster is public facing.	`private`
`--ssh-public-key`	This helps you assign an SSH public key for bastion server, then we may log in through the private key.	`~/.ssh/id_rsa.pub`
`--bastion`	This gives you an indication to create the bastion server.	N/A
`--yes`	This gives you the confirmation for executing immediately.	N/A

Now we are ready to compose the configurations into a command and fire it:

```
$ kops create cluster --name my-cluster.k8s-cookbook.net --
state=s3://kubernetes-cookbook --zones us-east-1a --cloud aws --network-
cidr 10.0.0.0/16 --master-size t2.large --node-size t2.medium --node-count
2 --networking calico --topology private --ssh-public-key ~/.ssh/id_rsa.pub
--bastion --yes
...
I0408 15:19:21.794035   13144 executor.go:91] Tasks: 105 done / 105 total;
0 can run
I0408 15:19:21.794111   13144 dns.go:153] Pre-creating DNS records
I0408 15:19:22.420077   13144 update_cluster.go:248] Exporting kubecfg for
cluster
kops has set your kubectl context to my-cluster.k8s-cookbook.net
Cluster is starting.  It should be ready in a few minutes.
...
```

After a few minutes, the command takes out the preceding logs showing what AWS services have been created and served for you kops-built Kubernetes cluster. You can even check your AWS console to verify their relationships, which will look similar to the following diagram:

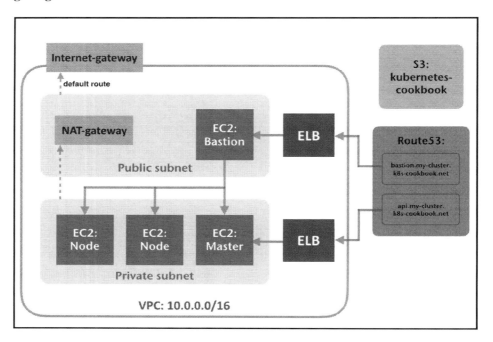

The components of Kubernetes cluster in AWS created by kops

How it works...

From localhost, users can interact with the cluster on AWS using the kops command:

```
//check the cluster
$ kops get cluster --state s3://kubernetes-cookbook
NAME                        CLOUD   ZONES
my-cluster.k8s-cookbook.net aws     us-east-1a
```

Working with kops-built AWS cluster

Furthermore, as you can see in the previous section, the last few logs of kops cluster creation shows that the environment of the client is also ready. It means that kops helps to bind the API server to our host securely as well. We may use the `kubectl` command like we were in Kubernetes master. What we need to do is install kubectl manually. It would be as simple as installing kops; just download the binary file:

```
// install kubectl on local
$ curl -LO https://storage.googleapis.com/kubernetes-release/release/$(curl
-s
https://storage.googleapis.com/kubernetes-release/release/stable.txt)/bin/l
inux/amd64/kubectl
$ chmod +x kubectl
$ sudo mv kubectl /usr/local/bin/
// check the nodes in cluster on AWS
$ kubectl get nodes
NAME                           STATUS    ROLES     AGE       VERSION
ip-10-0-39-216.ec2.internal    Ready     master    2m        v1.8.7
ip-10-0-40-26.ec2.internal     Ready     node      31s       v1.8.7
ip-10-0-50-147.ec2.internal    Ready     node      33s       v1.8.7
```

However, you can still access the nodes in the cluster. Since the cluster is set down in a private network, we will require to login to the bastion server first, and jump to the nodes for the next:

```
//add private key to ssh authentication agent
$ ssh-add ~/.ssh/id_rsa

//use your private key with flag "-i"
//we avoid it since the private key is in default location, ~/.ssh/id_rsa
//also use -A option to forward an authentication agent
$ ssh -A admin@bastion.my-cluster.k8s-cookbook.net

The programs included with the Debian GNU/Linux system are free software;
the exact distribution terms for each program are described in the
individual files in /usr/share/doc/*/copyright.

Debian GNU/Linux comes with ABSOLUTELY NO WARRANTY, to the extent
permitted by applicable law.
Last login: Sun Apr  8 19:37:31 2018 from 10.0.2.167
// access the master node with its private IP
admin@ip-10-0-0-70:~$ ssh 10.0.39.216

The programs included with the Debian GNU/Linux system are free software;
the exact distribution terms for each program are described in the
individual files in /usr/share/doc/*/copyright.
```

```
Debian GNU/Linux comes with ABSOLUTELY NO WARRANTY, to the extent
permitted by applicable law.
Last login: Sun Apr  8 19:36:22 2018 from 10.0.0.70
admin@ip-10-0-39-216:~$
```

Deleting kops-built AWS cluster

We can simply remove our cluster using the kops command as follows:

```
$ kops delete cluster --name my-cluster.k8s-cookbook.net --state
s3://kubernetes-cookbook --yes
Deleted cluster: "my-cluster.k8s-cookbook.net"
```

It will clean the AWS services for you. But some other services created by yourself: S3 bucket, IAM role with powerful authorization, and Route53 domain name; kops will not remove them on user's behavior. Remember to delete the no used AWS services on your side.

See also

- *Playing with Amazon Web Services*
- *Using AWS as Kubernetes Cloud Provider*
- *Managing Kubernetes cluster on AWS by kops*
- *Setting up the Kubernetes cluster on Linux by kubeadm* in Chapter 1, *Building your own Kubernetes Cluster*
- *Setting up Kubernetes cluster on Linux by kubespray* in Chapter 1, *Building your own Kubernetes Cluster*

Using AWS as Kubernetes Cloud Provider

From Kubernetes 1.6, **Cloud Controller Manager** (CCM) was introduced, which defines a set of interfaces so that different cloud providers could evolve their own implementations out of the Kubernetes release cycle. Talking to the cloud providers, you can't ignore the biggest player: Amazon Web Service. According to the Cloud Native Computing Foundation, in 2017, 63% of Kubernetes workloads run on AWS. AWS CloudProvider supports Service as **Elastic Load Balancer** (ELB) and Amazon **Elastic Block Store** (EBS) as StorageClass.

At the time this book was written, Amazon Elastic Container Service for Kubernetes (Amazon EKS) was under preview, which is a hosted Kubernetes service in AWS. Ideally, it'll have better integration with Kubernetes, such as **Application Load Balancer** (ALB) for Ingress, authorization, and networking. Currently in AWS, the limitation of routes per route tables in VPC is 50; it could be up to 100 as requested. However, network performance may be impacted if the routes exceed 50 according to the official documentation of AWS. While kops uses kubenet networking by default, which allocates a/24 CIDR to each node and configures the routes in route table in AWS VPC. This might lead to the performance hit if the cluster has more than 50 nodes. Using a CNI network could address this problem.

Getting ready

For following along with the examples in this recipe, you'll need to create a Kubernetes cluster in AWS. The following example is using kops to provision a Kubernetes cluster named `k8s-cookbook.net` in AWS; as the preceding recipes show, set `$KOPS_STATE_STORE` as a s3 bucket to store your kops configuration and metadata:

```
# kops create cluster --master-count 1 --node-count 2 --zones us-
east-1a,us-east-1b,us-east-1c --node-size t2.micro --master-size t2.small -
-topology private --networking calico --authorization=rbac --cloud-labels
"Environment=dev" --state $KOPS_STATE_STORE --name k8s-cookbook.net
I0408 16:10:12.212571 34744 create_cluster.go:1318] Using SSH public key:
/Users/k8s/.ssh/id_rsa.pub I0408 16:10:13.959274 34744
create_cluster.go:472] Inferred --cloud=aws from zone "us-east-1a"
I0408 16:10:14.418739 34744 subnets.go:184] Assigned CIDR 172.20.32.0/19 to
subnet us-east-1a
I0408 16:10:14.418769 34744 subnets.go:184] Assigned CIDR 172.20.64.0/19 to
subnet us-east-1b I0408 16:10:14.418777 34744 subnets.go:184] Assigned CIDR
172.20.96.0/19 to subnet us-east-1c
I0408 16:10:14.418785 34744 subnets.go:198] Assigned CIDR 172.20.0.0/22 to
subnet utility-us-east-1a I0408 16:10:14.418793 34744 subnets.go:198]
Assigned CIDR 172.20.4.0/22 to subnet utility-us-east-1b
I0408 16:10:14.418801 34744 subnets.go:198] Assigned CIDR 172.20.8.0/22 to
subnet utility-us-east-1c ...
Finally configure your cluster with: kops update cluster k8s-cookbook.net -
-yes
```

Once we run the recommended kops update cluster `<cluster_name>` `--yes` command, after a few minutes, the cluster is up and running. We can use the kops validate cluster to check whether the cluster components are all up:

```
# kops validate cluster
Using cluster from kubectl context: k8s-cookbook.net
Validating cluster k8s-cookbook.net
INSTANCE GROUPS
NAME                      ROLE     MACHINETYPE   MIN   MAX   SUBNETS
master-us-east-1a         Master   t2.small      1     1     us-east-1a
nodes                     Node     t2.micro      2     2     us-east-1a,us-
east-1b,us-east-1c
NODE STATUS
NAME                               ROLE      READY
ip-172-20-44-140.ec2.internal      node      True
ip-172-20-62-204.ec2.internal      master    True
ip-172-20-87-38.ec2.internal       node      True
Your cluster k8s-cookbook.net is ready
```

We're good to go!

How to do it...

When running Kubernetes in AWS, there are two possible integrations we could use: ELB as Service with `LoadBalancer` Type and Amazon Elastic Block Store as `StorageClass`.

Elastic load balancer as LoadBalancer service

Let's create a `LoadBalancer` Service with Pods underneath, which is what we learned in Chapter 3, *Playing with Containers*:

```
# cat aws-service.yaml
apiVersion: apps/v1
kind: Deployment
metadata:
  name: nginx
spec:
  replicas: 3
  selector:
    matchLabels:
      run: nginx
  template:
    metadata:
      labels:
```

```
        run: nginx
    spec:
      containers:
        - image: nginx
          name: nginx
          ports:
            - containerPort: 80
---
apiVersion: v1
kind: Service
metadata:
  name: nginx
spec:
  ports:
    - port: 80
      targetPort: 80
  type: LoadBalancer
  selector:
    run: nginx
```

In the preceding template, we declared one nginx Pod and associated it with the
LoadBalancer service. The service will direct the packet to container port 80:

```
# kubectl create -f aws-service.yaml
deployment.apps "nginx" created
service "nginx" created
```

Let's describe our nginx Service:

```
# kubectl describe svc nginx
Name:                     nginx
Namespace:                default
Labels:                   <none>
Annotations:              <none>
Selector:                 run=nginx
Type:                     LoadBalancer
IP:                       100.68.35.30
LoadBalancer Ingress:     a9da4ef1d402211e8b1240ef0c7f25d3-1251329976.us-
east-1.elb.amazonaws.com
Port:                     <unset>  80/TCP
TargetPort:               80/TCP
NodePort:                 <unset>  31384/TCP
Endpoints:
100.124.40.196:80,100.99.102.130:80,100.99.102.131:80
Session Affinity:         None
External Traffic Policy:  Cluster
Events:
  Type      Reason            Age      From              Message
```

```
   ----      ------                    ----   ----     -------
   Normal    EnsuringLoadBalancer      2m     service-controller   Ensuring load
balancer
   Normal    EnsuredLoadBalancer       2m     service-controller   Ensured load
balancer
```

After the service is created, we will find out that the AWS CloudProvider will provision a classic load balancer with the endpoint `adb576a05401911e8b1240ef0c7f25d3-1637943008.us-east-1.elb.amazonaws.com`. We can check its detailed settings via the aws command-line interface (`https://aws.amazon.com/cli/`).

 To install aws CLI, you can use pip to install in Mac or Linux (`pip install awscli`); for Windows users, you'll have to download the installer from the official website.

The combination of AWS CLI commands is `aws [options] <command> <subcommand> [<subcommand> ...] [parameters]`. For listing load balancers, we'll use `aws elb describe-load-balancers` as the major command. Using the `--load-balancer-names` parameter will filter load balancers by name, and for the `--output` parameter, you can choose text, JSON, or table:

```
# aws elb describe-load-balancers --load-balancer-names
a9da4ef1d402211e8b1240ef0c7f25d3 --output text
LOADBALANCERDESCRIPTIONS
a9da4ef1d402211e8b1240ef0c7f25d3-1251329976.us-east-1.elb.amazonaws.com
Z35SXDOTRQ7X7K 2018-04-14T20:30:45.990Z
a9da4ef1d402211e8b1240ef0c7f25d3-1251329976.us-east-1.elb.amazonaws.com
a9da4ef1d402211e8b1240ef0c7f25d3    internet-facing        vpc-07374a7c
AVAILABILITYZONES       us-east-1a
AVAILABILITYZONES       us-east-1b
AVAILABILITYZONES       us-east-1c
HEALTHCHECK    2       10      TCP:31384      5       6
INSTANCES      i-03cafedc27dca591b
INSTANCES      i-060f9d17d9b473074
LISTENER       31384   TCP     80      TCP
SECURITYGROUPS sg-3b4efb72
SOURCESECURITYGROUP     k8s-elb-a9da4ef1d402211e8b1240ef0c7f25d3
516726565417
SUBNETS subnet-088f9d27
SUBNETS subnet-e7ec0580
SUBNETS subnet-f38191ae
```

If we access this ELB endpoint port 80, we'll see the nginx welcome page:

Access ELB endpoint to access LoadBalancer Service

Behind the scene, AWS CloudProvider creates a AWS elastic load balancer and configures its ingress rules and listeners by the Service we just defined. The following is a diagram of how the traffic gets into the Pods:

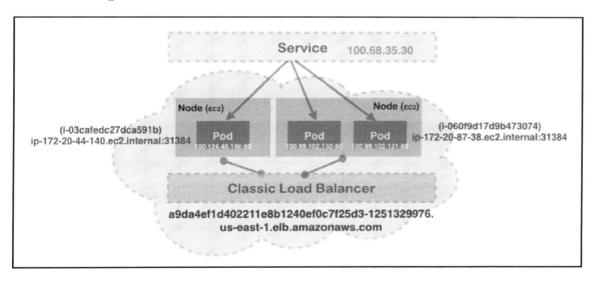

The illustration of Kubernetes resources and AWS resources for Service with LoadBalancer type

The external load balancer receives the requests and forwards them to EC2 instances using a round-robin algorithm. For Kubernetes, the traffic gets into the Service via NodePort and starts a Service-to-Pod communication. For more information about external-to-Service and Service-to-Pod communications, you can refer to Chapter 3, *Playing with Containers*.

Elastic Block Store as StorageClass

We've learned about Volumes in Chapter 2, *Walking through Kubernetes Concepts*. We know PersistentVolumeClaims is used to abstract storage resources from users. It can dynamically provision the PersistentVolume via StorageClass. The default provisioner in StorageClass in **AWS CloudProvider is Elastic Block Storage Service (aws-ebs)**. Whenever you request a PVC, aws-ebs provisioner will create a volume in AWS EBS.

Let's check the storage class in our cluster:

```
// list all storageclass
# kubectl get storageclass
NAME              PROVISIONER            AGE
default           kubernetes.io/aws-ebs  2h
gp2 (default)     kubernetes.io/aws-ebs  2h
In this recipe, we'll reuse the PVC example we mentioned in Chapter 2-6:
# cat chapter2/2-6_volumes/2-6-7_pvc.yaml
apiVersion: "v1"
kind: "PersistentVolumeClaim"
metadata:
  name: "pvclaim01"
spec:
  accessModes:
    - ReadWriteOnce
  resources:
    requests:
      storage: 1Gi
// create pvc
# kubectl create -f chapter2/2-6_volumes/2-6-7_pvc.yaml
persistentvolumeclaim "pvclaim01" created
// check pvc is created successfully.
# kubectl get pvc
NAME            STATUS    VOLUME                                          CAPACITY
pvclaim01       Bound     pvc-e3d881d4-402e-11e8-b124-0ef0c7f25d36        1Gi
ACCESS      MODES    STORAGECLASS    AGE
RWO                  gp2             16m
```

After PVC is created, an associated PV will be created:

```
# kubectl get pv
NAME                                      CAPACITY    ACCESS MODES
pvc-e3d881d4-402e-11e8-b124-0ef0c7f25d36  1Gi         RWO
RECLAIM POLICY   STATUS    CLAIM            STORAGECLASS   REASON    AGE
Delete           Bound     default/pvclaim01 gp2                     16m
```

You can take a closer look at PV here:

```
# kubectl describe pv pvc-e3d881d4-402e-11e8-b124-0ef0c7f25d36
Name:           pvc-e3d881d4-402e-11e8-b124-0ef0c7f25d36
Labels:         failure-domain.beta.kubernetes.io/region=us-east-1
                failure-domain.beta.kubernetes.io/zone=us-east-1a
Annotations:    kubernetes.io/createdby=aws-ebs-dynamic-provisioner
                pv.kubernetes.io/bound-by-controller=yes
                pv.kubernetes.io/provisioned-by=kubernetes.io/aws-ebs
Claim:          default/pvclaim01
...
Source:
    Type:       AWSElasticBlockStore (a Persistent Disk resource in AWS)
    VolumeID:   aws://us-east-1a/vol-035ca31b9cc1820d7
    FSType:     ext4
    Partition:  0
    ReadOnly:   false
```

We can find that it's associated with the claim we just created `pvclaim01` and the source type is `AWSElasticBlockStore`, as expected.

We can use AWS CLI to inspect the volume we created in EBS. Using the `--filter Name=tag-value` we can filter the volumes in EBS:

```
// aws ec2 describe-volumes --filter Name=tag-value,Values=$PV_NAME
# aws ec2 describe-volumes --filter Name=tag-value,Values="pvc-
e3d881d4-402e-11e8-b124-0ef0c7f25d36"{
    "Volumes": [
        {
            "AvailabilityZone": "us-east-1a",
            "Tags": [
                {   "Value": "k8s-cookbook.net",
                    "Key": "KubernetesCluster" },
                {   "Value": "default",
                    "Key": "kubernetes.io/created-for/pvc/namespace" },
                {   "Value": "k8s-cookbook.net-dynamic-pvc-
e3d881d4-402e-11e8-b124-0ef0c7f25d36",
                    "Key": "Name" },
                {   "Value": "pvclaim01",
```

```
                              "Key": "kubernetes.io/created-for/pvc/name" },
                    {         "Value": "owned",
                              "Key": "kubernetes.io/cluster/k8s-cookbook.net" },
                    {         "Value": "pvc-e3d881d4-402e-11e8-b124-0ef0c7f25d36",
                              "Key": "kubernetes.io/created-for/pv/name" }],
                    "VolumeType": "gp2",
                    "VolumeId": "vol-035ca31b9cc1820d7",
                ...
              }
          ]
      }
```

We can see that the EBS resource has been tagged with lots of different values: by observing these tags, we can know which Kubernetes cluster, namespace, PVC, and PV are associated with this EBS volume.

Thanks to dynamic provisioning that StorageClass and CloudProvider support, Volume management is no longer a huge pain. We can create and destroy PV on the fly.

There's more...

At the time of writing this book, there is no native way in Kubernetes 1.10 to support Ingress integration in AWS CloudProvider yet (ideally with application load balancer). Alternatively, kops provides addons that allow you to do so. The first one is ingress-nginx (https://github.com/kubernetes/kops/tree/master/addons/ingress-nginx), which is powered by nginx (https://nginx.org) and AWS Elastic Load Balancer. The requests will go through ELB to nginx, and nginx will dispatch the requests, based on the path definition in Ingress. Another alternative is running skipper as kubernetes-ingress-controller (https://zalando.github.io/skipper/dataclients/kubernetes). Kops also provides add-ons to help you deploy and leverage skipper and AWS Application Load Balancer (https://github.com/kubernetes/kops/tree/master/addons/kube-ingress-aws-controller).

We're expecting CCM and Amazon EKS (https://aws.amazon.com/eks/) to provide more native integration for Ingress via AWS Application Load Balancer, and there will be more to come!

Managing Kubernetes cluster on AWS by kops

In kops, both Kubernetes masters and nodes are running as auto-scaling groups in AWS. In kops, the concept is called **instance groups (ig)**, which indicate the same type of instances in your cluster. Similar to nodes across zones, or masters in each availability zone, we could check it via the kops command line:

```
// kops get instancegroups or kops get ig
# kops get instancegroups --name k8s-cookbook.net
NAME ROLE MACHINETYPE MIN MAX ZONES
master-us-east-1a Master t2.small 1 1 us-east-1a
nodes Node t2.micro 2 2 us-east-1a,us-east-1b,us-east-1c
```

With kops, you can change the instance type, resize instance groups (masters and nodes), rolling-update, and upgrade cluster. Kops also supports configuration for specific AWS features, such as enable AWS detailed monitoring for the instances in the cluster.

Getting ready

For performing this recipe, you'll need a Kubernetes cluster deployed by kops in AWS. You will need to follow the previous recipes in this chapter to launch a cluster. Here, we'll use the same cluster we created in the previous recipe:

```
# kops validate cluster
Using cluster from kubectl context: k8s-cookbook.net
Validating cluster k8s-cookbook.net
INSTANCE GROUPS
NAME                     ROLE    MACHINETYPE    MIN    MAX    SUBNETS
master-us-east-1a        Master  t2.small       1      1      us-east-1a
nodes                    Node    t2.micro       2      2      us-east-1a,us-
east-1b,us-east-1c
NODE STATUS
NAME                          ROLE      READY
ip-172-20-44-140.ec2.internal   node    True
ip-172-20-62-204.ec2.internal   master  True
ip-172-20-87-38.ec2.internal  node     True
Your cluster k8s-cookbook.net is ready
```

In the previous recipe, we've had the KOPS_STATE_STORE environment variable set as one of our S3 bucket names by the format s3://<bucket_name> to store the kops configuration and metadata.

How to do it...

The upcoming subsections cover some common operational examples that cluster administrators may run into.

Modifying and resizing instance groups

Modifying instance groups may be cumbersome if you deploy all instances manually. You'll need to update instances one by one or relaunch them. By kops, we can easily perform the update without pain.

Updating nodes

Using the kops edit command, we can modify the instance type and the node count:

```
// kops edit ig nodes
# kops edit instancegroups nodes --name k8s-cookbook.net
apiVersion: kops/v1alpha2
kind: InstanceGroup
metadata:
  creationTimestamp: 2018-04-14T19:06:47Z
  labels:
    kops.k8s.io/cluster: k8s-cookbook.net
  name: nodes
spec:
  image: kope.io/k8s-1.8-debian-jessie-amd64-hvm-ebs-2018-02-08
  machineType: t2.micro
  maxSize: 2
  minSize: 2
  nodeLabels:
    kops.k8s.io/instancegroup: nodes
  role: Node
  subnets:
  - us-east-1a
  - us-east-1b
  - us-east-1c
```

In this example, we modify both minSize and maxSize from 2 to 3. After the modification, we'll need to run the kops update to see it take effect:

```
# kops update cluster k8s-cookbook.net --yes
...
I0414 21:23:52.505171    16291 update_cluster.go:291] Exporting kubecfg for
cluster
kops has set your kubectl context to k8s-cookbook.net
Cluster changes have been applied to the cloud.
Changes may require instances to restart: kops rolling-update cluster
```

Some updates will need a rolling-update cluster. In this example, kops has updated the configuration in the AWS auto scaling group. AWS will then launch a new instance to accommodate the change. The following is a screenshot from AWS Auto Scaling Group's console:

nodes_in_AWS_Auto_Scaling_Groups

We can see that the configuration has been updated, and AWS is scaling a new instance. After few minutes, we can check cluster status via `kops validate` or `kubectl get nodes`:

```
# kops validate cluster
Using cluster from kubectl context: k8s-cookbook.net
Validating cluster k8s-cookbook.net
INSTANCE GROUPS
NAME                    ROLE    MACHINETYPE    MIN    MAX    SUBNETS
master-us-east-1a       Master  t2.small       1      1      us-east-1a
nodes                   Node    t2.micro       3      3      us-east-1a,us-
east-1b,us-east-1c
NODE STATUS
NAME                            ROLE    READY
ip-172-20-119-170.ec2.internal  node    True
ip-172-20-44-140.ec2.internal   node    True
ip-172-20-62-204.ec2.internal   master  True
ip-172-20-87-38.ec2.internal node    True
```

Everything looks good!

Updating masters

Updating masters is the same as updating nodes. Note that masters in the same availability zone are in one instance group. This means that you can't add additional subnets into the master instance group. In the following example, we'll resize the master count from 1 to 2.

 In this recipe, we only make the master count 1. In the real world, the recommended way is to deploy masters to at least two availability zones and have three masters per zone (one kops instance group). You can achieve that via the `--master-count` and `--master-zones` parameters when launching the cluster.

Now take a look at the following command:

```
# kops edit ig master-us-east-1a
apiVersion: kops/v1alpha2
kind: InstanceGroup
metadata:
  creationTimestamp: 2018-04-14T19:06:47Z
  labels:
    kops.k8s.io/cluster: k8s-cookbook.net
  name: master-us-east-1a
spec:
  image: kope.io/k8s-1.8-debian-jessie-amd64-hvm-ebs-2018-02-08
  machineType: t2.small
  maxSize: 1
  minSize: 1
  nodeLabels:
    kops.k8s.io/instancegroup: master-us-east-1a
  role: Master
  subnets:
  - us-east-1a
```

Before applying the change, we can run the update cluster command without `--yes` in the dry run mode:

```
# kops update cluster k8s-cookbook.net
...
Will modify resources:
  AutoscalingGroup/master-us-east-1a.masters.k8s-cookbook.net
      MinSize                 1 -> 2
      MaxSize                 1 -> 2
Must specify --yes to apply changes
```

After we verify the dry run message as expected, we can perform the update as follows. In this case, we'll have to perform a rolling update.

How to know whether a rolling update is needed

If we didn't run a kops rolling update in the preceding example, kops will show a validation error when running the kops validate cluster:

VALIDATION ERRORS

KIND   NAME   MESSAGE

InstanceGroup `master-us-east-1a` InstanceGroup `master-us-east-1a` did not have enough nodes 1 vs 2

Remember to replace k8s-cookbook.net with your cluster name.

```
# kops update cluster k8s-cookbook.net --yes && kops rolling-update cluster
...
Using cluster from kubectl context: k8s-cookbook.net
NAME                     STATUS  NEEDUPDATE     READY  MIN    MAX    NODES
master-us-east-1a        Ready   0              2      2      2      1
nodes                    Ready   0              3      3      3      3
No rolling-update required.
```

Just like modifying nodes, we can use both `kubectl get nodes` and `kops validate cluster` to check whether the new master has joined the cluster.

Upgrading a cluster

For demonstrating how we upgrade the Kubernetes version, we'll first launch the cluster with the 1.8.7 version. For detailed instructions of parameters, refer to the previous recipes in this chapter. Input the following command:

```
// launch a cluster with additional parameter --kubernetes-version 1.8.7 #
kops create cluster --master-count 1 --node-count 2 --zones us-east-1a,us-east-1b,us-east-1c --node-size t2.micro --master-size t2.small --topology
private --networking calico --authorization=rbac --cloud-labels
"Environment=dev" --state $KOPS_STATE_STORE --kubernetes-version 1.8.7 --name k8s-cookbook.net --yes
```

After few minutes, we can see that the master and the nodes are up with version 1.8.7:

```
# kubectl get nodes
NAME STATUS ROLES AGE VERSION
ip-172-20-44-128.ec2.internal Ready master 3m v1.8.7
ip-172-20-55-191.ec2.internal Ready node 1m v1.8.7
ip-172-20-64-30.ec2.internal Ready node 1m v1.8.7
```

In the following example, we'll walk through how to upgrade Kubernetes cluster from 1.8.7 to 1.9.3 using kops. Firstly, run the kops upgrade cluster command. Kops will show us the latest version that we could upgrade to:

```
# kops upgrade cluster k8s-cookbook.net --yes
ITEM PROPERTY OLD NEW
Cluster KubernetesVersion 1.8.7 1.9.3
Updates applied to configuration. You can now apply these changes,
using `kops update cluster k8s-cookbook.net`
```

It indicates that the configuration has been updated, and that we'll need to update the cluster now. We run command with the dryrun mode to check what will be modified first:

```
// update cluster
# kops update cluster k8s-cookbook.net
...
Will modify resources:
  LaunchConfiguration/master-us-east-1a.masters.k8s-cookbook.net
      UserData
                              ...
                              +     image: gcr.io/google_containers/kube-
apiserver:v1.9.3
                              -     image: gcr.io/google_containers/kube-
apiserver:v1.8.7
                              ...
                              +     image: gcr.io/google_containers/kube-
controller
manager:v1.9.3
                              -     image: gcr.io/google_containers/kube-
controller-manager:v1.8.7
                              ...
                                    hostnameOverride: '@aws'
                              +     image: gcr.io/google_containers/kube-
proxy:v1.9.3
                              -     image: gcr.io/google_containers/kube-
proxy:v1.8.7
                                    logLevel: 2
                                  kubeScheduler:
                              +     image: gcr.io/google_containers/kube-
scheduler:v1.9.3
                              -     image: gcr.io/google_containers/kube
scheduler:v1.8.7
                              ...
Must specify --yes to apply changes
```

We could see all of the components moved from v1.8.7 to v1.9.3 in Auto Scaling Launch Configuration. After verifying that everything is good, we can run the same command with the `--yes` parameter:

```
// run the same command with --yes
# kops update cluster k8s-cookbook.net --yes
...
kops has set your kubectl context to k8s-cookbook.net
Cluster changes have been applied to the cloud.
Changes may require instances to restart: kops rolling-update cluster
```

In this case, we need to run the rolling update for the cluster:

```
# kops rolling-update cluster --yes
Using cluster from kubectl context: k8s-cookbook.net
NAME                    STATUS          NEEDUPDATE      READY   MIN     MAX
NODES
master-us-east-1a       NeedsUpdate     1               0       1       1       1
nodes                   NeedsUpdate     2               0       2       2       2
I0414 22:45:05.887024    51333 rollingupdate.go:193] Rolling update
completed for cluster "k8s-cookbook.net"!
```

All the nodes have been upgraded to 1.9.3! When performing the rolling update, kops drains one instance first then cordons the node. The auto-scaling group will bring up another node with the updated user data, which contains the Kubernetes component images with the updates. For avoiding downtime, you should have multiple masters and nodes as the basic deployment.

After a rolling update is completed, we can check the cluster version via `kubectl get nodes`:

```
# kubectl get nodes
NAME                            STATUS      ROLES       AGE     VERSION
ip-172-20-116-81.ec2.internal   Ready       node        14m     v1.9.3
ip-172-20-41-113.ec2.internal   Ready       master      17m     v1.9.3
ip-172-20-56-230.ec2.internal   Ready       node        8m      v1.9.3
```

All the nodes have been upgraded to 1.9.3!

There's more...

In kops, there are lots of useful addons, such as autoscaling nodes (`https://github.com/kubernetes/kops/tree/master/addons/cluster-autoscaler`) and mapping the service to the record in Route53 (`https://github.com/kubernetes/kops/tree/master/addons/route53-mapper`). Refer to the add-ons page to find out more!

See also

- *Deployment API* in `Chapter 2`, *Walking through Kubernetes Concepts*
- *Building multiple masters* in `Chapter 4`, *Building High-Availability Clusters*
- *Managing Kubernetes cluster on GKE* in `Chapter 7`, *Building Kubernetes on GCP*

7
Building Kubernetes on GCP

In this chapter, we will use **Google Cloud Platform** (**GCP**) in the following recipes:

- Playing with GCP
- Setting up managed Kubernetes via **Google Kubernetes Engine** (**GKE**)
- Exploring Kubernetes CloudProvider on GKE
- Managing a Kubernetes cluster on GKE

Playing with GCP

GCP is getting popular in the public cloud industry. It has concepts similar to AWS, such as VPC, a compute engine, persistent disks, load balancing, and several managed services. The most interesting service is GKE, which is the managed Kubernetes cluster. We will explore how to use GCP and GKE.

Getting ready

To use GCP, you need to have a Google account such as Gmail (`https://mail.google.com/mail/`), which many people already have. Then sign up to GCP using your Google account by following these steps:

1. Go to the `https://cloud.google.com` website then click the **Try it free** button
2. Log in to Google using your Google account
3. Register with GCP and enter your personal information and billing information

That's it!

Once registration is complete, you'll see the GCP Web Console page. In the beginning, it may ask you to create one project; the default name could be **My First Project**. You can keep it, but we will create another project in this chapter, the better to help you understand.

The GCP Web Console is enough as a first step. But to keep using the Web Console is not recommended for DevOps, because human manual input always causes human errors and Google might change the Web Console design in the future.

Thus, we will use the CLI. GCP provides a CLI tool called Cloud SDK (`https://cloud.google.com/sdk/`). So, let's create one new GCP project and then install Cloud SDK on your machine.

Creating a GCP project

We will create a new project from scratch by following steps. It will help you to understand how does GCP project works:

1. Go to the project page by clicking the **My First Project** link:

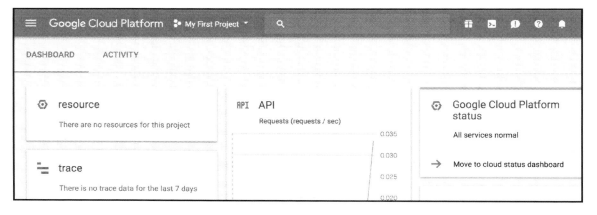

Navigating to the project link

2. You may see your own projects to choose from, but this time click the + button to create a new one:

Creating a new project

3. Type the project name as `Kubernetes Cookbook`. Then GCP will generate and assign a project ID such as **kubernetes-cookbook-12345**. Please remember this project ID.

You may notice that your project ID is NOT **kubernetes-cookbook,** like **kubernetes-cookbook-194302** in the screenshot as shown in the following screenshot. And even you click **Edit** to attempt to change it to **kubernetes-cookbook**, it doesn't allow it, because the project ID is a unique string for all GCP users. And we already took the **kubernetes-cookbook** project ID.

Project name and Project ID

4. After a few minutes, your project is ready to use. Go back to the project selection page on the top banner and then select your **Kubernetes Cookbook** project:

Selecting a Kubernetes Cookbook project

Done! You can at any time switch to your project and the **Kubernetes Cookbook** project. That is is isolated environment; any VPC, VM, IAM users and even billing methods are independent.

Installing Cloud SDK

Next, install Cloud SDK on your machine. It supports the Windows, Mac, and Linux platforms. All of these require a Python interpreter version 2.7, but most macOS and Linux installs use the defaults.

On the other hand, Windows does't have the Python interpreter by default. However, in the Cloud SDK installer for Windows, it is possible to install Python. Let's install Cloud SDK on Windows and macOS step by step.

Installing Cloud SDK on Windows

Cloud SDK provides an installer for Windows. It also include Python interpreter for Windows as well. Please follow the following steps to install on your Windows machine:

1. Download the Cloud SDK installer on Windows (`https://dl.google.com/dl/cloudsdk/channels/rapid/GoogleCloudSDKInstaller.exe`).

2. Run the Cloud SDK installer.

   If you've never installed a Python interpreter on your Windows machine, you have to choose the **Bundled Python** option:

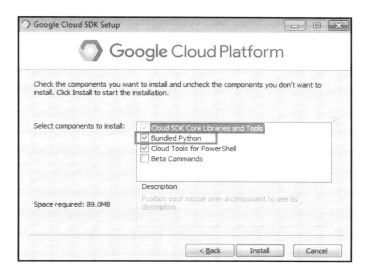

Cloud SDK installer for Windows

3. Other than that, proceed with the installation with the default options.
4. Once the installation is done, you can find **Google Cloud SDK Shell** in the **Google Cloud SDK** program group. Click it to launch a **Google Cloud SDK Shell**:

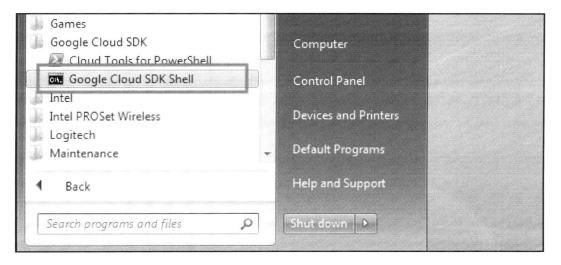

Google Cloud SDK Shell in the Google Cloud SDK program group

5. Type `gcloud info` to check whether you can see the Cloud SDK version:

Running the gcloud command on Windows

Installing Cloud SDK on Linux and macOS

Installing Cloud SDK on both Linux and macOS follows the steps listed here. Let's install Cloud SDK under your home directory:

1. Open the Terminal.
2. Type the following command to download and run the Cloud SDK installer:

```
$ curl https://sdk.cloud.google.com | bash
```

3. It asks for your desired installation directory. By default, it is under your home directory. So, type `return`:

```
Installation directory (this will create a google-cloud-sdk
subdirectory) (/Users/saito):
```

4. It asks whether to send user usage data; it will send some information when it crashes. Based on your privacy policy, if don't wish to send any data to Google, choose n. Otherwise choose Y to improve their quality:

```
Do you want to help improve the Google Cloud SDK (Y/n)? n
```

5. It asks whether to update `.bash_profile` by adding the `gcloud` command to your command search path; type `y` to proceed:

```
Modify profile to update your $PATH and enable shell command
completion?
Do you want to continue (Y/n)?  y
The Google Cloud SDK installer will now prompt you to update an
rc
file to bring the Google Cloud CLIs into your environment.
Enter a path to an rc file to update, or leave blank to use
[/Users/saito/.bash_profile]:
```

6. Open another Terminal or type `exec -l $SHELL` to refresh your command search path:

```
//reload .bash_profile
$ exec -l $SHELL

//check gcloud command is in your search path
$ which gcloud
/Users/saito/google-cloud-sdk/bin/gcloud
```

7. Type `gcloud info` to check whether you can see the Cloud SDK version:

```
$ gcloud info
Google Cloud SDK [187.0.0]
Platform: [Mac OS X, x86_64] ('Darwin', 'Hideto-Saito-no-
MacBook.local', '17.4.0', 'Darwin Kernel Version 17.4.0: Sun
Dec 17 09:19:54 PST 2017; root:xnu-4570.41.2~1/RELEASE_X86_64',
'x86_64', 'i386')
Python Version: [2.7.14 (default, Jan 21 2018, 12:22:04)  [GCC
4.2.1 Compatible Apple LLVM 9.0.0 (clang-900.0.38)]]
Python Location:
[/usr/local/Cellar/python/2.7.14_2/Frameworks/Python.framework/
Versions/2.7/Resources/Python.app/Contents/MacOS/Python]
```

Now you can start to configure Cloud SDK!

Configuring Cloud SDK

You can configure both Cloud SDK for Windows and for Linux/macOS, by using the following steps:

1. Launch **Google Cloud SDK Shell** (Windows) or open a Terminal (Linux/macOS).

2. Type `gcloud init`; it asks you to log on to your Google account. Type `y` and press return:

```
You must log in to continue. Would you like to log in (Y/n)? y
```

3. It will open a web browser to navigate to the Google logon page; proceed to log on using your Google Account with the GCP account.

4. It asks you whether Cloud SDK can access your Google account information. Click the **ALLOW** button.

5. Back to the Terminal—it asks you which project you want to use. Let's choose the **Kubernetes Cookbook** project you made:

```
Pick cloud project to use:
 [1] my-first-project-194302
 [2] kubernetes-cookbook
 [3] Create a new project
Please enter numeric choice or text value (must exactly match
list item):  2
```

6. It asks you whether to configure `Compute Engine` or not. Let's type n to skip it this time:

```
Do you want to configure Google Compute Engine
(https://cloud.google.com/compute) settings (Y/n)?  n
```

Now you can start to use Cloud SDK to control GCP. Let's create VPC, subnet, and firewall rules, then launch a VM instance to set up our own GCP infrastructure.

> If you chose the wrong project or you want to try again, at any time you can reconfigure your setup by the `gcloud init` command.

How to do it...

We will go through GCP's basic functionality to set up an infrastructure under the **Kubernetes Cookbook** project. By using the `gcloud` command, we will create these components:

- One new VPC
- Two subnets (`us-central1` and `us-east1`) in the VPC

- Three firewall rules (`public-ssh`, `public-http`, and `private-ssh`)
- We will add your ssh public key to a project-wide metadata

Overall, your infrastructure will resemble the following. Let's configure the components one by one:

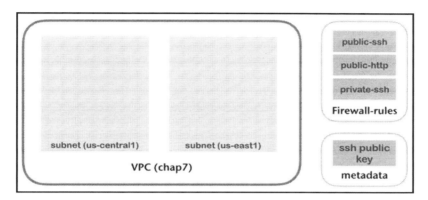

Target infrastructure

Creating a VPC

VPC in GCP is like AWS, but there's no need to bind a particular region, and also no need to set the CIDR address range. This means you can create a VPC that covers all regions. By default, your Kubernetes Cookbook project has a **default** VPC.

However, for a better understanding, let's create a new VPC by following these steps:

1. Run the `gcloud compute networks` command to create a new VPC. The name is `chap7` and subnet-mode is `custom`, which means subnets are not created automatically. So we will add it manually in the next step:

   ```
   $ gcloud compute networks create chap7 --subnet-mode=custom
   ```

2. Check the VPC list; you should have two VPCs, `default` VPC and `chap7` VPC:

   ```
   $ gcloud compute networks list
   NAME      SUBNET_MODE   BGP_ROUTING_MODE    IPV4_RANGE
   GATEWAY_IPV4
   chap7     CUSTOM        REGIONAL
   default   AUTO          REGIONAL
   ```

Creating subnets

Let's create two subnets under the `chap7` VPC (network) by following these steps:

1. In order to create a subnet, you have to choose the region. By typing `gcloud compute regions list` you will know which regions are available to you:

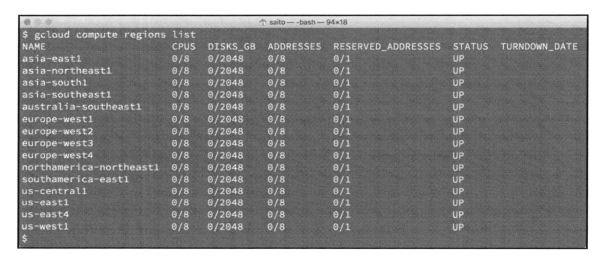

```
$ gcloud compute regions list
NAME                    CPUS  DISKS_GB  ADDRESSES  RESERVED_ADDRESSES  STATUS  TURNDOWN_DATE
asia-east1              0/8   0/2048    0/8        0/1                 UP
asia-northeast1         0/8   0/2048    0/8        0/1                 UP
asia-south1             0/8   0/2048    0/8        0/1                 UP
asia-southeast1         0/8   0/2048    0/8        0/1                 UP
australia-southeast1    0/8   0/2048    0/8        0/1                 UP
europe-west1            0/8   0/2048    0/8        0/1                 UP
europe-west2            0/8   0/2048    0/8        0/1                 UP
europe-west3            0/8   0/2048    0/8        0/1                 UP
europe-west4            0/8   0/2048    0/8        0/1                 UP
northamerica-northeast1 0/8   0/2048    0/8        0/1                 UP
southamerica-east1      0/8   0/2048    0/8        0/1                 UP
us-central1             0/8   0/2048    0/8        0/1                 UP
us-east1                0/8   0/2048    0/8        0/1                 UP
us-east4                0/8   0/2048    0/8        0/1                 UP
us-west1                0/8   0/2048    0/8        0/1                 UP
$
```

Displaying a GCP region list

2. Let's choose `us-central1` and `us-east1` to create two subnets under the `chap7` VPC with the following configuration:

Subnet name	VPC	CIDR range	Region
chap7-us-central1	chap7	192.168.1.0/24	us-central1
chap7-us-east1	chap7	192.168.2.0/24	us-east1

```
$ gcloud compute networks subnets create chap7-us-central1 --
network=chap7 --range=192.168.1.0/24 --region us-central1

$ gcloud compute networks subnets create chap7-us-east1 --
network=chap7 --range=192.168.2.0/24 --region us-east1
```

3. Check the following command to see whether subnets are configured properly or not:

```
$ gcloud compute networks subnets list --network=chap7
NAME               REGION      NETWORK   RANGE
chap7-us-east1     us-east1    chap7     192.168.2.0/24
```

```
chap7-us-central1   us-central1   chap7    192.168.1.0/24
```

Creating firewall rules

Firewall rules are similar to an AWS Security Group in that you can define incoming and outgoing packet filters. They use a network tag, which is a label, to distinguish between firewall rules and VM instances. So, VM instances can specify zero or some network tags, then the firewall rule will apply to the VM which has the same Network Tag.

Therefore, we need to set a **target network tag** while creating the firewall rule. Overall, we will create three firewall rules that have these configurations:

Firewall rule name	Target VPC	Allow port	Allow from	Target network tag
public-ssh	chap7	ssh (22/tcp)	All (0.0.0.0/0)	public
public-http	chap7	http (80/tcp)	All (0.0.0.0/0)	public
private-ssh	chap7	ssh (22/tcp)	Host which has a public network tag	private

1. Create a `public-ssh` rule:

   ```
   $ gcloud compute firewall-rules create public-ssh --
   network=chap7 --allow="tcp:22" --source-ranges="0.0.0.0/0" --
   target-tags="public"
   ```

2. Create a `public-http` rule:

   ```
   $ gcloud compute firewall-rules create public-http --
   network=chap7 --allow="tcp:80" --source-ranges="0.0.0.0/0" --
   target-tags="public"
   ```

3. Create a `private-ssh` rule:

   ```
   $ gcloud compute firewall-rules create private-ssh --
   network=chap7 --allow="tcp:22" --source-tags="public" --target-
   tags="private"
   ```

4. Check all firewall rules:

   ```
   $ gcloud compute firewall-rules list --filter='NETWORK=chap7'
   NAME           NETWORK    DIRECTION   PRIORITY   ALLOW      DENY
   private-ssh    chap7      INGRESS     1000       tcp:22
   public-http    chap7      INGRESS     1000       tcp:80
   public-ssh     chap7      INGRESS     1000       tcp:22
   ```

Adding your ssh public key to GCP

Before you launch VM instances, you need to upload your ssh public key in order to log on to the VM. If you don't have any ssh keys, you have to run the `ssh-keygen` command to generate a key pair (public key and private key). Let's assume you have a public key as `~/.ssh/id_rsa.pub` and a private key as `~/.ssh/id_rsa`

1. Check your login user name by using the `whoami` command, then use `gcloud compute config-ssh` to upload your key via the following command:

```
$ whoami
saito

$ gcloud compute config-ssh --ssh-key-file=~/.ssh/id_rsa
```

2. Check your ssh public key is registered as metadata:

```
$ gcloud compute project-info describe --format=json
{
  "commonInstanceMetadata": {
    "fingerprint": "fAqDGp0oSMs=",
    "items": [
      {
        "key": "ssh-keys",
        "value": "saito:ssh-rsa
AAAAB3NzaC1yc2EAAAADAQABAAABAQDAr1cHrrONuaPgN20sXCPH8uT2lOjWRB3
zEncOTxOI2lCW6DM6Mr31boboDe0kAtUMdoDU43yyMe4r734SmtMuh...
```

That's all. These are minimal configurations in order to launch a VM instance. So, let's launch some VM instances on this infrastructure.

How it works...

Now you have your own VPC, subnet, and firewall rules. This infrastructure will be used by the compute engine (VM instances), Kubernetes Engine, and some other GCP products. Let's deploy two VM instances onto your VPC, as in the following diagram, to see how it works:

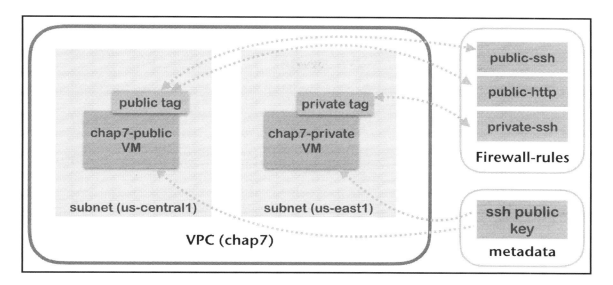

Final state

Launching VM instances

We will launch two VM instances on both `us-central1` and `us-east1` by using the following configuration:

VM Instance name	Target VPC	zone (see the following steps)	Target Subnet	Assign Network Tag
chap7-public	chap7	us-central1-a	chap7-us-central1	public
chap7-private	chap7	us-east1-b	chap7-us-east1	private

1. Check the available zones in `us-central1` and `us-east1` by using the following command:

```
$ gcloud compute zones list --filter='name:(us-east1,us-central1)'
NAME              REGION        STATUS   NEXT_MAINTENANCE   TURNDOWN_DATE
us-east1-b        us-east1      UP
us-east1-c        us-east1      UP
us-east1-d        us-east1      UP
us-central1-c     us-central1   UP
us-central1-a     us-central1   UP
```

```
us-central1-f   us-central1   UP
us-central1-b   us-central1   UP
```

So, let's choose us-central1-a for chap7-public and us-east1-b for chap7-private:

2. Type the following command to create two VM instances:

```
$ gcloud compute instances create chap7-public --network=chap7
--subnet=chap7-us-central1 --zone=us-central1-a --tags=public -
-machine-type=f1-micro

$ gcloud compute instances create chap7-private --network=chap7
--subnet=chap7-us-east1 --zone=us-east1-b --tags=private --
machine-type=f1-micro
```

3. Check the VM instance external IP address via the following command:

```
$ gcloud compute instances list
NAME            ZONE            MACHINE_TYPE   PREEMPTIBLE
INTERNAL_IP    EXTERNAL_IP     STATUS
chap7-public    us-central1-a   f1-micro
192.168.1.2    35.224.14.45    RUNNING
chap7-private   us-east1-b      f1-micro
192.168.2.2    35.229.95.179   RUNNING
```

4. Run ssh-agent to remember your ssh key:

```
$ ssh-add ~/.ssh/id_rsa
```

5. ssh from your machine to chap7-public using the -A option (forward authentication) and using an external IP address:

```
● ● ●                    .ssh — saito@chap7-public: ~ — ssh -A saito@35.224.14.45 — 94×15
$ ssh -A saito@35.224.14.45
The authenticity of host '35.224.14.45 (35.224.14.45)' can't be established.
ECDSA key fingerprint is SHA256:EM98+dknUIGbvH/nCm6ztVdeM+qqJ7nLmKBjBF0lLUA.
Are you sure you want to continue connecting (yes/no)? yes
Warning: Permanently added '35.224.14.45' (ECDSA) to the list of known hosts.
Linux chap7-public 4.9.0-5-amd64 #1 SMP Debian 4.9.65-3+deb9u2 (2018-01-04) x86_64

The programs included with the Debian GNU/Linux system are free software;
the exact distribution terms for each program are described in the
individual files in /usr/share/doc/*/copyright.

Debian GNU/Linux comes with ABSOLUTELY NO WARRANTY, to the extent
permitted by applicable law.
Last login: Mon Feb  5 07:19:34 2018 from 107.196.102.199
saito@chap7-public: $
```

ssh to the public VM instance

6. ssh from `chap7-public` to `chap7-private` via the internal IP address:

```
● ● ●                    .ssh — saito@chap7-private: ~ — ssh -A saito@35.224.14.45 — 94×14
saito@chap7-public: $ ssh saito@192.168.2.2
The authenticity of host '192.168.2.2 (192.168.2.2)' can't be established.
ECDSA key fingerprint is SHA256:WlhecoBpeuejmSrYrEEa/RD4louetw6bEau6NOAxa5k.
Are you sure you want to continue connecting (yes/no)? yes
Warning: Permanently added '192.168.2.2' (ECDSA) to the list of known hosts.
Linux chap7-private 4.9.0-5-amd64 #1 SMP Debian 4.9.65-3+deb9u2 (2018-01-04) x86_64

The programs included with the Debian GNU/Linux system are free software;
the exact distribution terms for each program are described in the
individual files in /usr/share/doc/*/copyright.

Debian GNU/Linux comes with ABSOLUTELY NO WARRANTY, to the extent
permitted by applicable law.
saito@chap7-private: $
```

ssh to private VM instance

7. Type the `exit` command to go back to the `chap7-public` host, then install `nginx` by using the `apt-get` command:

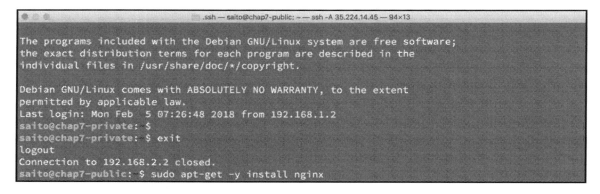

Installing nginx on a public VM instance

8. Launch `nginx` by using the following command:

```
$ sudo systemctl start nginx
```

9. Access `chap7-public` (via the external IP) using your web browser:

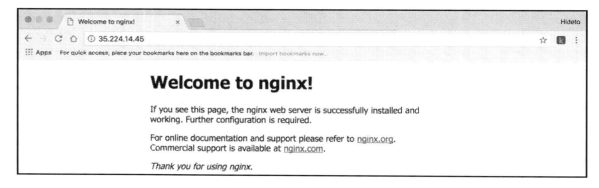

Accessing a nginx web server on a public VM instance

Congratulations! You have finished setting up a GCP VPC, Subnet, and firewall rules, and launch VM instances! These are very basic and common usages of Google Compute Engine. You can login and install software in these machines, or even build a Kubernetes cluster from scratch. However, GCP also has a managed Kubernetes product called Kubernetes Engine. We will explore it in this chapter.

Playing with Google Kubernetes Engine

Kubernetes was designed by google and widely used internally at Google for years. Google Cloud Platform offers the hosted GKE. With GKE, we don't need to build a cluster from scratch. Instead, clusters can be launched and turned down on demand.

Getting ready

We can use the Kubernetes Engine dashboard in the GCP console or the gcloud CLI to launched and configure a cluster. Using the console is very straightforward and intuitive. However, using CLI is a more flexible way to make the operation repeatable or to integrate it with your existing pipeline. In this recipe, we'll walk through how to use gcloud to launch and set up a Kubernetes cluster, along with some importants concept in GCP.

In GCP, everything is associated with a project. A GCP project is the basic unit for using GCP services, billing, and permission control. At first, we'll have to create a project from the GCP console `https://console.cloud.google.com`.

The project ID is globally unique in GCP. After the project is properly created, we'll see there is a unique project number assigned. In the home dashboard, we'll have a clear view of how many resources we've used. We can set permissions, storage, network, billing, and other resources from here. Before we can move forward, we'll need to install gcloud. gcloud is part of Google Cloud SDK. Other than gcloud, which can do most common operations in GCP, Google Cloud SDK also includes other common GCP tools, such as gsutil (to manage Cloud Storage), bq (a command-line tool for BigQuery), and core (Cloud SDK libraries). The tools are available at the Google cloud SDK download page: `https://cloud.google.com/sdk/docs/#install_the_latest_cloud_tools_version_cloudsdk_current_version`.

After gcloud is installed, run gcloud init to log in to set up your identity with gcloud and create a project named **k8s-cookbook-2e**. We can use gcloud to manipulate almost all the services in Google Cloud; the major command group is:

```
gcloud container [builds|clusters|images|node-pools|operations] | $COMMAND
$FLAG...
```

The gcloud container command line set is used to manage our containers and clusters in Google Kuberentes Engine. For launching a cluster, the most important parameters are network settings. Let's spend some time understanding network terminology in GCP here. Just like AWS, GCP has the VPC concept as well. It's a private and safer way to isolate your compute, storage, and cloud resources with the public internet. It can be peered across projects, or established as a VPN with on-premise datacenters to create a hybrid cloud environment:

```
// create GCP VPC, it might take few minutes.
# gcloud compute networks create k8s-network
Created
[https://www.googleapis.com/compute/v1/projects/kubernetes-cookbook/global/
networks/k8s-network].
NAME          SUBNET_MODE  BGP_ROUTING_MODE  IPV4_RANGE  GATEWAY_IPV4
k8s-network   AUTO         REGIONAL
```

Instances on this network will not be reachable until firewall rules are created. As an example, you can allow all internal traffic between instances as well as SSH, RDP, and ICMP by running:

```
$ gcloud compute firewall-rules create <FIREWALL_NAME> --network k8s-
network --allow tcp,udp,icmp --source-ranges <IP_RANGE>
$ gcloud compute firewall-rules create <FIREWALL_NAME> --network k8s-
network --allow tcp:22,tcp:3389,icmp
```

By default, the VPC is created in auto mode, which will create a one subnet per region. We can observe that via the subcommand `describe`:

```
// gcloud compute networks describe <VPC name>
# gcloud compute networks describe k8s-network
autoCreateSubnetworks: true
creationTimestamp: '2018-02-25T13:54:28.867-08:00'
id: '1580862590680993403'
kind: compute#network
name: k8s-network
routingConfig:
  routingMode: REGIONAL
selfLink:
https://www.googleapis.com/compute/v1/projects/kubernetes-cookbook/global/n
etworks/k8s-network
subnetworks:
-
https://www.googleapis.com/compute/v1/projects/kubernetes-cookbook/regions/
australia-southeast1/subnetworks/k8s-network
-
https://www.googleapis.com/compute/v1/projects/kubernetes-cookbook/regions/
```

```
europe-west4/subnetworks/k8s-network
-
https://www.googleapis.com/compute/v1/projects/kubernetes-cookbook/regions/
northamerica-northeast1/subnetworks/k8s-network
-
https://www.googleapis.com/compute/v1/projects/kubernetes-cookbook/regions/
europe-west1/subnetworks/k8s-network
-
https://www.googleapis.com/compute/v1/projects/kubernetes-cookbook/regions/
southamerica-east1/subnetworks/k8s-network
-
https://www.googleapis.com/compute/v1/projects/kubernetes-cookbook/regions/
us-central1/subnetworks/k8s-network
-
https://www.googleapis.com/compute/v1/projects/kubernetes-cookbook/regions/
us-east1/subnetworks/k8s-network
-
https://www.googleapis.com/compute/v1/projects/kubernetes-cookbook/regions/
asia-east1/subnetworks/k8s-network
-
https://www.googleapis.com/compute/v1/projects/kubernetes-cookbook/regions/
us-west1/subnetworks/k8s-network
-
https://www.googleapis.com/compute/v1/projects/kubernetes-cookbook/regions/
europe-west3/subnetworks/k8s-network
-
https://www.googleapis.com/compute/v1/projects/kubernetes-cookbook/regions/
asia-southeast1/subnetworks/k8s-network
-
https://www.googleapis.com/compute/v1/projects/kubernetes-cookbook/regions/
us-east4/subnetworks/k8s-network
-
https://www.googleapis.com/compute/v1/projects/kubernetes-cookbook/regions/
europe-west2/subnetworks/k8s-network
-
https://www.googleapis.com/compute/v1/projects/kubernetes-cookbook/regions/
asia-northeast1/subnetworks/k8s-network
-
https://www.googleapis.com/compute/v1/projects/kubernetes-cookbook/regions/
asia-south1/subnetworks/k8s-network
x_gcloud_bgp_routing_mode: REGIONAL
x_gcloud_subnet_mode: AUTO
```

In GCP, each subnet is across a zone. A zone is an isolated location in a region, which is a similar concept to availability zones in AWS.

Alternatively, you could create a network in custom mode by adding the parameter `--subnet-mode=custom`, which allows you to define your desired IP range, region, and all the routing rules. For more details, please refer to the previous section.

Auto mode also helps you set up all default routing rules. A route serves to define the destination for certain IP ranges. For example, this route will direct the packet to virtual network `10.158.0.0/20`:

□ Name ^	Destination IP ranges	Priority	Instance tags	Next hop
✓ default-route-23110207a699e1b8	10.158.0.0/20	1000	None	Virtual network

Default route example

There route which is used to direct the packet to the outside world. The next hop of this route is the default internet gateway, similar to the igw in AWS. In GCP, however, you don't need to explicitly create an internet gateway:

□ default-route-8f64e34aed068718	0.0.0.0/0	1000	None	Default internet gateway

Default route for internet access

Another important concept in a GCP network is firewall rules, used to control the ingress and egress for your instance. In GCP, the association between firewall rules and VM instances is implemented by network tags.

A firewall rule can also be assigned to all instances in the network or a group of instances with a specific service account (ingress only). The service account is the identity of a VM instance in GCP. One or more roles can be assigned to a service account, so it can have access to other GCP resources. This is similar to AWS instance profiles.

One VM instance can have more than one network tags, which implies multiple network routes could be applied. This diagram shows how tags work. In the following diagram, the first firewall rule is applied to VM1 and VM2, and VM2 has two firewall rules associated with it:

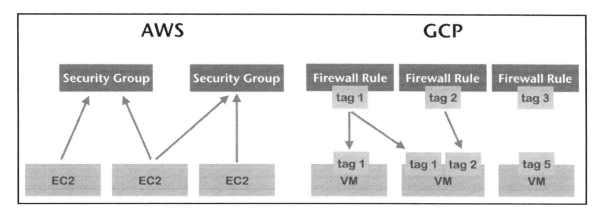

Illustration of AWS security groups and GCP firewall rules

In **AWS**, one or more ingress/egress rules are defined in a **Security Group**, and one or more Security Groups can be assigned to a **EC2** instance. In **GCP**, on the other hand, one or more firewall rules are defined, which are associated with one or more tags. One or more tags can be assigned to an instance. By mapping network tags, firewall rules can control and limit access in and out of your instances.

How to do it...

We've learned the basic network concept in GCP. Let's launch our first GKE cluster:

Parameter	Description	Value in example
`--cluster-version`	Supported cluster version (Refer to `https://cloud.google.com/kubernetes-engine/release-notes`)	`1.9.2-gke.1`
`--machine-type`	Instance type of nodes (Refer to `https://cloud.google.com/compute/docs/machine-types`)	`f1-micro`
`--num-nodes`	Number of nodes in the cluster	`3`
`--network`	Target VPC network	`k8s-network` (the one we just created)

`--zone`	Target zone	`us-central1-a` (you're free to use any zone)
`--tags`	Network tags to be attached to the nodes	`private`
`--service-account` | `--scopes`	Node identity (Refer to `https://cloud.google.com/sdk/gcloud/reference/container/clusters/create` for more scope value)	`storage-rw,compute-ro`

By referring preceding parameters, let's launch a three nodes cluster by `gcloud` command:

```
// create GKE cluster
$ gcloud container clusters create my-k8s-cluster --cluster-version 1.9.2-
gke.1 --machine-type f1-micro --num-nodes 3 --network k8s-network --zone
us-central1-a --tags private --scopes=storage-rw,compute-ro
WARNING: The behavior of --scopes will change in a future gcloud release:
service-control and service-management scopes will no longer be added to
what is specified in --scopes. To use these scopes, add them explicitly to
--scopes. To use the new behavior, set container/new_scopes_behavior
property (gcloud config set container/new_scopes_behavior true).
WARNING: Starting in Kubernetes v1.10, new clusters will no longer get
compute-rw and storage-ro scopes added to what is specified in --scopes
(though the latter will remain included in the default --scopes). To use
these scopes, add them explicitly to --scopes. To use the new behavior, set
container/new_scopes_behavior property (gcloud config set
container/new_scopes_behavior true).
Creating cluster my-k8s-cluster...done.
Created
[https://container.googleapis.com/v1/projects/kubernetes-cookbook/zones/us-
central1-a/clusters/my-k8s-cluster].
To inspect the contents of your cluster, go to:
https://console.cloud.google.com/kubernetes/workload_/gcloud/us-central1-a/
my-k8s-cluster?project=kubernetes-cookbook
kubeconfig entry generated for my-k8s-cluster.
NAME            LOCATION      MASTER_VERSION  MASTER_IP      MACHINE_TYPE
NODE_VERSION   NUM_NODES   STATUS
my-k8s-cluster  us-central1-a  1.9.2-gke.1      35.225.24.4  f1-micro
1.9.2-gke.1     3           RUNNING
```

After the cluster is up-and-running, we can start to connect to the cluster by configuring `kubectl`:

```
# gcloud container clusters get-credentials my-k8s-cluster --zone us-
central1-a --project kubernetes-cookbook
Fetching cluster endpoint and auth data.
```

```
kubeconfig entry generated for my-k8s-cluster.
```

Let's see if the cluster is healthy:

```
// list cluster components
# kubectl get componentstatuses
NAME                    STATUS     MESSAGE                 ERROR
controller-manager      Healthy    ok
scheduler               Healthy    ok
etcd-0                  Healthy    {"health": "true"}
etcd-1                  Healthy    {"health": "true"}
```

And we can check the nodes inside the cluster:

```
// list the nodes in cluster
# kubectl get nodes
NAME                                               STATUS    ROLES     AGE
VERSION
gke-my-k8s-cluster-default-pool-7d0359ed-0r18      Ready     <none>    21m
v1.9.2-gke.1
gke-my-k8s-cluster-default-pool-7d0359ed-1s2v      Ready     <none>    21m
v1.9.2-gke.1
gke-my-k8s-cluster-default-pool-7d0359ed-61px      Ready     <none>    21m
v1.9.2-gke.1
```

We can also use `kubectl` to check cluster info:

```
// list cluster info
# kubectl cluster-info
Kubernetes master is running at https://35.225.24.4
GLBCDefaultBackend is running at
https://35.225.24.4/api/v1/namespaces/kube-system/services/default-http-bac
kend:http/proxy
Heapster is running at
https://35.225.24.4/api/v1/namespaces/kube-system/services/heapster/proxy
KubeDNS is running at
https://35.225.24.4/api/v1/namespaces/kube-system/services/kube-dns:dns/pro
xy
kubernetes-dashboard is running at
https://35.225.24.4/api/v1/namespaces/kube-system/services/https:kubernetes
-dashboard:/proxy
Metrics-server is running at
https://35.225.24.4/api/v1/namespaces/kube-system/services/https:metrics-se
rver:/proxy
```

How it works...

Under the hood, gcloud creates a Kubernetes cluster with three nodes, along with a controller manager, scheduler, and etcd cluster with two members. We can also see that the master is launched with some services, including a default backend used by the controller, heapster (used for monitoring) KubeDNS for DNS services in the cluster, a dashboard for Kubernetes UI, and metrics-server for resource usage metrics.

We saw `Kubernetes-dashboard` has a URL; let's try and access it:

```
{
  "kind": "Status",
  "apiVersion": "v1",
  "metadata": {

  },
  "status": "Failure",
  "message": "services \"https:kubernetes-dashboard:\" is forbidden: User \"system:anonymous\" cannot get services/proxy in the namespace \"kube-system\": Unknown user \"system:anonymous\"",
  "reason": "Forbidden",
  "details": {
    "name": "https:kubernetes-dashboard:",
    "kind": "services"
  },
  "code": 403
}
```

Forbidden to access Kubernetes dashboard

We got `HTTP 403 Forbidden`. Where do we get the access and credentials though? One way to do it is running a proxy via the `kubectl proxy` command. It will bind the master IP to local `127.0.0.1:8001`:

```
# kubectl proxy
Starting to serve on 127.0.0.1:8001
```

After that, when we access `http://127.0.0.1:8001/ui`, it'll be redirected to `http://127.0.0.1:8001/api/v1/namespaces/kube-system/services/https:kubernetes-dashboard:/proxy`.

Since Kubernetes 1.7, the dashboard has supported user authentication based on a bearer token or `Kubeconfig` file:

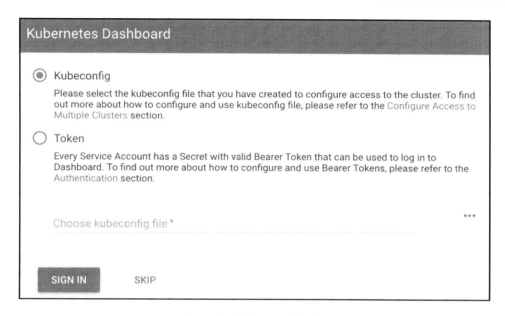

Logging in to the Kubernetes dashboard

You could create a user and bind it to the current context (please refer to the *Authentication and authorization* recipe in `Chapter 8`, *Advanced Cluster Administration*). Just for convenience, we can check if we have any existing users. Firstly, we need to know our current context name. Context combines of cluster information, users for authentication, and a namespace:

```
// check our current context name
# kubectl config current-context
gke_kubernetes-cookbook_us-central1-a_my-k8s-cluster
```

After we know the context name, we can describe it via the `kubectl` config view `$CONTEXT_NAME`:

```
// kubectl config view $CONTEXT_NAME
# kubectl config view gke_kubernetes-cookbook_us-central1-a_my-k8s-cluster
current-context: gke_kubernetes-cookbook_us-central1-a_my-k8s-cluster
kind: Config
preferences: {}
users:
- name: gke_kubernetes-cookbook_us-central1-a_my-k8s-cluster
  user:
    auth-provider:
      config:
        access-token: $ACCESS_TOKEN
        cmd-args: config config-helper --format=json
```

```
   cmd-path: /Users/chloelee/Downloads/google-cloud-sdk-2/bin/gcloud
   expiry: 2018-02-27T03:46:57Z
   expiry-key: '{.credential.token_expiry}'
   token-key: '{.credential.access_token}'
name: gcp
```

We may find there is a default user existing in our cluster; using its $ACCESS\_TOKEN$, you can glimpse the Kubernetes console.

Kubernetes dashboard overview

Our cluster in GKE is up-and-running! Let's try and see if we can run a simple deployment on it:

```
# kubectl run nginx --image nginx --replicas=2
deployment "nginx" created
# kubectl get pods
NAME                     READY     STATUS     RESTARTS    AGE
nginx-8586cf59-x27bj     1/1       Running    0           12s
nginx-8586cf59-zkl8j     1/1       Running    0           12s
```

Let's check our Kubernetes dashboard:

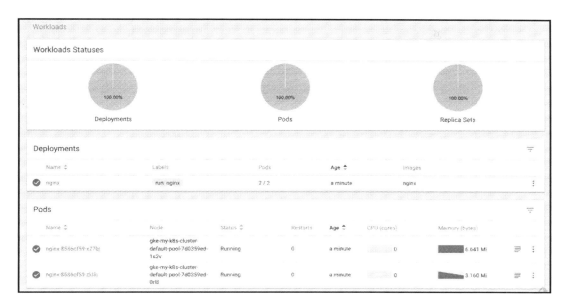

Workloads in Kubernetes dashboard

Hurray! The deployment is created and as a result two pods are scheduled and created.

See also

- *Advanced settings in kubeconfig* in Chapter 8, *Advanced Cluster Administration*
- *Setting resources in nodes* in Chapter 8, *Advanced Cluster Administration*
- *Playing with the Web UI* in Chapter 8, *Advanced Cluster Administration*
- *Setting up a DNS server in Kubernetes Cluster* in Chapter 8, *Advanced Cluster Administration*
- *Authentication and authorization* in Chapter 8, *Advanced Cluster Administration*

Exploring CloudProvider on GKE

GKE works as a native Kubernetes Cloud Provider, which integrates with resources in Kubernetes seamlessly and allows you to provision on demand, for example, VPC routes for the network, **Persistent Disk (PD)** for StorageClass, L4 load balancer for Service, and L4 load balancer for ingress.

Getting ready

By default, when you create the network and launch a Kubernetes cluster in Google Cloud Platform with proper routes, containers can already talk to each other without an explicit network being set up.Beyond the resources listed previously, we don't need to set any settings explicitly in most cases. GKE will just work.

How to do it...

Let's see how convenient GKE offers about storage, network and more.

StorageClass

In `Chapter 2`, *Walking through Kubernetes Concepts*, we learned how to declare `PersistentVolume` and `PersistentVolumeClaim`. With dynamic provisioning, you can define a set of `StorageClass` with different physical storage backends and use them in `PersistentVolume` or `PersistentVolumeClaim`. Let's see how it works.

To check the current default `StorageClass`, use `kubectl get storageclasses` command:

```
# kubectl get storageclasses
NAME                    PROVISIONER             AGE
standard (default)      kubernetes.io/gce-pd    1h
```

We can see we have a default storage class named standard and its provisioner is GCE PD.

Let's create a `PersistentVolumeClaim` request and use the standard `StorageClass` as the backend:

```
# cat gke-pvc.yaml
apiVersion: v1
kind: PersistentVolumeClaim
```

```
metadata:
    name: pvc-example-pv
spec:
  storageClassName: standard
  accessModes:
    - ReadWriteOnce
  resources:
    requests:
      storage: 10Gi

// create resources
# kubectl create -f gke-pvc.yaml
persistentvolumeclaim "pvc-example-pv" created
```

storageClassName is the place to put the name of the StorageClass. If you put in something that doesn't exist, PVC will not be created, since there is no proper mapped StorageClass to use:

```
// check pvc status
# kubectl get pvc
NAME               STATUS    VOLUME
CAPACITY    ACCESS MODES    STORAGECLASS    AGE
pvc-example-pv     Bound       pvc-1491b08e-1cfc-11e8-8589-42010a800360    10Gi
RWO             standard        12m

// describe the details of created PVC
# kubectl describe pvc pvc-example-pv
Name:          pvc-example-pv
Namespace:     default
StorageClass:  standard
Status:        Bound
Volume:        pvc-1491b08e-1cfc-11e8-8589-42010a800360
Labels:        <none>
Annotations:   pv.kubernetes.io/bind-completed=yes
               pv.kubernetes.io/bound-by-controller=yes
               volume.beta.kubernetes.io/storage-
provisioner=kubernetes.io/gce-pd
Finalizers:    []
Capacity:      10Gi
Access Modes:  RWO
Events:
  Type      Reason                  Age     From                               Message
  ----      ------                  ----    ----                               -------
  Normal    ProvisioningSucceeded   12m     persistentvolume-controller
Successfully provisioned volume pvc-1491b08e-1cfc-11e8-8589-42010a800360
using kubernetes.io/gce-pd
```

We can see volume `pvc-1491b08e-1cfc-11e8-8589-42010a800360` has been created and bounded. If we list GCP disks, we'll find there was a Persistent Disk created; the suffix of the disk name indicates the volume name in Kubernetes. That's the magic of dynamic volume provisioning:

```
# gcloud compute disks list
NAME                                                          ZONE
SIZE_GB  TYPE        STATUS
gke-my-k8s-cluster-5ef-pvc-1491b08e-1cfc-11e8-8589-42010a800360  us-
central1-a  10          pd-standard  READY
```

Besides the default `StorageClass`, you can also create your own. Recap this in `Chapter 2`, *Walking through Kubernetes Concepts*.

Service (LoadBalancer)

A `LoadBalancer` service type only works in the cloud environment that supports external load balancers. This allows outside traffic to be routed into target Pods. In GCP, a TCP load balancer will be created by a `LoadBalancer` service type:

1. The firewall rules for allowing traffic between the load balancer and nodes will be created automatically:

```
// leveraging LoadBalancer service
# cat gke-service.yaml
apiVersion: apps/v1
kind: Deployment
metadata:
  name: nginx
spec:
  replicas: 1
  selector:
    matchLabels:
      run: nginx
  template:
    metadata:
      labels:
        run: nginx
    spec:
      containers:
        - image: nginx
          name: nginx
          ports:
```

```
                - containerPort: 80
    ---
    apiVersion: v1
    kind: Service
    metadata:
      name: nginx
    spec:
      ports:
        - port: 80
          targetPort: 80
      type: LoadBalancer
      selector:
        run: nginx

    // create resources
    # kubectl create -f gke-service.yaml
    deployment "nginx" created
    service "nginx" created
```

2. Let's check the service. The `EXTERNAL-IP` will show `<pending>` if the load balancer is still provisioning. Wait a while and the load balancer IP will present itself eventually:

```
    # kubectl get svc nginx
    NAME        TYPE           CLUSTER-IP       EXTERNAL-IP
    PORT(S)         AGE
    nginx       LoadBalancer   10.35.250.183    35.225.223.151
    80:30383/TCP    11m
```

3. Let's curl `$EXTERNAL-IP:80`, to see if it works properly:

```
    # curl -I 35.225.223.151
    HTTP/1.1 200 OK
    Server: nginx/1.13.9
    Date: Thu, 01 Mar 2018 03:57:05 GMT
    Content-Type: text/html
    Content-Length: 612
    Last-Modified: Tue, 20 Feb 2018 12:21:20 GMT
    Connection: keep-alive
    ETag: "5a8c12c0-264"
    Accept-Ranges: bytes
```

4. If we check the forwarding rules in GCP, we can find a rule that defines how the traffic goes from external IP to the target pool:

```
    # gcloud compute forwarding-rules list
    NAME                            REGION       IP_ADDRESS
```

```
IP_PROTOCOL   TARGET
ae1f2ad0c1d0211e8858942010a80036  us-central1  35.225.223.151
TCP           us-
central1/targetPools/ae1f2ad0c1d0211e8858942010a80036
```

5. A target pool is a set of instances that receive the traffic from forwarding rules. We could inspect the target pool by using the gcloud command as well:

```
// list target pools
# gcloud compute target-pools list
NAME                                       REGION       SESSION_AFFINITY
BACKUP   HEALTH_CHECKS
ae1f2ad0c1d0211e8858942010a80036  us-central1  NONE
k8s-1a4c86537c370d21-node

// check target pools info, replace $GCP_REGION as your default
region.
# gcloud compute target-pools describe
ae1f2ad0c1d0211e8858942010a80036 --region=$GCP_REGION
creationTimestamp: '2018-02-28T19:45:46.052-08:00'
description: '{"kubernetes.io/service-name":"default/nginx"}'
healthChecks:
-
https://www.googleapis.com/compute/v1/projects/kubernetes-cookb
ook/global/httpHealthChecks/k8s-1a4c86537c370d21-node
id: '3515096241941432709'
instances:
-
https://www.googleapis.com/compute/v1/projects/kubernetes-cookb
ook/zones/us-central1-a/instances/gke-my-k8s-cluster-default-
pool-36121894-71wg
-
https://www.googleapis.com/compute/v1/projects/kubernetes-cookb
ook/zones/us-central1-a/instances/gke-my-k8s-cluster-default-
pool-36121894-04rv
-
https://www.googleapis.com/compute/v1/projects/kubernetes-cookb
ook/zones/us-central1-a/instances/gke-my-k8s-cluster-default-
pool-36121894-3mxm
kind: compute#targetPool
name: ae1f2ad0c1d0211e8858942010a80036
region:
https://www.googleapis.com/compute/v1/projects/kubernetes-cookb
ook/regions/us-central1
selfLink:
https://www.googleapis.com/compute/v1/projects/kubernetes-cookb
ook/regions/us-
```

```
central1/targetPools/ae1f2ad0c1d0211e8858942010a80036
sessionAffinity: NONE
```

We can see there are three nodes inside the pool. Those are the same three nodes in our Kubernetes cluster. Load balancer will dispatch the traffic to a node based on a hash of the source/definition IP and port. A service with `LoadBalancer` type looks handy; however, it can't do path-based routing. It's time for ingress to come into play. Ingress supports virtual hosts, path-based routing, and TLS termination, which is a more flexible approach to your web services.

Ingress

In `Chapter 5`, *Building Continuous Delivery Pipelines*, we learned about the concept of ingress , and when and how to use it. Ingress defines a set of rules allowing the inbound connection to access Kubernetes cluster services. It routes the traffic into cluster at L7, and the controller brings the traffic to the nodes. When GCP is the cloud provider, a L7 load balancer will be created if an ingress is created, as well as related firewall rules, health checks, backend services, forwarding rules, and a URL map. A URL map in GCP is a mechanism that contains a set of rules and forwards requests to the corresponding backend services.

In this recipe, we'll reuse the examples from `Chapter 5`, *Building Continuous Delivery Pipelines*, `Nodeport-deployment.yaml` and `echoserver.yaml`. Next is an illustration of how these two services work from `Chapter 5`, *Building Continuous Delivery Pipelines*:

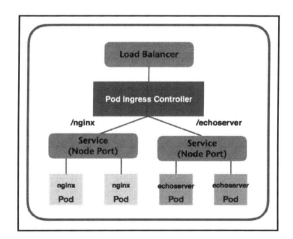

Ingress illustration

We will create an ingress for nginx and echoserver, that routes to different services. When the traffic comes in, the pod ingress controller will decide with service to route to.

Here is an example for ingress . Please note that you might want to add the host name inside the rules section if you want the underlying services to always be visited from a certain host name:

```
# cat INGRESS.yaml
apiVersion: extensions/v1beta1
kind: INGRESS
metadata:
  name: my-INGRESS
  annotations:
    INGRESS.kubernetes.io/rewrite-target: /
spec:
  rules:
    - http:
        paths:
          - path: /
            # default backend
            backend:
              serviceName: nodeport-svc
              servicePort: 8080
          - path: /nginx
            # nginx service
            backend:
              serviceName: nodeport-svc
              servicePort: 8080
          - path: /echoserver
            # echoserver service
            backend:
              serviceName: echoserver-svc
              servicePort: 8080

// create nodeport-svc (nginx) service
# kubectl create -f nodeport-deployment.yaml
deployment "nodeport-deploy" created
service "nodeport-svc" created

// create echoserver-svc (echoserver) service
# kubectl create -f echoserver.yaml
deployment "echoserver-deploy" created
service "echoserver-svc" created

// create INGRESS
# kubectl create -f INGRESS.yaml
INGRESS "my-INGRESS" created
```

Please double-check that the underlying service is configured as a `NodePort` type. Otherwise you might encounter errors such as `googleapi: Error 400: Invalid value for field 'namedPorts[1].port': '0'. Must be greater than or equal to 1, invalid error` from `loadbalancer-controller`.

After a few minutes, the L7 load balancer will be created and you'll be able to see it from the GCP console or by using the gcloud command. Let's use `kubectl` to check if the backend service in INGRESS is healthy:

```
// kubectl describe INGRESS $INGRESS_name
# kubectl describe INGRESS my-INGRESS

curl Name:            my-INGRESS
Namespace:         default
Address:           35.190.46.137
Default backend:  default-http-backend:80 (10.32.2.3:8080)
Rules:
  Host  Path  Backends
  ----  ----  --------
  *
        /              nodeport-svc:8080 (<none>)
        /nginx         nodeport-svc:8080 (<none>)
        /echoserver    echoserver-svc:8080 (<none>)
Annotations:
  backends:         {"k8s-be-31513--91cf30ccf285becb":"HEALTHY","k8s-
be-31780--91cf30ccf285becb":"HEALTHY","k8s-be-32691-
-91cf30ccf285becb":"HEALTHY"}
  forwarding-rule:  k8s-fw-default-my-INGRESS--91cf30ccf285becb
  rewrite-target:   /
  target-proxy:     k8s-tp-default-my-INGRESS--91cf30ccf285becb
  url-map:          k8s-um-default-my-INGRESS--91cf30ccf285becb
Events:
  Type      Reason    Age              From                   Message
  ----      ------    ----             ----                   -------
  Normal    Service   2m (x11 over 1h)  loadbalancer-controller  no user
specified default backend, using system default
```

We can see the three backends are healthy and the related forwarding rules, target proxy, and URL map have been all created. We can get a comprehensive view from the GCP console by visiting discovery and load balancing in GKE or the Load balancing tab in network services:

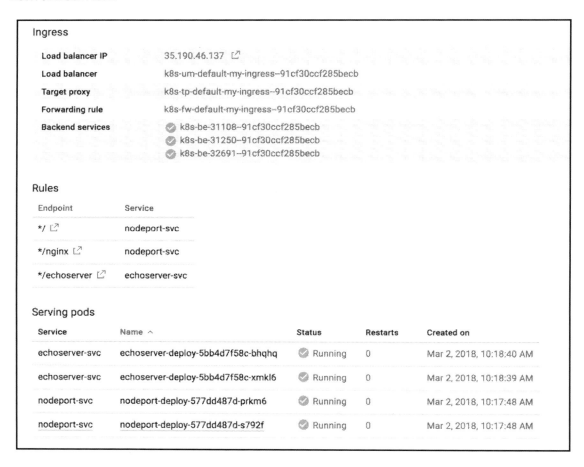

Discovery and Load balancing

The backend is illustrated here:

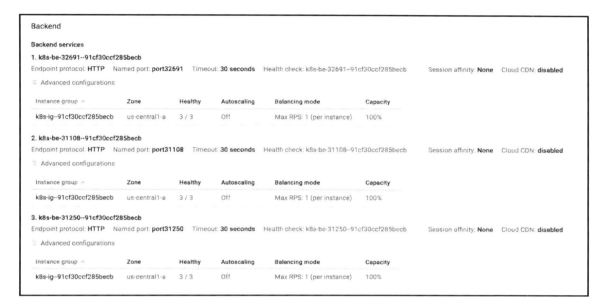

Backend services

From time to time, your ingress resource might encounter updates. When you redeploy it, there is no guarantee that GCP will allocate the same IP address to your load balancer. This might introduce a problem when the IP address is associated with a DNS name. The target IP address will need to be updated every time the IP is changed. This could be resolved by a static external IP address plus `kubernetes.io/INGRESS.global-static-ip-name` annotation:

```
// allocate static IP as my-external-ip
# gcloud compute addresses create my-external-ip –global


// check external-ip
# gcloud compute addresses list
NAME              REGION    ADDRESS         STATUS
my-external-ip              130.211.37.61   RESERVED
After external IP is prepared, we could start launching our INGRESS now.
# cat INGRESS-static-ip.yaml
apiVersion: extensions/v1beta1
kind: INGRESS
metadata:
  name: my-INGRESS-static-ip
```

```
  annotations:
    INGRESS.kubernetes.io/rewrite-target: /
    kubernetes.io/INGRESS.global-static-ip-name: my-external-ip
spec:
  rules:
  - http:
      paths:
      - path: /
        # default backend
        backend:
          serviceName: nodeport-svc
          servicePort: 8080
      - path: /nginx
        # nginx service
        backend:
          serviceName: nodeport-svc
          servicePort: 8080
      - path: /echoserver
        # echoserver service
        backend:
          serviceName: echoserver-svc
          servicePort: 8080
```

```
# kubectl create -f INGRESS-static-ip.yaml
INGRESS "my-INGRESS-stati-ip" created
```

Let's describe `my-INGRESS` **and see if it binds properly with the external IP we created :**

```
# kubectl describe INGRESS my-INGRESS
Name:             my-INGRESS
Namespace:        default
Address:          130.211.37.61
Default backend:  default-http-backend:80 (10.32.2.3:8080)
Rules:
  Host  Path  Backends
  ----  ----  --------
  *      /                 nodeport-svc:8080 (<none>)
         /nginx            nodeport-svc:8080 (<none>)          /echoserver
echoserver-svc:8080 (<none>)Annotations:
  backends:          {"k8s-be-31108--91cf30ccf285becb":"HEALTHY","k8s-
be-31250--91cf30ccf285becb":"HEALTHY","k8s-be-32691-
-91cf30ccf285becb":"HEALTHY"}  forwarding-rule:  k8s-fw-default-my-INGRESS-
-91cf30ccf285becb  rewrite-target:  /  target-proxy:    k8s-tp-default-
my-INGRESS--91cf30ccf285becb  url-map:        k8s-um-default-my-INGRESS-
-91cf30ccf285becbEvents: Type   Reason   Age              From
Message  ----   ------   ----             ----            ------
-  Normal  ADD      27m              loadbalancer-controller  default/my-
```

```
INGRESS  Normal  CREATE   25m               loadbalancer-controller  ip:
130.211.37.61
  Normal  Service  4m (x6 over 25m)  loadbalancer-controller  no user
specified default backend, using system default
```

We're all set. `Nginx` and `echoserver` can be visited via the external static IP
`130.211.37.61`, and we're able to associate a DNS name with it by using the cloud DNS
service in GCP.

There's more...

In Kubernetes v.1.9, the Kubernetes cloud controller manager was promoted to alpha.
Cloud controller manager aims to make the cloud provider release feature support via its
own release cycles, which could be independent from the Kubernetes release cycle. Then it
could be independent with Kubernetes core release cycle. It provides common interfaces
that each cloud provider can implement, which decoupling with Kubernetes Core logic. In
the near future, we'll see more comprehensive support from different cloud providers!

See also

- *Working with services* in `Chapter 2`, *Walking through Kubernetes Concepts*
- *Working with volumes* in `Chapter 2`, *Walking through Kubernetes Concepts*
- *Forwarding container ports* in `Chapter 3`, *Playing with Containers*

Managing Kubernetes clusters on GKE

Google Kubernetes Engines offers us the seamless experience of running Kubernetes; it also
makes Kubernetes administration so easy. Depending on the expected peak time, we might
want to scale the Kubernetes nodes out or in. Alternatively, we could use Autoscaler to do
auto-scaling for the nodes. Kubernetes is an evolving platform. The release pace is fast. We
might want to upgrade the cluster version from time to time, which is very easy to do. We
could also use the Autoupgrade feature to upgrade the cluster by enabling automatically
schedule feature in GKE. Let's see how to do it.

Getting ready

Before setting up the administration features that GCP offers, we'll have to have a cluster up and running. We'll reuse the cluster we created in the Playing with the Google Kubernetes Engine recipe in this chapter.

How to do it...

In this recipe, we'll introduce how to manage the number of nodes based on usage and requirements. Also, we'll learn how to deal with cluster upgrades. Finally, we'll see how to provision a multi-zone cluster in GKE, in order to prevent a physical zone outage.

Node pool

A node pool is a set of instances in GCP that share the same configuration. When we launch a cluster from the `gcloud` command, we pass `--num-node=3` and the rest of the arguments. Then three instances will be launched inside the same pool, sharing the same configuration, using the same method:

```
# gcloud compute instance-groups list NAME LOCATION SCOPE NETWORK MANAGED
INSTANCES gke-my-k8s-cluster-default-pool-36121894-grp us-central1-a zone
k8s-network Yes 3
```

Assume there is an expected heavy peak time for your service. As a Kubernetes administrator, you might want to resize your node pool inside the cluster.

```
# gcloud container clusters resize my-k8s-cluster --size 5 --zone us-
central1-a --node-pool default-pool
Pool [default-pool] for [my-k8s-cluster] will be resized to 5.
Do you want to continue (Y/n)?  y
Resizing my-k8s-cluster...done.
Updated
[https://container.googleapis.com/v1/projects/kubernetes-cookbook/zones/us-
central1-a/clusters/my-k8s-cluster].
# kubectl get nodes
NAME                                                      STATUS    ROLES     AGE
VERSION
gke-my-k8s-cluster-default-pool-36121894-04rv             Ready     <none>    6h
v1.9.2-gke.1
gke-my-k8s-cluster-default-pool-36121894-71wg             Ready     <none>    6h
v1.9.2-gke.1
gke-my-k8s-cluster-default-pool-36121894-8km3             Ready     <none>    39s
v1.9.2-gke.1
```

```
gke-my-k8s-cluster-default-pool-36121894-9j9p          Ready       <none>      31m
v1.9.2-gke.1
gke-my-k8s-cluster-default-pool-36121894-9jmv          Ready       <none>      36s
v1.9.2-gke.1
```

The resize command can help you scale out and in. If the node count after resizing is less than before, the scheduler will migrate the pods to run on available nodes.

You can set the compute resource boundary for each container in the spec. You set requests and limits to a pod container. Assume we have a super nginx which requires 1024 MB memory:

```
# cat super-nginx.yaml
apiVersion: apps/v1
kind: Deployment
metadata:
  name: super-nginx
  labels:
    app: nginx
spec:
  replicas: 1
  selector:
    matchLabels:
      app: nginx
  template:
    metadata:
      labels:
        app: nginx
    spec:
      containers:
      - name: nginx
        image: nginx
        resources:
          requests:
            memory: 1024Mi

// create super nginx deployment
# kubectl create -f super-nginx.yaml
deployment "super-nginx" created

# kubectl get pods
NAME                            READY       STATUS       RESTARTS     AGE
super-nginx-df79db98-5vfmv       0/1         Pending      0            10s
# kubectl describe po super-nginx-779494d88f-74xjp
Name:           super-nginx-df79db98-5vfmv
Namespace:      default
Node:           <none>
```

```
Labels:            app=nginx
                   pod-template-hash=89358654
Annotations:       kubernetes.io/limit-ranger=LimitRanger plugin set: cpu
request for container nginx
Status:            PendingIP:
Controlled By:     ReplicaSet/super-nginx-df79db98
...
Events:
  Type       Reason           Age               From              Message
  ----       ------           ----              ----              -------
  Warning    FailedScheduling 11s (x5 over 18s) default-scheduler 0/5
nodes are available: 5 Insufficient memory.
```

The node size we created is `f1-miro`, which only has 0.6 GM memory per node. It means the scheduler will never find a node with sufficient memory to run `super-nginx`. In this case, we can add more nodes with higher memory to the cluster by creating another node pool. We'll use `g1-small` as an example, which contains 1.7 GB memory:

```
// create a node pool named larger-mem-pool with n1-standard-1 instance
type
# gcloud container node-pools create larger-mem-pool --cluster my-k8s-
cluster --machine-type n1-standard-1 --num-nodes 2 --tags private --zone
us-central1-a --scopes=storage-rw,compute-ro
...
Creating node pool larger-mem-pool...done.
Created
[https://container.googleapis.com/v1/projects/kubernetes-cookbook/zones/us-
central1-a/clusters/my-k8s-cluster/nodePools/larger-mem-pool].
NAME            MACHINE_TYPE      DISK_SIZE_GB   NODE_VERSION
larger-mem-pool n1-standard-1     100            1.9.2-gke.1

// check node pools
# gcloud container node-pools list --cluster my-k8s-cluster --zone us-
central1-a
NAME            MACHINE_TYPE      DISK_SIZE_GB   NODE_VERSION
default-pool    f1-micro          100            1.9.2-gke.1
larger-mem-pool n1-standard-1     100            1.9.2-gke.1

// check current nodes
# kubectl get nodes
NAME                                                 STATUS   ROLES    AGE
VERSION
gke-my-k8s-cluster-default-pool-36121894-04rv        Ready    <none>   7h
v1.9.2-gke.1
gke-my-k8s-cluster-default-pool-36121894-71wg        Ready    <none>   7h
v1.9.2-gke.1
gke-my-k8s-cluster-default-pool-36121894-8km3        Ready    <none>   9m
```

```
v1.9.2-gke.1
gke-my-k8s-cluster-default-pool-36121894-9j9p        Ready        <none>        40m
v1.9.2-gke.1
gke-my-k8s-cluster-default-pool-36121894-9jmv        Ready        <none>        9m
v1.9.2-gke.1
gke-my-k8s-cluster-larger-mem-pool-a51c8da3-f1tb     Ready        <none>        1m
v1.9.2-gke.1
gke-my-k8s-cluster-larger-mem-pool-a51c8da3-scw1     Ready        <none>        1m
v1.9.2-gke.1
```

Looks like we have two more powerful nodes. Let's see the status of our super nginx:

```
# kubectl get pods
NAME                        READY     STATUS      RESTARTS     AGE
super-nginx-df79db98-5vfmv  1/1       Running     0            23m
```

It's running! Kubernetes scheduler will always try to find sufficient resources to schedule pods. In this case, there are two new nodes added to the cluster that can fulfill the resource requirement, so the pod is scheduled and run:

```
// check the event of super nginx
# kubectl describe pods super-nginx-df79db98-5vfmv
...
Events:
  Warning   FailedScheduling        3m (x7 over 4m)       default-scheduler
0/5 nodes are available: 5 Insufficient memory.
  Normal    Scheduled               1m                    default-scheduler
Successfully assigned super-nginx-df79db98-5vfmv to gke-my-k8s-cluster-
larger-mem-pool-a51c8da3-scw1
  Normal    SuccessfulMountVolume   1m                    kubelet, gke-my-k8s-
cluster-larger-mem-pool-a51c8da3-scw1  MountVolume.SetUp succeeded for
volume "default-token-bk8p2"
  Normal    Pulling                 1m                    kubelet, gke-my-k8s-
cluster-larger-mem-pool-a51c8da3-scw1  pulling image "nginx"
  Normal    Pulled                  1m                    kubelet, gke-my-k8s-
cluster-larger-mem-pool-a51c8da3-scw1  Successfully pulled image "nginx"
  Normal    Created                 1m                    kubelet, gke-my-k8s-
cluster-larger-mem-pool-a51c8da3-scw1  Created container
  Normal    Started                 1m                    kubelet, gke-my-k8s-
cluster-larger-mem-pool-a51c8da3-scw1  Started container
```

From the events of the pod, we know what path it ran through. Originally, it couldn't find any nodes with sufficient resources and eventually it's scheduled to the new node named gke-my-k8s-cluster-larger-mem-pool-a51c8da3-scw1.

For making the user preference on scheduling pods on certain nodes, `nodeSelector` was introduced. You could either use built-in node labels, such as `beta.kubernetes.io/instance-type: n1-standard-1` in pod spec, or use customized labels to achieve it. For more information, please refer to `https://kubernetes.io/docs/concepts/configuration/assign-pod-node`.

Kubernetes also supports **cluster autoscaler**, which automatically resizes your cluster based on capacity if all nodes have insufficient resources to run the requested pods. To do that, we add `--enable-autoscaling` and specify the maximum and minimum node count when we create the new node pool:

```
# cloud container node-pools create larger-mem-pool --cluster my-k8s-
cluster --machine-type n1-standard-1 --tags private --zone us-central1-a --
scopes=storage-rw,compute-ro --enable-autoscaling --min-nodes 1 --max-nodes
5
...
Creating node pool larger-mem-pool...done.
Created
[https://container.googleapis.com/v1/projects/kubernetes-cookbook/zones/us-
central1-a/clusters/my-k8s-cluster/nodePools/larger-mem-pool].
NAME            MACHINE_TYPE    DISK_SIZE_GB    NODE_VERSION
larger-mem-pool n1-standard-1   100             1.9.2-gke.1
```

After a few minutes, we can see there is a new node inside our cluster:

```
#  kubectl get nodes
NAME                                                STATUS    ROLES     AGE
VERSION
gke-my-k8s-cluster-default-pool-36121894-04rv       Ready     <none>    8h
v1.9.2-gke.1
gke-my-k8s-cluster-default-pool-36121894-71wg       Ready     <none>    8h
v1.9.2-gke.1
gke-my-k8s-cluster-default-pool-36121894-8km3       Ready     <none>    1h
v1.9.2-gke.1
gke-my-k8s-cluster-default-pool-36121894-9j9p       Ready     <none>    1h
v1.9.2-gke.1
gke-my-k8s-cluster-default-pool-36121894-9jmv       Ready     <none>    1h
v1.9.2-gke.1
gke-my-k8s-cluster-larger-mem-pool-a51c8da3-s6s6    Ready     <none>    15m
v1.9.2-gke.1
```

Now, let's change the replica of our super-nginx from 1 to 4 by using `kubectl` edit or creating a new deployment:

```
// check current pods
# kubectl get pods
NAME                        READY      STATUS      RESTARTS      AGE
super-nginx-df79db98-5q9mj  0/1        Pending     0             3m
super-nginx-df79db98-72fcz  1/1        Running     0             3m
super-nginx-df79db98-781br  0/1        Pending     0             3m
super-nginx-df79db98-fngp2  1/1        Running     0             3m
```

We find there are two pods with a pending status:

```
// check nodes status
# kubectl get nodes
NAME                                                STATUS      ROLES       AGE
VERSION
gke-my-k8s-cluster-default-pool-36121894-04rv       Ready       <none>      8h
v1.9.2-gke.1
gke-my-k8s-cluster-default-pool-36121894-71wg       Ready       <none>      8h
v1.9.2-gke.1
gke-my-k8s-cluster-default-pool-36121894-9j9p       Ready       <none>      2h
v1.9.2-gke.1
gke-my-k8s-cluster-larger-mem-pool-a51c8da3-d766    Ready       <none>      4m
v1.9.2-gke.1
gke-my-k8s-cluster-larger-mem-pool-a51c8da3-gtsn    Ready       <none>      3m
v1.9.2-gke.1
gke-my-k8s-cluster-larger-mem-pool-a51c8da3-s6s6    Ready       <none>      25m
v1.9.2-gke.1
```

After a few minutes, we see that there are new members in our larger mem pool, and all our pods get to run:

```
// check pods status
# kubectl get pods
NAME                        READY      STATUS      RESTARTS      AGE
super-nginx-df79db98-5q9mj  1/1        Running     0             3m
super-nginx-df79db98-72fcz  1/1        Running     0             3m
super-nginx-df79db98-781br  1/1        Running     0             3m
super-nginx-df79db98-fngp2  1/1        Running     0             3m
```

Cluster autoscaler comes in handy and is cost-effective. When the nodes are over-provisioned, the additional node in the node pool will be terminated automatically.

Multi-zone and regional clusters

Our `my-k8s-cluster` is currently deployed in the `us-central1-a` zone. While a zone is a physically isolated location in a region, it may suffer an outage. Google Kubernetes Engine supports multi-zone and regional deployment. Multi-zone clusters create a single master in a zone and provision nodes in multiple zones; on the other hand, a regional cluster creates multiple masters across three zones and provisions nodes in multiple zones.

Multi-zone clusters

To enable multi-zone cluster, add `--additional-zones $zone2, $zone3,` ... into the command when you create the cluster.

Just like AWS, GCP has service quota limits as well. You could use `gcloud compute project-info describe –project $PROJECT_NAME` to check the quota and request an increase from the GCP console if needed.

Let's launch a two-nodes cluster per zone first:

```
// launch a multi-zone cluster with 2 nodes per zone.
# gcloud container clusters create my-k8s-cluster --cluster-version 1.9.2-
gke.1 --machine-type f1-micro --num-nodes 2 --network k8s-network --tags
private --scopes=storage-rw,compute-ro --zone us-central1-a --additional-
zones us-central1-b,us-central1-c
Creating cluster my-k8s-cluster...done.
Created
[https://container.googleapis.com/v1/projects/kubernetes-cookbook/zones/us-
central1-a/clusters/my-k8s-cluster].
To inspect the contents of your cluster, go to:
https://console.cloud.google.com/kubernetes/workload_/gcloud/us-central1-a/
my-k8s-cluster?project=kubernetes-cookbook
kubeconfig entry generated for my-k8s-cluster.
NAME            LOCATION      MASTER_VERSION  MASTER_IP      MACHINE_TYPE
NODE_VERSION   NUM_NODES   STATUS
my-k8s-cluster  us-central1-a 1.9.2-gke.1     35.226.67.179  f1-micro
1.9.2-gke.1    6           RUNNING
```

We find we have six nodes now:

```
# kubectl get nodes
NAME                                                STATUS    ROLES     AGE
VERSION
gke-my-k8s-cluster-default-pool-068d31a2-q909       Ready     <none>    8m
v1.9.2-gke.1
```

```
gke-my-k8s-cluster-default-pool-068d31a2-rqzw    Ready    <none>    8m
v1.9.2-gke.1
gke-my-k8s-cluster-default-pool-64a6ead8-qf6z    Ready    <none>    8m
v1.9.2-gke.1
gke-my-k8s-cluster-default-pool-64a6ead8-x8cc    Ready    <none>    8m
v1.9.2-gke.1
gke-my-k8s-cluster-default-pool-798c4248-2r4p    Ready    <none>    8m
v1.9.2-gke.1
gke-my-k8s-cluster-default-pool-798c4248-skdn    Ready    <none>    8m
v1.9.2-gke.1
```

Let's check if the nodes are spread across the three zones we specified:

```
# gcloud compute instance-groups list NAME LOCATION SCOPE NETWORK MANAGED
INSTANCES gke-my-k8s-cluster-default-pool-068d31a2-grp us-central1-a zone
k8s-network Yes 2 gke-my-k8s-cluster-default-pool-64a6ead8-grp us-central1-
c zone k8s-network Yes 2 gke-my-k8s-cluster-default-pool-798c4248-grp us-
central1-b zone k8s-network Yes 2
```

Regional clusters

Regional clusters are still in the beta phase. To use these, we'll have to enable the gcloud
beta command. We can enable it via this command:

```
# export CLOUDSDK_CONTAINER_USE_V1_API_CLIENT=false # gcloud config set
container/use_v1_api false
Updated property [container/use_v1_api].
```

Then we should be able to use the gcloud v1beta command to launch the regional
cluster:

```
# gcloud beta container clusters create my-k8s-cluster --cluster-version
1.9.2-gke.1 --machine-type f1-micro --num-nodes 2 --network k8s-network --
tags private --scopes=storage-rw,compute-ro --region us-central1

Creating cluster my-k8s-cluster...done. Created
[https://container.googleapis.com/v1beta1/projects/kubernetes-cookbook/zone
s/us-central1/clusters/my-k8s-cluster]. To inspect the contents of your
cluster, go to:
https://console.cloud.google.com/kubernetes/workload_/gcloud/us-central1/my
-k8s-cluster?project=kubernetes-cookbook

kubeconfig entry generated for my-k8s-cluster. NAME LOCATION MASTER_VERSION
MASTER_IP MACHINE_TYPE NODE_VERSION NUM_NODES STATUS my-k8s-cluster us-
central1 1.9.2-gke.1 35.225.71.127 f1-micro 1.9.2-gke.1 6 RUNNING
```

The command is quite similar to the one that creates a cluster, just with two differences: a beta flag is added before the group name container which indicates it's a `v1beta` command. The second difference is changing `--zone` to `--region`:

```
// list instance groups
# gcloud compute instance-groups list
NAME                                              LOCATION      SCOPE   NETWORK
MANAGED   INSTANCES
gke-my-k8s-cluster-default-pool-074ab64e-grp      us-central1-a zone    k8s-
network   Yes     2
gke-my-k8s-cluster-default-pool-11492dfc-grp      us-central1-c zone    k8s-
network   Yes     2
gke-my-k8s-cluster-default-pool-f2c90100-grp      us-central1-b zone    k8s-
network   Yes     2
```

Cluster upgrades

Kubernetes is a fast-release project. GKE also keeps supporting new versions. It's not uncommon to have multiple minor version updates within a month. check the GKE console:

⊘ my-k8s-cluster			
Details	Storage	Nodes	
Cluster			
Master version	1.9.2-gke.1		Upgrade available
Endpoint	35.225.71.127		Show credentials

Upgrade available information in the GCP console

We see that an upgrade is available. **1.9.3-gke.1** in the screenshot has just been released and our cluster is able to upgrade:

Change Kubernetes version of master in my-k8s-cluster

○ 1.9.3-gke.0
● 1.9.2-gke.1 (current)

Changing the master version can result in several minutes of control plane downtime. During that period you will be unable to edit this cluster.

This operation starts immediately, and is not reversible.

Learn more   Release notes 🔗

CANCEL   CHANGE

Upgrade available to 1.9.3-gke.0

We can upgrade the cluster via the GKE console, or using gcloud command. We'll use the single zone (us-central1-a) cluster to demonstrate how to upgrade in the next example. When upgrading the cluster, the master is always the first citizen to do the upgrade. The desired node version cannot be greater than the current master version.

```
# gcloud container clusters upgrade my-k8s-cluster --zone us-central1-a --
cluster-version 1.9.3-gke.0 —master
Master of cluster [my-k8s-cluster] will be upgraded from version
[1.9.2-gke.1] to version [1.9.3-gke.0]. This operation is long-running
 and will block other operations on the cluster (including delete)
until it has run to completion.
Do you want to continue (Y/n)?  y
Upgrading my-k8s-cluster...done.
Updated
[https://container.googleapis.com/v1/projects/kubernetes-cookbook/zones/us-
central1-a/clusters/my-k8s-cluster].
```

Let's check the master's version:

```
# kubectl version
...
Server Version: version.Info{Major:"1", Minor:"9+", GitVersion:"v1.9.3-
gke.0", GitCommit:"a7b719f7d3463eb5431cf8a3caf5d485827b4210",
GitTreeState:"clean", BuildDate:"2018-02-16T18:26:01Z",
GoVersion:"go1.9.2b4", Compiler:"gc", Platform:"linux/amd64"}
```

Looks good. The master has been upgraded to `v1.9.3-gke.0`, but our nodes didn't get upgrade yet:

```
# kubectl get nodes
NAME                                             STATUS    ROLES     AGE
VERSION
gke-my-k8s-cluster-default-pool-978ca614-3jxx    Ready     <none>    8m
v1.9.2-gke.1
gke-my-k8s-cluster-default-pool-978ca614-njrs    Ready     <none>    8m
v1.9.2-gke.1
gke-my-k8s-cluster-default-pool-978ca614-xmlw    Ready     <none>    8m
v1.9.2-gke.1
```

For the node upgrade, instead of upgrading them all at once, GKE performs rolling upgrade. It will first drain and deregister a node from the node pool, delete an old instance, and provision a new instance with the desired version, then add it back to the cluster:

```
// perform node upgrades.
# gcloud container clusters upgrade my-k8s-cluster --zone us-central1-a --
cluster-version 1.9.3-gke.0
All nodes (3 nodes) of cluster [my-k8s-cluster] will be upgraded from
version [1.9.2-gke.1] to version [1.9.3-gke.0]. This operation is
long-running and will block other operations on the cluster (including
 delete) until it has run to completion.
Do you want to continue (Y/n)?  y
Upgrading my-k8s-cluster...done.
Updated
[https://container.googleapis.com/v1/projects/kubernetes-cookbook/zones/us-
central1-a/clusters/my-k8s-cluster].
```

The node pool can be configured to auto-upgrade via the `--enable-autoupgrade` flag during cluster creation, or using the gcloud container `node-pools` update command to update existing node pools. For more information, please refer to `https://cloud.google.com/kubernetes-engine/docs/concepts/node-auto-upgrades`.

It will take more than 10 minutes. After that, all the nodes in the cluster are upgraded to `1.9.3-gke.0`.

See also

- *Advanced settings in kubeconfig* in `Chapter 8`, *Advanced Cluster Administration*
- *Setting resources in nodes* in `Chapter 8`, *Advanced Cluster Administration*

8
Advanced Cluster Administration

In this chapter, we will cover the following recipes:

- Advanced settings in kubeconfig
- Setting resources in nodes
- Playing with WebUI
- Working with a RESTful API
- Working with Kubernetes DNS
- Authentication and authorization

Introduction

We will go through some advanced administration topics in this chapter. First, you will learn how to use kubeconfig to manage different clusters. Then, we will work on computing resources in nodes. Kubernetes provides a friendly user interface that illustrates the current status of resources, such as deployments, nodes, and pods. You will learn how to build and administrate it.

Next, you will learn how to work with the RESTful API that Kubernetes exposes. It will be a handy way to integrate with other systems. Finally, we want to build a secure cluster; the last section will go through how to set up authentication and authorization in Kubernetes.

Advanced settings in kubeconfig

kubeconfig is a configuration file that manages cluster, context, and authentication settings in Kubernetes, on the client side. Using the `kubeconfig` file, we are able to set different cluster credentials, users, and namespaces to switch between clusters or contexts within a cluster. It can be configured via the command line using the `kubectl config` subcommand or by updating a configuration file directly. In this section, we'll describe how to use `kubectl config` to manipulate kubeconfig and how to input a kubeconfig file directly.

If you have gone through the *Working with namespace* recipe in `Chapter 2`, *Walking through Kubernetes Concepts*, where we first mentioned kubeconfig, you will know of its basic concepts. Let's review some key points:

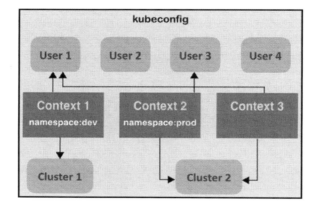

kubeconfig contains three parameters: user, cluster, and context

From the preceding diagram, we can note the following:

- **There are three parameters in kubeconfig**: User, cluster, and context—user has its own authentication, while cluster determines the specific API server with dedicated computing resources. Context is both *user* and cluster.
- **Building multiple contexts for various combinations of settings**: Users and clusters can be shared across different contexts.
- **Namespace can be aligned in one context**: The current context of a namespace sets up the rules. Any requests should follow the mapping user and cluster in the current context.

Getting ready

Please run two Kubernetes clusters and give them the specified host name. You may just update the hostfile (/etc/hosts) on the master nodes. One is under localhost with the API server endpoint http://localhost:8080 and the other is on the remote side with the endpoint http://$REMOTE_MASTER_NODE:8080. We will use these two clusters for our demonstration. The endpoints of the API server here are insecure channels. It is a simple configuration of an API server for the dummy accessing permissions.

Enableing the API server's insecure endpoint on kubeadm

We have to pass additional arguments to the API server while running kubeadm init. In this case, a custom configuration file indicated by flag --config should be applied:

```
// you can also get this file through code bundle
$ cat additional-kubeadm-config
apiVersion: kubeadm.k8s.io/v1alpha1
kind: MasterConfiguration
apiServerExtraArgs:
  insecure-bind-address: "0.0.0.0"
  insecure-port: "8080"
// start cluster with additional system settings
$ sudo kubeadm init --config ./additional-kubeadm-config
```

After you boot up two clusters that have an insecure-accessing API server endpoint, make sure you can approach them on the localhost cluster:

```
// on localhost cluster, the following commands should be successful
$ curl http://localhost:8080
$ curl http://$REMOTE_MASTER_NODE:8080
```

Please note that the insecure address configuration is just for our upcoming tutorial. Users should be careful to set it properly on a practical system.

Before we start, we should check the default kubeconfig in order to observe the changes after any updates. Fire the command kubectl config view to see your initial kubeconfig:

```
// the settings created by kubeadm
$ kubectl config view
apiVersion: v1
clusters:
- cluster:
```

```
      certificate-authority-data: REDACTED
      server: https://192.168.122.101:6443
    name: kubernetes
contexts:
- context:
    cluster: kubernetes
    user: kubernetes-admin
  name: kubernetes-admin@kubernetes
current-context: kubernetes-admin@kubernetes
kind: Config
preferences: {}
users:
- name: kubernetes-admin
  user:
    client-certificate-data: REDACTED
    client-key-data: REDACTED
```

There will be some different settings based on your installation method. But we may also find a basic context has been initialized by the tool, which is `kubernetes-admin@kubernetes` in kubeadm. Go ahead and copy the physical `kubeconfig` file as the base for later updating, and also for resuming our original environment after our practice.

```
// in default, the kubeconfig used by client is the one under $HOME
$ cp ~/.kube/config ~/original-kubeconfig
```

How to do it...

In this recipe, we'll use localhost cluster as the main console to switch the cluster via context changes. First, run a different number of `nginx` into both the clusters and make sure the pods are all running:

```
// in the terminal of localhost cluster
$ kubectl run local-nginx --image=nginx --replicas=2 --port=80
deployment "local-nginx" created
// check the running pods
$ kubectl get pod
NAME                            READY    STATUS    RESTARTS    AGE
local-nginx-6484bbb57d-xpjp2    1/1      Running   0           1m
local-nginx-6484bbb57d-z4qgp    1/1      Running   0           1m
// in the terminal of remote cluster
$ kubectl run remote-nginx --image=nginx --replicas=4 --port=80
deployment "remote-nginx" created
$ kubectl get pod
NAME                            READY    STATUS    RESTARTS    AGE
remote-nginx-5dd7b9cb7d-fxr9m   1/1      Running   0           29s
```

```
remote-nginx-5dd7b9cb7d-gj2ft    1/1        Running   0        29s
remote-nginx-5dd7b9cb7d-h7lmj    1/1        Running   0        29s
remote-nginx-5dd7b9cb7d-hz766    1/1        Running   0        29s
```

Setting new credentials

Next, we are going to set up two credentials for each cluster. Use the subcommand `set-credentials` as `kubectl config set-credentials <CREDENTIAL_NAME>` to add a credential into kubeconfig. There are different authentication methods supported in Kubernetes. We could use a password, client-certificate, or token. In this example, we'll use HTTP basic authentication to simplify the scenario. Kubernetes also supports client certificate and token authentications. For more information, please fire the `set-credentials` command with the flag `-h` for a detailed introduction to its functionalities:

```
// check the details of setting up credentials
$ kubectl config set-credentials -h
// in localhost cluster, copy the based file into a new one
$ cp ~/original-kubeconfig ~/new-kubeconfig
// add a user "user-local" with credential named "myself@localhost" in
kubeconfig "new-kubeconfig"
$ kubectl config set-credentials myself@localhost --username=user-local --
password=passwordlocal --kubeconfig="new-kubeconfig"
User "myself@local" set.
```

Through the preceding procedures, we successfully add a new credential in the "new-kubeconfig" kubeconfig file. The kubeconfig file will be formatted in YAML by default—you may check the file through a text editor. With this method, we are able to customize new configurations without interfering with the current settings. On the other hand, if there is no `--kubeconfig` flag, the update will be directly attached to the `live` kubeconfig:

```
// renew live kubeconfig file with previous update
$ cp ~/new-kubeconfig ~/.kube/config
// add another credential in localhost cluster, this time, let's update
current settings directly
$ kubectl config set-credentials myself@remote --username=user-remote --
password=passwordremote
User "myself@remote" set.
```

At this moment, check your live kubeconfig settings and find out the new credentials:

```
$ kubectl config view
...
users:
```

```
    - name: myself@local
      user:
        password: passwordlocal
        username: user-local
    - name: myself@remote
      user:
        password: passwordremote
        username: user-remote
```

Setting new clusters

To set a new cluster, we use the command `kubectl config set-cluster <CLUSTER_NAME>`. The additional flag `--server` is required to indicate the accessing cluster. Other flags work to define the security level, such as the `--insecure-skip-tls-verify` flag, which bypasses checking the server's certificate. If you are setting up a trusted server with HTTPS, you will need to use `--certificate-authority=$PATH_OF_CERT --embed-certs=true` instead. For more information, fire the command with the `-h` flag for more information. In the following commands, we set up two cluster configurations in our localhost environment:

```
    // in localhost cluster, create a cluster information pointing to itself
    $ kubectl config set-cluster local-cluster --insecure-skip-tls-verify=true
    --server=http://localhost:8080
    Cluster "local-cluster" set.
    // another cluster information is about the remote one
    $ kubectl config set-cluster remote-cluster --insecure-skip-tls-
    verify=true --server=http://$REMOTE_MASTER_NODE:8080
    Cluster "remote-cluster" set.
    // check kubeconfig in localhost cluster, in this example, the remote
    master node has the hostname "node01"
    $ kubectl config view
    apiVersion: v1
    clusters:
    ...
    - cluster:
        insecure-skip-tls-verify: true
        server: http://localhost:8080
      name: local-cluster
    - cluster:
        insecure-skip-tls-verify: true
        server: http://node01:8080
      name: remote-cluster
    ...
```

We do not associate anything with **users** and **clusters** yet. We will link them via **context** in the next section.

Setting contexts and changing current-context

One context contains a cluster, namespace, and user. According to the current context, the client will use the specified *user* information and namespace to send requests to the cluster. To set up a context, we will use the `kubectl config set-context <CONTEXT_NAME> --user=<CREDENTIAL_NAME> --namespace=<NAMESPACE> --cluster=<CLUSTER_NAME>` command to create or update it:

```
// in localhost cluster, create a context for accessing local cluster's
default namespace
$ kubectl config set-context default/local/myself --user=myself@local --
namespace=default --cluster=local-cluster
Context "default/local/myself" created.
// furthermore, create another context for remote cluster
$ kubectl config set-context default/remote/myself --user=myself@remote --
namespace=default --cluster=remote-cluster
Context "default/remote/myself" created.
```

Let's check our current kubeconfig. We can find two new contexts:

```
$ kubectl config view
...
contexts:
- context:
    cluster: local-cluster
    namespace: default
    user: myself@local
  name: default/local/myself
- context:
    cluster: remote-cluster
    namespace: default
    user: myself@remote
  name: default/remote/myself
...
```

After creating contexts, we can switch contexts in order to manage different clusters. Here, we will use the `kubectl config use-context <CONTEXT_NAME>` command:

```
// check current context
$ kubectl config current-context
```

```
kubernetes-admin@kubernetes

// use the new local context instead
$ kubectl config use-context default/local/myself
Switched to context "default/local/myself".
// check resource for the status of context
$ kubectl get pod
NAME                              READY   STATUS    RESTARTS   AGE
local-nginx-6484bbb57d-xpjp2      1/1     Running   0          2h
local-nginx-6484bbb57d-z4qgp      1/1     Running   0          2h
```

Yes, it looks fine. How about if we switch to the context with the remote cluster setting:

```
// switch to the context of remote cluster
$ kubectl config use-context default/remote/myself
Switched to context "default/remote/myself".
// check the pods
$ kubectl get pod
NAME                              READY   STATUS    RESTARTS   AGE
remote-nginx-5dd7b9cb7d-fxr9m     1/1     Running   0          2h
remote-nginx-5dd7b9cb7d-gj2ft     1/1     Running   0          2h
remote-nginx-5dd7b9cb7d-h7lmj     1/1     Running   0          2h
remote-nginx-5dd7b9cb7d-hz766     1/1     Running   0          2h
```

All the operations we have done are in the localhost cluster. kubeconfig makes the scenario of working on multiple clusters with multiple users easier.

Cleaning up kubeconfig

We can still leverage kubectl config to remove configurations in kubeconfig. For cluster sand context, you can delete the neglected one with the subcommands delete-cluster and delete-context. Alternatively, for these three categories, the unset subcommand can complete the deletion:

```
// delete the customized local context
$ kubectl config delete-cluster local-cluster
deleted cluster local-cluster from $HOME/.kube/config

// unset the local user
// to remove cluster, using property clusters.CLUSTER_NAME; to remove
contexts, using property contexts.CONTEXT_NAME
$ kubectl config unset users.myself@local
Property "users.myself@local" unset.
```

Although the effects of the preceding command would apply to the live kubeconfig right away, an even faster and more reliable way is updating another kubeconfig file for the replacement. A kubeconfig file is the text file `new-kubeconfig`, the one we just updated, or the one we copied from the initial statement, `original-kubeconfig`:

```
// remove all of our practices
$ cp ~/original-kubeconfig ~/.kube/config
// check your kubeconfig to make sure it has been cleaned
$ kubectl config view
```

There's more...

As we mentioned in the previous section, real use cases with credentials and permissions cannot be ignored like walking cross insecure endpoints, just like in our demonstration. To avoid security issues, you may take the official documentation (found at `https://kubernetes.io/docs/admin/authentication/`) while granting permissions to users.

See also

kubeconfig manages cluster, credential, and namespace settings. Check out the following recipes for complete concepts:

- The *Working with Secrets* recipe in `Chapter 2`, *Walking through Kubernetes Concepts*
- The *Working with Namespaces* recipe in `Chapter 2`, *Walking through Kubernetes Concepts*

Setting resources in nodes

Computing resource management is very important in any infrastructure. We should know our application well and preserve enough CPU and memory capacity to avoid running out of resources. In this section, we'll introduce how to manage node capacity in Kubernetes nodes. Furthermore, we'll also describe how to manage pod computing resources.

Kubernetes has the concept of resource **Quality of Service (QoS)**. It allows an administrator to prioritize pods to allocate resources. Based on the pod's setting, Kubernetes classifies each pod as one of the following:

- Guaranteed pod
- Burstable pod
- BestEffort pod

The priority is Guaranteed > Burstable > BestEffort. For example, if a BestEffort pod and a Guaranteed pod exist in the same Kubernetes node, and that node encounters CPU problems or runs out of memory, the Kubernetes master terminates the BestEffort pod first. Let's take a look at how it works.

Getting ready

There are two ways to set a Resource QoS: pod configuration or namespace configuration. If you set a Resource QoS to the Namespace, it will apply to all pods that belong to the same Namespace. If you set a Resource QoS to a pod, it will apply to the pod only. In addition, if you set it to both namespace and pod, it takes a value from the namespace configuration first, and then overwrite it with the pod configuration. Thus, we will set up two Namespaces, one which has a Resource QoS, and one that does not, to see how different they are:

1. Create two namespaces by using the `kubectl` command as follows:

```
$ kubectl create namespace chap8-no-qos
namespace "chap8-no-qos" created

$ kubectl create namespace chap8-qos
namespace "chap8-qos" created
```

2. Prepare a YAML file that sets `spec.limits.defaultRequest.cpu: 0.1` as follows:

```
$ cat resource-request-cpu.yml
apiVersion: v1
kind: LimitRange
metadata:
  name: resource-request-cpu
spec:
  limits:
  - defaultRequest:
      cpu: 0.1
```

```
        type: Container
```

3. Do this by typing the `kubectl` command so that it applies to the `chap8-qos` namespace only:

```
$ kubectl create -f resource-request-cpu.yml --namespace=chap8-
qos
limitrange "resource-request-cpu" created
```

4. Check the resource limit on both `chap8-qos` and `chap8-no-qos` with the `kubectl` command:

```
//chap8-no-qos doesn't have any resource limits value
$ kubectl describe namespaces chap8-no-qos
Name:         chap8-no-qos
Labels:       <none>
Annotations:  <none>
Status:       Active
No resource quota.
No resource limits.


//chap8-qos namespace has a resource limits value
$ kubectl describe namespaces chap8-qos
Name:         chap8-qos
Labels:       <none>
Annotations:  <none>
Status:       Active
No resource quota.
Resource Limits
 Type        Resource  Min  Max  Default Request  Default Limit  Max Limit/Request Ratio
 ----        --------  ---  ---  ---------------  -------------  -----------------------
 Container   cpu       -    -    100m             -              -
```

How to do it...

Let's configure a BestEffort pod, a Guaranteed pod, and then a Burstable pod step by step.

Configuring a BestEffort pod

The BestEffort pod has the lowest priority in the Resource QoS classes. Therefore, in the case of a resource shortage, this BestEffort pod will be terminated by the Kubernetes scheduler, then will yield CPU and memory resources to other, higher priority pods.

In order to configure a pod as a BestEffort, you need to set the resource limit as 0 (explicit), or specify no resource limit (implicit).

1. Prepare a pod configuration that explicitly sets the `spec.containers.resources.limits` as 0:

```
$ cat besteffort-explicit.yml
apiVersion: v1
kind: Pod
metadata:
  name: besteffort
spec:
  containers:
  - name: nginx
    image: nginx
    resources:
      limits:
        cpu: 0
        memory: 0
```

2. Create the pod on both the `chap8-qos` and `chap8-no-qos` namespaces:

```
$ kubectl create -f besteffort-explicit.yml --namespace=chap8-qos
pod "besteffort" created
```

```
$ kubectl create -f besteffort-explicit.yml --namespace=chap8-no-qos
pod "besteffort" created
```

3. Check the `QoS` class; both pods have the `BestEffort` class:

```
$ kubectl describe pods besteffort --namespace=chap8-qos | grep QoS
QoS Class:        BestEffort
```

```
$ kubectl describe pods besteffort --namespace=chap8-no-qos | grep QoS
QoS Class:        BestEffort
```

There is a pitfall : if you don't set any resource settings in the pod configuration, the pod takes a value from the namespace's default settings. Therefore, if you create a pod with no resource settings, the result will be different between chap8-qos and chap8-no-qos. The following example demonstrates how the namespace settings affect the result:

1. Delete the preceding pods from the chap8-qos and chap8-no-qos namespaces:

```
$ kubectl delete pod --all --namespace=chap8-qos
pod "besteffort" deleted

$ kubectl delete pod --all --namespace=chap8-no-qos
pod "besteffort" deleted
```

2. Prepare a pod configuration that doesn't have resource settings:

```
$ cat besteffort-implicit.yml
apiVersion: v1
kind: Pod
metadata:
  name: besteffort
spec:
  containers:
  - name: nginx
    image: nginx
```

3. Create the pod on both namespaces:

```
$ kubectl create -f besteffort-implicit.yml --namespace=chap8-
qos
pod "besteffort" created

$ kubectl create -f besteffort-implicit.yml --namespace=chap8-
no-qos
pod "besteffort" created
```

4. The result of the QoS class is different:

```
$ kubectl describe pods besteffort --namespace=chap8-no-qos
|grep QoS
QoS Class:        BestEffort

$ kubectl describe pods besteffort --namespace=chap8-qos |grep
QoS
QoS Class:        Burstable
```

Because the `chap8-qos` namespace has the default setting `request.cpu: 0.1`, it causes the pod to configure with the `Burstable` class. Therefore, we will use the `chap8-no-qos` namespace, which avoids this unexpected result.

Configuring a Guaranteed pod

The Guaranteed class has the highest priority of resource `QoS` classes. In the case of a resource shortage, the Kubernetes scheduler will try to retain the Guaranteed pod to the last.

In order to configure a pod to have the `guaranteed` class, explicitly set the resource limit and resource request as the same value, or only set the resource limit:

1. Prepare a pod configuration that has the same value for `resources.limit` and `resources.request`:

```
$ cat guaranteed.yml
apiVersion: v1
kind: Pod
metadata:
  name: guaranteed-pod
spec:
  containers:
  - name: nginx
    image: nginx
    resources:
      limits:
        cpu: 0.3
        memory: 350Mi
      requests:
        cpu: 0.3
        memory: 350Mi
```

2. Create the pod on the `chap8-no-qos` namespace:

```
$ kubectl create -f guaranteed.yml --namespace=chap8-no-qos
pod "guaranteed-pod" created
```

3. Check the `QoS class`; it has the `Guaranteed` class:

```
$ kubectl describe pods guaranteed-pod --namespace=chap8-no-qos
|grep QoS
QoS Class:        Guaranteed
```

Configuring a Burstable pod

The Burstable pod has a priority that is higher than BestEffort but lower than Guaranteed. In order to configure a pod to be a Burstable Pod, you need to set `resources.request`. `resources.limit` is optional, but the value of `resources.request` and `resources.limit` must not be equal:

1. Prepare a pod configuration that has `resources.request` only:

```
$ cat burstable.yml
apiVersion: v1
kind: Pod
metadata:
  name: burstable-pod
spec:
  containers:
  - name: nginx
    image: nginx
    resources:
      requests:
        cpu: 0.1
        memory: 10Mi
      limits:
        cpu: 0.5
        memory: 300Mi
```

2. Create the pod:

```
$ kubectl create -f burstable.yml --namespace=chap8-no-qos
pod "burstable-pod" created
```

3. Check the `QoS` class; it is `Burstable`:

```
$ kubectl describe pods burstable-pod --namespace=chap8-no-qos
|grep QoS
QoS Class:        Burstable
```

How it works...

Let's see how resource requests/limits affect resource management. A preceding burstable YAML configuration declares both requests and limits by a different threshold as follows:

Type of resource definition	Resource name	Value	Description
requests	CPU	0.1	At least 10% of 1CPU core
	Memory	10Mi	At least 10 Mbytes of memory
limits	CPU	0.5	Maximum 50% of 1 CPU core
	Memory	300Mi	Maximum 300 Mbytes of memory

For the CPU resources, acceptable value expressions are either cores (0.1, 0.2 ... 1.0, 2.0) or millicpu (100 m, 200 m ... 1000 m, 2000 m). 1000 m is equivalent to 1.0 core. For example, if a Kubernetes node has 2 cores CPU (or 1 core with hyperthreading), there are a total of 2.0 cores or 2000 millicpu, as shown in the following figure:

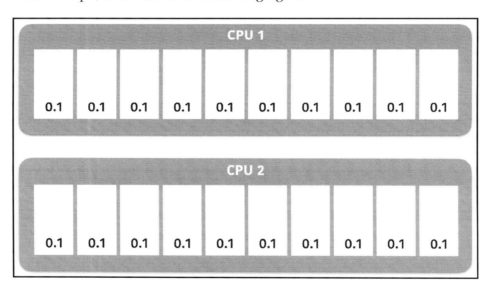

Representing a 2.0 CPU resource

By typing `kubectl describe node <node name>`, you can check what resources are available on the node:

```
//Find a node name
$ kubectl get nodes
NAME         STATUS    ROLES     AGE       VERSION
```

```
minikube    Ready      <none>    22h        v1.9.0


//Specify node name 'minikube'
$ kubectl describe nodes minikube
Name:              minikube
Roles:             <none>
Labels:            beta.kubernetes.io/arch=amd64
...
...
Allocatable:
  cpu:      2
  memory:   1945652Ki
  pods:     110
```

This shows the node `minikube`, which has 2.0 CPU and approximately 1,945 MB memory. If you run the nginx example (`requests.cpu: 0.1`), it occupies at least 0.1 core, as shown in the following figure:

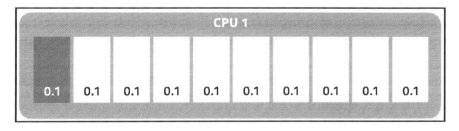

Requesting a 0.1 CPU resource

As long as the CPU has enough spaces, it may occupy up to 0.5 cores (`limits.cpu: 0.5`), as shown in the following figure:

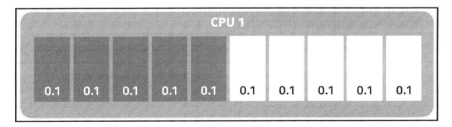

It can occupy up to 0.5 CPU resources

Therefore, if you set `requests.cpu` to be more than 2.0, the pod won't be assigned to this node, because the allocatable CPU is 2.0 and the nginx pod already occupies at least 0.1 CPU.

See also

In this section, you learned how to configure Resource QoS by setting a resource request and limit. The Namespace's default value affects the resulting pod configuration, so you should explicitly specify resource requests and limits.

Please revisit the following chapter to recap how to configure namespaces as well:

- *Working with Namespaces* in `Chapter 2`, *Walking through Kubernetes Concepts*

Playing with WebUI

Kubernetes has a WebUI that visualizes the status of resources and machines, and also works as an additional interface for managing your application without command lines. In this recipe, we are going to introduce Kubernetes dashboard.

Getting ready

Kubernetes dashboard (`https://github.com/kubernetes/dashboard`) is like a server-side application. In the beginning, just make sure you have a healthy Kubernetes cluster running, and we will go through the installation and related setup in the coming pages. Since the dashboard will be accessed by the browser, we can use a minikube-booted, laptop-running Kubernetes system, and reduce procedures for forwarding network ports or setting firewall rules.

For Kubernetes systems booting up by minikube, check that both minikube and the system itself are working:

```
// check if minikube runs well
$ minikube status
minikube: Running
cluster: Running
kubectl: Correctly Configured: pointing to minikube-vm at 192.168.99.100
// check the Kubernetes system by components
$ kubectl get cs
NAME                    STATUS    MESSAGE              ERROR
```

```
scheduler              Healthy    ok
controller-manager     Healthy    ok
etcd-0                 Healthy    {"health": "true"}
```

How to do it...

While booting up your Kubernetes system with minikube, it would help to create the dashboard by default. So, we will talk about both scenarios separately.

Relying on the dashboard created by minikube

Because the Kubernetes dashboard has been started, what we have do is to open the web UI with a specific URL. It is convenient; you just need to fire a command on your terminal:

```
$ minikube dashboard
Opening kubernetes dashboard in default browser...
```

Then, you will see your favourite browser opening a new webpage, as we introduced in Chapter 1, *Building Your Own Kubernetes Cluster*. Its URL will look like http://MINIKUBE_VM_IP:30000/#!/overview?namespace=default. Most of all, we bypass the expected network proxy and authentication procedures.

Creating a dashboard manually on a system using other booting tools

To run Kubernetes dashboard, we simply fire a command to apply a configuration file, and every resource is created automatically:

```
$ kubectl create -f
https://raw.githubusercontent.com/kubernetes/dashboard/master/src/deploy/re
commended/kubernetes-dashboard.yaml
secret "kubernetes-dashboard-certs" created
serviceaccount "kubernetes-dashboard" created
role "kubernetes-dashboard-minimal" created
rolebinding "kubernetes-dashboard-minimal" created
deployment "kubernetes-dashboard" created
service "kubernetes-dashboard" created
```

Next, let's use the command `kubectl proxy` to open a gateway connecting localhost and the API server. Then, we are good to access the dashboard via a browser:

```
$ kubectl proxy
Starting to serve on 127.0.0.1:8001
```

Once you see a halting result showing, as in the preceding code, you can now access the dashboard by URL: `http://localhost:8001/api/v1/namespaces/kube-system/services/https:kubernetes-dashboard:/proxy/`. There, you will see the following screen in your browser:

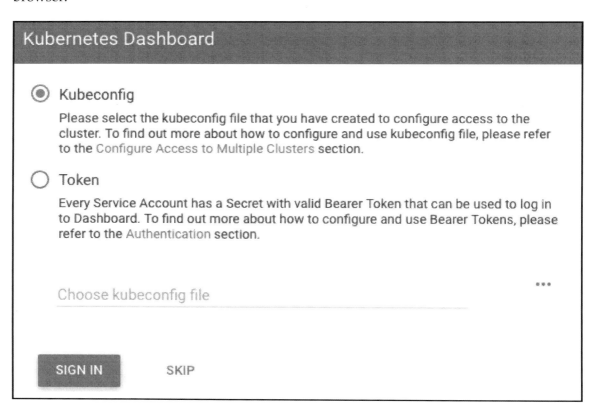

The login portal of Kubernetes dashboard

To step into our demonstration quickly, we will take the token of an existed service account to log in with. No matter what booting tool you use, leveraging the one created by the dashboard is suitable in every case:

```
// check the service account in your system
$ kubectl get secret -n kube-system
NAME                                    TYPE
DATA        AGE
default-token-7jfmd                     kubernetes.io/service-account-token    3
51d
kubernetes-dashboard-certs              Opaque                                 0
2d
kubernetes-dashboard-key-holder         Opaque                                 2
51d
kubernetes-dashboard-token-jw42n        kubernetes.io/service-account-token    3
2d
// grabbing token by checking the detail information of the service account
with prefix "kubernetes-dashboard-token-"
$ kubectl describe secret kubernetes-dashboard-token-jw42n -n kube-system
Name:          kubernetes-dashboard-token-jw42n
Namespace:     kube-system
Labels:        <none>
Annotations:   kubernetes.io/service-account.name=kubernetes-dashboard
               kubernetes.io/service-account.uid=253a1a8f-210b-11e8-
b301-8230b6ac4959
Type:   kubernetes.io/service-account-token
Data
====
ca.crt:        1066 bytes
namespace:     11 bytes
token:
eyJhbGciOiJSUzI1NiIsInR5cCI6IkpXVCJ9.eyJpc3MiOiJrdWJlcm5ldGVzL3NlcnZpY2VhY2
NvdW50Ii....
```

Copy the token and paste it into console on the browser, then, click **SIGN IN**:

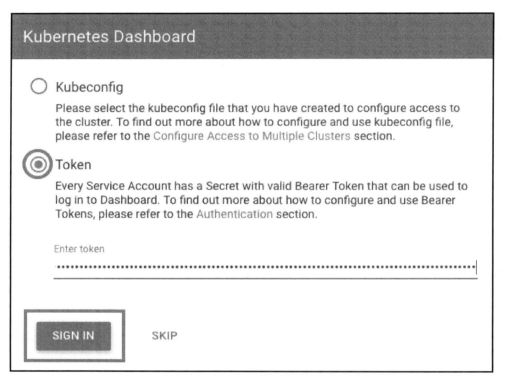

Authentication with the token of a service account

Welcome to the dashboard home page:

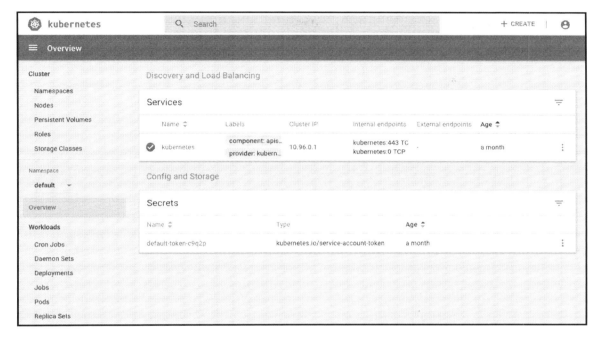

The home page of the Kubernetes dashboard

How it works...

Kubernetes dashboard has two main functions: inspecting the status of resources, and deploying resources. It can cover most of our works in the client terminal using the command kubectl, however, the graphic interface is more friendly.

Browsing your resource by dashboard

We can check both hardware and software resources on the dashboard. For example, to take a look at the nodes a cluster, click on **Nodes** under the **Cluster** section in the left-hand menu; every node in the current cluster will be shown on the page, with some basic information:

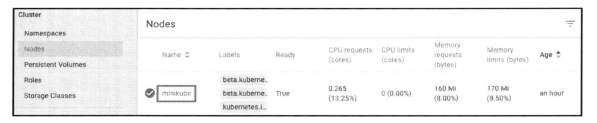

The status of Kubernetes nodes on the dashboard

Your result on screen may be different from the preceding screenshot, since it will be based on your environment. Go ahead and click on the name of one node; even more details will be shown. Some of them are illustrated in beautiful graphs:

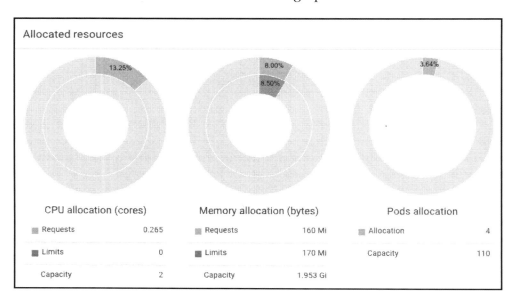

Computing the resource status of a node

To show software resources, let's take a look at the one holding this dashboard. In the left-hand menu, change the Namespace to **kube-system** and click **Overview**, which gathers all the resources under this Namespace. It is easy to find out any issue by putting resources together on a single page with a clear diagram:

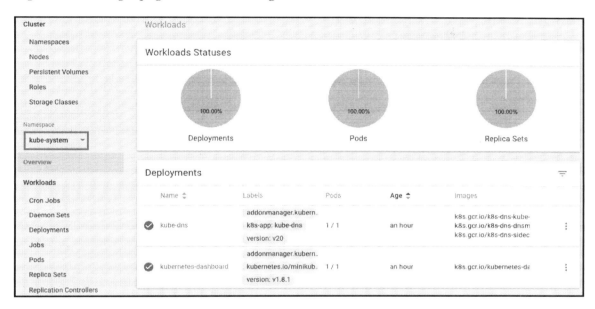

Resource overview of the namespace kube-system

There's more; click on the **Deployments** kubernetes-dashboard, and then click the small text-file icon on the right side of the only pod in the replica set. You can see the logs for the container:

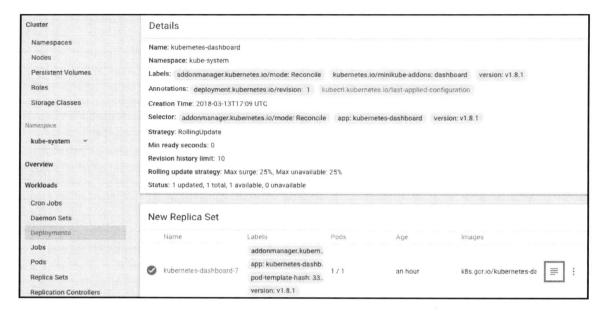

Deployment information of kubernetes-dashboard

Logs of the dashboard application

Now, we have seen that Kubernetes dashboard provides a brilliant interface for displaying resource status, covering nodes, Kubernetes workloads and controllers, and the application log.

Deploying resources by dashboard

Here, we will prepare a YAML configuration file for creating Kubernetes Deployments and related Services under a new Namespace. It will be used to build resources through the dashboard:

```
// the configuration file for creating Deployment and Service on new
Namespace: dashboard-test
```

```
$ cat my-nginx.yaml
apiVersion: apps/v1beta2
kind: Deployment
metadata:
  name: my-nginx
  namespace: dashboard-test
spec:
  replicas: 3
  selector:
    matchLabels:
      run: demo
  template:
    metadata:
      labels:
        run: demo
    spec:
      containers:
      - name: my-container
        image: nginx
        ports:
        - containerPort: 80
---
apiVersion: v1
kind: Service
metadata:
  name: my-nginx
  namespace: dashboard-test
spec:
  ports:
    - protocol: TCP
      port: 80
  type: NodePort
  selector:
    run: demo
```

First, click the **CREATE** button on the top right side of the web page.

There are three methods for deployment. Let's choose the second one and upload the configuration file introduced previously. Click the **UPLOAD** button:

Creating a resource by configuration file

Unfortunately, errors happened:

Deploying file has failed

Your file specifies a namespace that is inconsistent with the namespace currently selected in Dashboard. Either edit the namespace entry in your file or select a different namespace in Dashboard to deploy to (eg. 'All namespaces' or the correct namespace provided in the file).

CLOSE

Error message for problems due to bad deployment

Dashboard displays the resource according to a given Namespace, which is picked by *user* on the left-hand menu. This error message popped up and told users that the Namespace mentioned in the file does not match to dashboard one. What we have to do is to create a new Namespace and switch to it.

This time, we are going to create a Namespace using plain text. Click the **CREATE** button again, and pick the **create from text input** method. Paste the following lines for a new Namespace to the web page:

```
apiVersion: v1
kind: Namespace
metadata:
  name: dashboard-test
```

Now, we have a new Namespace, `dashboard-test`. Choose it as the main Namespace on the dashboard, and submit the `my-nginx.yaml` file again:

Picking a correct Namespace before submitting the configuration file

Now you can see the overview of this deployment! Yellow circles mean the pending status. They will turn to green once the pods are ready, or turn to red if they failed, but you will not see red ones if you are following these steps:

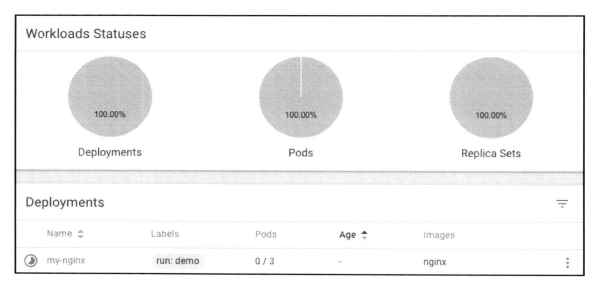

Status graph of creating a resource

Removing resources by dashboard

We can also remove Kubernetes resources through the dashboard. Try to find the Service `my-nginx` we just created by yourself! Perform the following:

- Change the Namespace on the left-hand menu to **dashboard-test**
- Click **Services** under the **Discovery and load balancing** section on left-hand menu
- Click the Service **my-nginx** on the hyperlinked name
- Click **DELETE** at the top right of the page, below the **CREATE** button

That's it! Once you see your screen launching a message for confirmation, just click it. Finally, you have not only created a resource but also removed it from the Kubernetes dashboard.

See also

This recipe described how to launch a web interface that will help with easily exploring and managing Kubernetes instances, such as pods, deployments, and services, without the `kubectl` command. Please refer to the following recipes on how to get detailed information via the `kubectl` command.

- The *Working with Pods, Deployment API*, and *Working with Services* recipes in `Chapter 2`, *Walking through Kubernetes Concepts*

Working with the RESTful API

Users can control Kubernetes clusters via the `kubectl` command; it supports local and remote execution. However, some administrators or operators may need to integrate a program to control the Kubernetes cluster.

Kubernetes has a RESTful API that controls Kubernetes clusters via an API, similar to the `kubectl` command. Let's learn how to manage Kubernetes resources by submitting API requests.

Getting ready

In this recipe, to bypass additional network settings and having to verify permissions, we will demonstrate the a *minikube*-created cluster with a Kubernetes proxy: it is easy to create a Kubernetes cluster on the host, and enable local proximity to an API server with a proxy entry.

First, run up a proxy for fast API request forwarding:

```
//curl by API endpoint
$ kubectl proxy
Starting to serve on 127.0.0.1:8001
```

Having worked with Kubernetes proxy for a while, you may find it is somehow annoying that the command `kubectl proxy` is a halt process on your terminal, forcing you to open a new channel for the following commands. To avoid this, just add & as the last parameter in your command. This & symbol in the shell will make your command run in the background:

```
$ kubectl proxy &
[1] 6372
Starting to serve on 127.0.0.1:8001
```

Be aware that you should kill this process manually if you don't use the proxy:

```
$ kill -j9 6372
```

Then, it is good to try the endpoint with a simple path, /api:

```
$ curl http://127.0.0.1:8001/api
{
  "kind": "APIVersions",
  "versions": [
    "v1"
  ],
  "serverAddressByClientCIDRs": [
    {
      "clientCIDR": "0.0.0.0/0",
      "serverAddress": "10.0.2.15:8443"
    }
  ]
}
```

Once you see some basic API server information showing as in the preceding code, congratulations! You can now play with the kubernetes RESTful API of Kubernetes.

A secured way to access the Kubernetes API server

However, if you consider accessing a more secure API server, likes a kubeadm cluster, the following items should be taken care of:

- The endpoint of the API server
- Token for authentication

We can get the required information through the following commands. And you can successfully fire the API request for the version:

```
$ APISERVER=$(kubectl config view | grep server | cut -f 2-
-d ":" | tr -d " ")
// get the token of default service account
$ TOKEN=$(kubectl get secret --field-selector
type=kubernetes.io/service-account-token -o name | grep
default-token- | head -n 1 | xargs kubectl get -o
'jsonpath={.data.token}' | base64 -d)
$ curl $APISERVER/api -H "Authorization: Bearer $TOKEN" --
insecure
```

On the other hand, you may see a message showing `permission denied` when accessing resources in kubeadm. If so, the solution is to bind the default service account to the role of administrator, that is `cluster-admin` in kubeadm system. We provide the configuration file `rbac.yaml` in the code bundle; please check it out if you need it:

```
$ curl $APISERVER/api/v1/namespaces/default/services -H
"Authorization: Bearer $TOKEN" --insecure
...
 "status": "Failure",
 "message": "services is forbidden: User
\"system:serviceaccount:default:default\" cannot list
services in the namespace \"default\"",
 "reason": "Forbidden",
...
$ kubectl create -f rbac.yaml
clusterrolebinding "fabric8-rbac" created
// now the API request is successful
$ curl $APISERVER/api/v1/namespaces/default/services -H
"Authorization: Bearer $TOKEN" --insecure
{
    "kind": "ServiceList",
    "apiVersion": "v1",
```

```
    "metadata": {
        "selfLink": "/api/v1/namespaces/default/services",
        "resourceVersion": "291954"
    },
    ...
```

Be careful of the --insecure flags, since the endpoint using HTTPS protocol, and -H, add headers with a token. These are the additional ones comparing with our naive demonstration settings.

How to do it...

In this section, we will show you how to manage resources through the RESTful API. Generally, the command line pattern of curl will cover the following ideas:

- **The operation**: curl without an indicating operation will fire GET by default. To specify your operation, add one with the X flag.
- **The body data**: Like creating a Kubernetes resource through kubectl, we apply resource configuration with the d flag. The value with symbol @ can attach a file. Additionally, the h flag helps to add request headers; here we need to add content type in the JSON format.
- **The URL**: There are various paths after the endpoint, based on different functions.

Let's create a deployment using the following JSON configuration file:

```
$ cat nginx-deployment.json
{
  "apiVersion": "apps/v1",
  "kind": "Deployment",
  "metadata": {
    "name": "my-nginx"
  },
  "spec": {
    "replicas": 2,
      "selector": {
      "matchLabels": {
        "app": "nginx"
      }
    },
    "template": {
      "metadata": {
```

```
        "labels": {
          "app": "nginx"
        }
      },
      "spec": {
        "containers": [
          {
            "image": "nginx",
            "name": "my-nginx"
          }
        ]
      }
    }
  }
}
```

We can get every function in the API reference page (`https://kubernetes.io/docs/ reference/generated/kubernetes-api/v1.10/`). It is similar to searching for the configuration of a resource while writing up a configuration file. To submit an API request, you should know what kind of resource to work on, and what operation to perform on it. Perform the following procedures to find the corresponding information on the reference webpage:

1. Choose an resource.
2. Choose an operation, for example, read or write.
3. Choose the details of the operation, for example, **Create** or **Delete**.
4. The information will show in the middle panel of the webpage. An optional step is to switch `kubectl` to `curl` on the top right of the console. More details such as command flags will show on the right panel.

To check the information for creating a Deployment, your web console may look as it does in this screenshot:

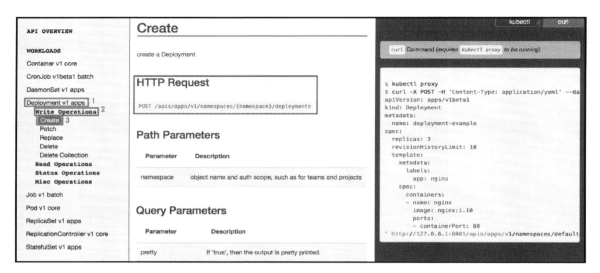

The steps finding the path for API using to create a deployment

Based on the reference page, we can combine a specified `curl` command and fire a request now:

```
$ curl -X POST -H "Content-type: application/json" -d @nginx-
deployment.json
http://localhost:8001/apis/apps/v1/namespaces/default/deployments
{
  "kind": "Deployment",
  "apiVersion": "apps/v1",
  "metadata": {
    "name": "my-nginx",
    "namespace": "default",
    "selfLink": "/apis/apps/v1/namespaces/default/deployments/my-nginx",
    "uid": "6eca324e-2cc8-11e8-806a-080027b04dc6",
    "resourceVersion": "209",
    "generation": 1,
    "creationTimestamp": "2018-03-21T05:26:39Z",
    "labels": {
      "app": "nginx"
    }
  },
  ...
```

For a successful request, the server returns the status of the resource. Go ahead and check if we can find the new Deployment through the `kubectl` command:

```
$ kubectl get deployment
NAME        DESIRED   CURRENT   UP-TO-DATE   AVAILABLE   AGE
my-nginx    2         2         2            2           1m
```

Of course, it also works while checking it via the RESTful API:

```
// the operation "-X GET" can be ignored, since
$ curl -X GET
http://localhost:8001/apis/apps/v1/namespaces/default/deployments
```

Next, try to delete this new Deployment, `my-nginx`, as well. It is a kind of `write` operation:

```
$ curl -X DELETE
http://localhost:8001/apis/apps/v1/namespaces/default/deployments/my-nginx
{
  "kind": "Status",
  "apiVersion": "v1",
  "metadata": {
  },
  "status": "Success",
  "details": {
    "name": "my-nginx",
    "group": "apps",
    "kind": "deployments",
    "uid": "386a3aaa-2d2d-11e8-9843-080027b04dc6"
  }
}
```

How it works...

The RESTful API allows CRUD (**Create**, **Read**, **Update**, and **Delete**) operations, which are the same concepts behind every modern web application. For more details, please refer to https://en.wikipedia.org/wiki/Create,_read,_update_and_delete.

According to the CRUD structure, the Kubernetes RESTful API has the following basic method:

Operation	HTTP Method	Example
Create	POST	POST /api/v1/namespaces/default/pods
Read	GET	GET /api/v1/componentstatuses
Update	PUT	PUT /apis/apps/v1/namespaces/default/deployments/my-nginx
Delete	DELETE	DELETE /api/v1/namespaces/default/services/nginx-service

As we mentioned in the recipe *Working with configuration files* in Chapter 3, *Playing with Containers*, Kubernetes builds the RESTful API with *swagger* (https://swagger.io/) and OpenAPI (https://www.openapis.org). We can open the swagger UI console of your cluster to check the API functions. Nevertheless, it is recommended that you check them through the official website, the one we demonstrated in the last section. The description on the website is more elaborate and user-friendly.

There's more...

An even more programmatic way to utilize Kubernetes API is to use the client library (https://kubernetes.io/docs/reference/client-libraries/). Making good use of these client tools not only saves you time in resource management, but also produce a robust and reliable CI/CD environment. Here, we would like to introduce the Kubernetes client library for Python: https://github.com/kubernetes-client/python. To start, you should install the Python library for Kubernetes:

```
$ pip install kubernetes
```

Then, please put the following Python file at the same location as the JSON configuration file, nginx-deployment.json, where firing kubectl does work on the system:

```
$ cat create_deployment.py
from kubernetes import client, config
import json
config.load_kube_config()
resource_config = json.load(open("./nginx-deployment.json"))
api_instance = client.AppsV1Api()
response = api_instance.create_namespaced_deployment(body=resource_config,
namespace="default")
print("success, status={}".format(response.status))
```

You don't even enable the Kubernetes proxy now; continue to run this script directly and see what happens:

```
$ python create_deployment.py
```

See also

This recipe described how to use the Kubernetes RESTful API via a program. It is important to integrate this with your automation program remotely. For detailed parameter and security enhancement, please refer to the following recipes:

- The *Working with configuration files* recipe in `Chapter 3`, *Playing with Containers*
- The *Authentication and authorization* recipe in `Chapter 7`, *Building Kubernetes on GCP*

Working with Kubernetes DNS

When you deploy many pods to a Kubernetes cluster, service discovery is one of the most important functions, because pods may depend on other pods but the IP address of a pod will be changed when it restarts. You need to have a flexible way to communicate a pod's IP address to other pods. Kubernetes has an add-on feature called `kube-dns` that helps in this scenario. It can register and look up an IP address for pods and Kubernetes Services.

In this section, we will explore how to use `kube-dns`, which gives you a flexible way to configure DNS in your Kubernetes cluster.

Getting ready

Since Kubernetes version 1.3, `kube-dns` has come with Kubernetes and is enabled by default. To check whether `kube-dns` is working or not, check the `kube-system` namespace with the following command:

```
$ kubectl get deploy kube-dns --namespace=kube-system
NAME        DESIRED   CURRENT   UP-TO-DATE   AVAILABLE   AGE
kube-dns    1         1         1            1           1d
```

If you are using minikube, type the following command to see the addon's status:

```
$ minikube addons list |grep kube-dns
- kube-dns: enabled
```

If it shows as disabled, you need to enable it using the following command:

```
$ minikube addons enable kube-dns
```

In addition, prepare two namespaces, chap8-domain1 and chap8-domain2, to demonstrate how kube-dns assigns domain names:

```
$ kubectl create namespace chap8-domain1
namespace "chap8-domain1" created

$ kubectl create namespace chap8-domain2
namespace "chap8-domain2" created

//check chap8-domain1 and chap8-domain2
$ kubectl get namespaces
NAME            STATUS   AGE
chap8-domain1   Active   16s
chap8-domain2   Active   14s
default         Active   4h
kube-public     Active   4h
kube-system     Active   4h
```

How to do it...

kube-dns assigns the **fully qualified domain name (FQDN)** to pods and Kubernetes Services. Let's look at some differences.

DNS for pod

Kubernetes assigns the domain name for the pod as `<IP address>.<Namespace name>.pod.cluster.local`. Because it uses the pod's IP address, FQDN is not guaranteed to be present permanently, but it is nice to have in case an application needs FQDN.

Let's deploy apache2 (httpd) on chap8-domain1 and chap8-domain2, as follows:

```
$ kubectl run my-apache --image=httpd --namespace chap8-domain1
deployment "my-apache" created
```

```
$ kubectl run my-apache --image=httpd --namespace chap8-domain2
deployment "my-apache" created
```

Type `kubectl get pod -o wide` to capture an IP address for those pods:

```
$ kubectl get pods -o wide --namespace=chap8-domain1
NAME                         READY    STATUS     RESTARTS    AGE        IP
NODE
my-apache-55fb679f49-qw58f   1/1      Running    0           27s
172.17.0.4    minikube


$ kubectl get pods -o wide --namespace=chap8-domain2
NAME                         READY    STATUS     RESTARTS    AGE        IP
NODE
my-apache-55fb679f49-z9gsr   1/1      Running    0           26s
172.17.0.5    minikube
```

This shows that `my-apache-55fb679f49-qw58f` on chap8-domain1 uses `172.17.0.4`. On the other hand, `my-apache-55fb679f49-z9gsr` on chap8-domain2 uses `172.17.0.5`.

In this case, the FQDN would be:

- `172-17-0-4.chap8-domain1.pod.cluster.local` (chap8-domain1)

- `172-17-0-5.chap8-domain2.pod.cluster.local` (chap8-domain2)

Note that the dots (.) in the IP address are changed to hyphens (–). This is because the dot is a delimiter to determine subdomains.

To check whether name resolution works or not, launch the busybox pod in the foreground (using the `-it` option). Then use the `nslookup` command to resolve FQDN to the IP address, as in the following steps:

1. Run `busybox` with the `-it` option:

    ```
    $ kubectl run -it busybox --restart=Never --image=busybox
    ```

2. In the busybox pod, type `nslookup` to resolve the FQDN of apache on chap8-domain1:

    ```
    # nslookup 172-17-0-4.chap8-domain1.pod.cluster.local
    ```

```
Server: 10.96.0.10
Address 1: 10.96.0.10 kube-dns.kube-system.svc.cluster.local

Name: 172-17-0-4.chap8-domain1.pod.cluster.local
Address 1: 172.17.0.4
```

3. Also, type `nslookup` to resolve the FQDN of apache on `chap8-domain2`:

```
# nslookup 172-17-0-5.chap8-domain2.pod.cluster.local
Server: 10.96.0.10
Address 1: 10.96.0.10 kube-dns.kube-system.svc.cluster.local

Name: 172-17-0-5.chap8-domain2.pod.cluster.local
Address 1: 172.17.0.5
```

4. Exit the busybox pod, then delete it to release a resource:

```
# exit
$ kubectl delete pod busybox
pod "busybox" deleted
```

DNS for Kubernetes Service

First of all, DNS for Kubernetes Service is most important from the service discovery point of view. This is because an application usually connects to Kubernetes Service instead of connecting to the pod. This is why the application looks up the DNS entry for Kubernetes Service more often than for the pod.

Secondly, the DNS entry for Kubernetes Service will use the name of Kubernetes Service instead of an IP address. For instance, it will look like this: `<Service Name>.<Namespace name>.svc.cluster.local`.

Lastly, Kubernetes Service has 2 different behaviors for DNS; either normal service or headless service. Normal service has its own IP address, while headless service uses the pod's IP address(es). Let's go through normal service first.

Normal service is the default Kubernetes Service. It will assign an IP address. Perform the following steps to create a normal service and check how DNS works:

1. Create a normal service for apache on `chap8-domain1` and `chap8-domain2`:

```
$ kubectl expose deploy my-apache --namespace=chap8-domain1 --
name=my-apache-svc --port=80 --type=ClusterIP
service "my-apache-svc" exposed
```

```
$ kubectl expose deploy my-apache --namespace=chap8-domain2 --
name=my-apache-svc --port=80 --type=ClusterIP
service "my-apache-svc" exposed
```

2. Check the IP address for those two services by running the following command:

```
$ kubectl get svc my-apache-svc --namespace=chap8-domain1
NAME              TYPE         CLUSTER-IP        EXTERNAL-IP
PORT(S)    AGE
my-apache-svc     ClusterIP    10.96.117.206     <none>
80/TCP     32s

$ kubectl get svc my-apache-svc --namespace=chap8-domain2
NAME              TYPE         CLUSTER-IP        EXTERNAL-IP
PORT(S)    AGE
my-apache-svc     ClusterIP    10.105.27.49      <none>        80/TCP
49s
```

3. In order to perform name resolution, use the busybox pod in the foreground:

```
$ kubectl run -it busybox --restart=Never --image=busybox
```

4. In the busybox pod, use the nslookup command to query the IP address of those two services:

```
//query Normal Service on chap8-domain1
# nslookup my-apache-svc.chap8-domain1.svc.cluster.local
Server: 10.96.0.10
Address 1: 10.96.0.10 kube-dns.kube-system.svc.cluster.local

Name: my-apache-svc.chap8-domain1.svc.cluster.local
Address 1: 10.96.117.206 my-apache-svc.chap8-
domain1.svc.cluster.local


//query Normal Service on chap8-domain2
# nslookup my-apache-svc.chap8-domain2.svc.cluster.local
Server: 10.96.0.10
Address 1: 10.96.0.10 kube-dns.kube-system.svc.cluster.local

Name: my-apache-svc.chap8-domain2.svc.cluster.local
Address 1: 10.105.27.49 my-apache-svc.chap8-
domain2.svc.cluster.local
```

5. Access to service for apache whether traffic can dispatch to the backend apache pod:

```
# wget -q -O - my-apache-svc.chap8-domain1.svc.cluster.local
<html><body><h1>It works!</h1></body></html>

# wget -q -O - my-apache-svc.chap8-domain2.svc.cluster.local
<html><body><h1>It works!</h1></body></html>
```

6. Quit the busybox pod and delete it:

```
# exit
$ kubectl delete pod busybox
pod "busybox" deleted
```

DNS for a normal service behaves as a proxy; traffic goes to the normal service, then dispatches to the pod. What about the headless service? This will be discussed in the *How it works...* section.

DNS for StatefulSet

StatefulSet was described in Chapter 3, *Playing with Containers*. It assigns a pod name with a sequence number—for example, my-nginx-0, my-nginx-1, my-nginx-2. StatefulSet also uses these pod names to assign a DNS entry instead of IP addresses. Because it uses Kubernetes Service, FQDN appear as follows: <StatefulSet name>-<sequence number>.<Service name>.<Namespace name>.svc.cluster.local.

Let's create StatefulSet to examine how DNS works in StatefulSet:

1. Prepare StatefulSet and normal service YAML configurations as follows:

```
$ cat nginx-sts.yaml
apiVersion: v1
kind: Service
metadata:
  name: nginx-sts-svc
  labels:
    app: nginx-sts
spec:
  ports:
  - port: 80
  selector:
    app: nginx-sts
---
```

```
apiVersion: apps/v1beta1
kind: StatefulSet
metadata:
  name: nginx-sts
spec:
  serviceName: "nginx-sts-svc"
  replicas: 3
  template:
    metadata:
      labels:
        app: nginx-sts
    spec:
      containers:
        - name: nginx-sts
          image: nginx
          ports:
          - containerPort: 80
      restartPolicy: Always
```

2. Create StatefulSet on chap8-domain2:

```
$ kubectl create -f nginx-sts.yaml --namespace=chap8-domain2
service "nginx-sts-svc" created
statefulset "nginx-sts" created
```

3. Use the kubectl command to check the status of the pod and service creation:

```
//check StatefulSet (in short sts)
$ kubectl get sts --namespace=chap8-domain2
NAME         DESIRED    CURRENT    AGE
nginx-sts    3          3          46s


//check Service (in short svc)
$ kubectl get svc nginx-sts-svc --namespace=chap8-domain2
NAME            TYPE        CLUSTER-IP       EXTERNAL-IP
PORT(S)   AGE
nginx-sts-svc   ClusterIP   10.104.63.124    <none>
80/TCP    8m


//check Pod with "-o wide" to show an IP address
$ kubectl get pods --namespace=chap8-domain2 -o wide
NAME                           READY   STATUS    RESTARTS   AGE
IP               NODE
my-apache-55fb679f49-z9gsr     1/1     Running   1          22h
172.17.0.4       minikube
nginx-sts-0                    1/1     Running   0          2m
```

```
          172.17.0.2     minikube
          nginx-sts-1                    1/1        Running   0        2m
          172.17.0.9     minikube
          nginx-sts-2                    1/1        Running   0        1m
          172.17.0.10    minikube
```

4. Launch the `busybox` pod in the foreground:

```
$ kubectl run -it busybox --restart=Never --image=busybox
```

5. Use the `nslookup` command to query the service's IP address:

```
# nslookup nginx-sts-svc.chap8-domain2.svc.cluster.local
Server:      10.96.0.10
Address 1: 10.96.0.10 kube-dns.kube-system.svc.cluster.local

Name:        nginx-sts-svc.chap8-domain2.svc.cluster.local
Address 1: 10.104.63.124 nginx-sts-svc.chap8-
domain2.svc.cluster.local
```

6. Use the `nslookup` command to query the individual pod's IP address:

```
# nslookup nginx-sts-0.nginx-sts-svc.chap8-
domain2.svc.cluster.local
Server:      10.96.0.10
Address 1: 10.96.0.10 kube-dns.kube-system.svc.cluster.local
Name:        nginx-sts-0.nginx-sts-svc.chap8-
domain2.svc.cluster.local
Address 1: 172.17.0.2 nginx-sts-0.nginx-sts-svc.chap8-
domain2.svc.cluster.local


# nslookup nginx-sts-1.nginx-sts-svc.chap8-
domain2.svc.cluster.local
Server:      10.96.0.10
Address 1: 10.96.0.10 kube-dns.kube-system.svc.cluster.local
Name:        nginx-sts-1.nginx-sts-svc.chap8-
domain2.svc.cluster.local
Address 1: 172.17.0.9 nginx-sts-1.nginx-sts-svc.chap8-
domain2.svc.cluster.local


# nslookup nginx-sts-2.nginx-sts-svc.chap8-
domain2.svc.cluster.local
Server:      10.96.0.10
Address 1: 10.96.0.10 kube-dns.kube-system.svc.cluster.local
Name:        nginx-sts-2.nginx-sts-svc.chap8-
domain2.svc.cluster.local
```

```
Address 1: 172.17.0.10 nginx-sts-2.nginx-sts-svc.chap8-
domain2.svc.cluster.local
```

7. Clean up the busybox pod:

```
# exit
$ kubectl delete pod busybox
pod "busybox" deleted
```

How it works...

We have set up several components to see how DNS entries are created initially. The Kubernetes Service name is especially important for determining the name of a DNS.

However, Kubernetes Service has 2 modes, either normal service or headless service. Normal service has already been described in the preceding section; it has its own IP address. On the other hand, headless service doesn't have an IP address.

Let's see how to create a headless service and how name resolution works:

1. Create a headless service (specify --cluster-ip=None) for apache on chap8-domain1 and chap8-domain2:

```
$ kubectl expose deploy my-apache --namespace=chap8-domain1 --
name=my-apache-svc-hl --port=80 --type=ClusterIP --cluster-
ip=None
service "my-apache-svc-hl" exposed

$ kubectl expose deploy my-apache --namespace=chap8-domain2 --
name=my-apache-svc-hl --port=80 --type=ClusterIP --cluster-
ip=None
service "my-apache-svc-hl" exposed
```

2. Check there is no IP address for those two headless services with the following command:

```
$ kubectl get svc my-apache-svc-hl --namespace=chap8-domain1
NAME                TYPE          CLUSTER-IP    EXTERNAL-IP
PORT(S)    AGE
my-apache-svc-hl    ClusterIP     None          <none>
80/TCP     13m


$ kubectl get svc my-apache-svc-hl --namespace=chap8-domain2
```

```
NAME                        TYPE          CLUSTER-IP    EXTERNAL-IP
PORT(S)       AGE
my-apache-svc-hl    ClusterIP     None          <none>
80/TCP        13m
```

3. Launch the `busybox` pod in the foreground:

   ```
   $ kubectl run -it busybox --restart=Never --image=busybox
   ```

4. In the `busybox` pod, query those two services. It must show the addresses as the pod's address (`172.168.0.4` and `172.168.0.5`):

   ```
   # nslookup my-apache-svc-hl.chap8-domain1.svc.cluster.local
   Server: 10.96.0.10
   Address 1: 10.96.0.10 kube-dns.kube-system.svc.cluster.local

   Name: my-apache-svc-hl.chap8-domain1.svc.cluster.local
   Address 1: 172.17.0.4


   # nslookup my-apache-svc-hl.chap8-domain2.svc.cluster.local
   Server: 10.96.0.10
   Address 1: 10.96.0.10 kube-dns.kube-system.svc.cluster.local

   Name: my-apache-svc-hl.chap8-domain2.svc.cluster.local
   Address 1: 172.17.0.5
   ```

5. Exit the `busybox` pod and delete it:

   ```
   # exit
   $ kubectl delete pod busybox
   pod "busybox" deleted
   ```

Headless service when pods scale out

The preceding example shows only one IP address, because we have been setup only one Pod. What happens if you increase an instance using the `kubectl scale` command?

Let's increase the Apache instances on `chap8-domain1` from 1 to 3, then see how the headless service DNS works:

```
//specify --replicas=3
$ kubectl scale deploy my-apache --namespace=chap8-domain1 --replicas=3
deployment "my-apache" scaled


//Now there are 3 Apache Pods
$ kubectl get pods --namespace=chap8-domain1 -o wide
NAME                         READY    STATUS     RESTARTS   AGE      IP
NODE
my-apache-55fb679f49-c8wg7   1/1      Running    0          1m
172.17.0.7    minikube
my-apache-55fb679f49-cgnj8   1/1      Running    0          1m
172.17.0.8    minikube
my-apache-55fb679f49-qw58f   1/1      Running    0          8h
172.17.0.4    minikube


//launch busybox to run nslookup command
$ kubectl run -it busybox --restart=Never --image=busybox


//query Headless service name
# nslookup my-apache-svc-hl.chap8-domain1.svc.cluster.local
Server: 10.96.0.10

Address 1: 10.96.0.10 kube-dns.kube-system.svc.cluster.local
Name: my-apache-svc-hl.chap8-domain1.svc.cluster.local
Address 1: 172.17.0.4
Address 2: 172.17.0.7
Address 3: 172.17.0.8


//quit busybox and release it
# exit
$ kubectl delete pod busybox
pod "busybox" deleted
```

The result is straightforward: one DNS entry, `my-apache-svc-hl.chap8-domain1.svc.cluster.local` returns 3 IP addresses. Therefore, when your HTTP client tries to access the Kubernetes Service `my-apache-svc-hl.chap8-domain1.svc.cluster.local`, it gets these 3 IP addresses from `kube-dns`, then accesses one of them directly, as shown in the following diagram:

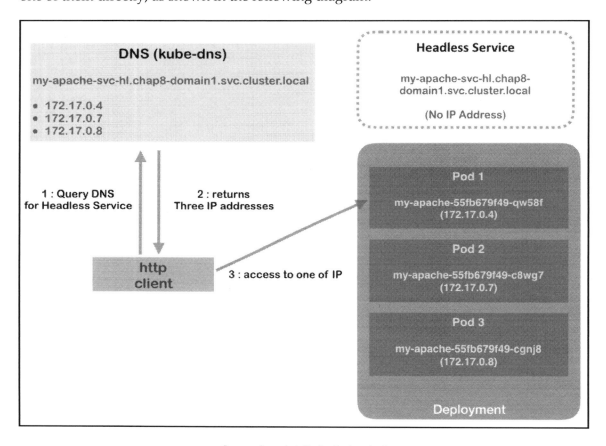

Sequence of accessing to Headless Service and pod

Therefore, Kubernetes headless service doesn't do any traffic dispatches. This is why it is called headless.

See also

This section described how `kube-dns` names pods and services in DNS. It is important to understand the differences between normal service and headless service to understand how to connect to your application. The StatefulSet use case was also described in the following recipe:

- *Ensuring flexible usage of your containers* in `Chapter 3`, *Playing with Containers*

Authentication and authorization

Authentication and authorization are both crucial for a platform such as Kubernetes. Authentication ensures users are who they claim to be. Authorization verifies if users have sufficient permission to perform certain operations. Kubernetes supports various authentication and authorization plugins.

Getting ready

When a request comes to an API server, it firstly establishes a TLS connection by validating the clients' certificate with the **certificate authority** (**CA**) in the API server. The CA in the API server is usually at `/etc/kubernetes/`, and the clients' certificate is usually at `$HOME/.kube/config`. After the handshake, it goes to the authentication stage. In Kubernetes, authentication modules are chain-based. We can use more than one authentication module. When the request comes, Kubernetes will try all the authenticators one by one until it succeeds. If the request fails on all authentication modules, it will be rejected as HTTP 401 unauthorized. Otherwise, one of the authenticators verifies the user's identity, and the requests are authenticated. Then, the Kubernetes authorization modules come into play. They verify if the *user* has the permission to do the action that they requested using a set of policies. Authorization modules are checked one by one. Just like authentication modules, if all modules are failed, the request will be denied. If the user is eligible to make the request, the request will pass through the authentication and authorization modules and go into admission control modules. The request will be checked by various admission controllers one by one. If any admission controller fails the request, the request will be rejected immediately.

The following diagram demonstrates this sequence:

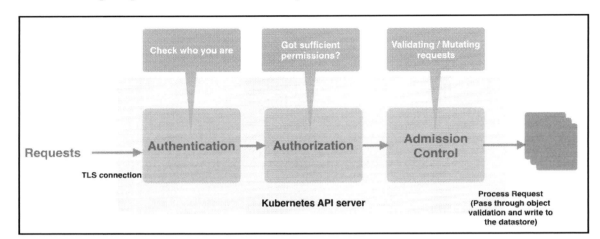

Requests passing through a Kubernetes API server

How to do it...

In Kubernetes, there are two types of account; service accounts and user accounts. The major difference between them is that user accounts are not stored and managed in Kubernetes itself. They cannot be added through API calls. The following table is a simple comparison:

	Service account	User account
Scope	Namespaced	Global
Used by	Processes	Normal user
Created by	API server or via API calls	Administrators, can't be added via API calls
Managed by	API server	Outside the cluster

Service accounts are used by processes inside a Pod to contact the API server. Kubernetes by default will create a service account named **default**. If there is no service account associated with a Pod, it'll be assigned to the default service account:

```
// check default service accoun
# kubectl describe serviceaccount default
Name:            default
Namespace:       default
Labels:          <none>
```

```
Annotations:           <none>
Image pull secrets:    <none>
Mountable secrets:     default-token-q4qdh
Tokens:                default-token-q4qdh
Events:                <none>
```

We may find there is a Secret associated with this service account. This is controlled by the token controller manager. When a new service account is created, the controller will create a token and associate it with the service account with the `kubernetes.io/service-account.name` annotation, allowing API access. Token is in the Secret format in Kubernetes. Anybody with the Secret view permission can see the token. The following is an example of creating a service account:

```
// configuration file of a ServiceAccount named chapter8-serviceaccount
# cat serviceaccount.yaml
apiVersion: v1
kind: ServiceAccount
metadata:
  name: chapter8-serviceaccount
// create service account
# kubectl create -f serviceaccount.yaml
serviceaccount "chapter8-serviceaccount" created
// describe the service account we just created
# kubectl describe serviceaccount chapter8-serviceaccount
Name:                  chapter8-serviceaccount
Namespace:             default
Labels:                <none>
Annotations:           <none>
Image pull secrets:    <none>
Mountable secrets:     chapter8-serviceaccount-token-nxh47
Tokens:                chapter8-serviceaccount-token-nxh47
Events:                <none>
```

Authentication

There are several account authentication strategies supported in Kuberentes, from client certificates, bearer tokens, and static files to OpenID connect tokens. More than one option could be chosen and combined with others in authentication chains. In this recipe, we'll introduce how to use token, client certs, and OpenID connect token authenticators.

Service account token authentication

We've created a service account in the previous section; now, let's see how to use a service account token to do the authentication. We'll have to retrieve the token first:

```
// check the details of the secret
# kubectl get secret chapter8-serviceaccount-token-nxh47 -o yaml
apiVersion: v1
data:
  ca.crt: <base64 encoded>
  namespace: ZGVmYXVsdA==
  token: <bearer token, base64 encoded>
kind: Secret
metadata:
  annotations:
    kubernetes.io/service-account.name: chapter8-serviceaccount
    name: chapter8-serviceaccount-token-nxh47
  namespace: default
  ...
type: kubernetes.io/service-account-token
```

We can see that the three items under the data are all base64-encoded. We can decode them easily with the `echo "encoded content" | base64 --decode` command in Linux. For example, we can decode encoded namespace content:

```
# echo "ZGVmYXVsdA==" | base64 --decode
default
```

Using the same command we can get the bearer token and use it in a request. The API server expects a HTTP header of `Authorization: Bearer $TOKEN` along with the request. The following is an example of how to use the token to authenticate and make a request directly to the API server.

Firstly, we'll have to get our decoded token:

```
// get the decoded token from secret chapter8-serviceaccount-token-nxh47
# TOKEN=`echo "<bearer token, base64 encoded>" | base64 --decode`
```

Secondly, we'll have to decode `ca.crt` as well:

```
// get the decoded ca.crt from secret chapter8-serviceaccount-token-nxh47
# echo "<ca.crt, base64 encoded>" | base64 --decode > cert
```

Next, we'll need to know what the API server is. Using the `kubectl config view` command, we can get a list of servers:

```
# kubectl config view
apiVersion: v1
clusters:
- cluster:
    certificate-authority-data: REDACTED
    server: https://api.demo-k8s.net
```

```
     name: demo-k8s.net
 - cluster:
     certificate-authority: /Users/chloelee/.minikube/ca.crt
     server: https://192.168.99.100:8443
   name: minikube
...
```

Find the one you're currently using. In this example, we're using minikube. The server is at `https://192.168.99.100:8443`.

You can use the `kubectl config current-context` command to find the current context.

Then we should be good to go! We'll request the API endpoint directly via `https://$APISERVER/api` with `--cacert` and `--header`

```
# curl --cacert cert https://192.168.99.100:8443/api --header
"Authorization: Bearer $TOKEN"
{
  "kind": "APIVersions",
  "versions": [
    "v1"
  ],
  "serverAddressByClientCIDRs": [
    {
      "clientCIDR": "0.0.0.0/0",
      "serverAddress": "10.0.2.15:8443"
    }
  ]
}
```

We can see that the available version is `v1`. Let's see what we have in `/api/v1` endpoint:

```
# curl --cacert cert https://192.168.99.100:8443/api/v1 --header
"Authorization: Bearer $TOKEN"
{
  "kind": "APIResourceList",
  "groupVersion": "v1",
  "resources": [
    ...
    {
      "name": "configmaps",
      "singularName": "",
      "namespaced": true,
      "kind": "ConfigMap",
```

```
      "verbs": [
        "create",
        "delete",
        "deletecollection",
        "get",
        "list",
        "patch",
        "update",
        "watch"
      ],
      "shortNames": ["cm"]
    }
  ], ...
}
```

It will list all the endpoints and verbs we requested. Let's take `configmaps` as an example and `grep` the name:

```
# curl --cacert cert https://192.168.99.100:8443/api/v1/configmaps --header
"Authorization: Bearer $TOKEN" |grep \"name\"
        "name": "extension-apiserver-authentication",
        "name": "ingress-controller-leader-nginx",
        "name": "kube-dns",
        "name": "nginx-load-balancer-conf",
```

There are four default configmaps listed in my cluster in this example. We can use `kubectl` to verify this. The result should match the ones we previously got:

```
# kubectl get configmaps --all-namespaces
NAMESPACE       NAME                                    DATA    AGE
kube-system     extension-apiserver-authentication      6       6d
kube-system     ingress-controller-leader-nginx         0       6d
kube-system     kube-dns                                0       6d
kube-system     nginx-load-balancer-conf                1       6d
```

X509 client certs

A common authentication strategy for user accounts is to use client certificates. In the following example, we'll create a user named Linda and generate a client cert for her:

```
// generate a private key for Linda
# openssl genrsa -out linda.key 2048
Generating RSA private key, 2048 bit long modulus
..............+++
..............+++
e is 65537 (0x10001)
// generate a certificate sign request (.csr) for Linda. Make sure /CN is
```

```
equal to the username.
# openssl req -new -key linda.key -out linda.csr -subj "/CN=linda"
```

Next, we'll generate a cert for Linda via a private key and sign request files, along with the CA and private key of our cluster:

 In minikube, it's under ~/.minikube/. For other self-hosted solutions, normally it's under /etc/kubernetes/. If you use kops to deploy the cluster, the location is under /srv/kubernetes, where you can find the path in the/etc/kubernetes/manifests/kube-apiserver.manifest file.

```
// generate a cert
# openssl x509 -req -in linda.csr -CA ca.crt -CAkey ca.key -CAcreateserial
-out linda.crt -days 30
Signature ok
subject=/CN=linda
Getting CA Private Key
```

We got Linda signed by our cluster cert; now we can set it into our kubeconfig file:

```
# kubectl config set-credentials linda --client-certificate=linda.crt --
client-key=linda.key
User "linda" set.
```

We can use kubectl config view to verify the user is set:

```
# kubectl config view
current-context: minikube
kind: Config
users:
  - name: linda
  user:
    client-certificate: /k8s-cookbooks-2e/ch8/linda.crt
    client-key: /k8s-cookbooks-2e/ch8/linda.key
...
```

After the user is created, we can create a context to associate the namespace and cluster with this user:

```
# kubectl config set-context linda-context --cluster=minikube --user=linda
```

After that, Kubernetes should be able to identify linda and pass it to the authorization stage.

OpenID connect tokens

Another popular authentication strategy is OpenID connect tokens. Delegating the identity verification to OAuth2 providers, is a convenient way to manage users. To enable the feature, two required flags have to be set to the API server: `--oidc-issuer-url`, which indicates the issuer URL that allows the API server to discover public signing keys, and `--oidc-client-id`, which is the client ID of your app to associate with your issuer. For full information, please refer to the official documentation `https://kubernetes.io/docs/admin/authentication/#configuring-the-api-server`. The following is an example of how we set Google OpenID authentication with our minikube cluster. The following steps can be programmed easily for authentication usage.

To start, we'll have to request a set consisting of the client ID, client secret, and redirect URL from Google. The following are the steps for requesting and downloading the secret from Google:

1. In GCP console, go to **APIs & Services** | **Credentials** | **Create credentials** | **OAuth client ID.**
2. Choose Other in application type and click **Create.**
3. Download the JSON file.

After this, the credential is successfully created. We can take a look at the JSON file. The following is the file we got from our example project kubernetes-cookbook:

```
# cat client_secret_140285873781-
f9h7d7bmi6ec1qa0892mk52t3o874j5d.apps.googleusercontent.com.json
{
    "installed":{
        "client_id":"140285873781
f9h7d7bmi6ec1qa0892mk52t3o874j5d.apps.googleusercontent.com",
        "project_id":"kubernetes-cookbook",
        "auth_uri":"https://accounts.google.com/o/oauth2/auth",
        "token_uri":"https://accounts.google.com/o/oauth2/token",
"auth_provider_x509_cert_url":"https://www.googleapis.com/oauth2/v1/certs",
        "client_secret":"Ez0m1L7436mlJQErhalp3Gda",
        "redirect_uris":[
            "urn:ietf:wg:oauth:2.0:oob",
            "http://localhost"
        ]
    }
}
```

Now, we should be able to start our cluster. Don't forget the OIDC flags have to be passed on. In minikube, this is done via the `--extra-config` parameter:

```
// start minikube cluster and passing oidc parameters.
# minikube start --extra-config=apiserver.Authorization.Mode=RBAC --extra-
config=apiserver.Authentication.OIDC.IssuerURL=https://accounts.google.com
--extra-config=apiserver.Authentication.OIDC.UsernameClaim=email --extra-
config=apiserver.Authentication.OIDC.ClientID="140285873781-
f9h7d7bmi6ec1qa0892mk52t3o874j5d.apps.googleusercontent.com"
```

After the cluster is started, the user has to log in to the identity provider in order to get `access_token`, `id_token`, and `refresh_token`. In Google, you'll get a code after login, and you pass the code with the request to get the tokens. Then we pass the token to the request to the API server via kubectl. The following is the sequence diagram for this:

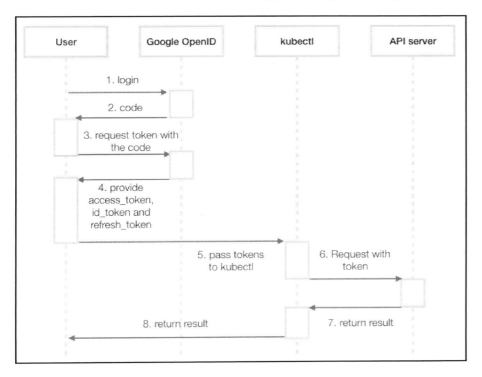

Time diagram of Google OpenID connect authentication

To request the code, your app should send the HTTP request in the following format:

```
//
https://accounts.google.com/o/oauth2/v2/auth?client_id=<client_id>&response
_type=code&scope=openid%20email&redirect_uri=urn:ietf:wg:oauth:2.0:oob
#
https://accounts.google.com/o/oauth2/v2/auth?client_id=140285873781-f9h7d7b
mi6ec1qa0892mk52t3o874j5d.apps.googleusercontent.com&response_type=code&sco
pe=openid%20email&redirect_uri=urn:ietf:wg:oauth:2.0:oob
```

Then, a browser window will pop out to ask for sign in to Google. After signing in, the code will be shown in the console:

```
Sign in

Please copy this code, switch to your application and paste it there:
4/AAAd5nqWFkpKmxo0b_HZGlcAh57zbJzggKmoOG0BH9gJhfgvQK0iu9w
```

Next, we pass the code for requesting the token to
`https://www.googleapis.com/oauth2/v4/token`. Then, we should be able to get
`access_token`, `refresh_token`, and `id_token` from the response:

```
// curl -d
"grant_type=authorization_code&client_id=<client_id>&client_secret=<client_
secret>&redirect_uri=urn:ietf:wg:oauth:2.0:oob&code=<code>" -X POST
https://www.googleapis.com/oauth2/v4/token
# curl -d "grant_type=authorization_code&client_id=140285873781-
f9h7d7bmi6ec1qa0892mk52t3o874j5d.apps.googleusercontent.com&client_secret=E
z0m1L7436mlJQErhalp3Gda&redirect_uri=urn:ietf:wg:oauth:2.0:oob&code=4/AAAd5
nqWFkpKmxo0b_HZGlcAh57zbJzggKmoOG0BH9gJhfgvQK0iu9w" -X POST
https://www.googleapis.com/oauth2/v4/token
{
  "access_token":
"ya29.GluJBQIhJy34vqJl7V6lPF9YSXmKauvvctjUJHwx72gKDDJikiKzQed9iUnmqEv8gLYg4
3H6zTSYn1qohkNce1Q3fMl6wbrGMCuXfRlipTcPtZnFt1jNalqMMTCm",
  "token_type": "Bearer",
  "expires_in": 3600,
  "refresh_token": "1/72xFflvdTRdqhjn70Bcar3qyWDiFw-8KoNm6LdFPorQ",
  "id_token": "eyJhbGc...mapQ"
}
```

Assume we'll have the user chloe-k8scookbook@gmail.com to associate with this Google account. Let's create it in our cluster. We can append user information into our kubeconfig. The default location of the file is $HOME/.kube/config:

```
// append to kubeconfig file.
- name: chloe-k8scookbook@gmail.com
 · user:
    auth-provider:
      config:
        client-id: 140285873781-
f9h7d7bmi6ec1qa0892mk52t3o874j5d.apps.googleusercontent.com
        client-secret: EzOm1L7436mlJQErhalp3Gda
        id-token: eyJhbGc...mapQ
        idp-issuer-url: https://accounts.google.com
        refresh-token: 1/72xFflvdTRdqhjn70Bcar3qyWDiFw-8KoNm6LdFPorQ
      name: oidc
```

After that, let's use the user to list nodes and see if it can pass the authentication:

```
# kubectl --user=chloe-k8scookbook@gmail.com get nodes
Error from server (Forbidden): nodes is forbidden: User "chloe-
k8scookbook@gmail.com" cannot list nodes at the cluster scope
```

We encounter an authorization error! After verifying the identity, the next step will be checking if the user has sufficient rights to perform the request.

Authorization

After passing the authentication phase, authorizers take place. Before we move on to authorization strategies, let's talk about Role and RoleBinding first.

Role and RoleBinding

Role in Kubernetes contains a set of rules. A rule defines a set of permissions for certain operations and resources by specifying apiGroups, resources, and verbs. For example, the following role defines a read-only rule for configmaps:

```
# cat role.yaml
kind: Role
apiVersion: rbac.authorization.k8s.io/v1
metadata:
  name: configmap-ro
rules:
  - apiGroups: ["*"]
    resources: ["configmaps"]
```

```
        verbs: ["watch", "get", "list"]
```

A `RoleBinding` is used to associate a role with a list of accounts. The following example shows we assign the `configmap-ro` role to a list of subjects. It only has the user `linda` in this case:

```
# cat rolebinding.yaml
kind: RoleBinding
apiVersion: rbac.authorization.k8s.io/v1
metadata:
  name: devops-role-binding
subjects:
- apiGroup: ""
  kind: User
  name: linda
roleRef:
  apiGroup: ""
  kind: Role
  name: configmap-ro
```

`Role` and `RoleBinding` are namespaced. Their scope is only within a single namespace. For accessing `cluster-wide` resources, we'll need `ClusterRole` and `ClusterRoleBinding`.

 For adding namespace into `Role` or `RoleBinding`, simply add a namespace field into the metadata in the configuration file.

ClusterRole and ClusterRoleBinding

`ClusterRole` and `ClusterRoleBinding` are basically similar to `Role` and `RoleBinding`. Unlike how `Role` and `RoleBinding` are scoped into a single namespace, `ClusterRole` and `ClusterRoleBinding` are used to grant cluster-wide resources. Therefore, access to resources across all namespaces, non-namespaced resources, and non-resource endpoints can be granted to `ClusterRole`, and we can use `ClusterRoleBinding` to bind the users and the role.

We can also bind a service account with `ClusterRole`. As a service account is namespaced, we'll have to specify its full name, which includes the namespace it's created in:

```
system:serviceaccount:<namespace>:<serviceaccountname>
```

The following is an example of `ClusterRole` and `ClusterRoleBinding`. In this role, we grant all operations for lots of resources, such as `deployments`, `replicasets`, `ingresses`, `pods`, and `services` to it, and we limit the permission to read-only for namespaces and events:

```
# cat serviceaccount_clusterrole.yaml
apiVersion: rbac.authorization.k8s.io/v1
kind: ClusterRole
metadata:
  name: cd-role
rules:
- apiGroups: ["extensions", "apps"]
  resources:
  - deployments
  - replicasets
  - ingresses
  verbs: ["*"]
- apiGroups: [""]
  resources:
  - namespaces
  - events
  verbs: ["get", "list", "watch"]
- apiGroups: [""]
  resources:
  - pods
  - services
  - secrets
  - replicationcontrollers
  - persistentvolumeclaims
  - jobs
  - cronjobs
  verbs: ["*"]---
apiVersion: rbac.authorization.k8s.io/v1
kind: ClusterRoleBinding
metadata:
  name: cd-role-binding
roleRef:
  apiGroup: rbac.authorization.k8s.io
  kind: ClusterRole
  name: cd-role
subjects:
- apiGroup: rbac.authorization.k8s.io
  kind: User
  name: system:serviceaccount:default:chapter8-serviceaccount
```

Note `[""]` in `apiGroup`; this indicates the core group in Kubernetes. To see the full list of resources and verbs, check out the Kubernetes API reference site: `https://kubernetes.io/docs/reference/`.

In this case, we create a `cd-role`, which is the role for performing continuous deployment. Also, we create a `ClusterRoleBinding` to associate the service account `chapter8-serviceaccount` with `cd-role`.

Role-based access control (RBAC)

The concept of role-based access control is surrounded by `Role`, `ClusterRole`, `RoleBinding`, and `ClusterRoleBinding`. By `role.yaml` and `rolebinding.yaml`, as we showed previously, Linda should get read-only access to the `configmaps` resource. To apply authorization rules to `chloe-k8scookbook@gmail.com`, simply associate a `ClusterRole` and `ClusterRoleBinding` with it:

```
# cat oidc_clusterrole.yaml
kind: ClusterRole
apiVersion: rbac.authorization.k8s.io/v1
metadata:
  name: oidc-admin-role
rules:
  - apiGroups: ["*"]
    resources: ["*"]
    verbs: ["*"]
---
kind: ClusterRoleBinding
apiVersion: rbac.authorization.k8s.io/v1
metadata:
  name: admin-binding
subjects:
  - kind: User
    name: chloe-k8scookbook@gmail.com
    apiGroup: rbac.authorization.k8s.io
roleRef:
  kind: ClusterRole
  name: oidc-admin-role
  apiGroup: rbac.authorization.k8s.io
```

Then, we should be able to see if we can get nodes with the `chloe-k8scookbook@gmail.com` user:

```
# kubectl --user=chloe-k8scookbook@gmail.com get nodes
NAME STATUS ROLES AGE VERSION minikube Ready <none> 6d v1.9.4
```

It works like a charm. We didn't encounter the Forbidden error anymore.

 Before RBAC, Kubernetes provided **Attribute-based access control** (**ABAC**), which allows a cluster administrator to define a set of user authorization polices into a file with one JSON per line format. However, the file has to exist when launching the API server, which makes it unusable in the real world. After RBAC was introduced in Kubernetes 1.6, ABAC became legacy and was deprecated.

Admission control

Admission control modules come into play after Kubernetes verifies who makes requests and whether the requester has sufficient permission to perform them. Unlike authentication and authorization, admission control can see the content of the request, or even have the ability to validate or mutate it. If the request doesn't pass through one of admission controllers, the request will be rejected immediately. For turning on admission controllers in Kubernetes, simply pass `--admission-control (version < 1.10) --enable-admission-plugins (version >= 1.10)` parameters when starting the API server.

 Depending on how you provision your cluster, the method for passing on the `--enable-admission-plugin` parameter may vary. In minikube, adding `--extra-config=apiserver.Admission.PluginNames=` `$ADMISSION_CONTROLLERS` and separate controllers with commas should do the trick.

Different admission controllers are designed for different purposes. In the following recipe, we'll introduce some important admission controllers and those that Kubernetes officially recommends that users have. The recommended list for version >= 1.6.0 is as follows: `NamespaceLifecycle`, `LimitRanger`, `ServiceAccount`, `PersistentVolumeLabel`, `DefaultStorageClass`, `DefaultTolerationSeconds`, `ResourceQuota`.

Please note that the sequence of admission controllers matters since the requests pass one by one in sequence (this is true for versions before 1.10, using the `--admission-control` option; in v1.10, the parameter is replaced by `--enable-admission-plugins` and the sequence no longer matters). We don't want to have `ResourceQuota` checking first and finding out that the resource information is outdated after checking the long chain of admission controllers.

If the version is >= 1.9.0, `MutatingAdmissionWebhook` and `ValidatingAdmissionWebhook` will be added before `ResourceQuota`. For more information about `MutatingAdmissionWebhook` and `ValidatingAdmissionWebhook`, please refer to the *There's more* section in this recipe.

NamespaceLifecycle

When a namespace is deleted, all objects in that namespace will be evicted as well. This plugin ensures no new object creation requests can be made in a namespace that is terminating or non-existent. It also saves Kubernetes native Namespaces from deletion.

LimitRanger

This plugin ensures `LimitRange` can work properly. With `LimitRange`, we can set default requests and limits in a namespace, be used when launching a pod without specifying the requests and limits.

ServiceAccount

The ServiceAccount plugin must be added if you intend to leverage ServiceAccount objects in your use cases. For more information about ServiceAccount, revisit ServiceAccount as we learned it in this recipe.

PersistentVolumeLabel (deprecated from v1.8)

`PersistentVolumeLabel` adds labels to newly-created PV's, based on the labels provided by the underlying cloud provider. This admission controller has been deprecated from 1.8. The function of this controller is now taken care of by cloud controller manager, which defines cloud-specific control logic and runs as a daemon.

DefaultStorageClass

This plugin ensures default storage classes can work as expected if no `StorageClass` is set in a `PersistentVolumeClaim`. Different provisioning tools with different cloud providers will leverage `DefaultStorageClass` (such as GKE, which uses Google Cloud Persistent Disk). Ensure you have this enabled.

DefaultTolerationSeconds

Taints and tolerations are used to prevent a set of pods from scheduling running on some nodes. Taints are applied to nodes, while tolerations are specified for pods. The value of taints could be `NoSchedule` or `NoExecute`. If pods running one tainted node have no matching toleration, the pods will be evicted.

The `DefaultTolerationSeconds` plugin is used to set those pods without any toleration set. It will then apply for the default toleration for the taints `notready:NoExecute` and **unreachable:NoExecute** for 300 s. If a node is not ready or unreachable, wait for 300 seconds before the pod is evicted from the node.

ResourceQuota

Just like `LimitRange`, if you're using the `ResourceQuota` object to administer different levels of QoS, this plugin must be enabled. The `ResourceQuota` should be always be put at the end of the admission control plugin list. As we mentioned in the `ResourceQuota` section, if the used quota is less than the hard quota, resource quota usage will be updated to ensure that clusters have sufficient resources to accept requests. Putting it into the end of ServiceAccount admission controller list could prevent the request from increasing quota usage prematurely if it eventually gets rejected by the following controllers.

DenyEscalatingExec

This plugin denies any kubectl exec and kubectl attach command escalated privilege mode. Pods with privilege mode have access to the host namespace, which could become a security risk.

AlwaysPullImages

The pull policy defines the behavior when kubelet is pulling images. The default pull policy is `IfNotPresent`; that is, it will pull the image if it is not present locally. If this plugin is enabled, the default pull policy will become Always, which is, always pull the latest image. This plugin also provides another benefit if your cluster is shared by different teams. Whenever a pod is scheduled, it'll always pull the latest image whether the image exists locally or not. Then we can ensure pod creation requests always go through an authorization check against the image.

For a full list of admission controllers, visit the official site (`https://kubernetes.io/docs/admin/admission-controllers`) for more information.

There's more...

Before Kubernetes 1.7, admission controllers needed to compile with the API server, and configure before the API server starts. **Dynamic admission control** is designed to break these limitations. As two major components in dynamic admission control are both not GA at the moment we wrote this book, excepting adding them into the admission control chain, additional runtime configuration is required in the API server: `--runtime-config=admissionregistration.k8s.io/v1alpha1`.

 In minikube, ServiceAccount runtime config is set to `api/all`, so it's enabled by default.

Initializers (alpha)

Initializers are a set of tasks during the object initialization stage. They could be a set of checks or mutations to perform force policies or inject defaults. For example, you could implement an initializer to inject a sidecar container or a volume containing test data to a pod. Initializers are configured in `metadata.initializers.pending` for an object. After the corresponding initializer controller (identified by name) performs the task, it'll remove its name from the metadata. If for some reasons one initializer doesn't work well, all the objects with that initializer will be stuck in ServiceAccount uninitialized stage, and not visible in the API. Use it with caution.

Webhook admission controllers (beta in v1.9)

There are two types of webhook admission controller as of v1.10:

- `ValidatingAdmissionWebhook`: It can do extra customized validation to reject the request
- `MutatingAdmissionWebhooks`: It can mutate the object to force default policies

For more implementation information, please refer to the official documents:
`https://kubernetes.io/docs/admin/extensible-admission-controllers/`

See also

The following recipes are of relevance to this section:

- *Working with Namespaces* in `Chapter 2`, *Walking through Kubernetes Concepts*
- *Setting up continuous delivery pipelines* in `Chapter 5`, *Building Continuous Delivery Pipelines*
- *Advanced settings in kubeconfig* in `Chapter 8`, *Advanced Cluster Administration*
- *Working with ServiceAccount RESTful API* in `Chapter 8`, *Advanced Cluster Administration*

Logging and Monitoring 9

This chapter will cover the following recipes:

- Working with EFK
- Working with Google Stackdriver
- Monitoring master and node

Introduction

Logging and monitoring are two of the most important tasks in Kubernetes. However, there are many ways to achieve logging and monitoring in Kubernetes, because there are a lot of logging and monitoring open source applications, as well as many public cloud services.

Kubernetes has a best practice for setting up a logging and monitoring infrastructure that most Kubernetes provisioning tools support as an add-on. In addition, managed Kubernetes services, such as Google Kubernetes Engine, integrate GCP log and a monitoring service out of the box.

Let's set up a logging and monitoring service on your Kubernetes cluster.

Working with EFK

In the Container world, log management always faces a technical difficulty, because Container has its own filesystem, and when Container is dead or evicted, the log files are gone. In addition, Kubernetes can easily scale out and scale down the Pods, so we need to care about a centralized log persistent mechanism.

Kubernetes has an add-on for setting up centralized log management, which is called EFK. EFK stands for **Elasticsearch**, **Fluentd**, and **Kibana**. These applications' stack bring you a full function of log collection, indexing, and UI.

Getting ready

In Chapter 1, *Building Your Own Kubernetes Cluster*, we set up our Kubernetes cluster with several different provisioning tools. Based on your Kubernetes provisioning tool, there is an easy way to set up EFK stack. Note that Elasticsearch and Kibana are heavy-duty Java applications. They require at least 2 GB of memory each.

Therefore, if you use minikube, your machine should have at least 8 GB of memory (16 GB is recommended). If you use kubespray or kops to set up Kubernetes cluster, Kubernetes node should have at least 4 core CPUs and 16 GB of memory in total (in other words, if you have 2 nodes, each node should have a minimum of 2 core CPUs and 8GB of memory).

In addition, in order to demonstrate how to gather the application logs efficiently, we create one additional namespace. It will help you to search your application log easily:

```
$ kubectl create namespace chap9
namespace "chap9" created
```

How to do it...

In this recipe, we will use the following Kubernetes provisioning tools to set up EFK stack. Based on your Kubernetes cluster, please read the appropriate section of this recipe:

- minikube
- kubespray (ansible)
- kops

 Note that for GKE on the Google Cloud Platform, we will introduce another way to set up logging infrastructure in the next recipe.

Setting up EFK with minikube

minikube provides an add-on feature for EFK out of the box, but it is disabled by default. So, you need to enable EFK on your minikube manually. EFK consumes a large amount of heap memory but minikube allocates only 2 GB by default, which is absolutely not sufficient to run the EFK stack in minikube. Therefore, we'll need to enlarge minikube's memory size explicitly.

In addition, you should use the latest version of minikube, due to several bug fixes made for EFK while writing this cookbook. So, we are using minikube version 0.25.2. Let's configure minikube to enable EFK using the following steps:

1. If you are already running `minikube`, stop `minikube` first:

    ```
    $ minikube stop
    ```

2. Update to the latest version of minikube:

    ```
    //if you are using macOS
    $ brew update
    $ brew cask upgrade
    ```

    ```
    //if you are using Windows, download a latest binary from
    https://github.com/kubernetes/minikube/releases
    ```

3. Since EFK consumes a large amount of heap memory, start `minikube` with 5 GB of memory:

    ```
    $ minikube start --vm-driver=hyperkit --memory 5120
    ```

4. Make sure, all Pods in the kube-system Namespace are up, because EFK relies on `kube-addon-manager-minikube`:

    ```
    $ kubectl get pods --all-namespaces
    NAMESPACE       NAME                                      READY
    STATUS      RESTARTS      AGE
    kube-system     kube-addon-manager-minikube               1/1
    Running     0             1m
    kube-system     kube-dns-54cccfbdf8-rc7gf                 3/3
    Running     0             1m
    kube-system     kubernetes-dashboard-77d8b98585-hkjrr     1/1
    Running     0             1m
    kube-system     storage-provisioner                       1/1
    Running     0             1m
    ```

5. Enable the `efk` add-on:

```
$ minikube addons enable efk
efk was successfully enabled
```

6. Wait for a while; Elasticsearch, fluentd and kibana Pod have been deployed in the kube-system namespace automatically. Wait for the STATUS to become Running. It should take at least 10 minutes to complete:

```
$ kubectl get pods --namespace=kube-system
NAME                                          READY     STATUS
RESTARTS    AGE
$ kubectl get pods --all-namespaces
NAMESPACE       NAME                              READY
STATUS      RESTARTS      AGE
kube-system     elasticsearch-logging-t5tq7       1/1
Running    0           9m
kube-system     fluentd-es-8z2tr                  1/1
Running    0           9m
kube-system     kibana-logging-dgql7              1/1
Running    0           9m
kube-system     kube-addon-manager-minikube       1/1
Running    1           34m
...
```

7. Use `kubectl logs` to watch a kibana that waits for the state to become green. This also takes an additional five minutes:

```
$ kubectl logs -f kibana-logging-dgql7  --namespace=kube-system
{"type":"log","@timestamp":"2018-03-25T18:53:54Z","tags":["info
","optimize"],"pid":1,"message":"Optimizing and caching bundles
for graph, ml, kibana, stateSessionStorageRedirect, timelion
and status_page. This may take a few minutes"}

(wait for around 5min)

{"type":"log","@timestamp":"2018-03-25T19:03:10Z","tags":["stat
us","plugin:elasticsearch@5.6.2","info"],"pid":1,"state":"yello
w","message":"Status changed from yellow to yellow - No
existing Kibana index
found","prevState":"yellow","prevMsg":"Waiting for
Elasticsearch"}
{"type":"log","@timestamp":"2018-03-25T19:03:15Z","tags":["stat
us","plugin:elasticsearch@5.6.2","info"],"pid":1,"state":"green
","message":"Status changed from yellow to green - Kibana index
ready","prevState":"yellow","prevMsg":"No existing Kibana index
found"}
```

8. Access the kibana service using the `minikube service` command:

```
$ minikube service kibana-logging --namespace=kube-system
Opening kubernetes service kube-system/kibana-logging in
default browser...
```

Now, you have access to the Kibana UI from your machine. You just need to set up an index. Since Fluentd keeps sending a log with the index name as `logstash-yyyy.mm.dd`, the index pattern is `logstash-*` by default. Click the **Create** button:

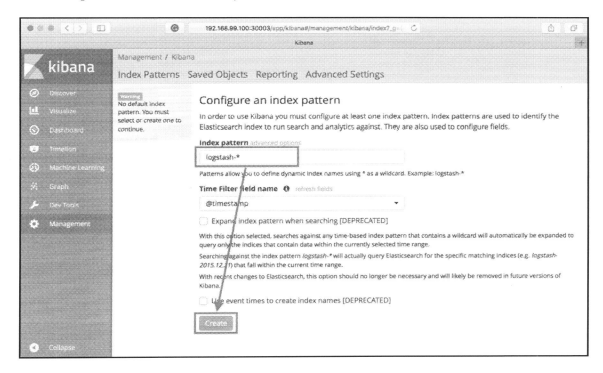

Setting up EFK with kubespray

kubespray has a configuration concerning whether or not to enable EFK. By default, it is disabled, so you need to enable it with the following steps:

1. Open `<kubespray dir>/inventory/mycluster/group_vars/k8s-cluster.yaml`.

2. Around line number 152 in the `k8s-cluster.yml` file, change the value of `efk_enabled` to `true`:

```
# Monitoring apps for k8s
efk_enabled: true
```

3. Run the `ansible-playbook` command to update your Kubernetes cluster:

```
$ ansible-playbook -b -i inventory/mycluster/hosts.ini
cluster.yml
```

4. Check to see if Elasticsearch, Fluentd, and Kibana Pod's **STATUS** became **Running** or not; if you see the **Pending** state for more than 10 minutes, check `kubectl describe pod <Pod name>` to see the status. In most cases, you will get an error saying insufficient memory. If so, you need to add more Nodes or increase the available RAM:

```
$ kubectl get pods --all-namespaces
NAMESPACE       NAME                                          READY
STATUS      RESTARTS    AGE
kube-system     calico-node-9wnwn                             1/1
Running   0         2m
kube-system     calico-node-jg67p                             1/1
Running   0         2m
kube-system     elasticsearch-logging-v1-776b8b856c-97qrq     1/1
Running   0         1m
kube-system     elasticsearch-logging-v1-776b8b856c-z7jhm     1/1
Running   0         1m
kube-system     fluentd-es-v1.22-gtvzg                        1/1
Running   0         49s
kube-system     fluentd-es-v1.22-h8r4h                        1/1
Running   0         49s
kube-system     kibana-logging-57d98b74f9-x8nz5               1/1
Running   0         44s
kube-system     kube-apiserver-master-1                       1/1
Running   0         3m
kube-system     kube-controller-manager-master-1             1/1
Running   0         3m
...
```

5. Check the kibana log to see if the status has become `green`:

```
$ kubectl logs -f kibana-logging-57d98b74f9-x8nz5 --
namespace=kube-system
ELASTICSEARCH_URL=http://elasticsearch-logging:9200
server.basePath: /api/v1/proxy/namespaces/kube-
system/services/kibana-logging
```

{"type":"log","@timestamp":"2018-03-25T05:11:10Z","tags":["info
","optimize"],"pid":5,"message":"Optimizing and caching bundles
for kibana and statusPage. This may take a few minutes"}

(wait for around 5min)

{"type":"log","@timestamp":"2018-03-25T05:17:55Z","tags":["stat
us","plugin:elasticsearch@1.0.0","info"],"pid":5,"state":"yello
w","message":"Status changed from yellow to yellow – No
existing Kibana index
found","prevState":"yellow","prevMsg":"Waiting for
Elasticsearch"}
{"type":"log","@timestamp":"2018-03-25T05:17:58Z","tags":["stat
us","plugin:elasticsearch@1.0.0","info"],"pid":5,"state":"green
","message":"Status changed from **yellow to green** – Kibana index
ready","prevState":"yellow","prevMsg":"No existing Kibana index
found"}

6. Run `kubectl cluster-info`, confirm Kibana is running, and capture the URL of Kibana:

```
$ kubectl cluster-info
Kubernetes master is running at http://localhost:8080
Elasticsearch is running at
http://localhost:8080/api/v1/namespaces/kube-system/services/el
asticsearch-logging/proxy
Kibana is running at
http://localhost:8080/api/v1/namespaces/kube-system/services/ki
bana-logging/proxy
KubeDNS is running at
http://localhost:8080/api/v1/namespaces/kube-system/services/ku
be-dns:dns/proxy
```

7. In order to access the Kibana WebUI from your machine remotely, it is easier to use ssh port forwarding from your machine to the Kubernetes master:

```
$ ssh -L 8080:127.0.0.1:8080 <Kubernetes master IP address>
```

8. Access the Kibana WebUI from your machine using the following URL: http://localhost:8080/api/v1/namespaces/kube-system/services/kibana-logging/proxy.

Now you can access Kibana from your machine. You also need to configure the index. Just make sure the index name has `logstash-*` as the default value. Then, click the **Create** button:

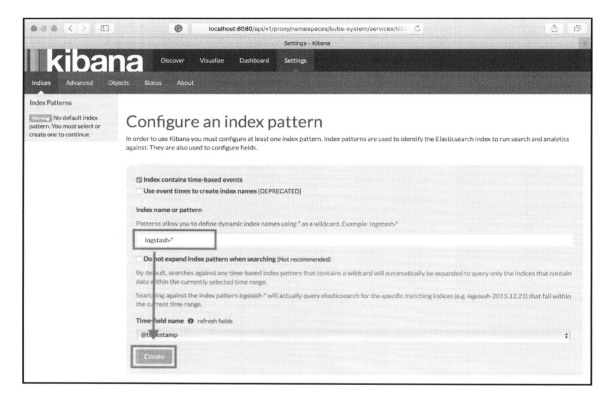

Setting up EFK with kops

kops also has an add-on for setting up the EFK stack on your Kubernetes cluster easily. Proceed through the following steps to run EFK stack on your Kubernetes:

1. Run `kubectl create` to specify the kops EFK add-on:

```
$ kubectl create -f
https://raw.githubusercontent.com/kubernetes/kops/master/addons
/logging-elasticsearch/v1.6.0.yaml
serviceaccount "elasticsearch-logging" created
clusterrole "elasticsearch-logging" created
clusterrolebinding "elasticsearch-logging" created
serviceaccount "fluentd-es" created
```

```
clusterrole "fluentd-es" created
clusterrolebinding "fluentd-es" created
daemonset "fluentd-es" created
service "elasticsearch-logging" created
statefulset "elasticsearch-logging" created
deployment "kibana-logging" created
service "kibana-logging" created
```

2. Wait for the STATUS of all Pods to become Running:

```
$ kubectl get pods --all-namespaces
NAMESPACE       NAME
READY       STATUS      RESTARTS     AGE
kube-system     dns-controller-dc46485d8-pql7r
1/1         Running     0            5m
kube-system     elasticsearch-logging-0
1/1         Running     0            1m
kube-system     elasticsearch-logging-1
1/1         Running     0            53s
kube-system     etcd-server-events-ip-10-0-48-239.ec2.internal
1/1         Running     0            5m
kube-system     etcd-server-ip-10-0-48-239.ec2.internal
1/1         Running     0            5m
kube-system     fluentd-es-29xh9
1/1         Running     0            1m
kube-system     fluentd-es-xfbd6
1/1         Running     0            1m
kube-system     kibana-logging-649d7dcc87-mrtzc
1/1         Running     0            1m
kube-system     kube-apiserver-ip-10-0-48-239.ec2.internal
1/1         Running     0            5m
...
```

3. Check Kibana's log and wait until the state becomes green:

```
$ kubectl logs -f kibana-logging-649d7dcc87-mrtzc --
namespace=kube-system
ELASTICSEARCH_URL=http://elasticsearch-logging:9200
server.basePath: /api/v1/proxy/namespaces/kube-
system/services/kibana-logging
{"type":"log","@timestamp":"2018-03-26T01:02:04Z","tags":["info
","optimize"],"pid":6,"message":"Optimizing and caching bundles
for kibana and statusPage. This may take a few minutes"}

(wait for around 5min)

{"type":"log","@timestamp":"2018-03-26T01:08:00Z","tags":["stat
us","plugin:elasticsearch@1.0.0","info"],"pid":6,"state":"yello
```

```
w","message":"Status changed from yellow to yellow - No
existing Kibana index
found","prevState":"yellow","prevMsg":"Waiting for
Elasticsearch"}
{"type":"log","@timestamp":"2018-03-26T01:08:03Z","tags":["stat
us","plugin:elasticsearch@1.0.0","info"],"pid":6,"state":"green
","message":"Status changed from yellow to green - Kibana index
ready","prevState":"yellow","prevMsg":"No existing Kibana index
found"}
```

4. Run `kubetl cluster-info` to capture the Kibana URL:

```
$ kubectl cluster-info
Kubernetes master is running at
https://api.chap9.k8s-devops.net
Elasticsearch is running at
https://api.chap9.k8s-devops.net/api/v1/namespaces/kube-system/
services/elasticsearch-logging/proxy
Kibana is running at https://api.chap9.k8s-
devops.net/api/v1/namespaces/kube-system/services/kibana-
logging/proxy
KubeDNS is running at
https://api.chap9.k8s-devops.net/api/v1/namespaces/kube-system/
services/kube-dns:dns/proxy
```

5. Use `kubectl proxy` to forward your machine to the Kubernetes API server:

```
$ kubectl proxy --port=8080
Starting to serve on 127.0.0.1:8080
```

6. Access the Kibana WebUI from your machine using the following URL:
`http://127.0.0.1:8080/api/v1/namespaces/kube-system/services/ki
bana-logging/proxy`. Note that the IP address is 127.0.0.1,
which is correct because we are using a kubectl proxy.

Now, you can start to use Kibana. Configure an index as described in the preceding minikube and kubespray sections.

How it works...

As you can see, the installed Kibana versions are different based on the Kubernetes provisioning tool. But this cookbook explores the basic functions of Kibana. Therefore, there are no version-specific operations to worry about.

Let's launch a sample application and then learn how to monitor your application log using Kibana:

1. Prepare a sample application that keeps printing a DateTime and hello message to the stdout:

```
$ cat myapp.yaml
apiVersion: v1
kind: Pod
metadata:
  name: myapp
spec:
  containers:
  - image: busybox
    name: application
    args:
      - /bin/sh
      - -c
      - >
        while true; do
        echo "$(date) INFO hello";
        sleep 1;
        done
```

2. Create a sample application in the chap9 namespace:

```
$ kubectl create -f myapp.yaml --namespace=chap9
pod "myapp" created
```

4. Access the Kibana WebUI, then click the **Discover** tab:

5. Make sure the time range is Last 15 minutes, then type kubernetes.namespace_name: chap9 in the search box and hit the *Enter* key:

Searching the chap9 namespace log in 15 minutes

6. You can see all of the logs in the `chap9` namespaces as follows. The screenshot shows much more information than you might have expected. By clicking the **add** button for `kubernetes.host`, `kubernetes.pod_name`, and `log` will display only the fields necessary for this purpose:

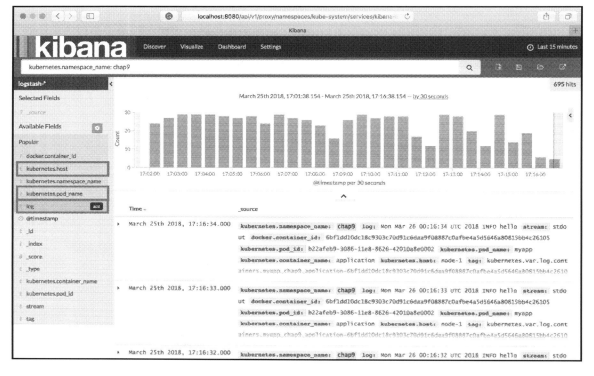

Choosing log columns

7. Now you can see a more simple log view for this application:

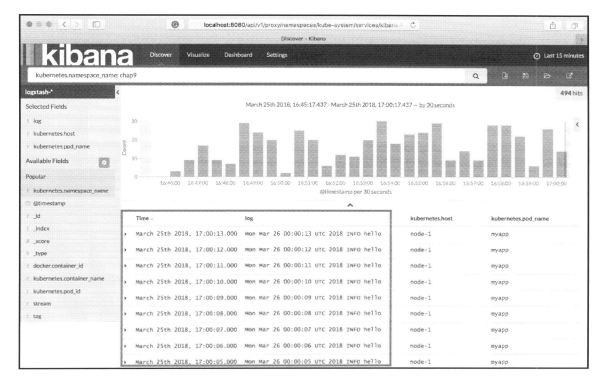

Showing the final state of a customized Kibana view

Congratulations! You now have have a centralized log management system in your Kubernetes cluster. You can observe the deployment of some Pods to see how you can see the application log.

There's more...

The preceding EFK stack collects Pods' logs only, because Fluentd is monitoring /var/log/containers/* in the Kubernetes node host. It is good enough to monitor an application's behavior, but, as a Kubernetes administrator, you also need some Kubernetes system logs such as master and node logs.

There is an easy way to achieve Kubernetes system log management that integrates with the EFK stack; add a Kubernetes Event Exporter, which keeps monitoring a Kubernetes event. When the new event has occurred, send a log to Elasticsearch. So, you can monitor a Kubernetes event with Kibana as well.

We have prepared an Eventer (Event Exporter) add-on (`https://raw.githubusercontent.com/kubernetes-cookbook/second-edition/master/chapter9/9-1/eventer.yml`). It is Heapster (`https://github.com/kubernetes/heapster`), based and expected to run on top of EFK add-ons. We can use this Eventer to monitor Kubernetes events through EFK:

 Details of Heapster will be described in the next section—*Monitoring master and nodes.*

1. Add eventer to your existing Kubernetes cluster:

```
$ kubectl create -f
https://raw.githubusercontent.com/kubernetes-cookbook/second-ed
ition/master/chapter9/9-1/eventer.yml
deployment "eventer-v1.5.2" created
serviceaccount "heapster" created
clusterrolebinding "heapster" created
```

2. Make sure Eventer Pod's STATUS is Running:

```
$ kubectl get pods --all-namespaces
NAMESPACE        NAME                                            READY
STATUS      RESTARTS      AGE
kube-system      elasticsearch-logging-v1-776b8b856c-9vvfl       1/1
Running     0             9m
kube-system      elasticsearch-logging-v1-776b8b856c-gg5gx       1/1
Running     0             9m
kube-system      eventer-v1.5.2-857bcc76d9-9gwn8                 1/1
Running     0             29s
kube-system      fluentd-es-v1.22-8prkn                          1/1
Running     0             9m
...
```

3. Use `kubectl logs` to keep observing Heapster and whether it can capture the event:

```
$ kubectl logs -f eventer-v1.5.2-857bcc76d9-9gwn8 --
namespace=kube-system
I0327 03:49:53.988961        1 eventer.go:68] /eventer --
source=kubernetes:'' --
sink=elasticsearch:http://elasticsearch-logging:9200?sniff=fals
e
I0327 03:49:53.989025        1 eventer.go:69] Eventer version
v1.5.2
I0327 03:49:54.087982        1 eventer.go:95] Starting with
ElasticSearch Sink sink
I0327 03:49:54.088040        1 eventer.go:109] Starting eventer
I0327 03:49:54.088048        1 eventer.go:117] Starting eventer
http service
I0327 03:50:00.000199        1 manager.go:100] Exporting 0
events
```

4. For testing purposes, open another terminal, and then create a `nginx` Pod:

```
$ kubectl run my-nginx --image=nginx
deployment "my-nginx" created
```

5. Observe Heapster's log; some new events have been captured:

```
I0327 03:52:00.000235        1 manager.go:100] Exporting 0
events
I0327 03:52:30.000166        1 manager.go:100] Exporting 8
events
I0327 03:53:00.000241        1 manager.go:100] Exporting 0
events
```

6. Open Kibana and navigate to **Settings** | **Indices** | **Add New**. This will add a new index.

7. Put the Index name as `heapster-*`, set the time-field name as `Metadata.creationTimestamp`, and then click **Create**:

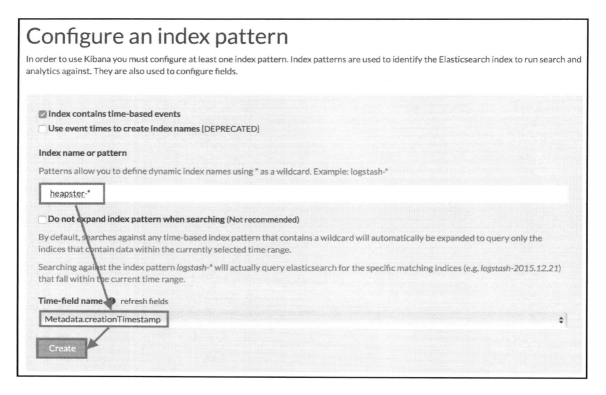

Configure an index pattern

In order to use Kibana you must configure at least one index pattern. Index patterns are used to identify the Elasticsearch index to run search and analytics against. They are also used to configure fields.

☑ **Index contains time-based events**
☐ **Use event times to create index names** [DEPRECATED]

Index name or pattern

Patterns allow you to define dynamic index names using * as a wildcard. Example: logstash-*

> heapster-*

☐ **Do not expand index pattern when searching** (Not recommended)

By default, searches against any time-based index pattern that contains a wildcard will automatically be expanded to query only the indices that contain data within the currently selected time range.

Searching against the index pattern *logstash-** will actually query elasticsearch for the specific matching indices (e.g. *logstash-2015.12.21*) that fall within the current time range.

Time-field name ↻ refresh fields

> Metadata.creationTimestamp   ⇕

> Create

Configuring a Heapster index

8. Go back to the **Discover** page, and then choose the `heapster-*` index from the left-hand panel.

9. Select (click the **Add** button) **Message**, **Source.component**, and **Source.host**:

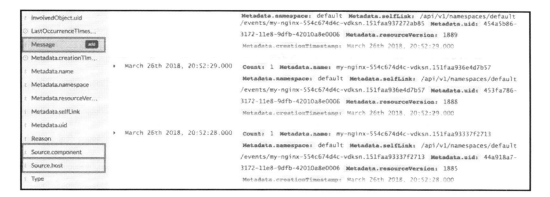

Choosing the necessary columns

10. Now you can see the Kubernetes system log, which shows the `nginx` Pod creation event as follows:

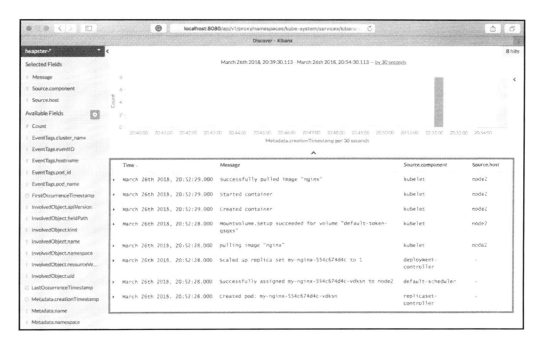

Showing the final state of the system log view in Kibana

Now you can monitor not only the application log, but also the Kubernetes system log in the EFK stack. Through switching indexes between either `logstash-*` (application log) or `heapster-*` (system log), you have a flexible log management environment.

See also

In this cookbook, we learned how to enable the EFK stack for your Kubernetes cluster. Kibana is a powerful tool that you can use to create your own dashboard and keep checking the logs more efficiently. Please visit Kibana's online documentation to understand how to use it:

- Kibana User Guide Reference: `https://www.elastic.co/guide/en/kibana/index.html`

Working with Google Stackdriver

In `Chapter 7`, *Building Kubernetes on GCP*, we introduced GKE. It has an integrated logging mechanism, which is called Google Stackdriver. In this section, we will explore the integration between GKE and Stackdriver.

Getting ready

To use a Stackdriver, you just need a GCP account. If you have never used GCP, please go back and read `Chapter 7`, *Building Kubernetes on GCP*, to set up a GCP account and the `gcloud` command-line interface.

To use Stackdriver on GKE, no action is needed, because GKE uses Stackdriver as a logging platform by default. But if you want to explicitly enable Stackdriver, specify `--enable-cloud-logging` while launching your Kubernetes by using the `gcloud` command, as follows:

```
$ gcloud container clusters create my-gke --cluster-version 1.9.4-gke.1 --
enable-cloud-logging --network default --zone us-west1-b
```

If, for some reason, you have a GKE that doesn't enable Stackdriver, you can use the `gcloud` command to enable it afterwards:

```
$ gcloud container clusters update my-gke --logging-service
logging.googleapis.com --zone us-west1-b
```

How to do it...

In order to demonstrate Stackdriver with GKE, we will create one namespace on Kubernetes, then launch a sample Pod to see some logs on the Stackdriver, as shown in the following steps:

1. Create the `chap9` namespace:

```
$ kubectl create namespace chap9
namespace "chap9" created
```

2. Prepare a sample application Pod:

```
$ cat myapp.yaml
apiVersion: v1
kind: Pod
metadata:
  name: myapp
spec:
  containers:
  - image: busybox
    name: application
    args:
      - /bin/sh
      - -c
      - >
        while true; do
        echo "$(date) INFO hello";
        sleep 1;
        done
```

3. Create the Pod on the `chap9` namespace:

```
$ kubectl create -f myapp.yaml --namespace=chap9
pod "myapp" created
```

4. Access the GCP Web Console and navigate to **Logging** | **Logs**.
5. Select **Audited Resources** | **GKE Container** | Your GKE cluster name (ex: **my-gke**) | **chap9** namespace:

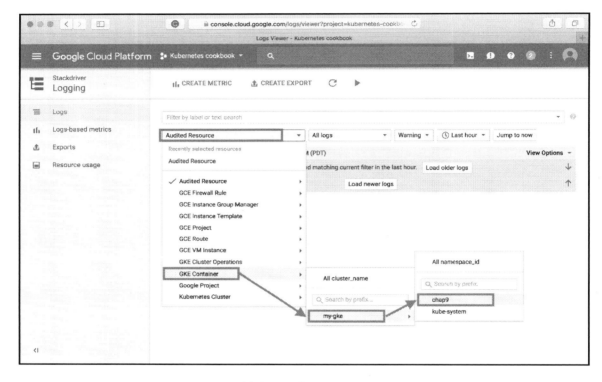

Selecting the chap9 namespace Pod log

6. As an alternative way of accessing the `chap9` namespace log, you can select an advanced filter. Then, type the following criteria to the text field and click the **Submit Filter** button:

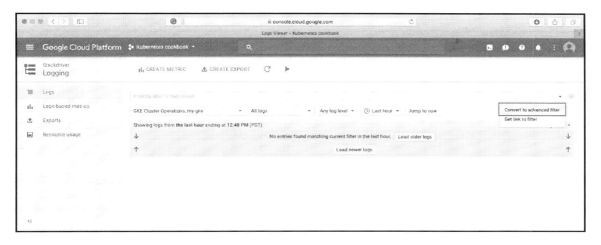

Using an advanced filter

```
resource.type="container"
resource.labels.cluster_name="<Your GKE name>"
resource.labels.namespace_id="chap9"
```

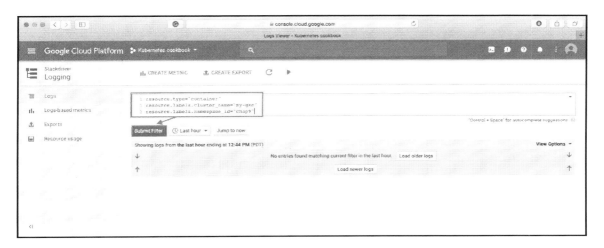

Input an advanced filter criterion

7. Now, you can see the `myapp` log on Stackdriver:

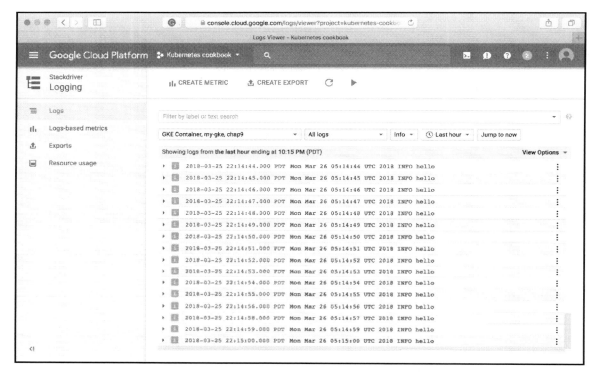

Showing the chap9 Pod log in Stackdriver

How it works...

Stackdriver has a basic functionality for narrowing down a date, severity, and keyword search. It helps to monitor an application's behavior. How about system-level behavior, such as master and node activities? Stackdriver also supports searching of the system-level log. Actually, `fluentd` captures not only the application log, but the system log as well. By performing the following steps, you can see the system log in Stackdriver:

1. Select **GKE Cluster Operation**s | Your GKE name (for example, **my-gke**) | **All location**:

> You should select **All location** instead of a particular location, because some Kubernetes operation logs do not contain location values.

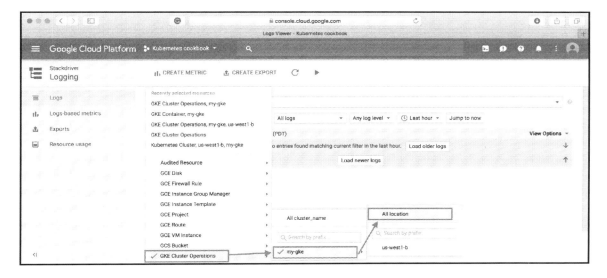

Choosing a GKE system log in Stackdriver

2. As an alternative, input an advanced filter as follows:

```
resource.type="gke_cluster"
resource.labels.cluster_name="<Your GKE name>"
```

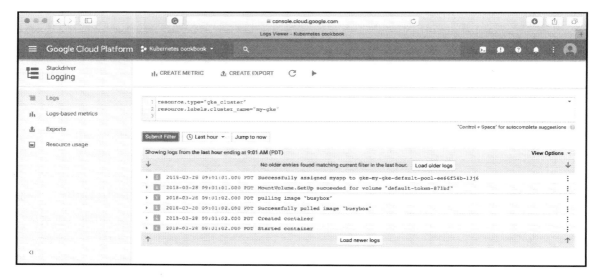

Showing a GKE system log in Stackdriver

See also

In this recipe, we introduced Google Stackdriver. It is a built-in function of Google Kubernetes Engine. Stackdriver is a simple but powerful log management tool. In addition, Stackdriver is capable of monitoring the system status. You can make built-in or custom metrics to monitor and provide alerts regarding events as well. This will be described in the next recipe.

In addition, please read the following chapter to recap the basics of GCP and GKE:

- `Chapter 7`, *Building Kubernetes on GCP*

Monitoring master and node

During the journey of the previous recipes, you learned how to build your own cluster, run various resources, enjoy different usage scenarios, and even enhance cluster administration. Now, here comes a new level of perspective for your Kubernetes cluster. In this recipe, we are going to talk about monitoring. Through the monitoring tool, users will not only learn about the resource consumption of nodes, but also the Pods. This will help us to have greater efficiency as regards resource utilization.

Getting ready

As with earlier recipes, all you have to prepare is a healthy Kubernetes cluster. The following command, along with `kubectl`, will help you to verify the status of your Kubernetes system:

```
// check the components
$ kubectl get cs
```

For demonstration later, we will deploy the monitoring system on a `minikube-booted` cluster. However, it works for any kind of well-installed clusters.

How to do it...

In this section, we will work on installing a monitoring system and introducing its dashboard. This monitoring system is based on *Heapster* (`https://github.com/kubernetes/heapster`), a resource usage collecting and analyzing tool. Heapster communicates with kubelet to get the resource usage of both machine and container. Along with Heapster, we have influxDB (`https://influxdata.com`) for storage and Grafana (`http://grafana.org`) as the frontend dashboard, which visualizes the status of resources in several user-friendly plots:

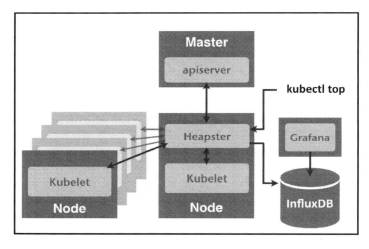

The interaction of monitoring components

Heapster gathers information from **kubelet** on each node and provides data for other platforms. In our case, an influxDB is a sink for saving historical data. It is available for users to do further data analysis, such as the prediction of peak workload, and then make corresponding resource adjustments. We have Grafana working as an affable web console; users can manage monitoring status through the browser. Moreover, `kubectl` has the subcommand `top`, which provides the ability to grep cluster-wide information through Heapster:

```
// try kubectl top before installing Heapster
$ kubectl top node
Error from server (NotFound): the server could not find the requested
resource (get services http:heapster:)
```

This command turns out an error message.

Installing a monitoring system could be much easier than anticipated. By applying configuration files from the open-source communities and companies, we can set up component monitoring on Kubernetes simply with the aid of a few commands:

```
// installing influxDB
$ kubectl create -f
https://raw.githubusercontent.com/kubernetes/heapster/master/deploy/kube-co
nfig/influxdb/influxdb.yaml
deployment "monitoring-influxdb" created
service "monitoring-influxdb" created
// installing Heapster
$ kubectl create -f
https://raw.githubusercontent.com/kubernetes/heapster/master/deploy/kube-co
nfig/influxdb/heapster.yaml
serviceaccount "heapster" created
deployment "heapster" created
//installing Grafana
$kubectl create -f
https://raw.githubusercontent.com/kubernetes/heapster/master/deploy/kube-co
nfig/influxdb/grafana.yaml
deployment "monitoring-grafana" created
service "monitoring-grafana" created
```

You could find that applying an online source is also feasible for creating Kubernetes applications.

How it works...

After you have installed influxDB, Heapster, and Grafana, let's learn how to get the status of the resource. First, you may use `kubectl top` now. Check the utilization of nodes and Pods, as well as verifying the functionality of monitoring:

```
// check the status of nodes
$ kubectl top node
NAME       CPU(cores)   CPU%     MEMORY(bytes)   MEMORY%
minikube   236m         11%      672Mi           35%
// check the status of Pods in Namespace kube-system
$ kubectl top pod -n kube-system
NAME                                    CPU(cores)   MEMORY(bytes)
heapster-5c448886d-k9wt7                1m           18Mi
kube-addon-manager-minikube             36m          32Mi
kube-dns-54cccfbdf8-j65x6               3m           22Mi
kubernetes-dashboard-77d8b98585-z8hch   0m           12Mi
monitoring-grafana-65757b9656-8cl6d     0m           13Mi
monitoring-influxdb-66946c9f58-hwv8g    1m           26Mi
```

Currently, `kubectl top` only covers nodes and Pods, and just shows their CPU and RAM usage.

According to the output of `kubectl top`, what does the **m** mean in terms of the quantity of CPU usage? It means "milli", as in millisecond and millimeter. Millicpu is regarded as 10^{-3} CPU. For example, if the Heapster Pod uses 1 m CPU, it only takes 0.1% CPU computation power at this moment.

Introducing the Grafana dashboard

Now, let's take a look at the Grafana dashboard. In our case, for the minikube-booted cluster, we should open a proxy to enable accessibility from the localhost to the Kubernetes cluster:

```
$ kubectl proxy
Starting to serve on 127.0.0.1:8001
```

You may access Grafana through this URL: `http://localhost:8001/api/v1/namespaces/kube-system/services/monitoring-grafana/proxy/`. The magic that enables us to see the web page is made by the Kubernetes DNS server and proxy:

Accessing the Grafana dashboard in an anti-minikube Kubernetes

To access Grafana through a browser, it depends on the network configuration of nodes and the Kubernetes service of Grafana. Follow these points for forwarding the web page to your client:

- **Upgrade Grafana's service type**: The configuration file we applied creates Grafana with a ClusterIP service. You should change it to `NodePort` or `LoadBalancer` for exposing Grafana to the outside world.
- **Check firewalls**: Make sure your clients or load balancer are able to access your node of the cluster.
- **Dashboard access through the target port**: Instead of using a detailed URL, like we did on the minikube cluster, you can access Grafana with simple ones such as `NODE_ENTRYPOINT:3000` (Grafana requests port 3000 in the configuration file by default) or the entry point of the load balancer.

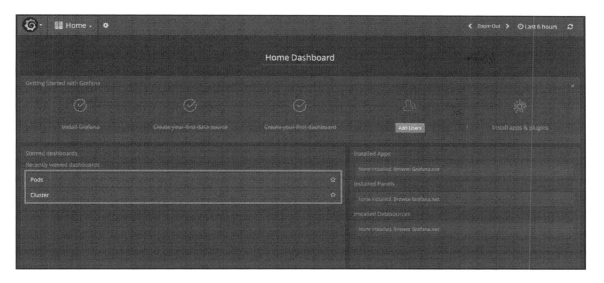

The home page of Grafana

In the default settings of Grafana, we have two dashboards, **Cluster** and **Pods**. The **Cluster** board covers the nodes' resource utilization, such as CPU, memory, network transaction, and storage. The **Pods** dashboard has similar plots for each Pod and you can check each container in a Pod:

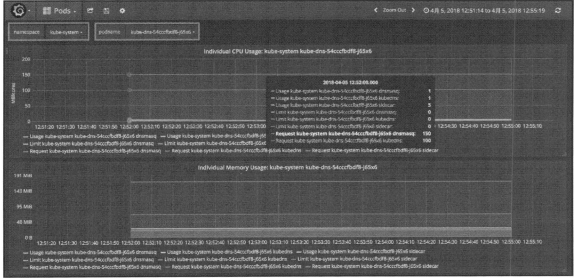

Viewing the Pod kube-dns by Pod dashboard

As the preceding screenshot show, for example, we can observe the CPU utilization of individual containers in the Pod `kube-dns` in the namespace `kube-system`, which is the cluster of the DNS server. You can find that there are three containers in this Pod, `kubedns`, `dnsmasq`, and `sidecar`, and the lines in the plot express the limit, request, and real usage of CPU for containers respectively.

Creating a new metric to monitor Pod

For a running application, metrics are the data we can collect and use to analyze its behavior and performance. Metrics can come from the system side, such as the usage of CPU, or be based on the functionality of an application, such as the request frequency of certain functions. There are several metrics for monitoring offered by Heapster (`https://github.com/kubernetes/heapster/blob/master/docs/storage-schema.md`). We are going to show you how to create a customized panel by yourself. Please take the following steps as a reference:

1. Go to the dashboard of Pod, and drag the web page to the bottom. There is a button called **ADD ROW**; click it to add a metric. Then, choose the first category **Graph** as a new panel for expressing this metric:

Adding a new metric with graph expression

2. An empty panel block appears. Go ahead and click on it for further configuration. Just choose **Edit** when the editing block shows up right after you pick the panel:

Starting to edit a panel

3. First, give your panel a name. For example, CPU Rate. We would like to create one showing the rate of CPU utilization:

Giving the panel a title on the "General" page

4. Set up the following parameters for specific data querying. Take the following screenshot as reference:
    - **FROM**: cpu/usage_rate
    - **WHERE**: type = pod_container
    - **AND**: namespace_name=$namespace, pod_name=$podname value
    - **GROUP BY**: tag(container_name)
    - **ALIAS BY**: $tag_container_name

Parameters of data querying for CPU-rate metric

5. Does any line of status show up? If not, modifying the configuration in the display page will help you build the best looking graph for you. Make the **Null value connected** and you will find lines showing out:

Editing the look of your metric. Checking the null value to be "connected" for showing the lines

6. Here you go! Feel free to close the edit mode. You now have a new metric for every Pod.

Just try to discover more functionality of the Grafana dashboard and the Heapster monitoring tool. You will obtain further details about your system, services, and containers through the information from the monitoring system.

There's more...

We built up a monitoring system based on Heapster, which is maintained by the Kubernetes group. Yet, several tools and platforms focusing on container cluster have sprung up to support the community, such as Prometheus (`https://prometheus.io`). On the other hand, public clouds may have run daemons on VM for grabbing the metrics by default, and provided services for corresponding actions. We don't have to build one within the cluster. Next, we are going to introduce the monitoring method on AWS and GCP. You may wish to check `Chapter 6`, *Building Kubernetes on AWS*, and `Chapter 7`, *Building Kubernetes on GCP*, to build a cluster and learn more concepts.

Monitoring your Kubernetes cluster on AWS

While working on AWS, we usually rely on AWS CloudWatch (`https://aws.amazon.com/cloudwatch/`) for monitoring. You can create a dashboard, and pick up any basic metrics you want. CloudWatch already collects a bunch of metrics for you:

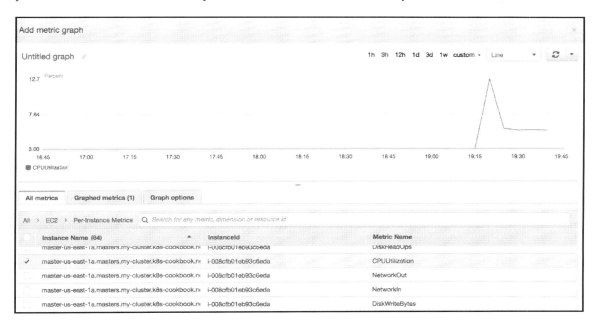

Create a new metric with AWS CloudWatch

But, for the resource of Kubernetes, such as Pods, customized metrics for them need to be sent out to CloudWatch with manual configuration. With a kops installation, it is recommended that you build your monitoring system with Heapster or Prometheus.

AWS has its own container cluster service, Amazon ECS. This may be the reason why AWS didn't support Kubernetes deeply and we have to build clusters through kops and terraform, along with other add-on services. Nevertheless, according to recent news, there will be a new service called **Amazon Elastic Container Service for Kubernetes** (**Amazon EKS**). We can look forward to the integration of Kubernetes and other AWS services.

Monitoring your Kubernetes cluster on GCP

Before we look at the monitoring platform of GCP, the nodes of GKE cluster should admit being scanned for any applied status:

```
// add nodes with monitoring scope
$ gcloud container clusters create my-k8s-cluster --cluster-version 1.9.7-
gke.0 - -machine-type f1-micro --num-nodes 3 --network k8s-network --zone
us-central1-a - -tags private --scopes=storage-rw,compute-ro,
https://www.googleapis.com/auth/monitoring
```

Google Stackdriver provides system monitoring in a hybrid cloud environment. Besides its own GCP, it can also cover your computing resources on AWS. To access its web console, you can find its section under the menu on the left-hand side. There are multiple service categories in Stackdriver. Select **Monitoring** to check related functionality.

As a new user, you will get a 30-day free trial. The initial configuration is simple; just enable an account and bind your project. You may avoid the agent installation and AWS account setup since we simply want to check the GKE cluster. Once you log in to Stackdriver successfully, click **Resources** on the left-side panel and choose **Kubernetes Engine** under infrastructure type:

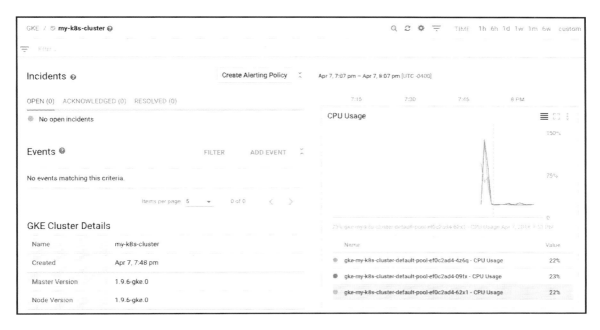

Main page for GKE on Strackdriver monitoring

There are several metrics set up already for computing resources from node to container. Take your time exploring and check the official introduction for more features: `https://cloud.google.com/kubernetes-engine/docs/how-to/monitoring`.

See also

This recipe showed you how to monitor your machines in the Kubernetes system. However, it is wise to study the recipes of the main components and daemons. You can get more ideas about working processes and resource usage. Moreover, since we have worked with several services to build our monitoring system, reviewing recipes about the Kubernetes services again will give you a clear idea about how you can build up this monitoring system:

- The *Exploring Architecture* recipe in `Chapter 1`, *Building Your Own Kubernetes Cluster*
- The *Working with Services* recipe in `Chapter 2`, *Walking through Kubernetes Concepts*

Kubernetes is a project that keeps moving forward and upgrading apace. The recommended way to catch up is to check out new features on its official website: `http://kubernetes.io`. Also, you can always get new Kubernetes versions on GitHub at `https://github.com/kubernetes/kubernetes/releases`. Keeping your Kubernetes system up to date, and learning new features practically, is the best method for accessing Kubernetes technology continuously.

Other Books You May Enjoy

If you enjoyed this book, you may be interested in these other books by Packt:

Mastering Kubernetes - Second Edition
Gigi Sayfan

ISBN: 978-1-78899-978-6

- Architect a robust Kubernetes cluster for long-time operation
- Discover the advantages of running Kubernetes on GCE, AWS, Azure, and bare metal
- Understand the identity model of Kubernetes, along with the options for cluster federation
- Monitor and troubleshoot Kubernetes clusters and run a highly available Kubernetes
- Create and configure custom Kubernetes resources and use third-party resources in your automation workflows
- Enjoy the art of running complex stateful applications in your container environment
- Deliver applications as standard packages

DevOps with Kubernetes
Hideto Saito, Hui-Chuan Chloe Lee, Cheng-Yang Wu

ISBN: 978-1-78839-664-6

- Learn fundamental and advanced DevOps skills and tools
- Get a comprehensive understanding for container
- Learn how to move your application to container world
- Learn how to manipulate your application by Kubernetes
- Learn how to work with Kubernetes in popular public cloud
- Improve time to market with Kubernetes and Continuous Delivery
- Learn how to monitor, log, and troubleshoot your application with Kubernetes

Leave a review - let other readers know what you think

Please share your thoughts on this book with others by leaving a review on the site that you bought it from. If you purchased the book from Amazon, please leave us an honest review on this book's Amazon page. This is vital so that other potential readers can see and use your unbiased opinion to make purchasing decisions, we can understand what our customers think about our products, and our authors can see your feedback on the title that they have worked with Packt to create. It will only take a few minutes of your time, but is valuable to other potential customers, our authors, and Packt. Thank you!

Index